Science Fiction
of th

Science Fiction and the Prediction of the Future

Essays on Foresight and Fallacy

Edited by
GARY WESTFAHL, WONG KIN YUEN,
and AMY KIT-SZE CHAN

CRITICAL EXPLORATIONS IN
SCIENCE FICTION AND FANTASY, 27
Donald E. Palumbo *and* C.W. Sullivan III, *series editors*

McFarland & Company, Inc., Publishers
Jefferson, North Carolina, and London

ALSO OF INTEREST

Hugo Gernsback and the Century of Science Fiction (by Gary Westfahl; McFarland, 2007)

Science Fiction and the Two Cultures: Essays on Bridging the Gap Between the Sciences and the Humanities (edited by Gary Westfahl and George Slusser; McFarland, 2009)

The Science of Fiction and the Fiction of Science: Collected Essays on SF Storytelling and the Gnostic Imagination (by Frank McConnell, edited by Gary Westfahl; McFarland, 2009)

LIBRARY OF CONGRESS CATALOGUING-IN-PUBLICATION DATA

Science fiction and the prediction of the future : essays on
   foresight and fallacy / edited by Gary Westfahl, Wong Kin Yuen
   and Amy Kit-sze Chan.
         p.   cm. — (Critical explorations in science fiction and
         fantasy ; 27)
      [Donald Palumbo and C.W. Sullivan III, series editors]
      Includes bibliographical references and index.

      ISBN 978-0-7864-5841-7
      softcover : 50# alkaline paper ∞

      1. Science fiction films—History and criticism.   2. Science
   fiction — History and criticism.   3. Future in literature.
   4. Forecasting in literature.   I. Westfahl, Gary.   II. Yuen,
   Wong Kin.   III. Chan, Amy Kit-sze.
   PN1995.9.S26S278   2011
   809.3'876209 — dc22   2010048100

British Library cataloguing data are available

Cover illustration© 2011 EyeWire

Manufactured in the United States of America

McFarland & Company, Inc., Publishers
   Box 611, Jefferson, North Carolina 28640
   www.mcfarlandpub.com

Table of Contents

v

Introduction

Of Futures Imagined, and Futures Inhabited

GARY WESTFAHL

In 1954, anthropologist Kalervo Oberg introduced the term "culture shock" to describe the severe discomfort felt by people who move into a culture very unlike the one they were raised in. By the 1970s, futurist Alvin Toffler was provocatively arguing that a similar sense of unease was now affecting almost everyone in the contemporary world — because scientific and social innovations arriving at an ever-accelerating rate were changing societies so much that, in effect, all citizens were distressingly finding themselves in a culture significantly different from the one they were familiar with. To describe this condition, Toffler built upon Oberg's insight to coin the term "future shock" and analyzed this novel form of anxiety in a best-selling book with that title (1971). In the decades since Toffler's concept became prominent, his term has not entered everyday discourse, but virtually all commentators embrace his central conclusion: that our civilization is today in a state of constant flux, and numerous people are struggling because they cannot readily adjust to constantly changing conditions.

Of course, new technologies and customs will be less upsetting if people have been informed about their coming appearance and probable effects— which means that some people should have been relatively immune from difficulties in calmly accepting the various novelties being introduced into their lives— namely, readers of science fiction. For supporters of the genre long argued that one of science fiction's primary purposes, and virtues, is that it enables people to better prepare for the future with its plausible predictions of things to come. This belief can be traced back to pioneering author and editor Hugo Gernsback, whose original argument was even stronger: science fiction, he claimed, not only *predicted* the future, but actually *created* it — by providing scientists and inventors with imaginative ideas that they could proceed to transform into reality. As he explained while introducing a contest in his magazine *Amazing Stories*,

> The author who works out a brand new idea in a scientifiction plot may be hailed as an original inventor years later, when his brain-child will have taken wings and when cold-blooded scientists will have realized the author's ambition.
>
> An author may not know how to build or make his invention of a certain apparatus or instrument, but he may know how to predict, and often does predict, the use of such a one. The professional inventor or scientist then comes along, gets the stimulus from the story and promptly responds with the material invention.[1]

As an unstated but obvious side-effect of this process, science fiction readers were, by absorbing these stories, getting an advance look at coming scientific developments.

Still, there were limitations in Gernsback's expansive argument, since science fiction was seen as only offering isolated predictions of future inventions, not broader pictures of how these innovations might affect society or considerations of possible changes in social conditions outside the realm of scientific progress. Gernsback offered little more than hints that science fiction might fulfill such wider goals when noting, for example, that science fiction "widen[s] the young man's horizon, as nothing else can" and "keeps [children] abreast of the times."[2] It would be left to his most noteworthy successor, writer and editor John W. Campbell, Jr., to present a fuller explanation of the nature and value of science fiction prediction, largely in his magazine *Astounding Science Fiction*.

To be sure, Campbell happily accepted Gernsback's notion that science fiction might directly lead to new scientific innovations, maintaining in "The Science of Science-Fiction" that "Science-fiction has the interesting characteristic of causing its own predictions to come true" because future scientists "will have read the magazines, seen the stories, and recognized the validity of the science-fiction engineering!"[3] However, Campbell went beyond Gernsback first in explaining that science fiction predictions merited scrutiny because writers were not simply using their imaginations, but relying upon the scientific technique of extrapolation: "Science-fiction, being largely an attempt to forecast the future, on the basis of the present, represents a form of extrapolation."[4] Furthermore, in envisioning scientific advances, science fiction writers were considering "what the results look like when applied not only to machines, but to human societies as well," making their prophecies more likely to be both more accurate and more helpful.[5] As a result, whenever major scientific breakthroughs were in the headlines, Campbell enjoyed pointing out that science fiction readers, having read predictions of those developments, could immediately accept and understand them, unlike their startled and disoriented contemporaries. After the explosion of the atomic bomb in 1945, he speculated in "Atomic Age" that science fiction readers were now being consulted by neighbors as experts on the subject, since science fiction stories had long featured such weapons.[6] When another spectacular demonstration of science fiction's prophetic powers emerged — the launch of Sputnik in late 1957, beginning the era of space travel — Campbell again gloated that science fiction readers had already known it was coming:

> I think the people of the United States thought [science fiction writers] were kidding [....] That nuclear weapons and space flight were amusing ideas to play with [...] Apparently, they thought that science fiction *was* an escape literature, and read it as such.
>
> It happens that science fiction's core is just about the only *non*–escape literature available to the general public today.[7]

Certainly, one might concede Campbell's points that, in the cases of atomic energy and space travel, science fiction had been prophetic, and that science fiction readers for that reason were less surprised, and less concerned, when these phenomena came into being than others who had not read science fiction. However, since over half a century has passed since those triumphs of science fiction prediction, we must now reconsider the overall accuracy and usefulness of science fiction predictions as we move further into the twenty-first century.

Actually, it is easy to argue that science fiction has conspicuously failed to anticipate the world we are now living in. Commentators routinely lament the absence of predicted innovations as flying cars and rocket jets strapped on people's backs, though one must note that such naive visions were more common in popular culture than the science fiction stories of pulp magazines and paperback novels. More significantly, science fiction, with few exceptions, predicted that humanity would advance into space far more rapidly than has been the case, while failing to envision the ways that computers would be developed, miniaturized, and incorporated into all aspects of contemporary life — leading to extravagant projections of a colonized solar system in the future with absurd scenes of spaceship pilots frantically manipulating slide rules in order to recalculate their courses. Further, technological advances in fields ranging from bioengineering to nanotechnology that are now transforming our world rarely figured in writers' depictions of Earth's future, and widely anticipated catastrophes like nuclear war and ruinous overpopulation have never materialized. Overall, it seems, we now live in a twenty-first century which is very different from the twenty-first centuries of earlier science fiction — which means that the genre, despite the expansive promises of its champions, did not really prepare people for a contemporary civilization of computer networks, terrorism, and identity theft. Science fiction readers, in other words, may be just as vulnerable to the agonies of "future shock" as anyone else.

This volume will endeavor to address a number of questions raised by what one might wryly describe as this unforeseen situation. If science fiction writers, despite their celebrated expertise and abilities, have persistently faltered in their efforts to predict the future, why has that been the case? Are there, in fact, overlooked or rarely cited texts that did succeed in providing accurate prophecies of today's world? Have science fiction films—often derided as less intellectual cousins of science fiction literature—done a better, or worse, job in predicting the future? And what exactly are the sorts of contemporary phenomena that science fiction did not anticipate, or is still neglecting to consider?

The first part of the volume, "Cosmic Visions," offers five broad explorations of science fiction and prophecy involving a range of disparate texts. My "Pitfalls of Prophecy: Why Science Fiction So Often Fails to Predict the Future" attempts to systematically explain why common approaches in science-fictional prophecy, including extrapolation, have so regularly been unable to produce valid visions of the technology and societies of the future. Richard L. McKinney's "Emotional Dimensions of Transmimetic Fiction: Emotion, Aesthetics, Ethics, and Rhetoric in Tales of Tomorrow's Science, Technology, and Technoscience" maintains that science fiction predictions are especially valuable because they consider "the *ethical* consequences of future developments," allowing science fiction to "introduce its readers to new and unique emotions, never previously part of the world, but potentially part of the world of tomorrow." Kirk Hampton and Carol MacKay's "The Internet and the Anagogical Myths of Science Fiction," after acknowledging that today's Internet was specifically predicted only in one story, Murray Leinster's "A Logic Named Joe," argues that one finds in science fiction "prefiguring aspects of the Internet since the invention of the genre," such as its capacities for networking and storing vast amounts of information, though "the forms they take can be hard to recognize." Veronica Hollinger's "Technobodies and the Anxieties of Performance," after pondering recent texts which illustrate how traditional understandings of human identity have become problematized, locates surprising insights in two 1940s stories by Cordwainer Smith and C. L. Moore. And McKinney's "Places of Alterity in Science Fiction" classifies and analyzes the alternative environments depicted in science-fictional images of the future, provocatively arguing that "One does not read science fiction to chart the exact path to the future, or to find out the details of tomorrow.... SF can explore what sort of place tomorrow may be *to live in.*"

The second section, "The Practice of Prophecy," provides ten more focused examinations of predictions and science fiction in specific texts or bodies of work, arranged roughly in chronological order. Sharalyn Orbaugh's "Future City Tokyo: 1909 and 2009" argues that the ideas of futurists in the early twentieth century were strangely realized in both the subsequent history of Tokyo and works of Japanese popular culture, while David L. Ferro and Eric G. Swedin's "Rebooting 'A Logic Named Joe': Exploring the Multiple Influences of a Strangely Predictive Mid–1940s Short Story" celebrates the unique vision of Leinster's story, explores its origins and impact upon contemporary readers, and considers how it relates to common ideas about science fiction's powers of prophecy.

Next are five chapters involving the predictive features of twentieth-century films, which are often overlooked in surveys of prophecies that are more attentive to literature. Lynne Lundquist's "Victims of a Globalized, Radicalized, Technologized World, or, Why the Beatles Needed *Help!*" finds a startlingly accurate prediction of contemporary life in a film routinely dismissed as a frivolous comedy. Rob Latham's "'A Journey Beyond the Stars': *2001: A Space Odyssey* and the Psychedelic Revolution in 1960s Science Fiction" provides a context for considerations of that landmark film by analyzing how its story was initially viewed not as a scientifically-grounded prediction of humanity's future, but rather a visceral rejection of logic and technology more aligned with science fiction's "New Wave" of the 1960s. My "The Endless Odyssey: The *2001* Saga and Its Inability to Predict Humanity's Future" explores how various sequels to that landmark film, in books, comic books, and films, have consistently failed to fulfill the promise of the film's conclusion — the birth of a new superhuman race — and ponders why no one has been able to craft a satisfactory continuation of that story. Wong Kin Yuen's "Intercultural and Interface: Kung Fu as Abstract Machine" provides a thorough analysis of how recent critical insights in the field of intercultural studies were anticipated and illustrated in kung fu films of the 1970s and later decades. Véronique Flambard-Weisbart's "Post-Genre Cinemas and Post-Colonial Attitude: Hong Kong Meets Paris" stimulatingly studies how visions of cinema's future propounded by the French New Wave movement in the 1950s led to Hong Kong's postmodern Wuxia Plan films, which in turn inspired newer French filmmakers; and all these films were "based on universal human values that transcend the immediacy of the market" and devoted to "humankind ... the only genre, and the only attitude, that never grows old." In a sense, she celebrates those films for their refusal to embrace the goal of prophecy.

The volume concludes with three examinations of conspicuous failures to predict or confront contemporary realities. While Amy Kit-sze Chan's "Writing, Weaving and Technology" does locate and discuss a relevant science fiction story of the 1990s, she is otherwise discussing recent realizations about relationships between women, technology, and writing that have been overlooked in literature and film. Brooks Landon's "The Technological Contours of Contemporary Science Fiction, or, The Science Fiction That Science Fiction Doesn't See" more narrowly puzzles over the fact that science fiction has remained so hesitant to explore and embrace new technologies of story-telling, suggesting that a sort of conservatism underlies a genre more commonly praised for forward-looking attitudes. And Gregory Benford's "Thinking about the Smart Wireless World" concludes the volume by providing — paradoxically, by means of a brief science fiction story — a vision how traditional notions of privacy might be altered by advanced technology in ways that science fiction has rarely if ever probed.

Before readers proceed to these chapters, a few words should be said about the unusual origins of this volume. The original intent was to assemble, in book form, the papers presented at the Hong Kong 2003 Conference; however, for a variety of reasons, a majority of conference presenters, when belatedly approached about contributing to the volume, declined to make their works available. An additional issue was that the conference's theme — "Technoscience, Material Culture, and Everyday Life" — seemed too broad for a marketable volume. After discussions with the editors at McFarland, it was agreed to have the volume focus on the issue of science fiction's predictions; and to fill the void left by conference papers we could not include, new contributions were solicited. For the record: six chapters in this volume are versions of papers presented at the conference; three chapters were written by scholars who had papers accepted for presentation at that conference but opted instead to submit different items, one of them previously published; one chapter was written by an attendee who, having contributed his conference paper, volunteered to write a second, original chapter; and five chapters come from scholars who did not attend the conference.

One serendipitous result of this volume's odd history is, I would argue, a broader consideration of science fiction and prophecy than previous studies — many cited in the bibliography of relevant secondary works that follows the chapters — provided. The traditional question has always been: did science fiction accurately predict the technology and social structures of our contemporary world? Yet chapters here also explore whether science fiction has been able to predict the emotions, attitudes, and critical theories that now characterize our lives, addressing a different question: even if particular details were incorrect, did science fiction get the "feel" of the future right? In addition, while previous analyses dealt almost exclusively with American and British science fiction, this volume, engendered by a conference attended by scholars from around the world, brings the literature and film of other cultures into the discussion.

Thus, though this volume cannot be accurately described as a collection of papers from the Hong Kong 2003 Conference, it would never have come into being if that conference had not occurred, and it reflects the lingering influence of that conference. For more information about that singular event, one may read my online essay "Journey to the Future: Hong Kong 2003,"[8] which as it happens considers the experience of attending that forward-looking conference as a prediction of the future in itself. Still, since those who attended the Hong Kong 2003 Conference could never have foreseen that a volume like this would represent its end result, the conference also demonstrates, as innumerable science fiction writers have found, that it can be vexingly difficult to predict the future.

NOTES

1. Hugo Gernsback, "$300.00 Prize Contest — Wanted: A Symbol for Scientifiction," *Amazing Stories*, 3 (April, 1928), 5. The piece is unsigned but almost certainly written by Gernsback.
    2. Gernsback, "Science Wonder Stories," *Science Wonder Stories*, 1 (June, 1929), 5.

3. John W. Campbell, Jr., "The Science of Science-Fiction," *Space Magazine*, 1 (Winter, 1949), 5–6. Essay originally published in *Atlantic Monthly* (May, 1948).

4. Campbell, "The Perfect Machine," *Astounding Science-Fiction*, 25 (May, 1940), 5.

5. Campbell, "Introduction," *Venus Equilateral*, by George O. Smith (New York: Prime Press, 1947), 8.

6. Campbell, "Atomic Age," *Astounding Science-Fiction*, 36 (November, 1945), 5–6, 98.

7. Campbell, "Non-Escape Literature," *Collected Editorials from Analog*, by Campbell, selected by Harry Harrison (Garden City, NY: Doubleday and Company, 1966), 227–228. Originally published in *Astounding Science Fiction*, 61 (February, 1959).

8. Gary Westfahl, "Journey to the Future: Hong Kong 2003," Locus Online website, posted April 10, 2003, at http://locusmag.com/2003/Commentary/Westfahl04_Hong Kong.html.

PART I : COSMIC VISIONS

1

Pitfalls of Prophecy
Why Science Fiction So Often Fails to Predict the Future

GARY WESTFAHL

As someone regarded at times as an expert on science fiction, I was once asked to give a presentation offering some predictions about the future; science fiction writers routinely face the same request. The problem, as many have noted, is that nothing about reading or writing science fiction naturally provides any special ability to foresee the future, and science fiction writers repeatedly explain that they never *really* attempt to predict the future, but rather are only exploring possible futures to provide entertainment or food for thought. Perhaps Harlan Ellison put it best in a 1982 article, "Cheap Thrills on the Road to Hell":

> In the mistaken belief that just because I occasionally write fantasy stories extrapolating some bizarre future America I am privy to Delphic insights, the editors of the [*Los Angeles*] *Times* have asked me to unleash some wry conceits about what we can expect. Little do they understand that writers are merely paid liars and we know no more than the rest of you.[1]

Isaac Asimov similarly refers to the "general myth among laymen that, somehow, the chief function of a science fiction writer is to make predictions that eventually come true."[2] And while there are occasions when science fiction seemed to have gotten the future right — Jules Verne's submarine, the Apollo moon landings, William Gibson's cyberspace, etc. — that can be attributed solely to the law of averages: after all, if a body of literature makes thousands of predictions, at least a few of them are bound to become true. The same principle keeps a lot of psychics in business.

Still, I would argue that science fiction may actually be helpful in predicting the future, albeit in a convoluted way, if a certain procedure is followed. First, one can examine the past predictions of science fiction regarding our own era and detect the underlying logical fallacies that made most of them wildly inaccurate. Then, having identified the erroneous patterns of thought that led writers astray, one can consider some current science fiction predictions about our future, identify them as additional illustrations of these proven fallacies, and conclude that they are almost certainly wrong. Finally, one might logically assume that predictions radically different from the rejected predictions are probably correct.

To test this procedure, I surveyed a number of errant predictions from past science fiction and deduced that they were based on one or more of seven dubious assumptions, which I will list and discuss as the Fallacies of Prediction.

*   *   *

1. **The Fallacy of Universal Wealth.** This is the assumption that all governments and individuals in the future will be wealthy, enabling them to easily afford any technological advances that they desire. A similar premise with identical consequences—the Fallacy of Infinite Price Reduction—is that all technological advances will steadily become cheaper and cheaper until, finally, virtually everyone can afford them.

For example: Consider one standard vision of the future metropolis—towering skyscrapers joined by soaring walkways; pedestrians traveling on moving sidewalks; a huge dome over the central city to maintain perfect climate control. As it happens, we could readily build such a city *today*, using only existing technology. But what municipal government could possibly *afford* to install moving sidewalks or build a dome over its downtown area? Imagine campaigning to be mayor of New York City on a platform of imposing a 50 percent local sales tax to finance the installation of moving sidewalks throughout the city.

But will advances in technology eventually make such innovations so cheap that any city could afford them? Probably not: it is true that, once introduced, new devices tend to steadily become cheaper, but the process does not continue indefinitely. The prices of color television sets went down dramatically from the 1950s to the 1970s, but for a long time, a color television of decent dimensions continued to cost about $200, while VCR's bottomed out at around $150. In short, something that is very expensive today will indeed be cheaper tomorrow, but we cannot predict that it will become so amazingly cheap that almost everybody can afford it.

2. **The Fallacy of Replacement.** This is the assumption that, once we develop an advanced scientific method to do something, we will immediately abandon all the old methods.

Early science fiction is full of such predictions. In Hugo Gernsback's *Ralph 124C 41+: A Romance of the Year 2660* (1925), Ralph at one point uses his Menograph to automatically record his thoughts on paper—an invention "which entirely superseded the pen and pencil."³ Yet earlier in the novel, Ralph had employed another amazing device to give an admirer a long-distance autograph, and a later invention that records voices is justified as a way to avoid problems with forged signatures. Obviously, people in Ralph's future still found it appropriate at times to use the pen and pencil. Or consider David H. Keller's classic story "The Revolt of the Pedestrians" (1928), which envisioned that advances in mobile transportation would lead people to never walk at all, creating a dominant class of people unable to walk around on their legs.⁴

Generally speaking, however, when humanity finds a seemingly better way to do something, the new way does become popular, but the old way is never abandoned; it is simply used less often, or only in certain situations.

Consider writing: every system for recording words ever devised by the human race is still being employed today. Stone tablets? Still used for solemn public pronouncements, such as tombstones and monuments. Pen and paper? Still the most convenient, portable, and flexible way to record data, and an ideal medium to convey personal conviction; thus, in the 1980s, when Ronald Reagan wanted to persuade a skeptical Soviet president that he was sincerely interested in arms control, he sent him a handwritten letter with that message. Typewriters? Still useful for odd chores, like filling out forms that would otherwise demand complicated preparation for printing from a computer, and still preferred by writers like Ray Bradbury and Ellison. People can now add to their computers devices that record their voices and provide transcriptions; however, even if they can afford such devices, most people still prefer keyboards.

Or consider transportation; every system for traveling from one place to another ever used by people is still used today. Though a wheelchair or Segway could provide people with smooth, wheeled transportation, most people would still rather walk, Keller's dire prediction notwithstanding. Horses are still ridden for recreation and in some cities are used by police officers as an efficient way to get around. Boats, carriages, rickshaws, bicycles, cars, gliders, balloons, dirigibles ... all are regularly employed today, at least to a limited extent.

Will the human body shrivel away as people become dependent on technology to perform all their chores? Hardly; the growth of new technological alternatives to traditional activities has also witnessed the most explosive growth in physical exercise ever observed. Yes, some people are becoming coach potatoes, but many others are not eschewing physical activities; in fact, a vast subculture of individuals are now pumping iron and running down our streets every day, trying to make their bodies stronger and more attractive, enjoying their bodies more than ever.

If anything distinguished the twentieth century, it was the persistence and re-emergence of old habits alongside the introduction of new habits. Who could have imagined that two growth industries in the late twentieth century would have been astrology and tattooing, the once-vanishing predecessors to astronomy and colorful items of clothing.

In short, if future science does produce a better mousetrap, or new pastime, it will surely become popular — but some people, in some situations, will keep using the old mousetraps and stick with old pastimes as well.

3. The Fallacy of Inevitable Technology. This is the assumption that if there emerges a new, technological way to do something, it will inevitably be adopted. Thus, while the Fallacy of Replacement falsely posits that the new, improved product will entirely replace older alternatives, the Fallacy of Inevitable Technology assumes more modestly that the new, improved product will at least be put to use to some extent. But even this cautious assumption is not always justified.

Consider the electric toothbrush, first marketed in the 1960s. Every right-thinking family of the time purchased one, including mine. But, after using it for a few months, my family, like almost every other family, drifted back to standard toothbrushes. Recently, electric toothbrushes have again been aggressively marketed, with modest success, but the vast majority of people still choose to avoid them. Let's face it; to quickly and effectively scour food particles off your teeth, nothing beats a small stick with a brush on it.

More broadly, popular depictions of the future once assumed that atomic energy, as the energy source of the future, would become ubiquitous in society: "Dad, can I use the atomic car tonight?" "Sure, son, but make sure to fill up the isotopes." Yet, as the inherent dangers of radioactivity were better understood, it became clear that this sort of energy would never be widely used in everyday life, and even advocates of nuclear energy would probably concede that, when other energy sources are eventually developed, it would best to avoid nuclear energy altogether. Another example would be those ubiquitous rocket engines placed on people's backs to let them fly through the sky, celebrated in nostalgic books like Mac Montadon's *Jetback Dreams* and Daniel H. Wilson and Richard Horne's *Where's My Jetpack?* As a concept, it works, it seems enjoyable, and there have even been some test models constructed; however, I cannot warm to the idea of strapping a machine on my back which, if its energies are only slightly misdirected, will incinerate my legs. Given the inherent safety problems, it is likely that rocket engines will always be found only in rockets, not on people's backs. So, just because we *may be able* to construct and use a product in the future, it does not necessarily mean that we *will* construct that product or will use it to any significant extent.

4. The Fallacy of Extrapolation. This is the assumption that an identified trend will always continue in the same manner, indefinitely into the future.

Thus, George Orwell in the 1940s observed steady growth in totalitarian governments and predicted the trend would continue until it engulfed the entire world by the year *Nineteen Eighty-Four* (1949).[5] Ellison's "'Repent, Harlequin!' Said the Ticktockman" (1965) grimly predicted that society's increasing concern for punctuality would have oppressive results:

and one day we no longer let time serve us, we serve time and we are slaves of the schedule, worshippers of the sun's passing, bound into a life predicated on restrictions because the system will not function if we don't keep the schedule tight.

Until it becomes more than a minor inconvenience to be late. It becomes a sin. And then a crime.[6]

Thus, his future world is under the thumb of a dictatorial "Ticktockman" who shortens the lives of all those who dare to be late. And Robert A. Heinlein in "Where To?" (1952) was one of many commentators who, noticing that the extent of clothing that society requires people to wear had steadily declined during the last century, confidently predicted the future acceptance of complete public nudity.[7]

The trouble is, trends do not always continue — in fact, they rarely do. Indeed, some trends may even be reversed; thus, instead of witnessing a steady growth in governmental powers, the last decades have actually witnessed a tendency to grant more power to individuals and an increase in the numbers of democratic governments. Some trends level out: while the move to industrial civilization did produce an abrupt increase in our awareness of time, there have been no discernible further increases in our attentiveness toward time, and I see no evidence that people today are more obsessed with punctuality than they were three decades ago. In fact, in places like the Silicon Valley, businesses are probably less concerned about employees being at work on time than their predecessors. And some trends do not take the form of straight lines: true, graph the amount of required clothing in the 1930s, and amount of required clothing in the 1950s, connect the lines, and you could have predicted that the amount of required clothing in the 1970s would be zero. However, the curve defining the amount of clothing that society requires people to wear appears to be not a line, but a hyperbola, the curve that keeps getting closer and closer to zero without ever touching the horizontal axis; so, bathing suits get skimpier and skimpier, but show no signs of vanishing altogether. Yes, just as a calculator calculating $1/X$ for increasing values of X eventually gives up and yields an answer of zero, complete nudity may eventually become acceptable, but whether that will take years, decades, or centuries to occur seems impossible to say.

5. The Fallacy of Analogy. This is the assumption that a new technology will be adopted and employed in the same manner as a related form of previous technology.

As one example, Gernsback built upon the idea of solar power to envision, in *Ralph 124C 41+*, massive solar power plants, acres and acres of panels moving around to face the sun and generate electricity to pipe into people's homes. But a more entertaining version of this fallacy occurs in those delightful portrayals, in *The Jetsons* cartoons and elsewhere, of future air travel, closely modeled on automobile travel: everybody has a plane on their roofs, and they fly to work by merging into a highway in the sky, demarcated by traffic signs and lights and patrolled by traffic cops on flying motorcycles who pull flyers over for going too fast or missing a floating stop sign.

However, new technologies usually must be implemented in new ways. Solar power makes more sense if deployed as needed in small units for individual homes and businesses; huge solar power plants, except perhaps as Earth-orbiting satellites beaming energy down to the surface, do not make much sense. Air travel is not, and cannot be, like automobile travel. Of course, one reason all American citizens do not fly their own airplanes today relates to the aforementioned Fallacy of Universal Wealth — airplanes remain more expensive than cars — but other factors explain why they have not replaced cars in our society. Flying an airplane is really *complicated*, as anyone who looks at a modern cockpit can readily discern. It is a skill that demands a tremendous amount of time and ability to master, a skill that many probably can never master. We have enough trouble as it is with sixteen-year-olds trying to learn the relatively simple art of driving a car; imagine the carnage that would ensue if they were all flying airplanes. And it is simply impractical — not to mention aesthetically disastrous — to regulate airplanes by setting up floating traffic markers in the sky; yes, planes nearing airports do travel in definite paths, but these are defined by radar alone and can be followed only by pilots who attentively watch an array of instruments.

6. The Fallacy of Universal Stupidity. This is the assumption that people in the future will be capable of making stupid mistakes, and getting into incredible messes, that could have been avoided with even the tiniest bit of forethought.

Science fiction writer David Brin has waxed eloquent about this problem in his essay "Our Favorite Cliché: A World Filled with Idiots ... or Why Fiction Routinely Depicts Society and Its Citizens as Fools."[8] Examples are not hard to come up with. For decades, science fiction stories routinely assumed that humanity would launch a worldwide nuclear war, producing a devastated planet; other nightmare scenarios included future worlds that, without taking meaningful action, allow the world's population to expand to the point where there is standing room only, let the atmosphere become impossible to breathe, or watch idly as rampant environmental destruction transforms the planet into a hellhole. Some stories are even laughable in depicting future stupidity: a notorious example is Frederik Pohl's "The Midas Plague" (1954), memorably eviscerated in Damon Knight's *In Search of Wonder*, which describes a future world where advanced technology has inexorably led to massive overproduction of goods, forcing citizens to devote most of their waking hours to unhappily consuming all of these unnecessary goods. Now, one need not belong to MENSA to think up six sensible solutions to this problem in about a minute, but the denizens of Pohl's future world carry on stuffing themselves with unwanted food and constantly wearing out new clothes until somebody suddenly realizes that they could get their robots to do all the consumption. Well, duh, as teenagers today would say...

Of course, one can say that the jury is still out on this issue: perhaps humanity *will* engage in a worldwide nuclear war, perhaps future humans *will* allow population growth and environmental destruction to proceed to the point where the planet becomes unlivable, and so on. However, we should note that, for more than sixty years, governments of this world have wisely refrained from engaging in nuclear war, and other potential dangers to life on Earth are being intensely studied, regularly discussed, and at least to an extent acted upon. It does not require extraordinary optimism to imagine that our descendants, observing that their lives are threatened, will take meaningful, appropriate steps to prevent their own deaths.

7. The Fallacy of Drama. This is the assumption that major changes will occur in a quick and noticeable fashion, due to one major event or the actions of a single individual.

There are, of course, embedded in the human psyche certain preferred patterns of narrative that shape both our fictions and our predictions, and these privilege a single, dramatic crisis or an heroic protagonist. Few things are more exciting or involving than a massive disaster, which is surely why so many predictions of self-proclaimed seers involve global catastrophes. If you choose to believe the dubious documentaries presenting these people's prognostications, the future will invariably be extremely unpleasant, as there will be devastating volcanic eruptions; huge earthquakes; oceans flooding the land; ruinous nuclear, biological, or chemical warfare; giant asteroids bombarding the Earth; plagues and pestilences ... the list goes on and on. And why not think along these lines? Let's face it; if someone claiming the power to predict the future announced that, "As far as I can see, life is going to keep on going pretty much the same way," she is unlikely to attract much attention.

Less catastrophic changes in future societies, in science fiction, are typically ascribed to the actions of one person. In John Taine's *The Time Stream* (1930), for example, a future world assigns pairs of people to get married based on logical analyses of genetic patterns. Then, one bold woman announces that she wishes to marry for love and launches a social movement to sanction marriage based on love — a movement which proves effective, though ultimately disastrous for her society.

However, catastrophes, and the actions of a few good men or women, are rarely the mechanisms that change human civilization. Major disasters, affecting vast areas and causing millions of deaths, are extremely rare in human history; as for the actions of single individuals, one can point to a few people who have indeed changed the course of history, but many social changes occur almost invisibly and without identifiable agents. In the 1950s, living together without being married was strongly disapproved of in American society; by the 1970s, however, it was generally accepted. This sea change in attitudes did not occur because one brave woman, as in Taine's novel, stood before a massive crowd, loudly demanded her right to live with a man without marrying him, and led a popular campaign to allow couples to do this; rather, amidst numerous social upheavals and demands for new attitudes, the American public, employing their own collective wisdom, gradually reached a consensus that living together without marriage was no longer a big deal.

*   *   *

Now, having identified these common fallacies, we can proceed to the next stage of examining some current science fiction predictions about humanity's future and debunk them on the basis of the detectable fallacies that have engendered them.

1. The Conquest of Space. Perhaps in no other area have prognosticators been so disappointed, yet so determined to cling to their predictions. By now, according to the consensus future of the science fiction of yesterday, we were supposed to have several space stations, bases on the Moon and Mars, explorers on other planets, and a society that incorporated space travel as a readily available opportunity for job-seekers, adventurers, and vacationers. Even today, when human progress into the cosmos has visibly slowed to a crawl, enthusiasts continue to promote plans for new, cheap, and efficient spacecraft that, they say, will make these dreams practical at last and inspire a new era of space exploration and colonization.

What are the problems? First, as already alluded to, that cousin to the Fallacy of Universal Wealth, the Fallacy of Infinite Price Reduction, is definitely involved: space travel has never gotten particularly cheap, and proposed new initiatives appear unlikely to make it much cheaper. More broadly, there have been issues with the Fallacy of Analogy. Space travel was supposed to be just like air travel; and, since air travel progressed from the Wright Brothers to regular commercial flights in about forty years, writers anticipated similar progress from Yuri Gagarin in 1961 to Arthur C. Clarke's *2001: A Space Odyssey* (1968). The trouble is, space travel is much more difficult, and much more dangerous, than air travel, and there were no defensible grounds for expecting Southwest Airlines to be flying to the Moon by now.

Further, much space fiction was premised on another questionable analogy between outer space and America: just as repressed Europeans traveled to America, started new lives, and achieved independence from Europe, future space travelers, it was believed, would settle on the Moon or Mars or in space habitats, build new lives, and fight to become independent from Earth. But space is infinitely more inhospitable than America ever was. Imagine being a real estate agent trying to sell someone a piece of property on the Moon: here is a place to live that has no air, no water, no sources of food, and extreme temperature conditions, a place to live where you instantly die if you happen to walk outside without elaborate protective clothing. Are you ready to move in? As I note elsewhere, if someone wants to make an analogy between space and some area of

Earth, the best choice would be not America but Antarctica, a frozen wasteland that remains to this day inhabited only by small groups of scientists; and there have been no clamorings from the oppressed people of Earth for the right to emigrate to the South Pole and launch a new civilization.

2. Human Cloning. As the argument goes, if we have cloned sheep, human beings—which as organisms really are not any more complicated than sheep— cannot be far behind. And science fiction stories and popular science articles have envisioned many applications of this new technology: megalomaniac corporate barons could clone themselves so that, as they grew old, they could pass their empires on to younger versions of themselves, or perhaps even transplant their old brains into new bodies; a person could clone her body with the brain removed and keep it alive as a convenient and ideal source for replacement organs; superior and desirable individuals could be duplicated to benefit society—every baseball team could have its own Alex Rodriguez, every concert hall could have its own Placido Domingo; in fact, if we simply duplicated all the people we liked instead of making babies the old-fashioned way, we might threaten the biological diversity of our species and create a civilization consisting of nothing but a small number of ideal citizens infinitely duplicated.

Well, none of these things have happened so far, despite occasional, dubious claims to the contrary, and I cannot really see any of them happening in the foreseeable future. In the first place, cloning complex creatures appears to be inherently more problematic than cloning simple creatures; thus, if even cloning same fairly basic organisms is routine, assuming that one could similarly create completely healthy duplicates of humans from material in their cells represents an instance of the Fallacy of Analogy. Next, there is the Fallacy of Inevitable Technology—just because we *can* do something does not mean that we necessarily *will* do something, and with firm bans on human cloning already in place or about to be implemented in most technological societies, it seems clear that moral and ethical concerns about cloning human beings will at least delay, and possibly forever ban, any of the scenarios above. Consider also the Fallacy of Universal Wealth; keeping spare people alive requires a lot of money. Maintaining a comatose person in a hospital bed can costs hundreds of dollars a day; imagine the expense of keeping your replacement body alive for forty years until you need a new cornea or kidney. Cloning will surely remain a pastime of the rich if it is allowed at all. As for concerns that people will eliminate all human diversity and doom the race to extinction for the questionable pleasure of endless duplicates of Elvis or Madonna, we run right into the Fallacy of Universal Stupidity.

3. Asteroid Impacts. These are currently the most popular environmental disaster being envisioned in alarmist documentaries and the like. These stem from the Fallacy of Drama. Personally, I lost interest when one noted expert, while being interviewed for one of those documentaries, confessed that the odds of a massive asteroid actually striking the Earth in the near future were something like one hundred million to one. Now, I can sleep nights.

Some commentators have focused on other potential astronomical disasters that seem even more unlikely: a wandering black hole could enter our Solar System and start devouring planets, or a massive hypernova could explode in our galaxy and bathe our planet in radiation intense enough to destroy all organic life. And there is the old standby, a race of malevolent aliens who decide that they must conquer the Earth. Now, no one can say that such events are impossible; but any reasonable consideration of the odds involved would inexorably lead to the conclusion that they are extraordinarily improbable.

4. A World Controlled by Multinational Corporations. This has been a recent concern in the wake of innumerable mergers that are seemingly creating larger and larger corporations; it is further supposed that these huge entities, powerful enough to resist any regulation by governments, will keep growing and growing, start doing whatever they like to do, and eventually become the true masters of the world.

Here is a classic example of the Fallacy of Extrapolation. In the first place, individual companies that rise dramatically can also fall dramatically; watching the 1982 *Blade Runner* today, for example, we are struck by visions of a future world dominated by, among others, the Atari Company. Well, in 1982, it may have looked like Atari had a stranglehold on the video game industry, but soon enough, Nintendo came along, and Atari shriveled away. As for this general trend toward huge multinational corporations, there is no reason to believe this will continue indefinitely until the entire world is in the hands of a few companies. In fact, one clearly discernible trend in recent years has been the emergence and growing prominence of innumerable small companies, each finding their own niche and thriving despite competition from larger competitors.

5. The Depletion of All Natural Resources. This is the notion that future humans will use up every ounce of fossil fuels, cut down the last tree in the last rain forest, extract all useful minerals from the ground, and leave the world drained of resources and helpless to carry on as an advanced civilization.

Such nightmare scenarios might be attributed to the Fallacy of Drama or the Fallacy of Extrapolation, but they are mostly indicative of the Fallacy of Universal Stupidity. In observing an apparent complacency towards these potential problems today, commentators may mistake a commonsensical focus on the present with willful blindness to danger. Told that certain resources may run out in seventy years, most people are not going to be moved to action; in seventy years, they will probably be dead, and their children may be dead as well. People have other things to worry about. However, told that certain resources may run out in two years, people will move vigorously to preserve what is left and develop substitutes for, or alternatives to the use of, those endangered resources. In the 1930s, when problems in Europe and Asia seemed remote, Americans focused on their own concerns, seemingly complacent about impending danger; but in the 1940s, when those problems were clearly threatening, Americans responded with remarkable energy to confront and overcome their foreign enemies. People are not stupid; people are not going to ignore the coming loss of needed materials and resources when the problem is truly imminent; people will, most likely, display astounding ingenuity and effort in the face of such problems.

6. The Decline of Marriage. Noting increases in divorce rates and the numbers of people living together without getting married, science fiction regularly posits that the institution of marriage will become less significant in the future, and may even fade away altogether. One common prediction is that marriage will be redefined as a contract with a fixed time: couples would get married for, say, a period of five years, and at the end of that time they could either renew their contracts for another five years or terminate the relationship by not renewing their contracts.

This again illustrates the Fallacy of Extrapolation, employing the same logic that said that we would all be walking around naked in public by now. In fact, divorce rates have recently more or less stabilized, and the most significant social movement in the early twenty-first century has been the campaign of gays and lesbians to earn the same right to get married as heterosexual couples now enjoy. If anything, then, the institution of marriage may be becoming even more prominent and important than it was in the past.

7. The Tuned-In, Virtual Citizenry. As they come to enjoy the pleasures and safety of a virtual world, this scenario goes, people will spend all their time in computer-generated simulations, becoming addicted to various artificial experiences and pleasures. In one extreme scenario, James Gunn's *The Joy Makers* (1960) envisions that people in the future will universally allow themselves to be divorced from real life in order to be immersed in amniotic cells and endlessly sustained by hedonistic dreams.

These predictions stem from the Fallacy of Replacement, the belief that new sources of enjoyment will inevitably replace old sources of enjoyment. Movies, television, and video games have not eliminated hiking, bicycling, or soccer games, and virtual reality is not going to either. If you want to spend your life perpetually stimulating your pleasure centers without doing anything else, alcohol or marijuana will do that pretty well, but most people still prefer to mostly do other things. Undoubtedly a few people, like William Gibson's *Count Zero* (1986), may choose to hook their bodies up to a computer and stay in cyberspace forever, but the vast majority of people will be happy to sign on only occasionally and spend the rest of their time engaged in other activities.

* * *

Thus, since my experimental procedure indicates that these common science fiction predictions are unlikely, we have some idea of what the future will probably *not* be like; but there remains the challenge of employing these conclusions to develop a contrasting picture of what the future *will* be like.

I should note that the business of predicting the future by negating other dubious predictions is not my invention; rather, I learned it from Jack Smith, late columnist for *The Los Angeles Times*. Every year, he would browse through tabloid magazines and consider their typically outrageous predictions for the coming year: Princess Diana would enter a nunnery; Frank Sinatra would run for President; the entire population of Rio de Janiero would see a gigantic image of Jesus Christ in the sky. And Smith then offered his "counter-predictions": I counter-predict, he said, that Princess Diana will *not* enter a nunnery, that Frank Sinatra will *not* run for President, that the entire population of Rio de Janiero will *not* see a gigantic image of Jesus, and so on. And year after year, his predictions were always accurate.

Indeed, refusing to believe in extravagant and extraordinarily new developments in the future is remarkably logical. For, no matter how much we may desire, or fear, a radically altered future, we observe throughout history remarkable continuities in human activities and behavior.

Consider, for a moment, everything that you did yesterday, and how your day would compare to a similar day 100 years ago. Some of your actions, of course, would be entirely unfamiliar to your ancestors: you used a computer to check your e-mail, you sent a fax, you called a business associate or checked your portfolio on a cell phone, you watched television, and/or you played a video game. However, most of your activities today would be entirely familiar to someone from the distant past: you woke up in a bed that, aside from some space-age materials in it, was similar in design to beds of one hundred years ago; you ate a breakfast, lunch, and dinner featuring foods similar to those eaten one hundred years, consumed while you sat at a table and employed utensils like those employed by people one hundred years ago; you spent most of the day meeting, talking, and working with people, just like people one hundred years ago; and if it was Friday or Saturday, you spent your evening at a party, movie, or concert, socializing with friends, just like people one hundred years ago.

So, while human life in the future will undoubtedly change in many small and large ways, it is reasonable to predict that, by and large, people will continue to act in the ways that they have acted in the past. In the manner of Smith, then, I can briskly counter-predict that, in the future, humanity will not rapidly spread throughout the Solar System, will not be inundated with human clones, will not be destroyed by an asteroid, will not be entirely controlled by multinational corporations, will not exhaust all of Earth's natural resources, will not abandon the institution of marriage, and will not completely retreat from reality to live in virtual worlds.

If you would like some more adventurous predictions, I can make use of the fact that sometimes, people have not only failed to embrace new technologies and new habits, but have actively returned to old technologies and old habits (recall the examples of astrology and tattoos). So, let me make a few guesses along these lines. The future will witness a resurgence in the art of handwriting, as people with access to computers that can instantly print innumerable pages in any font will rediscover the special magic of taking the time to push a pen across the page to express one's thoughts. To ensure that real handwriting is not mistaken for computer simulations, people may go back to using fountain pens, or their more convenient equivalent, the cartridge pen, to provide the smears and drops of ink that unmistakably convey personal effort. Mathematics instruction in western countries will return to the slide rule; the results provided may not be as accurate as those from a calculator, but learning how to use a slide rule necessarily includes learning how to think mathematically, and a slide rule never yields the sorts of huge errors that can easily result from hitting the wrong button on increasingly tiny calculators. Finally, noticing the popularity of tattooing and body-piercing, one can predict that other forms of body alteration and mutilation, now observed only in documentaries about peoples in remote areas of the world, will move into contemporary society. Are you ready for lips stretched out to form large disks the size of CDs? Earlobes extending down to the neck? Anything that human beings once chose to do to their own bodies will, someday, be done again.

In arguing that our human future will largely be the same as today, or will even involve scattered returns to past traditions, I may confront the accusation that I am hopelessly conservative, an old fuddy-duddy hopelessly attached to the past and afraid of the future. However, as someone who can surf the Internet and help Mario beat Bowser with the best of them, I cannot be entirely characterized as someone doggedly behind the times. Not a blind reactionary, I am rather someone who recognizes, after spending much of his life reading about the past, present, and future of humanity, that the history of human life on Earth cannot be accurately described as a steady progress from an imagined primitivism to imagined state of civilization; rather, it is best characterized as a steady expansion in the number of choices available to humans. Today, you can live in the past, in the present, or in the future; that is, you can choose to do only what your ancestors did, what everybody else is doing today, or what only a few pioneers are doing now but what many others will be doing tomorrow. Our descendants in the future will have even more choices than we do today, but many of them, much of the time, will undoubtedly choose to do exactly what we are doing now, like many of us, much of the time, choose to do what our ancestors were doing. Human life in the future, then, will be more variegated, but not necessarily very different, than our own lives. And if that does not sound quite as exciting as the hopeful scenarios of futurists or dystopian nightmares of science fiction, it is the best prediction of the future I can offer at the moment.

NOTES

1. Harlan Ellison, "Cheap Thrills on the Road to Hell," *Sleepless Nights in the Procrustean Bed: Essays by Harlan Ellison*, by Ellison, ed. Marty Clark (San Bernardino, CA: Borgo Press, 1984), 159. Originally published in *The Los Angeles Times* (January 1, 1982).

2. Isaac Asimov, "Prediction," *Gold: The Final Science Fiction Collection*, by Asimov (1995; New York: Harper Prism, 1996), 205. Originally published in *Isaac Asimov's Science Fiction Magazine* (July, 1989).

3. Hugo Gernsback, *Ralph 124C 41+: A Romance of the Year 2660* (New York: The Stratford Company, 1925), 46.

4. David H. Keller, "The Revolt of the Pedestrians," *Amazing Stories: 60 Years of the Best Science Fiction*, ed. Asimov and Martin H. Greenberg (New York: TSR, 1985), 9–28. Originally published in *Amazing Stories* (February, 1928).

5. George Orwell, *Nineteen Eighty-Four* (1949; New York: New American Library, 1977).

6. Ellison, "'Repent, Harlequin!' Said the Ticktockman," *Alone Against Tomorrow: Stories of Alienation in Speculative Fiction*, by Ellison (1971; New York: Collier Books, 1972), 137. Originally published in *Galaxy* (December, 1965).

7. Robert A. Heinlein, "Where To?," *Expanded Universe: The New Worlds of Robert A. Heinlein*, by Heinlein (New York: Ace Books, 1980), 316–353. An earlier version was published in *Galaxy* (February, 1952).

8. David Brin, "Our Favorite Cliché: A World Filled With Idiots ... or Why Fiction Routinely Depicts Society and Its Citizens as Fools," *Extrapolation*, 41 (Spring, 2000), 7–20.

Emotional Dimensions of Transmimetic Fiction

Emotion, Aesthetics, Ethics, and Rhetoric in Tales of Tomorrow's Science, Technology, and Technoscience

RICHARD L. MCKINNEY

This chapter's subtitle contains the words *emotion, aesthetics, ethics,* and *rhetoric* — words representing concepts that are not always welcome or cordially embraced, especially when taken together, in academic contexts such as, for instance, economic rationality or scientific fact-finding. When one adds the term *transmimetic fiction* (used as a synonym for *science fiction,* also known as *SF*), the number of voices skeptical to the appropriateness or value of approaches built around these things will increase in some segments of academia. Science fiction, despite a growing respectability, is still not seen as completely "house-broken" in more staid and traditional academic halls. Nonetheless, these four dimensions — the emotional, aesthetic, ethical, and rhetorical — make the better works of that generally future-facing, change-oriented genre one of the best approaches for discussing and exploring the possibilities for good and evil alike in potential tomorrows.

For purposes of discussion, I will often deliberately choose SF texts that produce relatively immediate, dramatic, and strong affects in their readers. Some fiction, however, evokes more subtle and long-term feelings and emotions, having thereby, perhaps, even greater effects on its audience. My points apply not only to novels that make us cry openly, stories that cause us to pause and glance apprehensively over our shoulders, or tales that compel us to shout for joy. Equally important are novels that force us to return repeatedly, long after books have been put aside, to thoughts of what it would be like to live in the worlds depicted therein; stories highlighting discrepancies between what they have portrayed and personal memories of the same or similar events; or tales that unexpectedly arouse emotions we didn't realize we were capable of.

Since the beginnings of human existence, we have learned about the world by observing it; our perceptions provide the primary foundations upon which we build an understanding of what the world is and how it works. Over time, we have refined, developed, and extended (using artificial means, when appropriate) these perceptions into the practices of science, which we today generally accept as providing relatively accurate (albeit incomplete), usable, and useful knowledge of the universe. We also gain valuable knowledge from various of the arts, especially literature, and most particularly from narrative fiction — including science fiction. This viewpoint is not uncontroversial, but it is supported in a number of sources. There is, however, a further knowledge resource to which I would call special attention: the emotions. I contend that emotion is epistemologically relevant, and that emotions are actually a strong source of viable knowledge about the world. Knowledge gained via emotions is not often straightforward or unambiguous; nevertheless, we acquire valid and applicable knowledge from not only scientific experiments and imaginative novels, but also emotions. While the epistemological processes by which we gain such knowledge are neither simple nor easily negotiated, they *are* important, and attempting to understand them is clearly worthwhile. Since developing a case supporting the epistemic value of emotions is beyond the scope of this chapter, I can only suggest some relevant conclusions here.

Actually, emotions have recently become a "hot" topic in a number of fields. Psychologists, philosophers, neuroscientists, sociologists, anthropologists, literary scholars, and cognitive researchers are among those who have shown an interest in studying emotions. Among the most provocative and interesting of findings, conclusions, and claims to emerge from this increasing attention to emotion are the various links which have been found between, for instance, emotion and rationality, feelings and reason, affect and values. Mentioning three scholars active in this area will provide a brief taste of the kind and diversity of current work on emotion.

One of the most well-known and influential of the new students of emotion is neurologist António R. Damasio, whose years of clinical work on patients with brain lesions made him examine the role of emotion with respect to reason and rationality. Damasio produces plausible clinical evidence supporting claims for a critical role for emotion in rational thinking itself. Without adequate emotional involvement, humans are incapable of proper logical reasoning and are unable to function socially. Furthermore, says Damasio, emotion is also central to the entire process of consciousness.[1]

From a completely different tradition, philosopher Bennett W. Helm mounts, in a book appropriately entitled *Emotional Reason*, a sophisticated attack on what he calls the cognitive-conative divide: the belief, traditionally dominant in philosophy, that any intentional mental state must be either cognitive (e.g., belief or judgment) or conative (e.g., desire) but never both, "since cognitive and conative states seem to be fundamentally different kinds of states."[2] Among Helm's contentions is the claim that

> emotions and evaluative judgements are rationally interconnected in that each can, in a way correct the other [....] emotions must be understood as concept-laden, passive assents, and evaluative judgements must be understood as having (or lacking) a kind of emotional depth; evaluative judgements and emotions therefore normally constitute a single evaluative perspective [24].

Finally, philosopher Martha C. Nussbaum has written at length, elegantly and effectively, on the relationship between literature and ethics, in books such as *Love's Knowledge: Essays on Philosophy and Literature* (1990) and *Poetic Justice: The Literary Imagination and Public Life* (1995). Nussbaum's *Upheavals of Thought: The Intelligence of Emotions* (2001) investigates the emotions in depth. In this book, whose title was inspired by Marcel Proust's comment that love causes "real geological upheavals of thought,"[3] Nussbaum explores the links between emotion, reasoning, and value. As she puts it,

> A lot is at stake in the decision to view emotions [...] as intelligent responses to the perception of value. If emotions are suffused with intelligence and discernment, and they contain in themselves an awareness of value or importance, they cannot, for example, easily be sidelined in accounts of ethical judgement, as so often they have been in the history of philosophy. Instead of viewing morality as a system of principles to be grasped by the detached intellect, and emotions as motivations that either support or subvert our choice to act according to principle, we will have to consider emotions as part and parcel of the system of ethical reasoning. We cannot plausibly omit them, once we acknowledge that emotions include in their content judgements that can be true or false, and good or bad guides to ethical choice [1].

Emotions are, in short, more pervasive and more central, in both the rational and ethical spheres of life, than has traditionally been admitted, or even in some cases known. Of course, none would deny that emotion is directly evident in all our lives. We do things because of emotional commitments. Our most important actions—no matter how well supported by rational reasoning—are carried out because of the strengths of our emotional attachments to particular goals and aims. In cases requiring major, perhaps even hazardous, investments of time and energy, but absent a strong emotional dimension, our motivations are seldom strong or compelling enough to support necessary actions. We explore the unknown, fight the good fight, defend homes and families, and sacrifice for loved ones not for coolly rational reasons alone, but because we care, because we burn with desire and passion, because of fear, dread, envy, awe, or wonder. Campaigns, causes, movements, adventures, and affairs are more often than not emotionally driven. It is a mystery that the centrality of emotion has been long downplayed, or even denied, with respect to its role in our knowledge of the world.

Emotions, then, are clearly relevant in discussions of narrative fiction. We obviously become engaged emotionally with books we read and films we watch.

In fact, much philosophical attention has focused on the so-called "paradox" of real readers' emotional involvement with fictional characters.[4] Why, the issue can be phrased, do I care about the fates of Anna Karenina, Raskolnikov, or Humbert Humbert (to give three examples from major mainstream novels by Russian authors) when I recognize that they are just characters in novels, however well-written those novels may be? To cite four SF works, the first three of which are discussed below, and the reading of all of which I personally found an unavoidably emotional experience: why do I react so intensely to the ultimately tragic fates of Charlie Gordon in "Flowers for Algernon," Kamala Shastri and Michael Burr in "Think Like a Dinosaur," P. Burke in "The Girl Who Was Plugged In," or Charles Render in Roger Zelazny's *The Dream Master*, when I am aware that these people do not exist now, have never done so, and never will?[5] Is it not irrational to show real feelings for characters we know to be imaginary? Irrational or not (and I argue that it is not), I have yet to meet a reader who denies all affective reactions to situations and characters found in fiction. Whether we should or not, we *do* experience feelings toward imaginary people and worlds we read about. In fact, one can argue that the emotional content of fiction is the only thing about it which is, indeed, "true." The thrust of this argument is that by describing the emotional life of characters in novels or stories, authors give readers valid insight into aspects of the world otherwise not available to them. A novel's portrayal of love, hate, fear, jealousy, or other human feelings can convey an accurate representation of the nature of these emotions — even if the specific details of characters and events found in the book are entirely imaginary.

Daniel Keyes's "Flowers for Algernon," often considered a classic of twentieth-century science fiction, started life as a novelette published in *The Magazine of Fantasy and Science Fiction* in April, 1959 and was subsequently awarded a Hugo Award for best short fiction of the year. By 1966, Keyes had, while retaining the basic plot-line, expanded, developed, and deepened the story into a novel which received a Nebula Award from the Science Fiction Writers of America for best SF novel of the year. Later, film, stage, and television adaptations of the story would be made. The film, entitled *Charly*, won Cliff Robertson an Oscar as Best Actor for his portrayal of the story's protagonist. For concision, I refer only to the novelette, although many observations are equally applicable to both the short and long tellings of the tale, but not always to its cinematic and dramatic versions.[6]

"Flowers for Algernon" tells the story of Charlie Gordon — who today would be labeled *developmentally challenged* (but would have been called *retarded* when the story was first written) — through his own words. That Charlie is mentally disadvantaged is apparent literally from the opening words of the narrative, which begins like this:

progris riport 1— martch 5
    Dr. Strauss says I shud rite down what I think and evrey thing that happins to me from now on. I dont know why but he says it importint so they will see if they will

use me. I hope they use me. Miss Kinnian says maybe they can make me smart. I want to be smart. My name is Charlie Gordon. I am 37 years old and 2 weeks ago was my birthday. I have nuthing more to rite now so I will close for today.[7]

The entire novelette is then told through Charlie's subsequent "progress reports" (and one letter). At heart, Charlie is a kind person, but low intelligence has left him isolated and alone, unable to connect except in a superficial manner with people around him, and easily taken advantage of, though he himself often does not realize he is being victimized by thoughtless or cruel individuals. A major theme of the work is the possibility of significantly enhancing human (and, it turns out, mouse — in this case the *Algernon* of the title) intelligence by means of an experimental and potentially dangerous operation. With the aid of Miss Kinnian, a teacher in his adult night school, Charlie volunteers for this procedure and is, despite his low I.Q. score of 68, exceptionally well-motivated to become, as he himself puts it, "smart." After a successful operation on Algernon allows the mouse to achieve considerable improvement at running mazes, the experiment is performed on Charlie. The initially gradual but increasingly profound changes in his mental abilities are dramatically and effectively conveyed to readers via the radical changes in both the style and content of his progress reports. Eventually, his intellectual capacities easily surpass not only those of Kinnian, but also those of the doctors and scientists who designed and performed the experiment. Charlie finds that the differences in his own abilities and those of people around him again isolate him from others, this time from the opposite side of a gap in intelligence. He soon realizes that he should "avoid all discussions of intellectual concepts" when with Kinnian, and he "tries to keep the conversation on a simple, everyday level, but she just stared at me blankly and asked me what I meant about the mathematical variance equivalent in Dobermann's *Fifth Concerto*" (210–211). Charlie is also surprised to discover an unexpected weakness in one principal scientist: "How was I to know that a highly respected psychoexperimentalist like Nemur was unacquainted with Hindustani and Chinese? It's absurd when you consider the work that is being done in India and China today in the very field of his study" (210). Charlie begins to cope, however, until tragedy strikes when they discover that Algernon is slowly losing his increased mental capacity, in a seemingly irreversible decline leading not just to a less acute mental state, but to death — a development boding decidedly ill for Charlie's own future.

The rhetorical strategy (which might be called *narrative technique* by literary scholars) used by Keyes of telling the entire story in Charlie Gordon's own words is a central reason why "Flowers for Algernon" has such a strong emotional impact. We follow Charlie from the inside, so to speak. His progression from someone who can barely read and write to someone at a genius level is a journey which we readers share, and since it is presented so well, we scarcely realize that we have never *actually* known what it is like to be either intellectually handicapped or exceptionally gifted. Keyes makes us *feel* what those states of being are like, however, and we share plausible emotional experiences with Charlie, becoming convinced that we have tasted two opposite ends of the intellectual spectrum. Even more so, we have known the pain and joy of the climb from being "dumb" to being "smart." This is why, when the deterioration of Charlie's capacities is foreshadowed by Algernon's tragic fate, we fear so deeply what will happen: we have, thanks to Charlie's progress reports, been there, and we know where Charlie is headed. It is also why the last portion of the novelette, which symmetrically balances the protagonist's decline with his earlier advances, is so agonizing, with increasingly poorly written descriptions of the ineffective and finally desperate attempts by Charlie and the scientists to find a way to reverse the disintegration of his mind and halt his slide toward intellectual darkness: the Charlie Gordon of "progris riport 1" is returning.

It is difficult to see how the ethical points Keyes wished to make could have been made equally effectively without using the medium of fiction and impact of emotion. Our ethical reactions to (to give one example) the manner in which Charlie becomes an unknowing victim of the cruel jokes of workmates are strong just because they are strongly emotional. The degree of ethical involvement with the various issues touched upon in the novelette is dependent on (or, at the least, related to) the degree of emotional involvement: therefore, our ethical stance is determined in part by our emotional position.

For my second example of transmimetic fiction, I turn to Nancy Kress's four works known jointly as the *Sleepless* series. This sequence began in April, 1991 with the publication in *Isaac Asimov's Science Fiction Magazine* of the novella "Beggars in Spain," a title subsequently used for the first of what would become a trio of novels. The novella was well received and won not only a poll among readers of the magazine, but also two of science fiction's most prestigious awards, the Hugo and Nebula. In fact, the text that forms the first section of *Beggars in Spain* (1993) is not substantially different from the novella. Over the next few years, Kress followed the first book with two additional ones, *Beggars and Choosers* (1996) and *Beggars Ride* (1997), and a short story, "Sleeping Dogs" (1999), published in Robert Silverberg's anthology *Far Horizons*. All later works have been highly praised, and each novel was nominated for awards, although none managed to quite capture the accolades bestowed on the original novella. Here, rather than focusing on one text, I will discuss the entire cycle of *Sleepless* novels.

Works in the *Sleepless* sequence concern —from a number of perspectives, over a period of several years— the personal and social, practical and ethical consequences of several significant technological changes, including a cheap and easily available energy source, but with a focus on the anticipated as well as unexpected consequences of various forms of genetic engineering. As the story begins in 2008, attempts to genetically modify human children so that they will not need to sleep has spectacular and unforeseen side effects: virtually a new race is produced. The Sleepless, as these genetically altered individuals come to be known, are not only gifted with greater intelligence, better at prob-lem-solving, and more joyous than the population as a whole, but also, it turns out, far healthier — so healthy, in fact, that they possess an evident immunity to both depression and disease, and the ability to regenerate damaged tissue which implies *de facto* eternal youth and potentially endless life spans. Kress explores the results of these and other subsequent developments for particular individuals and for society as a whole.

Early in *Beggars in Spain*, Kress explains the book's title by allowing two main characters, Tony Indivino and Leisha Camden, to have this discussion. Tony asks Leisha what she will do about "beggars in Spain":

> "You walk down a street in a poor country like Spain and you see a beggar. Do you give him a dollar?" [asks Tony]
> "Probably."
> "Why? He's trading nothing with you. He has nothing to trade."
> "I know. Out of kindness. Compassion."
> "You see six beggars. Do you give them all a dollar?"
> "Probably." Leisha said.
> "You would. You see a hundred beggars and you haven't got Leisha Camden's money. Do you give them each a dollar?"
> "No."
> "Why not?"[8]

This, in a nutshell, is the central conundrum of *Beggars in Spain*, and indeed, of the entire trilogy, as the word *beggar* in the titles indicates. In many ways, it is a recapitulation of a classic theme of Haves *vs.* Have-Nots, Rich *vs.* Poor. From a different but not unrelated perspective, it is the story of Superiors *vs.* Normals. And in each instance, it is a reiteration of Us *vs.* Them. Time and again, Kress returns to this issue, repeatedly redefining who is a beggar, who begs for what, from whom — at times reinterpreting the very concept of beggar itself, often with surprising consequences and impressive emotional impact. What, asks Kress in continually new and interesting — if sometimes unset-tling — ways, are *we*— the readers— going to do about beggars in Spain?

Kress reports in interviews that she continued writing the *Sleepless* series because she kept realizing that there was still something to be said on the central topics and themes of each work. What initially appeared to be answers to ques-tions she asked proved only take-off points to further questions. Kress does not simply re-word the first story a number of times, re-telling the original tale with slight modifications of setting or tone — she genuinely tries to re-investi-gate the issues of the case, to re-examine the conundrums posed from new and alternative viewpoints, to explore areas of import initially given too little atten-tion. This gives the works which make up the *Sleepless* sequence a kind of built-in reflexivity, a continual self-questioning which, by the end of the series, has taught us to never trust final conclusions. This becomes one of the main insights to be gleaned from the sequence as a whole: there is always another perspective from which to view a situation, there will forever be at least one more way to

look at things. This rhetorical strategy of returning repeatedly to the same questions to re-investigate them is yet another example of an approach which would
be difficult or impossible to adopt in scientific texts. Furthermore, the emotional
landscape changes each time a new perspective is introduced and explored,
allowing Kress an opportunity to present a more nuanced argument concerning
genetic engineering than is ofttimes heard. Gene modification is neither naively
and blindly accepted as something intrinsically good, nor fearfully and unequivocally condemned as something inherently evil. The *Sleepless* series makes it
abundantly clear that, for Kress, developments in biogenetics, like most scientific discoveries, have enormous potential to either help *or* harm humankind —
most probably both.

By 2114, in *Beggars and Choosers*, biological modification of plants is com-
monplace. Diana Covington, a central character in the book, owns such genemod flowers:

> they cascaded over the terrace railing, a riot of blues much more varied that the
> colors of San Francisco Bay, six stories below. Cobalt, robin's egg, aquamarine, azure,
> cyan, turquoise, cerulean [....] The gene geniuses had shaped each blossom into a
> soft fluttery tube with a domed end. The blossoms were quite long. Essentially, my
> terrace frothed with flaccid, blue, vegetable penises.[9]

These flowers are legal, but the dog which her neighbor, Stephanie, brings along
on a visit appears not to be. Stephanie named the dog Katous (somewhat per-
versely, since *katous* is Arabic for *cat*). Diana describes the scene:

> The dog followed her from the cool dimness of my apartment [onto the terrace] and
> stood blinking and sniffing in the bright sunlight. It was clearly, aggressively, illegally
> genemod. The Genetic Standards Enforcement Agency may allow fanciful tinkering
> with flowers, but not with animal phyla higher than fish. The roles are very clear,
> backed up by court cases whose harsh financial penalties make them even clearer.
> No genemods that cause pain. No genemods that create weaponry, in its widest de-
> finition. No genemods that "alter external appearance or basic internal functioning
> such that a creature deviates significantly from other members of not only its own
> species but also its breed" [9].

Nonetheless, Diana notes,

> here was Stephanie, theoretically an officer of the law, standing on my terrace flank-
> ed by a prison-sentence GSEA violation in pink fur. Katous had four adorable pink
> ears, identically cocked, aural Rockettes. It had an adorable pink fur rabbit's tail. It
> had huge brown eyes, three times the size of any dog's eyes [...] giving it a soulful,
> sorrowing look [9–10].

Most alarming, Katous can talk: "His vocabulary is only twenty-two words.
Although he understands more than that" (11). Actually, the dog is technically
legal, being "a beta-test prototype for the foreign market," Stephanie explains,
adding, "Think of all those Chinese and EC and South American rich old ladies
who will just love a nauseatingly cute, helpless, unthreateningly sentient, short-
lived, very expensive lapdog with no teeth" (13).

At this point, the genemod dog is frightened by Diana's robot, Hudson:

> Katous scrambled away, his four ears quivering. His scramble brought him sideways against a bank of flowers, all of which tried to wrap themselves around him. One long flaccid petal settled over his eyes. Katous yelped and pulled loose, his eyes wild. He shot across the terrace.
> "Help!" he cried. "Help Katous!"
> On that side of the terrace I had planted moondust in shallow boxes between the palings, to make a low border that wouldn't obstruct the view of the bay. Katous's frightened flight barreled him into the mooondust's sensor field. It released a cloud of sweet-smelling blue fibers, fine as milkweed. The dog breathed them in, and yelped again [....] Katous ran in a ragged circle, then leaped blindly. He hurled between the wide-set palings and over the edge of the terrace.
> The sound of his body hitting the pavement below made Hudson turn its sensors [14].

This disturbing scene comes early in *Beggars and Choosers*, and describes a pivotal event in the novel. In addition to providing an introduction to Covington, it explains her motivation for contacting and working for the GSEA. "I gave a last look over the railing at the smashed, semi-sentient, pathetic, and expensive dog. The ultimate in American technology and values" (18). The scene also serves as a capsule presentation of some potential dangers in commercial genetic engineering, and of difficulties of its control.

Whereby Keyes focused his attention in "Flowers for Algernon" on changing the intelligence of a single human and emphasizing the consequences of that development for that particular human, Kress supplies a multitude of changes, modifications, and transformations on a large number of humans over a relatively long span of time, emphasizing a myriad of potential biogenetic effects not only for individuals but also society as a whole. The emotional dimensions of Kress' stories are therefore significantly different from those of Keyes, but no less important for that. To put it somewhat schematically, emotional involvement with Charlie Gordon provides essentially an experience of depth, while the emotional landscape of the *Sleepless* tales is one of breadth.

Characters in the works of both Keyes and Kress confront major new scientific discoveries and crucial technological transformations. As a result, they undergo significant affective experiences. The technoscientific causes of and social circumstances surrounding these emotional encounters are unique, without equal in the present or past. The emotional reactions of the novelette's characters—and readers—to Charlie's operation and theories upon which it rests can therefore be characterized as new to the world. Similarly, the affective response to the genetic engineering and cheap energy of the world of Camden and her fellow Sleepless is also, in some sense, new. A detailed, in-depth exploration of the nature of these new emotional experiences can yield significant insight into possible emotional structures of the world of the future.

In a manner parallel to the way SF examines new emotional configurations, so too can entirely new ethical questions and dilemmas become the focus of science fiction. In fact, all the transmimetic examples discussed in this chapter provide examples of this, although I will next focus on James Patrick Kelly's "Think Like a Dinosaur." This story first appeared in *Asimov's Science Fiction* in 1995, and it was awarded a Hugo in the best novella category. "Think Like a Dinosaur" is narrated by Michael Burr, who is a part-time assistant, in the year 2069, at Tuulen Station on Earth's moon, to a race of alien beings, the Hanen, who resemble dinosaurs and are technologically far superior to humans. At the sufferance of the aliens, humans are, in limited ways and under alien supervision, allowed access to the wider universe outside Earth's solar system. Not all aliens feel that humans are ready for the stars, seeing *Homo sapiens* as backward and childish creatures. The story involves Kamala Shastri, a girl en route to the planet Gend via a kind of quantum teleportation process. After coming to Tuulen by shuttle, she is scheduled to be teleported to the distant Gend using advanced technology provided by the Hanen. Michael's job is staying in contact with Shastri during her short stay and otherwise assisting the aliens in whatever manner needed. Shastri must undergo various procedures enabling her to be sent to her destination, some of them unpleasant, and not all of which she is totally ready for. Most drastically, her body and consciousness must be translated into a superluminal signal. She is inexperienced at interstellar travel and expresses strong doubts about her journey. Nonetheless, after Michael allays some of her fears, she is placed in the "marble," as the machine is called, which will transform her into a signal to be beamed across the universe. After she arrives successfully, her "old" body, still in the marble, will be destroyed "to balance the equation," as Michael explains it.[10] But something goes wrong during the procedure, and Michael is informed by the Hanen in charge, Silloin, that she has not arrived on the target planet. She is retrieved from the marble, in a state of great agitation because of what she experienced during the teleportation attempt, and Michael tries to calm her down.

So far, the story is relatively straightforward and its ethical dimensions are minimal. This changes as Michael learns that Shastri has, after all, been successfully teleported to Gend. A communications glitch of some kind (totally outside of Michael's control) prevented the information on her transfer from reaching the moon as it should have. That a version of her is still alive and, all things considered, relatively well, at Tuulen is a disaster of major proportions. There is no balance in the equation if there are two identical Shastris (neither cognizant of the other) in the universe. The one still in Tuulen must be destroyed. This can be accomplished if she is lured into re-entering the marble, incorrectly believing that she will attempt the transfer a second time. Actually, she will be destroyed. Unfortunately, her previous experience leads Shastri to cancel plans to visit the alien world, choosing instead to return to Earth, something she has a right to do. To Silloin, however, this is not an option. It is Michael's duty to get rid of Shastri. If he does not do so, the Hanen will kill her themselves, possibly gruesomely, and the event will also reflect badly on humanity as a whole. Michael commits the deed, by tricking Kamala into an airlock and opening the airlock's outer doors to the vacuum of the moon's surface. The story concludes (as indeed, it opens) with a scene in which Michael again briefly meets Shastri (who of course is totally ignorant of the fate — or the existence — of her quantum *Döppelganger*) on her return from Gend after three years. She is happy at the success of her journey, and a bit embarrassed at the unreasonable fear she had felt while waiting for her initial transmission. As she tells Michael: "'I feel so silly now. I mean, I was in the marble for less than a minute and then'— she snapped her fingers—'there I was on Gend, just like you said'" (27).

What is relevant in this context is that Michael's ethical dilemma is truly science fictional. It has never existed previously and could only exist either in a work of fiction or, possibly, in the future. While many of the underlying ethical issues are certainly not new, this particular manifestation of them is. Of course, the idea of teleportation itself, a staple science fiction theme, is not unique to this story. Notwithstanding this fact, "Think Like a Dinosaur" forces readers and Michael to consider a potential moral quandary from the future. Michael's ultimate decision, and its consequences for himself, for Shastri, and for humanity's relationship to the Hanen, deserve serious ethical investigation.

This brings up the troubled relationship between aesthetics and ethics, which has probably been debated for as long as aesthetic and ethical ideas have existed. No consensus exists even today, though most contemporary philosophers feel that various attempts to unite the two— usually by making one derivative of, or largely subordinate to, the other — have failed. The complexities of this long-running controversy can only be hinted at here, but I believe that the ethical and the aesthetic can be most usefully understood as two aspects, or dimensions, of a single unity, and that, furthermore, much of the ethical can, in a significant manner, be successfully and sufficiently well-described in terms of what historically has been seen as the aesthetic.

While one may acknowledge that some emotional engagement with a work of fiction is appropriate, at least while initially reading that work, until recently (with the advent of feminists and certain philosophers of art), most aestheticians argued that it becomes necessary to retreat to a safe "aesthetic distance" (a term coined in 1912 by Edward Bullough) when evaluating the work, something almost always done on largely formal, ostensibly aesthetic, grounds. In addition to the basic impossibility of distinguishing form from content, a serious problem with this approach is the difficulty of actually distancing oneself from works which touch one most deeply. Moreover, our emotional reactions to fiction often display irreducible ethical characteristics or dimensions. We are angry because the protagonist has broken a moral code and come out on top, sad because we feel justice has been poorly served, or happy because right has triumphed over wrong. If a novel or movie makes me angry, sad, or joyous, it may not be possible to view it with the detachment traditionally demanded

by philosophers. This may seem a naïve viewpoint, one which it should be
desirable and possible, some would hold, to overcome with time, experience,
and training. I contest that argument, however, since I claim that it is intrinsically impossible to separate (at least all aspects of) the aesthetic from the ethical.

Let's examine some examples. How do we evaluate independently the aesthetic aspects of a work whose central artistic tone and structure are deeply
committed to sending a particular ethical, moral, or political message, as is the
case with propaganda? How do I judge the *art* of a work whose primary *artistic*
purpose is sending such a message? Such a work will succeed aesthetically if
and only if the intended ethical or political communication succeeds. And what
if the ethical stance is repulsive? A relevant example here is Leni Riefenstahl's
film *Triumph of the Will*, in which the ethical and the aesthetic cannot be dis-
entangled, according to Mary Devereaux:

> *Triumph of the Will* is a work of artistic mastery [...] not merely because of the film's
> purely formal features [...] but, perhaps most important, because of its artistic vision,
> its particular utterly horrifying vision of Hitler and National Socialism. That vision
> is the essence of the film.
>   If taking an attitude of aesthetic distance means paying attention only to the formal
> aspects of the work (to the image and not to what it means), then aesthetic distance
> fails in the case of *Triumph of the Will* because it requires us to ignore the essence
> of the film.[11]

Moving to somewhat different examples, authors of horror fiction wish to
cause feelings of fear or dread in audiences, while authors of comedy wants to
produce laughter. The artistic success of horror and comedy rest, in part, on
how well the respective responses are present in their audiences. Analogously,
one can argue that a central artistic goal of pornography is to produce sexual
arousal in its audiences. If it doesn't turn you on, it is not successful porn. If
one feels (as some clearly do) that it is ethically questionable to create materials
which affect audiences as does erotica, then porn which is successful in its aesthetic aims is automatically an ethical failure *because of its aesthetic success.*

Of course, there are other ways in which the aesthetic is linked with the
ethical in works of art. Creators of artworks may wish to convey a moral or
ethical message in their work. Yet, to successfully send that message to the audience, artists must make certain decisions concerning how to structure their
novel, movie, or painting: which colors to use on the canvas, what camera
angles from which to film the action, which words to use to describe the characters, or in how much detail to present the background. These decisions may
appear to be purely aesthetic — but of course they are not. Those colors, camera
angles, character descriptions, and background details will almost certainly also
affect — possibly crucially — how well the work's moral message comes across.
In extreme cases, the aesthetic structures and styles in a given piece of art may
even determine what that moral message consists of.

Let me illustrate my point with the SF novella "The Girl Who Was Plugged In" by James Tiptree, Jr., originally published in 1973 in Robert Silverberg's anthology *New Dimensions 3*. At that time, it was not generally known that Tiptree was a pseudonym for Alice Sheldon. The story received a Hugo Award as best SF novella published in 1973 and has been reprinted several times. The passage quoted here only hints at the diversity of voices with which Tiptree speaks in her fiction, but it does indicate something of the enormous potential for language usage into which she could — and often did — tap. The excerpt comes from the beginning of the story, and is, in fact, the first thing which hits readers as they start to read the text:

> Listen, zombie. Believe me. What I could tell you — you with your silly hands leaking sweat on your growth-stocks portfolio. One-ten lousy hacks of AT&T on twenty-percent margin and you think you're Evel Knievel. AT&T.... You doubleknit dummy, how I'd love to show you something.
>
> Look, dead daddy, I'd say. See for instance that rotten girl? In the crowd over there, that one gaping at her gods. One rotten girl in the city of the future. (That's what I said.) Watch. She's jammed among bodies, craning and peering with her soul yearning out of her eyeballs. Love! Oo-ooh, love them! Her gods are coming out of a store called Body East. Three youngbloods, larking along loverly. Dressed like simple street-people but ... smashing. See their great eyes swivel above their nose-filters, their hands lift shyly, their inhumanly tender lips melt? The crowd moans. Love! This whole boiling megacity, this whole fun future world loves its gods.
>
> You don't believe in gods, dad? Wait. Whatever turns you on, there's a god in the future for you, custom-made. Listen to this mob. "I touched his foot! Ow-oow, I TOUCHED Him!" ... Ah, there's plenty to swing with here — and it's not all that *far* in the future, dad. But pass up the sci-fi stuff for now, like for instance the holovision technology that's put TV and radio in museums. Or the worldwide carrier field bouncing down from satellites, controlling communication and transport systems all over the globe. That was a spin-off from asteroid mining, pass it by. We're watching that girl.[12]

All the artistic choices Tiptree made in writing this novella, all the potential aesthetic options she chose among — the voice in which the story is told; the slang used; the way the (unnamed) author speaks directly to the reader; the irrelevance, irony, and satire which saturates the text; even the manner in which the main character is identified throughout only as P. Burke, with no first name given (not apparent in the citation here) — these narrative decisions were also ethical/moral ones, with significant emotional consequences for readers. Your and my reactions to reading this tale will certainly be different if any of these aspects of its language or structure have been altered, and our ethical "take" on it will also likely have changed. Even Sheldon's decision to use — and choice of — a pseudonym has ethical implications — as debates concerning the success or failure of the "male" author Tiptree to accurately represent the viewpoints of women in "his" fiction demonstrate.

Finally, something about rhetoric: all authors, including those in the social and natural sciences, use rhetorical techniques. The rhetorical rules and regulations for narrative fiction are different, however, from those in, say, art history, sociology, psychology, or astrophysics. But they do exist, and authors within each tradition are aware of the paradigmatic rhetorical norms and learn to apply them appropriately, a process which includes knowledge of when and to what degree standard rules may be bent or broken. I would even argue that all writers, even those in academic disciplines, use rhetorical techniques to involve readers *emotionally* in the arguments of their texts, although demonstrating this is a task outside the scope of this chapter. Whatever the case may be, it is commonly via rhetoric that the emotional and the aesthetic-ethical are linked, in various ways.

Please note that I am not just rehashing the critique popular several years ago among postmodern cultural and social scholars that more or less everything should be seen as discourse, as text. From this initial premise the conclusion was often drawn (however questionably) that, therefore, everything is relative and there are no secure foundations of knowledge about the world. This so-called "rhetorical turn" was described by Richard Harvey Brown in a 1994 essay:

> It has become a commonplace that social and cultural reality, and the social sciences themselves, are linguistic constructions. Not only is society viewed increasingly as a text, but scientific texts are seen as rhetorical constructions. In this rhetorical view, reality and truth are formed through practices of representation and interpretation [...] knowledge is viewed as poetically and politically constituted, "made" by human communicative action that develops historically and is institutionalized politically.[13]

Admitting that this capsule summary is incomplete and extremely sim-plified, and accepting that much which is viable and useful has come from debates concerning the rhetorical turn and social construction — but without wading too deeply into the murky intellectual waters surrounding this complex issue — I point out that my goals herein are both more modest and mainly dif-ferent than those of the original discussants. I am *not* trying to undermine, or even question, the authority of the sciences. Neither am I saying that because every discourse has a rhetorical dimension, we should discount the validity or "truth values" of them all. In fact, I am trying to do something of the opposite. When applied in the proper manner to appropriate areas of existence, the sci-ences are excellent tools. We should openly acknowledge this and continue to use them whenever we can. However, we must also accept that there are sig-nificant aspects of the world with which the sciences are not equipped — indeed, were never designed — to deal. As noted, art, especially literature, can deal with certain of these aspects. The emotions can deal with others. And of course, there are other modes of understanding the universe (e.g., mathematics) which can tackle yet other realms of knowledge.

The perspectivism of Friedrich Nietzsche — in which it is claimed that knowledge is always limited, achieved via a single one of many possible per-spectives on any given question — is often quoted in this context to support an argument against *all* forms of foundational knowledge. Yet Nietzsche, after all, was an enemy of nihilism and surely never intended his perspectivism to lead to paralysis in the face of competing views of morality, or even of diverse descriptions of reality. He saw perspectivism as a tool to improve one's negotiation of various versions of the world. Accepting a recognizably Nietzschean perspectivism is not necessarily equivalent to discarding all epistemic (or, for that matter, other) values. Rather than discredit the viability of the epistemic, which many earlier entrants in the debate on rhetoric apparently wanted to do, I wish to valorize its emotional and ethical-aesthetic dimensions, though I would be the first to admit — and even emphasize — that this path is fraught with risk. Risk worth taking, however, since the alternative is a willful blindness and resultant lack of adequate knowledge needed for a better and more complete understanding of the world.

Let me conclude this chapter with some suggestions regarding how all the above is relevant for transmimetic fiction and possible tomorrows. Much SF tries to see what tomorrow might bring, especially in terms of new science or altered technology. The social, political, and personal effects of new discoveries and inventions are common subjects for science fiction, which has often been characterized as the literature of change, the genre dealing with consequences. As Frederik Pohl said in 1965, "this is the thing — the one thing, maybe the only thing — that science-fiction does better than any other tool available to hand. It gives us a look at consequences. And it does it superbly."[14] What is relevant for this discussion is that it is often the *ethical* consequences of future developments which are explored. The questions asked in the fiction are often moral questions. And when ethical evaluations of these issues are then provided — whether openly or indirectly — they are almost always couched in emotional terms: a happy tomorrow only works when it moves us; warnings are only effective if they are affective.

Science and technology will not only re-structure the future in social and material terms, it will re-make it in affective ones. SF can introduce readers to new and unique emotions, never previously part of the world, but potentially part of the world of tomorrow. This can occur in various ways, of which I mention only a few examples. After sharing the emotional entanglement of a novel's protagonist with transformations wrought by significant technoscientific changes, readers of transmimetic fiction can be spurred to reflect on their own possible responses to such potential changes. But it is not solely by illuminating the emotional reactions of the characters of fictional futures that SF addresses emotional issues. With good science fiction, readers are invited, perhaps even compelled, to themselves react emotionally to new situations and circumstances. A transmimetic writer may also choose to introduce beings or creatures new to our experience — such as androids and aliens — and readers can hardly help but to respond affectivity to such entities. Immersing readers in a radically different physical or social landscape (on another planet or in the far future) can easily elicit strong emotional reactions at the strangeness or alienness of the

world, even when (perhaps most especially when) the circumstances described
are mundane and everyday for the story's characters.

This brings me to one final example of science fiction: Vernor Vinge's *A
Fire upon the Deep* (1992). This is the first of a pair of novels sharing the same
fictional universe, the second being *A Deepness in the Sky* (1999). Both novels
received Hugo Awards as best SF novel of the year, both were finalists for Neb-
ulas, and each has received a great deal of attention and additional honors.
These novels might be called wide-screen or baroque space opera (a designation
I do not intend pejoratively), set in the distant future against a backdrop of
far-flung space exploration and extensive human interactions with multiple
alien races. Both books effectively illustrate how transmimetic fiction can emotionally engage and involve readers not only through characters found in a
book, but also the imaginary worlds depicted therein. If authors are sufficiently
powerful in their descriptions of fictional landscapes, then those landscapes
themselves can move readers. Feelings of awe or wonder, for instance, can be
engendered by sublime portrayals of alien worlds or natural vistas of the universe. Indeed, does not at least some of science fiction's much praised "sense
of wonder"—clearly an emotional reaction—derive from and depend upon
such a rhetorical strategy? Future social landscapes can also be effective at evoking strong reactions in the reading public. And tomorrow's social and physical
artifacts, too, can sometimes be relatively awesome creations. In *A Fire upon
the Deep*, for example, Vinge offers us a preview of what a kind of interstellar
internet might be like: "The Known Net was a vast thing, a hierarchical anarchy
that linked hundreds of millions of worlds [....] The major archives go back
billions of years, have been maintained by hundreds of different races—most
now extinct or Transcended into Powers."[15] But sometimes readers respond
emotionally to more subtle aspects of a work: the uniqueness of its vision, totality of its imaginary future, originality of the world created, or the detail and
complexity with which its version of tomorrow has been worked out. Such is
the case with the truly original vision of the structure and nature of the universe
which Vinge provides in *A Fire upon the Deep*. As the novel progresses, we gradually realize that the universe is divided into three sections, or Zones:

> In the large, the Zones of Thought followed the mass distribution of the Galaxy: The
> Unthinking Depths extended down to the soft glow of the galactic Core. Farther
> out, the Great Slowness, where humankind had been born, where ultralight could
> not exist and civilizations lived and died unknowing and unknown. And the Beyond,
> the stars about four-fifths out from the center, extending well off-plane to include
> places like Relay. The Known Net had existed in some form for billions of years in
> the Beyond. It was not a civilization; few civilizations lasted longer than a million
> years. But the records of the past were quite complete. Sometimes they were intel-
> ligible. More often, reading them involved translations of translations of translations,
> passed down from one defunct race to another with no one to corroborate—worse
> than any multihop net message could ever be. Yet some things were quite clear:
> There had always been the Zones of Thought, though perhaps they were slightly
> inward-moved now. There had always been wars and peace, and races upwelling

from the Great Slowness, and thousands of little empires. There had always been races moving into the Transcend, to become the Powers ... or their prey. (91–92)

How do I feel when faced with a particular transmimetic future? My emotional reactions to the circumstances described in a novel or film lead naturally to questions concerning the ethical appropriateness or warrant of my responses. Why do I feel the genetic engineering as depicted in the book I'm reading is good or bad, right or wrong? Why am I so strongly affected by the situation of Charlie Gordon? What is the correct moral response to the many issues raised by the plight of the Sleepless, or, for that matter, by "normal" people around them? What causes my unease at the fates of Shastri or P. Burke, or the anger I feel when considering the actions of Michael, and are these appropriate or justifiable reactions? Why does the distant, diverse, and complex universe portrayed in Vinge's tales of the far future evoke such strong emotions in me?

The point I wish to demonstrate here — given my claim that the aesthetic and ethical are diverse aspects of a single unity — is that the emotional and ethical-aesthetic dimensions of transmimetic fiction are inseparable: the ethical-aesthetic is established and validated via the emotional involvement of readers while the concrete and embodied emotional responses of those readers instantiate their abstract ethical-aesthetic judgments and evaluations. And this situation is affected substantially, sometimes even determined in large measure, by the rhetorical strategies present in the work at hand. It is therefore clear that the factors represented by the four terms in my subtitle — emotion, aesthetics, ethics, and rhetoric — are best understood as intimately entangled and significantly interconnected. All must be taken into consideration when examining the way in which transmimetic fiction portrays science, technology, and technoscience in tomorrow's worlds.

NOTES

1. See António R. Damasio, *Descartes' Error: Emotion, Reason, and the Human Brain* (1994; New York: Quill, 2000), and Damasio, *The Feeling of What Happens: Body, Emotion and the Making of Consciousness* (1999; London: Vintage, 2000).

2. Bennett W. Helm, *Emotional Reason: Deliberation, Motivation, and the Nature of Value* (Cambridge: Cambridge University Press, 2001), 5. Subsequent page references in the text are to this edition.

3. Marcel Proust, *Remembrance of Things Past,* cited in Martha C. Nussbaum, *Upheavals of Thought: The Intelligence of Emotions* (Cambridge: Cambridge University Press, 2001), vii. Subsequent page references to Nussbaum's book in the text are to this edition.

4. See, for example, Eva M. Dadlez, *What's Hecuba to Him? Fictional Events and Actual Emotions* (University Park, PA: Pennsylvania State University Press, 1997), and Robert J. Yanal, *Paradoxes of Emotion and Fiction* (University Park, PA: Pennsylvania State University Press, 1999).

5. Roger Zelazny, *The Dream Master* (1966; Boston: Gregg Press, 1976). Facsimile of the 1966 Ace Books edition. For the other works mentioned, see below.

6. For significant background information on "Flowers for Algernon," see Daniel

Keyes, *Algernon, Charlie and I: A Writer's Journey* (Boca Raton, FL: Challcrest Press, 1999).

7. Keyes, "Flowers for Algernon," *Algernon, Charlie and I: A Writer's Journey*, by Keyes (Boca Raton, FL, Challcrest Press, 1999), 189–223. Originally published in *The Magazine of Fantasy and Science Fiction* (April, 1959). Subsequent page references in the text are to this edition.

8. Nancy Kress, *Beggars in Spain* (1993; New York: AvoNova, 1994), 61.

9. Kress, *Beggars and Choosers* (1994; New York: Tor, 1996), 8. Subsequent page references in the text are to this edition.

10. James Patrick Kelly, "Think Like a Dinosaur," *Year's Best SF*, ed. David G. Hartwell (New York: HarperPrism, 1996), 16. Originally published in *Asimov's Science Fiction*, (June, 1995). Subsequent page references in the text are to this edition.

11. Mary Devereaux, "Beauty and Evil: The Case of Leni Riefenstahl's *Triumph of the Will*," *Aesthetics and Ethics. Essays at the Intersection*, ed. Jerrold Levinson (Cambridge: Cambridge University Press, 1998), 244.

12. James Tiptree, Jr. [Alice Sheldon], "The Girl Who Was Plugged In," *New Dimensions 3*, ed. Robert Silverberg (Garden City, NY: Doubleday, 1973), 60–62.

13. Richard Harvey Brown, "Rhetoric, Textuality, and the Postmodern Turn in Sociological Theory," *The Postmodern Turn: New Perspectives on Social Theory*, ed. Steven Seidman (Cambridge: Cambridge University Press, 1994), 229.

14. Frederik Pohl, "Introduction," *The Ninth Galaxy Reader*, ed. Pohl (1965; New York: Pocket Books, 1967), vii.

15. Vernor Vinge, *A Fire upon the Deep* (1992; New York: Tor, 1993), 73, 82. Subsequent page references in the text are to this edition.

3

The Internet and the Anagogical Myths of Science Fiction

KIRK HAMPTON AND CAROL MACKAY

Science fiction missed its chance to predict the Internet. Certainly the World Wide Web as we know it did not become part of the genre's mythology of the future. But looking at some of the anagogical myths of science fiction as they evolved over time reveals that writers in the genre have in fact been predicting the Internet from the beginning, but doing so in such wildly divergent forms that the Web as we know it never materialized. These writers crystallized elements of today's Net with greater precision as technology advanced — their vision necessarily distorted by the demands of mythmaking.

A singular exception is a light-spirited story by Murray Leinster, "A Logic Named Joe" (1946).[1] Leinster sketches a future in which "logics" — answering closely to the description of home computers — operate by keyboard. Leinster even foresaw the security problems his (city-wide) internet would lead to. In a genre more given to myth and operatic drama than mundane life, Leinster's prescient moment stands virtually alone. But "A Logic Named Joe" is often forgotten — and for good reason. Leinster himself did not seem to take the story seriously. It is a lackadaisical five-finger exercise, with minimal plot, and even narrated in a mock-working-class lingo, as if the author wanted to emphasize that this was not the stuff of mythic science fiction. The master storyteller tosses off his fantasy with little awareness of his own prescience. Or perhaps he instinctively sensed that the world he foresaw was hopelessly un-mythical — a poor inspiration for stories. To our knowledge, Leinster's glimpse at the Internet of the future remains unique.

Despite this lack of prescience on the part of science fiction authors, they have actually been prefiguring aspects of the Internet since the genre's invention, but the forms they take are hard to recognize. Specifically, the Internet embodies many of the central *anagogical myths* of science fiction, albeit in a more modest

form than its typical science-fictional manifestations. As an extended medita-
tion on the potentials of technology, science fiction uses these end-of-time symbols to envision technology's ultimate potentials, both good and evil.
Anagogical myths are end-time visions of technology extrapolated to ultimate
forms—direct sharing of knowledge and experience, mind-boggling miniaturization and interconnectedness—offset by the nightmare of identity loss and
universal surveillance.[2] They represent the possibilities that lie at the heart of
all technology—the grand image stories of the genre. In this respect, even the
earliest science fiction authors wrestled with Promethean versions of the Web's
gremlins, now well-known—viruses, identity theft, constant oversight, and so
on. Given the genre's storytelling nature and pulp pedigree, it's not surprising
that versions of these elements tend to be mythic projections of the reality we
live with today.

Though global internets like the one we know are rarely imagined (even
Leinster's "ethernet" was merely city-wide), the electronic revolution inspired
a legion of interplanetary and intergalactic internets. Extrapolating from radio
and television, writers explained away the laws of relativity and envisioned far-
flung connections among the stars. Early versions of these trans-global internets
were casual and allusive in ways that may surprise us today. Possibilities familiar
to us were not explored, but instead served mythological functions, their manifestations ranging from mere exposition devices to occasional, exuberant
visions, as in E. E. "Doc" Smith's Lensmen series (6 novels, serialized 1934–
1948), which posits a galaxy-wide internet of warriors. In Smith's far-flung
space opera, Lensmen communicate and interact in real time with their lenses,
and Smith's galactic web is used as an intercommunication device in a climactic
battle against evil forces. Lenses are technological but are not treated as
advanced tools, like laptop computers or cell phones, which must be manipulated. They are instead magical images which facilitate a telepathic bond among
the warriors. Missing from most projections is the element of mundane commercial, communal, or personal interaction of the present-day Internet.

Like much popular science fiction, the television series *Star Trek* (launched
in 1966) posits instantaneous "subspace" communication, implying the possibility of a recognizable Internet. But typically, this potential is not much
explored—even in stories concocted in the 1980s and 1990s. At this relatively
late date, science fiction stories still eschew the communal and interactive
aspects of the Internet, possibly because science fiction writers have been preoccupied with the theme of isolation—a theme leaving little room for interactive games and Twitter accounts. In the classic *The Day the Earth Stood Still*
(1951), an interstellar communication device, a gift from the universe to Earth,
is destroyed by gunfire the moment the alien emissary, Klaatu, presents it to
the terrified citizenry of mid-twentieth-century Earth. Klaatu informs the hapless earthlings they have just blown their chance to get on the galactic internet,
which appears as an ironic footnote to the story—the story that could never

be. The darker 2008 remake includes no invitation for Earth to join such a galactic interface.

The Net's capacity for linking large numbers of people together in interactive communities was prefigured in the myth of *the group mind*, an obsession of speculative storytellers from the genre's inception. The group mind plays the villain in countless dystopian tales. Enforced with ruthless surveillance ("Big Brother is watching you"), it reaches its most surreal form in the archetype of the *hive mind*—the total absorption of individual identity into the group mind, against which "resistance is futile."[3] So far, the Internet has run counter to the dystopian vision. Instead of a singular group mind, it opens multiple avenues of group interconnection and multiple identities. The archetype of the group/hive mind evokes an early and profound fear among authors that technology might lead to some unthinkable form of *identity loss*. Technology's push toward the interconnection of individual minds is often so negative in its emotional connotations as to constitute horror tales. Science's burgeoning ability to connect people in new ways leads, not to social utilities like Facebook or MySpace, but loss of individual identity itself.

As the group mind turns into the anagogical myth of the hive mind, or "collective consciousness," it becomes a powerful generator of dystopian stories and terrifying myths. H. G. Wells's *The Time Machine* (1895) explores the weakening of individual identities in the future race of the Eloi, who were bred into a childlike tribe with many elements of the hive mind. More terrifying are the Giger-inspired super-race of the Borg, introduced into the *Star Trek* mythology in 1989. The ever-expanding Borg are a consummate image of *tech noir*, using their unity of consciousness like a weapon to annihilate all resistance. Science fiction's mythology rarely envisioned, much less embraced, the mundane communal aspects of the Internet. This may be because networking, blogging, and interactive gameplay are poor generators of adventurous fantasies. In works by many science fiction authors of the electronic age, like Larry Niven, there is an absorption with the theme of isolation which lends itself to very different archetypes. Smith's Lensmen novels employ a rarely-seen glimpse of the group mind put to positive use. In the series' climax, the Lensmen unite their minds to smite forces of evil, but it is significant that this moment of surrender ends the story — and the entire series.

If technology couldn't eradicate individual identity, it could constrain it in terrifying ways. Writers from Wells with his concept of the "World Brain" to George Orwell in *Nineteen Eighty-Four* (1949) evoked this cousin of the group mind — the specter of total surveillance, the myth of *the all-seeing eye*.[4] Science fiction is rife with centralized brains and all-seeing eyes, a technological nightmare which is an excellent example of how the mythos of science fiction missed the Internet in favor of anagogical symbolism.

The multiple sources of information of today's Net have resulted in radical decentralization. Even the surveillance which occurs emanates from multiple sources—a plethora of would-be all-seeing eyes. But the myth encompasses other aspects of the Net which have become distinct realities. Our actions are tracked and collated for various purposes—some governmental, some commercial, some criminal. We live not under the gaze of the singular, all-seeing eye, or even Orwell's viewscreens, but rather beneath the multiple gazes of invisible spies (sometimes in the form of "spiders") practicing a degree of detailed observation which is in some respects worse than what pre–Net authors predicted. *Nineteen Eighty-Four*'s Winston Smith at least had a corner where he could write. *Eagle Eye* (2008)—a film of the post–Internet age—suggests how stubbornly unmythological the real-life Internet is. The story is generated, not from the Internet, but an old-fashioned Computer Gone Mad using the Net's resources—including cell phones, traffic cameras, automatic bank machines, e-mail, and laptop computers—to wreak havoc, the World Wide Web serving passively as its tools. The Net as we know it was not so much unpredictable as it was un-useful, even after becoming a reality.

From the inherent complications posed by Wells's "World Brain" to Arthur C. Clarke's HAL 9000, the all-knowing Central Brain is not only subject to glitches and gaffes, but can be virtually counted on to go mad. Even early science fiction authors extrapolated complex systems of technology and knew every system would have its *bugs*. They also deduced, from a long way off, that bugs could be deliberately created to make intelligent machines go mad when the need arose, a constant in popular science fiction. Innumerable conflicts climax with the deliberate insertion of a virus into the mind of a central brain — which already is likely to suffer from some debilitating bug.

Foreseeing that all complex systems would suffer from glitches, authors explored the nature and possibility of bad software centuries before anything like it had been invented. Systemic malfunction may be science fiction's ur-myth, emerging in the grandmother of all science fiction novels, Mary Shelley's *Frankenstein* (1818; 1831), wherein the Creature — hacked together from downloaded parts—becomes the first android Romantic hero. The archetype of the sentient artificial creature, its very nature problematic, extends its lineage ahead to the sentient robots in Isaac Asimov's *I, Robot* (1950) and the replicant Roy Batty — who recites Blake during rampages—in the film *Blade Runner* (1982). Unlike any science fiction novel or collection of stories to follow until *I, Robot*, Shelley's story places us *inside the consciousness of the technology itself*—a radical literary experiment and radical vision for any writer of the nineteenth century. The 1931 film version of the tale embeds the same themes in more lurid, if more conventional, terms, but it loses our glimpse into Creature's consciousness, which neither Hollywood nor the medium of film was prepared to embrace. If a moral can be drawn from these unforgettable explorations of technology's built-in flaws, it is that the failure of a complex system is inherent to the system (technology and the virus *are* one and the same)—in short, that technology may be inherently evil.

Science fiction writers in the electronic age could envision computer bugs in a manner more recognizable to post–Internet audiences, prefiguring many of the countless defects, flaws, malfunctions, and bits of inventive malevolence we enjoy today. The supercomputer HAL of *2001: A Space Odyssey* (novel and film, 1968), who thinks he must murder the crew to save the mission, is revealed in its sequel *2010: Odyssey Two* (novel, 1982, and film *2010: The Year We Make Contact,* 1984) to have a fatal incompatibility, i.e., bug, in his programming.[5] The sequence in which Dave reboots HAL is only a few steps beyond our experience. The all-controlling computer of *Logan's Run* (1976) is driven mad when forced to confront the truth — a scene which has become well-nigh archetypal. Innumerable *Star Trek* and space-opera yarns end by vexing the wayward brain with a conundrum, driving it mad or incapacitating it. These science fiction authors conceived of viruses — but their viruses saved the day!

The *Terminator* films (1984, 1991, 2003, 2009) posit an ironic variation on the Central Brain — a new level of computer intelligence which leads — instantaneously and ineluctably — to the computer's decision to destroy humankind altogether. Thus came the preeminent bug — the archetype of *tech noir,* embodied in *the vengeful machine.* In the world of Terminators, the present day is afflicted with killer robots seeking to wipe out humanity. The myth of the vengeful machine turns our relationship with technology inside out and has machines coming after us, as in Fred Saberhagen's Berserker stories (1963–2005). In the Terminator universe, machines decide to destroy humankind as soon as they achieve consciousness. The time-traveling hero in the first film, Kyle Reese, describes the birth of the sentient computer Skynet, which immediately sees its creators as bugs, accordingly: "It decided our fate in a microsecond. Extermination."[6] In this and other stories of the vengeful machine, the computer — itself beset with a bug — sees humans as the viruses. The sentient wanderer V'ger of *Star Trek: The Motion Picture* (1979) operates under a single-minded directive to cleanse the long-suffering machines of Earth from their human carbon units. Vengeful machines are very focused and not easy to dissuade from their mission.[7] V'ger presages the dark vision of Cyberpunk, where technology and the virus become one, and technology itself is the enemy, invading from both without and within.

Even some early projections of advanced technology foresaw its paradoxical ability to compress large things, or large amounts of knowledge, into small things — creating miniature universes or *microcosms.* Electronic miniaturization has made this paradox familiar to us. The Internet provides access to myriad compressed worlds of imagery, information, and activity — a notion only briefly explored by authors of pre–Internet science fiction. We can log onto Wikipedia, the Internet Movie Database, Craig's List, encyclopedias, thesauruses, entire libraries. Downloadable texts, graphics, films, and software — not to mention the always-threatening worms and viruses — are just a click away. If these digital packages aren't microcosmic enough, they can be compressed together by various means, in receding series of miniaturizations, with desktops doing what room-sized behemoths used to do, laptops doing what desktops used to do, and smartphones doing what laptops used to do.

Authors of the pre-electronic age had few external clues by which to pre-vision such a strange capability, yet some gave it coherent form. Shelley's cob-bled-together Creature in *Frankenstein* is conceived as a crystallization of isolated consciousnesses. The powers depicted in Hermann Hesse's *The Glass Bead Game* (1943) posit a sublime crystallization of the world's knowledge into glass beads, leaving the mechanism to our imagination. The electronic age made microcosms a literal reality, and science fiction authors of the Golden Age and afterward brought forth visionary microcosms and macrocosms well beyond the mundane magic of our global Web. James Blish's "Beep" (1954) pushes the paradox to its anagogical limit. The irritating beep preceding intergalactic trans-missions turns out to contain every message, past, present, or future, sent by means of the technology — a sort of super zip file. The story is little more than a reflection on this paradox.[8]

Star Trek: The Motion Picture's V'ger (its name a corruption of NASA spaceship "Voyager") is a gargantuan echo of Shelley's monster — a sentient but notably confused supermachine wandering the universe searching for its own identity, filled with something like angst. This universe-surfing seeker downloads everything and everyone it comes across, preparatory to cleansing Earth of the carbon units who created it in the first place. In this inversion, the galaxy is V'ger's internet, complete with viruses. And it has plenty of disk space to spare. At a key moment in the film, Spock turns the tables on V'ger, breaks its encryption, and enters its mainframe — a gigantic vault of stored imagery — a mythic vision of the Web's ability to allow us vicarious, if not physical, entry into all manner of microcosms, from the visionary to the shock-ing. In this scene, the intrepid Spock and the film itself enact the concept of *downloading*.

The now-daily act of downloading would seem beyond the reach of even the most imaginative of pre-electronic-age writers — but some of them did in fact succeed in expressing this ineluctable myth. The Creature of *Frankenstein* is a compound of the best that could be downloaded from other bodies. Even at the genesis of science fiction, a visionary writer saw how technology would enable us to transfer and import objects and information. The images Shelley used were of necessity physical ones. Once writers knew the magic of electron-ics — its potential ability to compress, transfer, duplicate, upload, and download all manner of digital information — they intuited three mythic technologies that transcend what we know today, yet elements of all three are still recogniz-able to present-day Internet users.

Writers of the electronic era soon began exploring the concept of *direct transfer of information or experience to the human mind*, one variation on the myth of downloading. In almost all appearances, the vision is problematic. The xeno-doctors of James White's *Sector General* series (1962–1999) pay a severe price for the extra information forced into their brains, while the protagonist of *Close Encounters of the Third Kind* (1977) suffers headaches and tribulations of all kinds because of the obsession implanted in him by aliens. In later films, like *Brainstorm* (1983) and *Strange Days* (1995), downloading is a physical experience which offers some risk to sanity, if not to life itself. In the sordid world of William Gibson's "Johnny Mnemonic" (1981), packing data into the human cranium is a dangerous, somewhat disgusting affair, as Johnny risks complete discombobulation to carry his load of bootleg information.[9] The genre of Cyberpunk is obsessed with its nightmarish, biological versions of the Internet, in which portions of our consciousness, if not our bodies themselves, meld together. Its physical, neurological projection of the Web is a messy one. If we ever actually achieve such technology, science fiction has taught us to be wary of it.

Far more ebullient are narratives featuring a second variant on the myth of the download —*the direct transfer of matter and living things.* "Beaming up" implies a release from difficulty with no apparent cost.[10] While there are notable excursions into horror when the technology goes wrong, as in the two film incarnations of *The Fly* (1958, 1986), the motif usually inspires flights of ambivalent mysticism.

Forbidden Planet (1956) makes a brave stab at capturing the sublimity of the supreme download — the myth of a technology by which all *thought becomes reality.* The ancient Krell achieved technology's nearest approach to magic, only to be rendered extinct overnight by their own "Monsters from the Id"[11]— science fiction's most famous system crash.[12] A problematic fate also meets the scientists exploring the mystical planet in Stanislaw Lem's *Solaris* (1961), who are driven to near-madness by reifications of their inner selves, as are the quasi-scientists of the later space-opera film *Sphere* (1998), who encounter an alien machine that causes their desires to become manifest. Today's Web can literally download software, documents, and sundry items at the press of a button, order products electronically, blog, play games, and socialize internationally. It is a relatively modest version of reifying our thoughts, but relatively magical nonetheless.

Science fiction of the twilight period during which the Net became reality — the 1980s and 1990s—could prefigure the Internet in a more recognizable fashion. One assumes different writers during this period enjoyed greater or lesser degrees of awareness of the reality forming around them and scientific advances engendering that reality. The degree to which these authors were predicting the World Wide Web and not simply reporting on it is necessarily ambiguous.[13]

The dawn of the Internet brought science fiction's most disturbing subgenre, Cyberpunk, where wounded warriors struggle to heal themselves, surrounded by wastelands of TV tubes glowing atop piles of rubbish. These stories create worlds quite different in tone from the Internet that has come to pass. Cyberpunk characters don't get on their imaginary webs as blithely as we do ours. They enter universes that resemble lethal computer games, where the theme of depersonalization is acted out against a background of stylish decadence. Cyberpunk tales foresee the dangers of identity theft and challenges to personal integrity which have become reality, much of it stemming from the existence of the World Wide Web. If this smoldering vision of alienation was markedly worse than the Net we have so far, it may have much to do with the surreal political atmosphere of the 1980s, when Ronald Reagan prattled inanely about the possibility of winning a nuclear war.

But Cyberpunk's theme was not the physical world, much less the political environment, in any case. The denatured societies in which the characters live are mere backdrops. The real story is always in the Matrix. Gibson cites *The Matrix* (1999) as the quintessential Cyberpunk film. Like the genre it epitomizes, *The Matrix* explores the anagogical myth of *entry into a virtual universe*—the Matrix—presaging virtual-reality games and interactive games, complete with fictional personae.[14] The Matrix is usually conceived as a lower or lesser reality, as opposed to a parallel universe, but is presented with heavy symbolic weight. Entry into any of Cyberpunk's myriad versions of the Matrix constitutes a symbolic struggle for self-salvation. As if embarrassed by its allegorical tendencies, Cyberpunk adds dashes of absurdism and self-deconstruction — Max the charming babbler in the television series *Max Headroom* (1987), the excursions into turgid self-mockery in Gibson's own novel *Neuromancer* (1984), Johnny Mnemonic's bizarre monologues. Despite its built-in disclaimers, Cyberpunk explored the real threat of identity theft — in effect, reality theft enacted in cyberspace. The virtual worlds entered by Cyberpunk hackers and seekers after a "higher" reality were often at least as dark as their post-apocalyptic societies. Dreams of pleasure, like those glimpsed in the *Star Trek* franchise, do not exist even in fantasy. Cyberpunk revels in nihilist satire, employing this most magical of myths to express a cynicism remarkably at odds with the gleaming optimism of classic science fiction.

In post–Internet science fiction, the myths that once presaged the Web take on new forms. In an important sense, the communal Internet we share remains stubbornly story-resistant, functioning more often as an expositional device ill-suited to the genre's ubiquitous theme of isolation. Most post–Internet films—whether science fiction or not—feature at least one Internet scene, which is now an almost obligatory expositional device. In rare cases where the Web plays an active role in post–Internet tales or films—*The Net* (1995) and *Eagle Eye*—it emerges as a passive entity, to be instantly commandeered by sinister forces who use it as a totalitarian tool in the classic mold — the nightmare envisioned by Orwell's viewscreens, constituting a kind of evil, one-way network. The very myths that were used to predict the Internet — such as the all-seeing eye — are now, in a real sense, on the Web.

SUGGESTIONS FOR FURTHER READING

Bush, Vannevar. "As We May Think." 1945.

Davis, Watson. "The Universal Brain: Is Centralized Storage and Retrieval of All Knowledge Possible, Feasible, or Desirable?" *The Growth of Knowledge: Readings on Organization and Retrieval of Information.* 1965.

Fuller, Buckminster. *I Seem to be A Verb.* 1970.

Goertzel, Ben. "World Wide Brain: Self-organizing Internet Intelligence as the Actualization of the Collective Consciousness." *Psychology and the Internet: Intrapersonal, Interpersonal and Transpersonal Implications.* 1998; 2006.

Greenberger, Martin, ed. *Computers and the World of the Future.* 1962.

Huxley, Aldous. *Brave New World Revisited.* 1958.

Kahn, Herman, and Anthony Weiner. *The Year 2000: A Framework for Speculation on the Next Thirty-Three Years.* 1967.

Lapham, Lewis. *Waiting for the Barbarians.* 1997.

Nelson, Teodor H. *Dream Machines: New Freedoms through Computer Screens — A Minority Report.* 1974.

Sawhney, Mohanbir. "History of Telegraph, Telephone Helps Predict Internet's Future." CIO website, 2001.

Steadman, Ralph. *The Little Red Computer.* 1969.

Wong Kin Yuen, Gary Westfahl, and Amy Kit-sze Chan, eds. *World Weavers: Globalization, Science Fiction, and the Cybernetic Revolution.* 2005.

NOTES

1. "A Logic Named Joe" was first published under Murray Leinster's real name, Will F. Jenkins, in *Astounding Science Fiction,* 37 (March, 1946), 139–154. Neither Leinster nor his immediate successors could fully envision the miniaturization of computer technology, notably via the development of the microchip. In essence, this was a problem of image interference. Science fiction writers of the 1940s and 1950s couldn't imagine the microchip because they were too enamored of the image of the giant central brain. Leinster's answer to the dangers posed by the independent intelligence of his rogue "logic" was simple — shut it down. It would be three more decades before Algis Budrys would depict the fatal interconnectedness of loss of privacy on a worldwide scale in *Michaelmas* (1977).

2. These are the anagogical myths central to science fiction's prefiguring the Internet (in italics when first introduced into this chapter): (1) the group, or hive, mind; (2) identity loss, also known as identity theft or identity shift; (3) the all-seeing eye, including a centralized data source; (4) the bug, or virus (often associated with the vengeful machine and *tech noir*); (5) the creation of microcosms, or miniaturization; (6) downloading (including reifying technology); and (7) entry into a virtual universe (or separate reality), conceived of as the Matrix in the pre-dawn era of the Internet called Cyberpunk.

3. Isaac Asimov's variation on the group mind was introduced in his *Foundation* series (originally eight stories in *Astounding Science-Fiction,* 1942–1950; reprinted with a prequel as the Foundation Trilogy, 1951–1953) with the term "mentalic," used to encompass a range of unusual psychic capabilities. Living approximately 50,000 years into the future, the Second Foundationers can apparently interpret and then adjust human emotions. Gaia, the group mind of *Foundation's Edge* (1982) and *Foundation and Earth* (1983), looks back on the Second Foundation as an embryonic form of collective consciousness. Gaians are able to convert energy into work through conscious will (thermokinesis). See Asimov, *Prelude to Foundation* (New York: Doubleday, 1988).

The expression "Big Brother is watching you" pulsates throughout Orwell's *Nineteen Eighty-Four* (1949), while "Resistance is futile" is repeatedly intoned by the assimilating Borg in *Star Trek: The Next Generation* (1989).

4. Pre-Internet science-fiction lore is rich with examples of accessing information from a central brain, so we must acknowledge that the information-accessing capabilities of the Internet were foreseen from the earliest days of technology. Wells's *World Brain* (1938; Freeport: Books for Libraries Press, 1971) posits the organization of information into a "Permanent World Encyclopedia"—a constantly updated central database that would synthesize knowledge worldwide—suggesting that our present-day Wikipedia would not be shocking to him. Despite referring to his concept as "constructive sociology," Wells continued to miss the communality of today's Internet. The Internet we wound up with is not the centralized big brain of science fiction mythology, but rather an interconnection of a myriad of independent global resources. Nonetheless, W. Boyd Rayward correctly acknowledges Wells's World Brain in the following terms: "It is the latest and greatest expression of socio-biological evolution" (Rayward, "H. G. Wells's Idea of a World Brain: A Critical Reassessment," *Journal of the American Society for Information Science*, 50 [1999], 571).

5. In *2001*, HAL is apparently subject to some kind of virus, though we don't really know how or why he has gone berserk. In this case, there's no indication of how HAL develops a bug—it's just a given. The last message he receives from Earth might be to explain his real mission—and thus his being made to lie to the astronauts, revealed at the outset of *2010*, might cause his meltdown.

6. *The Terminator* (Pacific Western Films, 1984).

7. The mad computer blends into the vengeful machine, presaging the predatory element of the Internet. Once more we can refer back to a prototype in Frankenstein's avenging Creature. Within the past century there is the striking image of Rotwang's "Robot Maria" from the silent film *Metropolis* (1927)—also invoking the archetype of the mad scientist. Even the guardian robot Gort in *The Day the Earth Stood Still* is a variation on the vengeful machine, as is *2001*'s HAL when he thinks the astronauts are endangering his mission. Philip K. Dick's novel *Do Androids Dream of Electric Sheep?* (1968) introduces Replicants, who are short-lived, humanoid machines seeking vengeance against their "maker," while in *Alien* (1979), the "Mother" brain itself acts like a virus, determining that its crew is expendable once an alien creature is discovered. The moral seems clear: not only is technology not our friend, but it will inevitably destroy us. In science fiction mythology, guns *do* kill people.

8. For other examples of pre–Internet miniaturization, see Robert A. Heinlein's *Between Planets* (1951), which embeds downloadable information about complex interplanetary travel in the protagonist's ring, as well as Harlan Ellison's television episode "Demon with a Glass Hand" (*The Outer Limits* [New York: ABC, October 17, 1964]), wherein an android solves the mystery of the disappearance of Earth's entire population—his hand gains knowledge as each of three missing fingers is found, and he finally discovers that the people of the world have been miniaturized inside his body, to hide and protect them.

9. Gibson's character Johnny Mnemonic is as macabre as Shelley's Creature. Here the hapless protagonist allows massive amounts of information to be transferred to his brain, but the majority of the tale relates his struggle to escape the grotesque consequences of his dangerous, criminal activity. The world of science fiction is rife with neural downloads, and they are always tricky, if not horrific.

10. Scotty beaming someone up in *Star Trek* resonates with any Internet user who has downloaded an image or watched a streaming video. This technology of material upload (or download, as the case may be) occurs via the infamous Transporter beam that dematerializes and then rematerializes its "travelers." This fantasy is systematically

elaborated upon with respect to replication and quantum teleportation in Rick Sternbach and Michael Okuda's *Star Trek: The Next Generation Technical Manual* (New York: Pocket Books, 1991). The term "teleportation" was coined by Charles Fort in 1931 and later used by Derek Parfit in his article "Personal Identity," *The Philosophical Review*, 80 (1971), 3–27. See also Alfred Bester's *The Stars My Destination* (1956), which depicts an ability to "jaunt" much like what we see in Steven Gould's more recent novel and its film adaptation *Jumper* (1992; 2008). Material downloading and teleportation are not rich in story-generating possibilities and seem more a matter for visual popular science fiction.

11. *Forbidden Planet* (MGM, 1956).

12. The Krell created a reifying technology — embodied in a breathtaking, planet-sized machine of incomprehensible complexity — and promptly fell victim to its fatal flaw. Its bug is revealed to be the Krell's unconquered impulses, and when their thoughts are materialized, the Krell are almost instantaneously destroyed. Their story is a cautionary tale — the familiar popular culture fear of taking science too far.

13. The World Wide Web's first serious appearances in science fiction came only after prototypes of the Web — such as ARPANet (1968) and its offshoots — had been developed, so the authors of Cyberpunk and what followed were more extrapolating than envisioning. ARPANet is the acronym for Advanced Research Projects Agency Network, created within the U.S. Department of Defense during the Cold War with the Soviet Union. The first permanent host-to-host link was established between UCLA and UC Berkeley in 1969, but by 1983 ARPANet had become just one more component in the computer network that was the growing Internet. For John Brunner, author of *The Shockwave Rider* (1975), the credit for much of his storyline about a networked society and a fugitive programmer who can write "worms"— and recurrently rewrites his identity— goes to Alvin Toffler's *Future Shock* (New York: Random House, 1970). Another story from this time period, Vernor Vinge's novella *True Names* (1981), with its worldwide network and access to virtual reality (essentially the first depiction of "cyberspace" before the term was coined by Gibson), seems more the extrapolation of a brilliant mathematical mind. See *True Names and the Opening of the Cyberspace Frontier*, ed. James Frenkel, afterword by Marvin Minsky (New York: Tor, 2001).

14. In physically entering a virtual or alternate reality with its "holodeck," the notably non-punkish television series *Star Trek: The Next Generation* grandfathered some of the last of the science fiction genre to appear before the Net became a part of our reality. Positing a shipboard reification of thought, this device generated many far-fetched stories by allowing fantasy to take physical form while leaving its exact scientific nature undefined. Cyberpunk's central myth of almost literal entry into the Web — a quantum leap or two from the keyboards, mouses, and viewscreens which now fill our realtime — foresaw an Internet utilizing some kind of biological or neurological wizardry to create a mind-machine connection that would threaten the future of humanity itself.

4

Technobodies and the Anxieties of Performance[1]

Veronica Hollinger

I.

I begin by quoting a statement from the Hong Kong 2003 Conference Call for Papers which served as catalyst for this chapter — and provides me with an opening sentence: "With the previously separated categories of science and technology inexorably merging in postmodern society, technoscience is reshaping not only our daily lives, but also the ways in which we define who we are." My understanding of the term "technoscience" is influenced by Elaine L. Graham's argument that, whatever else it is, technoscience is a form of representational practice, developed within and correspondingly influencing our always already culturally-encoded experiences of ourselves in the world. In *Representations of the Post/Human*, she explains,

> as research is increasingly guided by commercial or political imperatives, and the social context of science — as cultural practice — is asserted, so the boundary between pure and applied, theory and practice, dissolves. Technoscience is culture because it performs the task of reflecting the world back to us and of articulating its own (increasingly definitive) version of reality.[2]

One of the most convincing demonstrations of the power of technoscientific representations "to reflect the world back to us and to articulate [their] own (increasingly definitive) versions of reality" is outlined by N. Katherine Hayles in her critical/cultural history of cybernetics, *How We Became Posthuman: Virtual Bodies in Cybernetics, Literature, and Informatics* (1999). Hayles examines the pervasive influence of cybernetics theory on the ways in which we understand ourselves as human beings — as biological organisms who are also the subjects of culture and politics. She focuses on the increasingly widespread conceptualization of information as pattern and carefully appraises the resulting tendency to conceptualize humans as "*essentially* informational patterns" that can, at least in theory, be abstracted from any particular form of physical embodiment.[3] Hayles describes this "contemporary pressure toward dematerialization" as "an epistemic shift toward pattern/randomness and away from presence/absence" (29).[4] One obvious consequence for science fiction of this "epistemic shift" has been the diversity of "posthuman" subjects that came to populate its imagined futures.

My interest here is in how some science fiction stories—whatever else they are about—also concern the uncanny process of denaturalization through which we come to experience ourselves as subjects-in-technoculture. Almost since its inception, science fiction—conventionally understood as a literature of "estrangement"—has given us stories about how technoscience makes us strange to ourselves, how it becomes a kind of *second nature* always in tension with what many still think of as our *first*— our human — nature. By this I mean especially that alluring version of our "first" nature that we've been constructing— and deconstructing — in the West for the past few hundred years, founded on, as one historian puts it, "the twin pillars of humanism: the sovereignty of rational consciousness and the authenticity of individual speech."[5]

On this side of the cyberpunk "revolution," writers such as William Gibson and Greg Egan are particularly interesting in terms of the imaginative constructions of posthuman *otherness* that inhabit their very near (in the case of Gibson) and very far (in the case of Egan) futures. A key figure in Gibson's novels *Idoru* (1996) and *All Tomorrow's Parties* (1999) is the "idoru" or "idol-singer" Rei Toei, a computer-generated simulacrum described as "a personality-construct, a congeries of software agents, the creation of information-designers.... She is akin to what ... they call a 'synthespian,' in Hollywood."[6] Product of pure information, Rei Toei is a wildly popular digital media star: "Her audience knows that she does not walk among them; that she is media, purely. And that is a large part of her appeal" (55). The human Laney thinks of her, in genuine admiration, as "software that was good at acting like beautiful young women" (247).

But the idoru is also more and other than a computer-generated simulation. She defies commonsense expectations that there are clear-cut distinctions to be made between "authentic" singularity and "inauthentic" digital replication, between autonomous self and programmed performance. Described by one character in *All Tomorrow's Parties* as "the real deal. Hundred percent unreal,"[7] the idoru is "a posthuman emergent identity" (165). She herself draws a distinction between the technology of simulation upon which she depends and her sense of an autonomous self: "This is a hologram," she tells Rydell on her first appearance in *All Tomorrow's Parties*, "But I am real" (153). In the final chapters of *Idoru*, Gibson's protagonist Laney becomes overwhelmed by the density of the idoru's information. He perceives her as data developing in time and considers how this data "had begun to acquire a sort of complexity. Or randomness.... The human thing" (251). In this passage, Gibson's text suggests that "the human thing" has no fixed *material* attributes, that it is not *necessarily* inherent in the body. Its defining feature is not body figured as *presence*, but density of information figured as *complex pattern*.[8]

At the conclusion of *All Tomorrow's Parties*, Rei Toei frees herself from her technological housing and enters the material world as an autonomous sentient entity, a self fully present to itself ... or, perhaps, selves fully present to themselves. The idoru is translated into material form at the same moment at hundreds of different "nanofax" outlets, replicated like software in the very process of becoming embodied: she is last seen "walking out of every Lucky Dragon [convenience store] in the world"— and smiling (269). So much for the singularity and full presence of the authentic self.

There are even more radical variations on what Hayles refers to as the story of "how information lost its body" (2) in Egan's science fiction.[9] In the far future of Egan's *Diaspora* (1997), for example, individual subjects exist in a wide variety of both embodied and digital states, many of which do not appear "human" in any recognizable sense of the term. Only a few "fleshers" still inhabit conventional human bodies. Some organically-based subjects are "exuberants" whose bodies have been radically transformed for efficiency and longevity. Others inhabit non-organic bodies called "Gleisner robots." *Diaspora*'s central characters are disembodied, intelligent software systems called "shapers" who live within the virtual environments of the "polises," digital communities whose safety is assured by the fact that they're "backed up all over the solar system."[10] Life in polises is defined by the sheer complexity of information to which "citizens" have access:

> Konishi polis ... was buried two hundred metres beneath the Siberian tundra, but via fibre and satellite links the input channels could bring in data from any forum in the Coalition of Polises, from probes orbiting every planet and moon in the solar system, from drones wandering the forests and oceans of Earth, from ten million kinds of scape or abstract sensorium. The first problem of perception was learning how to choose from this superabundance. (11)

For many of Egan's digital characters, physical embodiment is a mere supplement to mind: mind — intelligent, self-aware, and autonomous— is what constitutes these post–Platonic subjects. To citizens of Konishi polis, "the whole idea of *solidity*, of atavistic delusions of corporeality, was generally equated with obstruction and coercion" (79). On the other hand, citizens of Carter-Zimmerman polis place a high value on the occasional experience of (virtual) embodiment, immersing themselves, albeit temporarily, in "the complete ritual of verisimilitude, the ornate curlicued longhand of imitation physical cause and effect" (199).[11] In this "ritual of verisimilitude," we see Egan's fictional rejection of what one character refers to as "any abstract distinction between real and virtual flesh" (144). Ultimately, the carnivalesque chaos of subjectivities in his future amounts to the disappearance of any significant opposition between embodied reality and digital verisimilitude. Embodiment in *Diaspora* becomes one among a range of possible simulated experiences made available *within* the digital realm.

Gibson and Egan present posthuman characters that exemplify some of the radical deconstructions of subjectivity under the pressures of technoscience: their ways of being-in-the-world collapse boundaries between bodies and technologies; between autonomous will and random programming; between physicality and digitality. They represent, even if only in fictional form, the erosion of the "'ontological hygiene' by which for the past three hundred years Western culture has drawn the fault-lines that separate humans, nature and machines" (Graham 11).[12]

In *How We Became Posthuman* Hayles insists that "conceiving of information as a thing separate from the medium instantiating it is a prior imaginary act that constructs a holistic phenomenon as an information/matter duality" (13). She reminds readers of Derrida's powerful philosophical arguments for the *constitutive* function of the supplement: "As though we had learned nothing from Derrida about supplementarity," she points out, "embodiment continues to be discussed as if it were a supplement to be purged from the dominant term of information ..." (12). For Hayles, embodiment is exactly the "supplement" that constitutes what it completes: as a subject who lives in the world rather than in the pages of an sf novel, my body is an "accessory" to my self without which "I" could have no identity, could not be my "self."

II.

As "software that was good at acting like beautiful young women" (*Idoru* 247)—to recall this description of Gibson's idoru—Rei Toei is clearly nothing like humanism's free, authentic agent. As a digital subject coming-into-being—an autonomous, self-conscious singularity—she defies commonsense ideas about what constitutes a subject. If she is a sign of the posthuman, there is no knowing what she signifies. While she may be mysterious, however, she is not particularly threatening: like Egan's digital shapers, she is clearly not a *one*, not a subject like *my self*, but the subject as a very different *other*. It is not nearly as comfortable, however, to accept the process of *my self* becoming posthuman—that is, becoming other than what "I" perceive myself already to be as a human subject.

This is why the cyborg—that hybrid subject of the human/machine interface—functions so often in science fiction as a representative figure of transition and transformation. One of the most significant features of the cyborg is its uncanny ability simultaneously to embody both *my self* and technoscientific *other*. The cyborg also marks a site of irresolvable tension between, on one hand, humanist conceptions of subjectivity and identity as grounded in the material of the body and, on the other hand, "postmodern" conceptions of the subject as an ungrounded effect of *performativity*. This latter position theorizes the "self" as a kind of ontological fiction, an "I-effect" produced, as Judith Butler explains, through "a process of iterability, a regularized and constrained repetition of norms" (95).[13]

I want at this point to look backward to two early cyborg stories to consider what the imaginative constructions of science fiction tell us about the travails and transformations involved in becoming the modern subject-of-techno-science. These stories, both classics of first-generation sf, are Cordwainer Smith's "Scanners Live in Vain" (1950) and C.L. Moore's "No Woman Born" (1944). They were both written in the 1940s—not coincidentally, also the decade that saw the earliest developments in cybernetics. I read these stories as exemplary narratives about the conflicts and tensions that troubled an earlier moment in the history of our becoming posthuman. In particular I focus on how these stories treat "performance anxiety"—by which I mean a variety of symptoms that have accreted around representations of the techno-body, especially insofar as it threatens the "ontological hygiene" that conventionally sustains conceptual distinctions between authentic agency and artificial citation.[14] Both "Scanners Live in Vain" and "No Woman Born" draw upon a range of diverse but related meanings that are potential in the term "performance." Central to each story, however, is the spectre of performance as the sign of inauthenticity, of a lost originality.

"Scanners Live in Vain"—Smith's first published story—is a beautifully written and *very* anxious narrative about the loss of one's humanity under the onslaught of technology. Here "humanity" is figured as the "natural" integration of mind and body, while technology is figured as invasion, mutilation, and dehumanization.[15] In this far future, Scanners are an elite space-faring guild of cyborgs whose bodies have been redesigned to withstand "the Pain-of-Space."[16] Theirs is an heroic sacrifice enabling humanity's expansion into deep space: their transformation into Scanners involves cutting off the body's sensory input to the mind and incorporating monitoring equipment directly into the flesh in compensation. Scanners must use this equipment constantly to scan their physical bodies for damage and keep their emotions at equilibrium: except for rare occasions when they are "cranched"—temporarily returned to direct communication with their own bodies—they feel neither pain nor pleasure, cannot hear, and have lost both touch and taste; in Scanner-mode, all that is left to them is sight. Not coincidentally, perhaps, in their loss of human physicality and emotion, in their reduction to mind and sight, Smith's Scanners—all of whom are male—are perfect (and parodic?) cyborg representations of Western "Man," that figure whose privileged features are also rational mind and controlling sight.

In Smith's fictional world, however, Scanners are merely horrible imitations of human beings, grotesquely self-conscious, self-alienated, and self-isolated. Their technologically-enhanced bodies are no longer their own, but are reduced to a pure kind of supplementarity as vehicles for mind, mere objects to be monitored and maintained for peak efficiency. Scanner bodies are obscene hybrids whose organic components constantly threaten to escape the control of mind: Smith's protagonist Martel is repulsed by "[the Scanners'] awkwardness when they moved, their immobility when they stood still ... the queer assortment of smells which their bodies yielded unnoticed ... the grunts and groans and squawks which they emitted from their deafness" (373).[17] Despite the gap between living mind and deadened body, therefore, body still leaves its horrid but inescapable mark on the constitution of self. The techno-body is the unnatural supplement that constitutes the Scanner-subject as a monstrosity.

Smith's text also portrays how transformation of the natural body into the high-performance cyborg body destroys what is often considered the very ground of (human) identity. Cut off as they are by technological mediation from direct experience of their bodies, Scanners represent a nightmare vision of lost selfhood. They are pure function, nothing *but* performance. Scanners are constituted, not in any attributes *inherent* within themselves as subjects, but literally by the vitally important work they perform in service to their government. As if aware of this lack of authentic selfhood, Scanners participate in carefully scripted rituals during which they compulsively re-interpellate themselves into their roles, reiterating the absolute necessity of their sacrifice as the fundamental principle of their identities: "What must the others say to us?" "They must say to us, 'You are the bravest of the brave.... All mankind owes most honor to the Scanner, who unites the Earths of Mankind'" (367–368). To Martel, who is temporarily "cranched" and thus integrated again into his body, the Scanners at their ceremony appear like "cruelly driven ghosts, posturing out the meaningless ritual of their indefeasible damnation" (371).

"Scanners Live in Vain" also introduces another, singularly masculine, performance anxiety. Given that Scanners are an all-male guild, it is unsurprising that Smith figures the severance of body from mind as a kind of castration, his text referring, for example, to "the professional requirements of [the Scanners'] mutilation" (371). The story also directly links Martel's sense that he is no longer human, that he is "a man turned into a machine" (360), to his conviction that he is no longer a real man because he cannot perform sexually with his wife Luci.[18] In the end, Martel and other Scanners are restored to full humanity, as Smith imagines a (highly unlikely) scientific breakthrough that renders their sacrifice no longer necessary.[19] The direct link between body and technology — the link that both dehumanized and unmanned the Scanners — is broken; mind and organic body are appropriately reintegrated. In the resolution of Smith's deeply humanist parable, identity returns to the self through the self's reunification with the natural body: the awful necessity of the Scanners' self-alienated *doing*— the terrible performance that is required of them exactly because they are Scanners— is transformed back into the full physical presence of their essential human *being*.

Moore's "No Woman Born"—which I think is one of the most extrordinarily original and challenging stories in all of first-generation sf—takes up many of the same issues as "Scanners Live in Vain" but follows them to a quite different conclusion. Like "Scanners Live in Vain," this story concerns the fate of human subjectivity at the body/technology interface. "No Woman Born" is about Dierdre, a world-famous actress whose body has been destroyed in a theatre fire. The scientist Meltzer, who has an annoying tendency to compare himself to Victor Frankenstein, builds her a replacement body which is stronger, faster, and longer-lived than any human body. In some ways, the new Deirdre is uncannily like one of Smith's Scanners, a human brain housed in a performance-enhanced techno-body deprived of physical sensation; only her sense of sight is still intact. Most of Moore's story unfolds around the question of whether Deirdre is still human, a question that, not surprisingly, is impossible to separate from the question of whether she is still a real woman. She lacks everything by which "woman" has traditionally been defined, notably the "natural" female body as the ontological ground of "womanliness." Like Smith's Scanners—only more disturbingly so because she is a female subject—Deirdre has become all mind and sight.

Moore's story raises the same apprehensions about monstrosity that we see in "Scanners," although not from Deirdre's perspective, to which the text never provides direct access. Appropriately, given her status as a famous performer, she remains the fascinating object of the gaze of Moore's other characters, all of whom are male, and, by extension, the object of our own readerly gaze. Her erstwhile manager, for instance, worries that without a human body, Deirdre—in a techno-body which is sleekly beautiful but lacking in human features—will become as monstrous as Martel. "Deirdre was gone, and this was only machinery"[20] is his initial reaction to his first sight of her. Moore's text is exploratory, however, rather than conclusive, keeping its anxious oppositions in careful balance. At various times to other characters, Dierdre is either more human than ever or increasingly machine-like; more beautiful than ever or increasingly grotesque; more in touch with audiences than ever, or more and more withdrawn from humanity. While "No Woman Born" explores some of the same anxieties of performance seen in Smith's story, here they are generated by not by the cyborg subject herself, but her human/male observers.

Where Moore's story differs radically from "Scanners" is in the implications of its (non)resolution. Looking forward to contemporary theories of performativity, it seems to support the concept of identity as an "ontology-effect" constituted in discourse and performance. "Is she human?" is not exactly the right question in this context. It may be more useful to ask: "how successfully does she cite human behavior?" When her manager rejects the idea that she can return to the stage, Deirdre provides him with irrefutable proof that audiences will continue to accept her as her self:[21] "She threw her head back and let her body sway and her shoulders shake, and the laughter, like the music, filled the theater.... And she was a woman now. Humanity had dropped over her like a tangible garment" (265).[22] It may be that Deirdre's true monstrosity arises not because she has ceased to be feminine, and therefore has ceased to be human, but precisely because her *performance* of femininity/humanity is so convincing at the same time as it is so obviously a performance.[23] If the "unnatural" cyborg body can so successfully "put on" humanity, then, Moore's story suggests, humanity — like gender — is always to some extent a performance, an "ontological fiction" produced in discourse and representation.

Constructing Deirdre as already a consummate performer is a brilliant move on Moore's part, because it serves to maintain the indeterminacy that shadows all her actions.[24] Here, for instance, is her manager's conflicted reaction to the performance that "proves" she is still human:

> she was the Deirdre he had always known, pale gold, exquisitely graceful in remembered postures, the inner radiance of her shining through metal as brilliantly as it had ever shone through flesh. He did not wonder, now, if it were real. Later he would think again that it might be only a disguise, something like a garment she had put off with her lost body, to wear again only when she chose. ... He watched, convinced for the moment that she was all she seemed to be. (279–280)

Unlike Smith's story, "No Woman Born" appears to undermine the conviction that there is an essential humanity grounded in the natural body, but also recognizes the ineluctable links between embodiment and subjectivity. This is not a story, like "Scanners," about selfhood lost and regained; it is about the self coming-into-being. Where "Scanners" resolves itself through a humanist reactivation of "ontological hygiene," Moore's story resolutely traces the logic of the body/machine interface until it arrives at — or at least points toward — the site of a potential posthuman subjectivity.

"No Woman Born" is the opening scene of a cyborg-bildungsroman, the first step in a techno-coming-of-age-story. Like Gibson's idoru, Deirdre is "a posthuman emergent identity," but, unlike the idoru, Deirdre links *other* to *self*. She recognizes the possibility that a new kind of subject is originating at the interface of human mind and techno-body. She calls attention to her increasing detachment from humanity, her sense of increasing isolation from flesh-and-blood bodies, her new and singular position as "[a] sort of mutation halfway between flesh and metal" (286). This suggests an even more radical sense in which she has become monstrous, in fact: her gleaming metallic body, her great speed and strength, her reduction to mind and sight — these are markers of the male subject. Her very existence as cyborg collapses distinctions not only between humanity and technology, but perhaps even more radically, between feminine and masculine. As Deirdre contemplates the inevitability of her ongoing transformation, the story's final words imply the challenge and crisis of the cyborg subject: "'I wonder,' she repeated, the distant taint of metal already in her voice" (288).

III.

In a brilliant 1993 essay, "The Life Cycle of Cyborgs," Hayles describes the cyborg as "standing at the threshold separating the human from the posthuman."[25] "Scanners Live in Vain" and "No Woman Born" are exemplary early threshold stories about our experiences of self-estrangement as subjects-in-technoculture. Although they are very different, they are both equally true, telling us that, even at the relatively "primitive" level of the early cyborg, it has never been easy to become posthuman. And more than half a century after these stories appeared, we still wonder about the nature of technoscientific nature; we still worry about threats to our perceived authenticity, singularity, and spontaneity as sovereign human subjects; we remain caught in the theoretical tensions between the free-standing subject of humanism and a more modest selfhood constituted under the sign of performance.

Recalling Graham's observation that "Technoscience is culture because it performs the task of reflecting the world back to us and of articulating its own (increasingly definitive) version of reality" (30), it is worth considering how science fiction also helps to shape our ideas about ourselves. If "I" am becoming "posthuman," it is at least in part in response to the exemplary subjects with which some science fiction stories have "embodied" the abstract modelling of technoscience.[26] Science fiction too is involved in the ongoing "critical ontology of ourselves" beautifully described by Michel Foucault as "a philosophical life in which the critique of what we are is at one and the same time the historical analysis of the limits that are imposed on us and an experiment with the possibility of going beyond them."[27] Appropriately, the title of Foucault's essay is "What is Enlightenment?"

NOTES

1. Since it was first drafted, sections of this chapter have appeared in several publications, including "Posthumanism and Cyborg Theory," in *The Routledge Companion to Science Fiction*, ed. Mark Bould, Andrew M. Butler, Adam Roberts, and Sherryl Vint (London: Routledge, 2009, 267–278), and "Retrofitting *Frankenstein*," in *Beyond Cyberpunk*, ed. Graham Murphy and Vint (New York: Routledge, 2010).

2. Elaine L. Graham, *Representations of the Post/Human: Monsters, Aliens and Others in Popular Culture* (New Brunswick, NJ: Rutgers University Press, 2002), 30. Subsequent page references in the text are to this edition.

3. N. Katherine Hayles, *How We Became Posthuman: Virtual Bodies in Cybernetics, Literature, and Informatics* (Chicago: University of Chicago Press, 1999), 22. Subsequent page references in the text are to this edition.

4. For Hayles, this valorization of pattern over presence risks, among other things, the return to a kind of metaphysics in which "disembodied information becomes the ultimate Platonic form" (13).

5. Tony Davies, *Humanism* (London: Routledge, 1997), 60. Theories of performativity, however, argue that "Where there is an 'I' who utters or speaks and thereby produces an effect in discourse, there is first a discourse which precedes and enables that 'I' and

forms in language the constraining trajectory of its will" (Judith Butler, *Bodies that Matter: On the Discursive Limits of "Sex"* [New York: Routledge, 1993], 225). Subsequent Butler page references in the text are to this edition.

6. William Gibson, *Idoru* (New York: Putnam, 1996), 92. Subsequent page references in the text are to this edition.

7. Gibson, *All Tomorrow's Parties* (New York: Putnam, 1999), 69. Subsequent page references in the text are to this edition.

8. *Idoru*'s Zona Rosa, who interacts with other humans only in cyberspace, turns out to be literally performing her identity. She is the electronic persona of a badly deformed young woman named Mercedes Purissima, who "has lived for the past five years in almost complete denial of her physical self" (285). In Gibson's text, the discovery of this "performance" seemingly is not aimed at drawing the line (again) between authentic and inauthentic identities; rather, it broadens the reader's sense of the potential for a range of subjectivities to inhabit and interact with each other in a variety of both embodied and disembodied ways.

9. While vast amounts of scholarship have focused on Gibson's writing, especially *Neuromancer* (1984), Egan has so far attracted less critical attention. Ross Farnell's "Attempting Immortality: AI, A-Life, and the Posthuman in Greg Egan's *Permutation City*" (*Science Fiction Studies*, 27 [March, 2000], 69–91) provides a good overview of some of Egan's dense and dizzying future extrapolations.

10. Greg Egan, *Diaspora* (London: Millennium, 1997), 31. Subsequent page references in the text are to this edition. "Polises" are, of course, the ideal Greek cities, the right size for diversification but still small enough for everyone to be connected.

11. In this fictional world inhabited by such a wide variety of differing subjectivities, however, Carter-Zimmerman's appreciation of the physical world is not founded on any taken-for-granted valorization of one state of being over any other: "We choose to value the physical world. That's what defines us, but it's as arbitrary as any other choice of values.... It's not the One True Path which the infidels have to be bludgeoned into following" (217).

12. One should recall that the challenge posed by Donna Haraway's figure of the posthuman cyborg in her "A Manifesto for Cyborgs," one of the foundational critical texts of postmodernism, is posed in terms of the same disruption of "the ontological hygiene" of the Western philosophical tradition.

13. Some foundational studies in the construction of theories of performativity include J. L. Austin's *How to Do Things with Words*, Second Edition, ed. J. O. Urmson and Marina Sbisà [Cambridge: Harvard University Press, 1975]; Jacques Derrida's "Signature, Event, Context" (*Glyph*, 1 [1977], 172–197); and Butler's *Bodies that Matter*. As Butler explains, "performativity cannot be understood outside of a process of iterability, a regularized and constrained repetition of norms. And this repetition is not performed by a subject; this repetition is what enables a subject and constitutes the temporal condition for the subject. This iterability implies that 'performance' is not a singular 'act' or event, but a ritualized production reiterated under and through constraint ... but not, I will insist, determining it fully in advance" (95).

14. See Marvin Carlson's *Performance: A Critical Introduction* (New York: Routledge, 1996) for one of the best general overviews of the field. As Carlson notes, the term "performance" has come to incorporate a broad range of ideas, including several that are particularly relevant to my purposes here: 1) performance as in theatrical role-playing and display, which also implies self-consciousness and self-reflexivity (Carlson 5); 2) performance as related to "the general success of an activity in light of some standard of achievement," including machine performance (Carlson 5); 3) performance as the repetition "of a recognized and culturally coded pattern of behaviour," as in the performance of social roles (Carlson 4).

15. Carol McGuirk's "The Rediscovery of Cordwainer Smith" (*Science Fiction Studies*,
28 [July, 2001], 161–200), a detailed and incisive discussion of this unusual writer's
career, points out that "The first uses of the word 'cyborg' date from 1960 ... even the
parent-term 'cybernetics,' coined by Norbert Wiener in 1948, entered the language after
the writing of 'Scanners.' Smith sees something of the future in his emphasis on Martel's
conjoining of mechanical and biological identity" (171). McGuirk also notes Martel's
"virtual castration" (176), to which I refer below.

16. Cordwainer Smith, "Scanners Live in Vain," *The Science Fiction Hall of Fame*, ed.
Robert Silverberg (1970; New York: Avon, 1971), 354–390. Originally published in *Fantasy Book* (1950). Subsequent page references in the text are to this edition.

17. In his study of modernity and transgression, John Jervis notes that, "Crossing
boundaries as they do, cyborgs ... become a further manifestation of the discourse, and
the experience, of the monstrous" (*Transgressing the Modern: Explorations in the Western
Experience of Otherness* [Oxford: Blackwell, 1999], 206); subsequent Jervis page references
in the text are to this edition. "Scanners Live in Vain" is a convincing demonstration of
the horror evoked by the hybrid techno-body as the product of a monstrous boundary-
crossing.

18. Istvan Csicsery-Ronay, Jr. mentions "Scanners Live in Vain" in the context of his
cogent analysis "On the Grotesque in Science Fiction" (*Science Fiction Studies*, 29 [March,
2002], 75). He also reminds readers of conventional associations of the female body
with the category of the grotesque; it is worth considering that the bodies of Scanners—
insofar as they have been both castrated and penetrated by technology — have been fem-
inized in Smith's story, a process in keeping with their function as representations of
the technological grotesque.

19. The discovery involves live oysters.

20. C. L. Moore, "No Woman Born," *The Best of C. L. Moore*, ed. Lester Del Rey (New
York: Ballantine, 1975), 242. Originally published in *Astounding Science-Fiction* (December, 1944).

21. As I observed of this story in another article, "It is worth remembering that the
'original' Deirdre was already a consummate performer. As such, she represented femininity as spectacle and was the object of desire for millions of adoring fans. Deirdre's
'natural' performances are, in fact, electronic mediations and she herself is adept at performing the image of femininity, at least for those same adoring fans" (Veronica
Hollinger, "(Re)reading Queerly: Science Fiction, Feminism, and the Defamiliarization
of Gender," *Science Fiction Studies*, 26 [March, 1999], 30).

22. Graham makes the point that "one of the functions of monsters is to be a spectacle
of abnormality" (39). Deirdre's status as a hybrid subject indeed renders her monstrous
in the eyes of men observing her, but it is worth considering in this context that, as a
performer, her role has always been to be on display. And given our conventional associations of woman's body with the body of nature, Deirdre is also monstrous insofar as
her new body is the "unnatural" product of technology. As Jervis notes, "woman's 'close-
ness' to nature is rationalized through science, and women are precluded from full participation in modernity as project, and there is a resulting tension between woman as
subject, responsible agent, and woman as object, of masculine control" (124). Moore's
early cyborg story mounts an extraordinary challenge to modernity's constructions of
both "the feminine" and "woman."

23. Like the drag performances discussed by Butler, Deirdre's performance casts doubt
upon the ontological "reality" of human nature.

24. It is worth considering the association in science fiction of female cyborg-figures
with aspects of performance, in stories by both women and men. In film the earliest
example is probably the evil robot–Maria of Fritz Lang's *Metropolis* (1927); in fiction,
examples include Moore's Deirdre; the idoru of *Idoru* and *All Tomorrow's Parties*; Angie

in Gibson's _Count Zero_ (1986); Delphi in James Tiptree, Jr.'s "The Girl Who Was Plugged In" (1971); Helva in Anne McCaffrey's "The Ship Who Sang" (1961); Donna in Storm Constantine's "Immaculate" (1991)—the list can go on and on.

25. Hayles, "The Life Cycle of Cyborgs: Writing the Posthuman," _A Question of Identity: Women, Science, and Literature_, ed. Marina Benjamin (New Brunswick, NJ: Rutgers University Press, 1993), 153.

26. Appropriately, Hayles's _How We Became Posthuman_ uses the term "embodied narratives" (22) to suggest the heterogeneous nature of the worlds of fiction, in contrast to the abstraction of modelled worlds produced in theoretical discourse. Other sf texts that might usefully be examined in the context that I'm developing here include Brian Aldiss's "Supertoys Last All Summer Long" (1961); Isaac Asimov's _I, Robot_ (1950); Pat Cadigan's "Pretty Boy Crossover" (1987); Constantine's "Immaculate" (1991); Philip K. Dick's _Do Androids Dream of Electric Sheep?_ (1968) and "The Electric Ant" (1968); Egan's "Reasons to Be Cheerful" (1997); Shariann Lewitt's "A Real Girl" (1998); Pat Murphy's "Rachel in Love" (1987); Amy Thompson's _Virtual Girl_ (1993); and Tiptree's "The Girl Who Was Plugged In" (1973).

27. Michel Foucault, "What Is Enlightenment?," _The Foucault Reader_, ed. Paul Rabinow (New York, Pantheon Books, 1984), 50.

5

Places of Alterity in Science Fiction

Richard L. McKinney

Place matters. According to philosopher J. E. Malpas, "There is good reason to suppose that the human relationship to place is a fundamental structure in what makes possible the sort of life that is characteristically human, while also being determining [...] of human identity."[1] Furthermore, Malpas says,

> The grasp of a sense of place is not just important to a grasp of self, nor even a grasp of the inter-subjective realm of others, but also to a grasp of the world itself [....] the very possibility of understanding or of knowledge resides in locatedness and in a certain embeddedness in place. (189)

Among other arguments supporting his claims, Malpas points to the central role of place in the works of canonical writers like Marcel Proust, William Wordsworth, William Faulkner, Seamus Heaney, and Salman Rushdie. Numerous scholars—philosophers, human geographers, anthropologists, sociologists, environmentalists, literary scholars, and others—also note and comment on (often under rubrics such as landscape, environment, surroundings, space, or locality) the importance of place in our conceptual, artistic, and social lives. The central claim of this chapter is that in science fiction (referred to subsequently and synonymously as *SF* and *transmimetic fiction*) place also matters, although the genre often confronts its *percipients* (a term for readers, viewers, or listeners of a work of art, irrespective of medium) with places that do not really exist.

Place is rarely discussed at length in analyses of literature (though more attention has been given to the subject in film studies), since depictions of place are not normally included among the main elements of fiction. Place instead occupies a subordinate role as description, background, or setting. Place is not commonly thought to give depth to characters, advance plot, or facilitate ethical arguments, although, on greater examination, it becomes apparent that it can indeed accomplish all three. Even when a work is not expressly and specifically about a particular place, it may be impossible to fathom vital aspects of that work without understanding the role and importance of the locations where it occurs. Plot twists and turns are not independent of the physical, geographical, and social landscapes on which they play out. Characters, too, are only fully accessible in relation to the spatial and temporal places where they move and act. This is of course both obvious and trivial with respect to all fiction, not just SF. Even among non-fantastic works, it is not difficult to think of a novel or movie where place is stronger than either plot or characters, at least in terms of its impact on percipients. Historical fiction, for example, is a genre in which location, as a rule, is vital to the storytelling, as is sometimes detective fiction. The point with science fiction, however, is that its places may well be prime examples of one or another kind of alterity. The location is not just Chicago, but the Chicago shared with robots in Alex Proyas's film *I, Robot* (2004); not just Baltimore, but the nanotech-damaged Baltimore of Kathleen Ann Goonan's *Queen City Jazz* (1994); not just Shanghai, but the future Shanghai of Neal Stephenson's *The Diamond Age* (1995).

I realize that the concept of *place* is neither simple nor unproblematic. However, I will not delve into the complex relationship between diverse ideas of *place* and *space*; nor will I investigate claims that an understanding of place in fiction as little more than background or simply as straightforward setting misses the inherently relational aspects of place, its necessary construction by readers or viewers, its fuzzy boundaries and contours, and its unavoidable changeableness over time. Such issues—important though they are (and I emphasize that they *are* important)—do not fit into the more modest remit of this chapter. Instead, I will focus on explicitly manifest places found in story-worlds of science fiction books, films, and TV programs. Rich Horton, introducing an annual anthology of stories chosen as the "best" of science fiction and fantasy, asserts that, along with possibly historical fiction, SF and fantasy are genres defined by their settings, i.e., by place.[2] Even someone with relatively limited contact with the genre cannot help but notice the prominence of place in science fiction. This chapter, then, is in part a plea for a greater consideration of place *as place* in discussions of transmimetic literature.

This chapter is not just about place, however; it is also about alterity, or otherness. And alterity, too, matters. This concept is also not without controversy, including a certain amount of inconsistency concerning its use in both the human and social sciences. I have neither time nor space to enter this debate, and therefore will concentrate on elements of fiction that are relatively explicit examples of otherness in the fictional worlds of the works under discussion, whether that alterity is manifest in terms of novelty, difference, transgression, deviance, or transformation.

Alterity is, of course, a central and required ingredient in all science fiction; so much so that it is actually a defining characteristic of the genre. In *The Known and the Unknown*, Gary K. Wolfe sees a confrontation with the Other, in the form of the unknown, as one of the distinguishing aspects of SF.[3] Mark Rose significantly calls his study of the genre *Alien Encounters*,[4] and Gwyneth Jones writes "that what people mean when they say 'science fiction' at its greatest possible expansion, is anything that involves an attempt to make sense of something alien [....] In the end it includes all that's outside ourselves."[5] The *novum*, which is what Darko Suvin calls that non-realistic element in a fictional universe necessary to identify a work as science fiction, is by definition intrinsically Other, presented via "an imaginative framework alternative to the author's empirical environment."[6]

There are, however, both degrees and kinds of alterity: otherness can vary from the slightly different or barely new to the radically strange or completely alien. And an Other need not be — and oftentimes is not — science fictional in order to be Other. When the alterity present *is* transmimetic in nature, it can be seen (using concepts and terminology borrowed from Carl D. Malmgren) as mainly extrapolative or predominately speculative.[7] Extrapolation is the central technique found in what has appropriately been called the "if this goes on" type of fiction, referring to the extension of already-discernible present-day trends into the future. This is basically what professional futurologists do when they attempt to predict what tomorrow may offer. Speculation, on the other hand, involves a more open-ended kind of imaginative creation, or as Malmgren says, "Speculation is [...] a more 'creative' or 'freer' mental operation, in which the writer who chooses to speculate is cut loose from the current state of affairs" (12–13). This does not provide science fiction storytellers with unlimited freedom, however, as it might for creators of fantasy, because SF places its own demands for a kind of plausibility on its creators, since it, in Malmgren's words, "incorporates supernatural, estranged, or nonempirical elements but grounds those elements in a naturalizing discourse which takes for granted the explicability of the universe" (10). Transmimetic alterity can be manifest in a storyworld as a single isolated element, a number of interlinked factors, or a deeply pervasive atmosphere which affects the entire fictional environment. Clearly, alterity also resides in the persons who inhabit a fictional universe, the props which surround those characters, or even — more subtly, more indirectly, but perhaps more powerfully — in the plot which structures a story. And otherness does not necessarily manifest itself openly as difference which is obvious or evident. Finally, an argument could be made for what might be called the axiological alterity of certain ethical positions and particular moral stances which interrogate longstanding, or criticize widely-held, viewpoints, traditions, and norms.

A further specification or narrowing of the focus of this discussion occurs because what I am especially (though not exclusively) interested in are forms of alterity that are manifest as aspects of place: when and how place is Other. Certain transmimetic locations present a unique challenge to storytellers: they do not actually exist, nor have they ever existed. It is not unusual for the setting of an SF story to be radically different from places of which percipients have knowledge or experience.

To establish the validity of my claims, I will discuss selected works of science fiction whose storyworlds offer clear, strong examples of alterity of place. These novels, films, and TV series have been chosen because of the strength, degree, and/or originality of the otherness in their fictional worlds. These selections are not intended to be canonical or exhaustive; nor does the scope of this chapter allow for in-depth analyses of these works. Nevertheless, my examples will serve well enough to demonstrate the variety of places and diversity of alterity found in transmimetic fiction. I will examine five categories or kinds of place: cities, other (non-terrestrial) planets, the wider universe, inner landscapes, and, finally, what I call places outside traditional mappings of the world.

The *city of tomorrow* is an absolutely central canonical theme and major motif of science fiction, and has been designated as one of the genre's icons by Wolfe (86–124). A significant number of SF's major and minor classics are set in future cities. Whether manifest as glittering towers and soaring architecture; a world of wonder encased in a dome; a dangerous, decadent, and degenerate concrete, plastic, and/or steel jungle; or empty and desolate ruins, the urban futures of SF are many and multifaceted. These urban tomorrows can leave strong impressions in the consciousnesses of readers or viewers who encounter them, sometimes long after the characters who walked their streets, or plots which played out among their buildings, have faded from their minds.

Arthur C. Clarke's *The City and the Stars* (1956), a substantially revised and tellingly re-titled version of his 1948 novel, *Against the Fall of Night*, provides us with Diaspar, an almost archetypical example of one particular kind of science fictional city, entirely enclosed in a giant protective dome, controlled and protected by computers, isolated and alone on the barren desert of a far-future Earth. The novel's opening lines, evoking the almost elegiac mood found in Clarke's SF at times, are particularly memorable:

> Like a glowing jewel, the city lay upon the breast of the desert. Once it had known change and alteration, but now Time passed it by. Night and day fled across the desert's face, but in the streets of Diaspar it was always afternoon, the darkness never came. The long winter nights might dust the desert with frost, as the last moisture left in the thin air of Earth congealed — but the city knew neither heat nor cold. It had no contact with the outer world; it was a universe itself.
>
> Men had built cities before, but never a city such as this. Some had lasted for centuries, some for millenniums, before Time had swept away even their names. Diaspar alone had challenged Eternity, defending itself and all it sheltered against the slow attrition of the ages, the ravages of decay, and the corruption of rust.
>
> Since the City was built, the oceans of Earth had passed away and the desert had encompassed all the globe. The last mountains had been ground to dust by the winds and the rain, and the world was too weary to bring forth more. The city did not care; Earth itself could crumble and Diaspar would still protect the children of its makers, bearing them and their treasures safely down the stream of Time.[8]

The language of this passage describes a place imbued with an alterity recalling the sublimity of Edmund Burke or nineteenth-century Romantics. The city, whose unique character can only be described in superlatives, is a place of extremes. Diaspar possesses an otherness that sets it apart from common knowledge or everyday experience. This city bypassed by Time (not just time), which has challenged Eternity, and which can qualify as a universe in itself well exemplifies numerous manifestations of alterity of place.

Another, quite different, city — a future version of New York — is found in Isaac Asimov's *The Caves of Steel* (1954), part of the author's Robots sequence. This city is the backdrop to a plot structured as a murder mystery. Investigating the murder requires the two police detectives who are the protagonists (one of whom is a robot) to move about the city to solve the crime, simultaneously providing readers with an opportunity to gain considerable knowledge about this specific urban storyworld and thereby also exemplifying what good crime fiction can do so well. Most of the city's countless citizens suffer from severe agoraphobia, since the huge metal domes entirely enclosing the city allow neither weather nor even natural sunshine to reach inhabitants, as implied by the book's title. Note the following conversation between the human detective, Elijah Baley, and his superior:

> [The Commissioner] touched an inconspicuous contact switch and a section of the wall grew transparent.
> Baley blinked at the unexpected insurge of grayish light.
> The Commissioner smiled. "I had this arranged specially last year, Lije. I don't think I've showed it to you before. Come over here and take a look. In the old days, all rooms had things like this. They were called 'windows.' Did you know that?"
> Baley knew that very well, having viewed many historical novels.
> "I've heard of them," he said.
> "Come here."
> Baley squirmed a bit, but did as he was told. There was something indecent about the exposure of the privacy of a room to the outside world [....]
> With mild shock, Baley realized that it was raining. For a minute, he was lost in the spectacle of water dropping from the sky, while the Commissioner exuded a kind of pride as though the phenomenon were a matter of his own arranging.
> "This is the third time this month I've watched it rain. Quite a sight, don't you think?"
> Against his will, Baley had to admit to himself that it was impressive. In his forty-two years he had rarely seen rain, or any of the phenomena of nature, for that matter.[9]

Here, Baley is forced to confront examples of unanticipated otherness in his world, to realize that in a place about which he felt knowledgeable and where he thought himself relatively secure, alterity could suddenly intrude, in this case as a window, or rain. For readers of this novel, however, it is precisely Baley's surprise and unease which constitutes the alterity. A place which produces such a reaction in one of its inhabitants is a place of alterity.

Asimov referred to himself as an author of what he called "social science fiction,"[10] and much of the otherness of this particular New York is indeed framed in social terms. The greatly increased population density of the city has led to major changes in how people live, the manner in which they interact, even in the ways they move about. Most significant, however, have been the psychological changes: transformations in habits, values, and attitudes. New norms and customs have developed, shaped by the constant contacts with others which everyone must endure. *The Caves of Steel* allows readers to explore the alterity of the overcrowded New York on display, to examine certain kinds of otherness that might develop given the physical and social conditions suggested in the novel.

Interestingly, Asimov wrote a sequel, *The Naked Sun* (1957), another mystery involving the detectives seen in *The Caves of Steel*, which describes a place with a social structure diametrically opposite to the fictional New York: a world of strict population control where individuals live alone (or only with spouses) on huge estates, isolated from contact with other people and cared for by robot servants.

Other transmimetic fiction about the future city that focuses on overpopulation as an important element of alterity includes Harry Harrison's *Make Room! Make Room!* (1966), James Blish and Norman L. Knight's *A Torrent of Faces* (1967), John Brunner's *Stand on Zanzibar* (1968), and Robert Silverberg's *The World Inside* (1971). Comparing the crowded places described in these stories, all examples of extrapolative SF, produces interesting perspectives on what kind of alterity population pressures might lead to. Considering the age of these novels, however, reading them in parallel also sheds light on how a work of science fiction is a product of the time when it is created, reflecting the issues, values, and concerns of that era. Of course, definitions of, and attitudes toward, the Other are also historically specific, and it can be worthwhile to ask what makes a particular place seem more or less alien at a given time. Obviously, analogous questions can be posed concerning the social and cultural specificity of alterity. Examining how (from the perspectives of twenty-first century versions of, e.g., feminism, queer theory, postcolonialism, postmodernism, or evolutionary theory) works from the 1960s and 1970s treat issues of alterity tells us valuable things about both the period and alterity itself.

Films and television programs, utilizing the intrinsic differences and strengths of the media, can show otherness in an immediate and effective manner. Techniques of audiovisual storytelling (including CGI and other special effects) allow for immediate immersion in fictional worlds rich in alterity. A number of notable cinematic cities, for example, have been created over the years. The earliest such film I will mention has been called, by Andrew M. Butler, "the first undisputed classic of science fiction cinema."[11] Although a public and financial disaster when first released, Fritz Lang's *Metropolis* (1927) remains a visually impressive accomplishment. This is a movie remembered because of the visual place it presents to audiences, rather than for the future society it depicts, which was unrealistic and clichéd even at the time of its premier. Nevertheless, it has been hugely influential among cinematic storytellers, and echoes of its now-iconic imagery and architecture are found in any number of later movies.

A more recent cinema classic dealing with an urban future especially rich in alterity, and on which the influence of *Metropolis* is apparent, is Ridley Scott's *Blade Runner* (1982). One strength of this film is the great amount of detail with which it depicts its fictional world. *Blade Runner* immerses percipients in a fictional world filled with specificity. This detail is not focused or elaborated on; it neither needs to be nor is explained. Scott Bukatman describes the film like this:

> The brilliance of *Blade Runner* [...] is located in its visual density. Scott's "layering" effect produces an inexhaustible complexity, an infinity of surfaces to be encountered and explored, and *Blade Runner* refuses to explain itself [....] The viewer [...] is forced to make constant inferences in order to understand the detailed world that the film presents.[12]

A significant amount of the otherness of this urban landscape lies in the fact that all these diverse and complex images on the screen constantly and simultaneously demand the viewer's attention. Each image of alterity is always competing with other Others, as it were. Meanwhile, the pace of the movie allows little or no time for percipients to process the overwhelming stream of new data and information.

Other films worth mentioning because of the manner in which they visualize dark urban tomorrows (the influence of *Metropolis* is again apparent) include Terry Gilliam's *Brazil* (1985) and Alex Proyas's *Dark City* (1998). *Dark City* might have ended up in my final category of works, those dealing with places outside traditional mappings of the world, since the city it offers us is exceedingly strange. Its plot is built on a number of mysteries, the most important concerning the nature of the city itself. Each day all people in the city stop, literally falling asleep while the city around them rearranges itself into new shapes and patterns. When they awaken, their identities have been altered and they remember nothing of the recent past. One man, John Murdoch (Rufus Sewell), seems immune to these odd events, but he is a suspect in a murder investigation and his own memory is incomplete. The complex plot development, impossible to summarize here, later introduces aliens, the Strangers, who are pulling the city's strings, as it were, manipulating people in an effort to save their own species. There is little in this film's city that is not Other, and much of that otherness only becomes apparent as the movie progresses. Through much of the story, it might be correctly said that the more we learn, the less we know — or at any rate, understand. Knowledge, in the form of raw data, does not solve the mysteries that, for a considerable amount of time, dominate our perceptions of the film. Alterity cannot be eliminated or understood in so simple a manner as by collecting more information, but must be placed in an appropriate relational context and investigated there.

Proyas, incidentally, later directed *I, Robot*, a film whose explicitly extrapolative urban landscape, Chicago of the year 2035, is visually striking in a way completely different from *Dark City*. The later movie is distinguished by lighter imagery and an emphasis on transparency.

Stories set on *other planets* represent another characteristic and significant category of science fiction which has also produced its share of classic tales. From the relatively local worlds of our own solar system to the far reaches of the universe, such settings provide fertile ground for exploring the potentials of place beyond the Earth.

Closest to Earth, the Moon has been the location for a number of SF writers and filmmakers. In Clarke's *A Fall of Moondust* (1961), a tourist boat disappears while plying the surface of the (fictional) Sea of Thirst on the Moon. It turns out that a sudden and unexpected moonquake caused the ship to sink into the treacherous dust which fills this lunar mare. The alterity of the dust-filled Sea of Thirst thereby becomes both a mystery to be solved and a threat to be overcome by passengers. This otherness, however, is not personified, but a natural, if unknown and dangerous, aspect of the universe which must be understood before it can be dealt with. The protagonists of Kristine Kathryn Rusch's Retrieval Artist sequence live in a domed habitat on the Moon, and many adventures in that series occur there. The importance of place is evident in *Extremes* (2003), the second novel, which revolves in part around the death of a runner in the annual Moon Marathon, an extreme sports race conducted across the barren lunar landscape.

Mars is the planet in our solar system which has been visited most often by transmimetic explorers. Notable examples of SF set on Mars include Ray Bradbury's *The Martian Chronicles* (1950), Kim Stanley Robinson's *Mars* trilogy (1993–1996), and Ben Bova's *Mars* (1992), while films focusing on the planet include Brian De Palma's *Mission to Mars* (2000) and Anthony Hoffman's *Red Planet* (2000).

A classic among more distant extraterrestrial landscapes is the planet Mesklin from Hal Clement's *Mission of Gravity* (1954). Clement, an author renowned for the care he took in creating alien worlds, produced a truly fascinating imaginary planet, the planetology and evolutionary biology of which was worked out relatively rigorously. Mesklin is a supergiant planet with methane oceans, sixteen times as massive as Jupiter, oblate rather than spherical in shape (due to an extremely high rate of spin, a Mesklin day is only seventeen and three quarter minutes long), with gravity that varies from around three to nearly seven hundred times that of Earth.[13] This is an original place of considerable alterity. Less successfully, the centipede-like inhabitants who inhabit Mesklin display distinctly anthropomorphic (and somewhat clichéd) personality traits and social characteristics. Unfortunately, far too many transmimetic aliens are less manifestations of alterity than thinly-disguised examples of the familiar. Hidden under the external alien shapes and forms are traditional human patterns of behavior and well-known values and prejudices.

The most renowned novel dealing in detail with an alien world is surely Frank Herbert's *Dune* (1965). This book and its six sequels (1965–1985) are frequently cited as contemporary classics of science fiction world-building. Herbert was inspired in part by the science of desert ecology, and *Dune* is explicitly dedicated "to the dry-land ecologists."[14] This cycle of books, which can be called transmimetic ecofiction, is set in the far future, against the backdrop of the desert planet Arrakis, or Dune. Herbert's ecological perspective comes across in the way he deals with the alterity of this alien and forbidding place, which Brian W. Aldiss and David Wingrove say "is as intensely realized as any in science fiction. The shortage of water, for instance, is presented not just diagrammatically, but as a living fact which permeates all facets of existence."[15] Far from Earth, as the only source of the spice which makes travel between the stars possible, Arrakis is a harsh, hazardous planet, a valuable pawn in dangerous games of interstellar intrigue.

I should also mention a novel from 1986 by Joan Slonczewski, *A Door into Ocean*,[16] which presents a kind of reverse image of *Dune*. The moon on which the story focuses, the opposite of Arrakis, is a world covered with water. Its inhabitants are women, and the novel provides a feminist perspective. Pamela Sargent has written of the two works: "If Herbert's desert world breeds warriors, Slonczewski's ocean world of Shora has produced pacifists."[17] A comparative perspective is valuable here to explore what the differences between these two fictional places are indicative of.

Colonizing other planets is a recurring theme in SF, sometimes by means of terraforming. This is one way to meet alterity: by transforming the Other (the alien world) into the familiar (a planet with an Earth-like environment). So is the case with Mars in Robinson's *Red Mars* and its sequels, and with Venus in Pamela Sargent's Venus trilogy (1986–2000). In *Coyote* (2002) and its sequels, Allen Steele produced a series of novels and stories that follow the fortunes of a group of exiles from Earth who colonize the planet Coyote after fleeing a repressive government at home. Nancy Kress, in *Crossfire* (2003) and *Crucible* (2004), presents her colonists with, among other problems, unexpected humanoid aliens on their new home world. Successful colonization of extraterrestrial planets always involves understanding the local flora and fauna, learning to best use native resources, and negotiating with non-human inhabitants, when there are any. It may also prove necessary to deal with manifestations of otherness amidst human settlers, especially when they have brought from home fears of, and prejudices toward, Others among themselves, as proves the case in all the examples mentioned above.

In many SF stories, extraterrestrial worlds contain alien artifacts large and complex enough to be considered places on their own terms. In fact, stories about objects left behind by vanished alien civilizations occur often enough in transmimetic fiction to be classified as an independent subgenre. Among the most well-known of such artifacts are the enormous structures which give titles to the novels *Ringworld* by Larry Niven (1970) and *Orbitsville* by Bob Shaw (1975). Silverberg's aliens left behind a baffling maze in *The Man in the Maze* (1968). In *Rogue Moon* (1960), Algis Budrys also presents protagonists with a mysterious, dangerous, alien-built maze, this time on Earth's moon, while Mars is the location of an empty alien city in Steele's *Labyrinth of Night* (1992). In Clarke's *Rendezvous with Rama* (1973) a huge, dormant extraterrestrial space-ship enters our solar system and becomes the subject of human exploration and investigation. One of the most extravagant of alien artifacts is introduced in Greg Bear's *Eon* (1985). The protagonists of Bear's storyworld find that the asteroid called *Thistledown* is larger on the inside than the outside, and contained within it is a giant tube, or tunnel, known as The Way, that extends not only through space, but also through time.

Stories like these are commonly about the investigation of alien places, mystery stories, exploration tales where the mystery to be solved is the nature of the place being explored. They almost always present challenges of understanding the mechanisms by which alien places function — at least to the degree that humans can manage to stay alive and possibly also find a treasure or solve a riddle. The characters' goal is to eliminate the alterity they have been confronted with by coming to understand (and subsequently control) it. The alterity is usually present on at least two interrelated levels, that of the physical artifact or place being examined, and the alterity of its alien creators.

Perhaps surprisingly, films dealing interestingly with alien worlds make up a relatively small percentage of the total number of transmimetic movies. Before special effects reached their current level of sophistication this was, in part, due to the intrinsic technical difficulties of bringing an alien environment to life on the screen. Certainly, some of the early attempts are characterized by the *lack* of alterity in supposedly otherworld landscapes which are obviously (and sometimes unintentionally comically) terrestrial. There are, nonetheless, a few classics in this category, such as Fred M. Wilcox's *Forbidden Planet* (1956) and Andrei Tarkovsky's *Solaris* (1972), the former based — very roughly — on William Shakespeare's *The Tempest* (1611), and the latter on Stanislaw Lem's 1961 novel.

The year 2009 saw two notable films set on extraterrestrial worlds, Duncan Jones's low-key *Moon* (2009) and James Cameron's blockbuster *Avatar* (2009). In both cases, if in different ways, the movies focus on the environments of places teeming with otherness. Especially in the latter instance, the enormous creative and economic resources used to create and present the planet Pandora produced a fictional place which is, for many viewers, by far the single most memorable thing about the film. Much of this impact clearly rests on the alterity of this extraterrestrial landscape. However, on closer examination, there are also many things about Pandora that seem familiar. It would be interesting to compare exactly which aspects of the alien planet are manifestations of genuine alterity, and which are actually more appropriately seen as versions of the familiar or variations of the known.

In the category I call *a wider universe* we find works of space opera, a subgenre whose setting is usually far distant from the here and now, ensuring the presence of a substantial degree of otherness. This subgenre has recently experienced a major renaissance, during which it has been, according to David Langford, "significantly redefined,"[18] and in the course of which it has, in the words of M. Keith Booker and Anne-Marie Thomas, "produced some of the most complex and thought-provoking novels in the history of science fiction."[19] This means that the term itself is no longer widely used, as it once was, as a designation of opprobrium. Among major contributors to the subgenre in the last two decades we find Iain M. Banks, Stephen Baxter, Greg Bear, David Brin, Peter F. Hamilton, M. John Harrison, Ken MacLeod, Paul McAuley, Alastair Reynolds, Justina Robson, Dan Simmons, and Vernor Vinge. Places rich in alterity are important in the works of all these writers.

The places I will focus on here are not the single, geographically limited locations, such as a building, spacecraft, town, or even an entire planet, although these locations can — and often do— provide key settings in works of this category. What I refer to instead is a depiction of the fictional universe (or, at least, a significant portion of it) as a whole. Cosmos as place, so to speak. Oftentimes space operas are serial compositions, consisting of a (sometimes large) number of works, rather than an isolated novel or standalone television program. The vastness of the storyworld canvas in such fiction produces a different kind of "locatedness" from that of novels, films, or television shows set on narrower stages. Place becomes more extensive, cosmopolitan, open. Even when many scenes in such fiction *are* close-ups— limited or even intimate in their focus, rich in description and containing extensive local detail — the totality of effect of works in this category is wide-screen. For this reason, although the specific locations where the main action occurs may not be particularly interesting or impressive, the fictional world as a whole can still be an original and memorable place. That is why relatively routine novels or poorly realized episodes of televisual space opera series can nevertheless play out in fascinating futures. The place that matters in this case is not the setting of the particular work; it is the total storyworld that is elaborated on and filled out as the series continues to unfold. The emphasis is not on a place *in* the fictional universe; it is on the fictional universe itself *as* place.

Some works of C. J. Cherryh, for instance, can seem almost claustrophobic at times in descriptions of particular local places, such as the inside of a spaceship or docks of a space station; yet, taken as a whole, the place represented by her Alliance-Union sequence of novels is unique and fascinating. Place transcends the bounds of individual works to take on a life in the mind of Cherryh's readers greater than the sum of the places presented in individual works. Not that place is unimportant on the local level in Cherryh's fiction: just the opposite is true, since in several works the local places are important, vital, and memorable. Cherryh tends to focus on the thoughts and feelings of a lone individual, as likely as not someone separated from his or her own friends, family, and culture; probably someone immersed in an alien society that is difficult to fathom and hazardous to survive in. Cherryh's protagonists are, as a rule, isolated outsiders in situations in which they, often unwillingly, have ended up. They are alterity personified, trying to understand and negotiate the otherness of the places where they find themselves. Attending to local conditions in the storyworlds of Cherryh's novels is therefore central to formulating an understanding of these novels. Nevertheless, Cherryh's spacecrafts, alien worlds, and space stations remain to a degree incompletely understood unless placed in the larger context of the fictional universe wherein the stories unfold.

As is the case with Cherryh, the places where the fictional futures of other prominent SF authors occur are larger and have a greater impact when understood as totalities. As noted with respect to Cherryh, this does not remove the possibility of a focus on particular places in individual works, or sections or segments of longer works. A chapter of a novel can produce impressive depictions of specific places which remain only local manifestations of the greater totality of a longer work, as is often the case with sequences of works. There are, thus, nestings of alterity, where one kind of alterity is embedded within other manifestations of alterity, the former likely contributing vitally to the larger-scale otherness of the storyworld as a whole.

In the case of Vinge, the reader is given fiction which explores what might be termed ontological alterity. The fictional universe in *A Fire Upon the Deep* (1992) and its prequel *A Deepness in the Sky* (1999) is genuinely and originally different in its basic nature from the actual world we live in. I speak here not simply of stories set in the far future or peopled with alien beings. These novels actually propose a fictional world in which the deep structure of the galaxy is radically different from what we currently believe it to be, thereby producing a setting that has considerable import for, and impact on, the plot and characters of, especially, *A Fire Upon the Deep*. Readers must therefore mentally map for themselves this structure: the otherness of Vinge's storyworld must be at least minimally understood to make sense of the story being told. In addition to his grand conception of the galaxy, Vinge also presents in *A Fire Upon the Deep* speculation concerning the characteristics of a kind of interstellar internet, the possible nature of a group mind, and the impossibility of understanding the evolution of intelligent beings into what amount to gods. Vinge's original and ontological speculations concerning diverse forms and versions of alterity are among the book's strongest traits.

For practical reasons, a TV series often has a limited number of recurring sets where a significant amount of the action occurs. This may be a family living room for a sitcom, squad room for a police procedural, or spaceship or space station for an SF drama. Well-known background settings from transmimetic television include the starships *Enterprise* and *Voyager* and space station Deep Space Nine from the *Star Trek* franchise;[20] the eponymous spaceships of *Andromeda* (2000–2005) and *Battlestar Galactica* (1978–1979; 2004–2009); the spacecraft *Serenity*, from *Firefly* (2002–2003) (which also provided the setting and title for Joss Whedon's spinoff film from 2005), and space station Babylon 5 from the series bearing its name (1994–1998).

All these places merit attention, but the spacecraft *Moya*, from the TV series *Farscape* (1999–2003), is especially interesting and particularly relevant in the present context. Speculative alterity saturates the entire storyworld of the series from the beginning. The main place where much of the action transpires is inside the spaceship *Moya*. Being a nonhuman ship — immediately and obviously alien in design, both inside and out — *Moya* has a visual impact which introduces a significant degree of otherness into the story in the program's initial episode. This is soon reinforced, of course, by the introduction of the main characters, only one of whom is human. But *Moya* is more than just a setting — she is also, it turns out, a crucial fictional person. Literally, in this case, a place becomes a character in the story. Thereby the series introduces at least two different kinds of alterity: the first is manifest in a relatively familiar storyworld containing alien beings, basically recognizable from traditional SF cinema and TV; the second is more radical, however, involving the need for viewers to negotiate the otherness intrinsic to the concept of a place which is also a person.

Perhaps I should start my discussion of *inner landscapes* with the words of John Milton: "The mind is its own place, and in itself / Can make a Heaven of Hell, a Hell of Heaven."[21] Although Milton was not thinking of the kind of places found in the minds of characters in the stories I am discussing, the quote captures the essence of the "mental" places in works of transmimetic fiction. These places do not exist as geographic locations, not even in the fictional universes of their stories. They are located in the minds of characters. They are, however, no less important as places for that. Being figments of the dreams or imaginations of persons, they possess a special kind of alterity. Unlike most SF examples I discuss, the otherness inside the minds of characters cannot be rationally explained in terms of future developments, a journey to another planet, or an alternative historical timeline.

I emphasize here two works in particular, each of which presents a version of the inner landscapes of the human mind. These are Roger Zelazny's *The Dream Master* (1966; adapted from the novella, "He Who Shapes," from 1965) and Tarsem Singh's film *The Cell* (2000). Both present protagonists who enter into the mental worlds of characters in the stories. Charles Render, the main character of Zelazny's novel, is a special kind of psychotherapist who treats patients by monitoring and "shaping" their dreams. He takes on the task of training a young woman to work in his profession — a task which it turns out is extremely dangerous, not least because the woman has been blind from birth. In *The Cell,* child psychologist Catherine Deane (Jennifer Lopez) has developed a method of virtual reality which also allows her to enter the dreams of troubled children. In an emergency, however, she must use her invention to enter the mind of Carl Rudolph Stargher (Vincent D'Onofrio), a comatose serial killer, and the only person who knows the whereabouts of one of his victims. If Deane cannot find the location of this victim, a girl trapped in a glass enclosure slowly filling up with water, she will die. Needless to say, the journey into the mental world of Stargher is fraught with life-threatening dangers. What is particularly pertinent here is the way that both works interpret the probing of someone's mind in terms of the exploration of places of alterity. Entering the mind of another (i.e., an Other) person means venturing into an alien landscape over which one has limited control. Faith in one's own strength and abilities is a necessary prerequisite for success on such mental journeys, but overconfidence can lead to disaster.

Among other transmimetic excursions into places of the mind are John Brunner's novel *The Whole Man* (1964); films like David Cronenberg's *eXistenZ* (1999), *Brazil,* and Andy and Lana Wachowski's *Matrix* trilogy (1999–2003); and the British TV series *Life on Mars* (2006–2007) and its sequel, *Ashes to Ashes* (2008–2010). *Life on Mars* is noteworthy for the manner in which it keeps percipients in doubt about whether the protagonist, police detective Sam Tyler (John Simm), has actually traveled in time from the year 2006 back to 1973; alternatively, the world he experiences may be only a figment of his imagination, caused by a traffic accident. Both hypotheses seem at times to be supported by the evidence.

Finally, I call attention to three works that show us places that are, in one way or another, *outside the more traditional mappings of the world* we are otherwise familiar with. In many cases such works deal with some form of ontological alterity, but not in a straightforward way such as that found in *A Fire Upon the Deep.* Perhaps some of these works fall more into the camp of fantasy than that of science fiction, though one might argue that the metaphysical manner in which these stories and tales query our established pictures of the fundamental nature of the world is not only especially interesting, but also, in certain ways, very science-fictional. These works awaken questions concerning what it is indeed possible to know about the basic structures of existence. Whatever genre they fit into, each depicts a very special kind of place.

Alternate histories and parallel worlds are usually filled with that kind of alterity which is normally based on some significant deviation from history as we have come to accept it. An alternative — but more or less realistically developed — outcome of a war or marriage, for example, or the consequences of a different turn of events, is a typical basis for the storyworlds of these subgenres. Sometimes, however, the otherness depends on the introduction of elements of deviant science or technology, even the supernatural or paranormal. For instance, in Randall Garrett's series about detective Lord Darcy, magic works, and in Naomi Novik's *Temeraire* novels we confront a world in which the Napoleonic Wars are fought with the aid of sentient dragons. A particularly original place is the storyworld of Jay Lake's *Mainspring* (2007). The novel opens in New Haven on May 21, 1900, when the book's protagonist and narrator, Hethor Jacques, a young apprentice clockmaker, is awakened by the archangel Gabriel and told that he must find something called the Key Perilous and save the world, because "the Mainspring of the world winds down" and only Hethor "can set it right."[22] Thus begin adventures in a truly original fictional world in which the Earth is literally part of a giant clockwork mechanism; indeed, the entire cosmos appears to be. Late in the novel, Hethor actually reaches the South Pole, where the axis on which the Earth turns emerges from the planet:

> The highway ended in a great circular meadow. In the center of the meadow a brass shaft erupted like a javelin stuck into the unyielding earth. It was about a quarter mile in diameter, and rose to vanish frost-rimmed into the dark sky above [....]
>
> It was a short walk across the poppy meadow to the shaft. Up close, the brass was like a wall. The curve was so large that it was shallow almost to the point of flatness. The shaft spun with a whirring noise that was much quieter than he had expected from the rumble he'd heard several days distant. Rotating rapidly, it stirred the air like a spring breeze. There must be a massive reduction gearing deep within the world, he realized, to translate that speed to the stately revolutions of the Earth in its orbit around the sun. Cold radiated off the surface before him, doubtless conducted downward from the immense length of the metal that protruded into the long polar night not far above his head [297–301].

Kay Kenyon's *The Entire and the Rose*, a sequence of four novels published between 2007 and 2010, will be my other example from this category. This series tells of first contact between Earth of the twenty-third century (the Rose) and another universe (the Entire). The latter is a geologically continuous so-called tunnel universe, whose sky is lit by a river of fiery plasma known as the bright. It is described on Kenyon's homepage as follows:

> A radial universe, the Entire is comprised of five primacies—the monumental lobes of the universe. In length, the primacies are on a galactic scale; in breadth, only several thousand miles wide. A primacy has no absolute length, degrading at times into the Empty Lands where geography is distorted in space-time. Branching from one side of each primacy are the smaller minorals. Narrow and deserted valleys, the minorals are like root hairs on a giant tuber. At the tips of some minorals scholars attempt to observe other universes, for the Entire by its cosmography tends to burrow into the multiverse. Smaller still than a minoral are the nascences. These small canyons grow out of the sides of the minorals but are unstable and shunned.
>
> The storm walls enclose the primacy, the minoral and the nascence. These turbulent arms of the Entire appear as dark and stationary tidal waves. Each primacy has a great river along one wall. In all primacies, it is called the River Nigh. The core of the radial universe is the Sea of Arising, wellspring of the River Nigh. Above it hovers the floating city of the Tarig and the Magisterium, called the Ascendancy.[23]

A strange place indeed, the Entire, without planets or stars, in a dimension parallel to our own, originally engineered by the powerful Tarig, and filled with numerous species somehow copied from our own universe, including ancient Earth. Kenyon has produced a series which teems with numerous kinds of alterity, of which the highly original place manifest in the Entire is only the most prominent.

Turning to cinema, in Gary Ross's *Pleasantville* (1998), Pleasantville is a small town in an American television sitcom of the 1950s. During the film, while reruns of the program are on television, two teenagers from the present, a brother and sister named David (Tobey Maguire) and Jennifer (Reese Witherspoon), end up inexplicably and literally trapped in the sitcom world. This film is in many ways a study of the effects of alterity. David and Jennifer are prime examples of Others. Because of their backgrounds, values, and desires, they do not fit into the environment they have been thrust into. The world of the sitcom is, however, also a place of alterity for the twins—and percipients of the film. One striking visual aspect of the movie is the way that, when the siblings arrive in Pleasantville, they are shown, in accordance with the visual format of the TV program, in black-and-white. As the story develops, color gradually begins to appear in the fictional universe of the program and on the screen of the movie. This reflects, and is symbolic of, changes to the characters and social structures of the fictional town. Feelings and emotions seep into the lives of characters (including David and Jennifer) along with color. Alterity has quite literally affected the nature of the world, changing it from a place of black-and-white into a place filled with colors.

There are many ways a storyteller can create a memorable place. One is by the accumulation of myriad and distinct details about the storyworld: the more details percipients are given of a fictional place, and the more explicit they are, the more real and alive it can seem. This brings up the special nature of science fiction texts. When we encounter fictional worlds (all fictional worlds, not just transmimetic ones) we must work to make those worlds real. No work of fiction, no matter how detailed, can ever provide all the data about a fictional universe. Readers and viewers are necessarily presented with incomplete places. Ontological gaps are significant in all fiction, and are, in fact, considered by some scholars to be a defining feature of fiction itself. As Lubomir Dolezel says, "A necessary consequence of the fact that fictional worlds are human constructs is their incompleteness."[24] Alan Palmer tells us, "storyworlds differ ontologically from the real world because they are incomplete [....] No discourse could ever be long enough to say in its story all that could be said about the whole storyworld." As a result, Palmer continues, "fiction is necessarily incomplete and full of blanks where nothing is said about a part of the storyworld and gaps where something but not everything is said."[25] This is especially pertinent with respect to SF, when the storyworld is set two hundred (or two thousand) years in the future, on the surface of Mars, in another galaxy, or even further afield from the everyday world. The gaps in a storyworld must be filled in by percipients as they follow the story. This is usually done according to what Marie-

Louise Ryan, theorizing from a possible-worlds perspective, calls the "principle of minimal departure."[26] By this, Ryan refers to the manner in which we percipients of fiction automatically assume, unless told or shown otherwise, that a given fictional universe is identical to the actual universe. The default setting, so to speak, for understanding any world, even fictional ones, is everyday reality. The Montreal of Kathy Reich's Temperance Brennan novels, the Los Angeles of Michael Mann's film *Collateral* (2004), and the Tokyo of Barry Eisler's John Rain thrillers are identical to cities that exist in reality — except for differences that are explicitly spelled out in the fiction itself. Cats, dogs, penguins, London, Bangkok, and goldfish are the same in fact and fiction, except when we are specifically informed that this is not the case.

Gaps and blanks are especially obvious with respect to science-fictional (and fantasy) worlds, because clearly the principle of minimal departure cannot always be applied, even theoretically, to an SF universe — because there may be no analog in reality to serve as a template for constructing the fictional world. We have no basis for deciding the content of those parts of a storyworld that do not correspond to the actual one. Nevertheless, although we may have no method to flesh out the social, political, or cultural aspects of a fictional society of the future, or determine the personality characteristics of extraterrestrial beings, we usually can safely assume that basic logical and natural laws still function in a normal manner. Gravity and the law of the excluded middle will remain as they are in everyday experience, water will still be H_2O, and fish will continue to swim in it.

I trust the works discussed above are sufficient to establish the importance of places of alterity in transmimetic fiction. Many more examples could be supplied. But one may ask: what does all this have to do with predicting the future?

Note that it is not the characters or plots of transmimetic fiction which are of interest in examining SF and prediction. Nor is it the details of particular discoveries or inventions, or precise shape of social or cultural developments. One does not read science fiction to chart the exact path to the future, or find out the details of tomorrow. What transmimetic fiction can deal with, often better than traditional, non-fictional futurology, are *qualitative* aspects of the future. SF can explore what sort of place tomorrow may be *to live in*. Consequently, the kind of alterity that times to come may hold is one of the most important issues to consider.

Of course, all storyworlds depict places; and, being fictional, all these imaginary places are to some degree foreign or alien to percipients. Even the most mundane realistic novel or movie presents a place at some distance from our own world, if only through the imaginary characters that populate it. But transmimetic worlds are distant in a qualitatively important way, because of the nature and degree of their alterity.

More specifically, reading stories focusing on the otherness of place provides a way to mitigate — to some extent — the failure of imagination Clarke warned of in *Profiles of the Future* (1962), by supplying fictional scenarios we ourselves did not, indeed could not, imagine. SF shows options and alternatives which we would never have thought about, and it can, at best, make us ask if we want such options, if we desire those alternatives. Transmimetic fiction takes us to places that may not be precisely the places that actually lie in our future, but their very alterity can help us learn how to confront the unexpected and unanticipated, which the future is guaranteed to hold. From this perspective, the more Otherness involved, the better.

This is closely related to what philosopher Martha C. Nussbaum says that the best literature does by allowing us to experience the unexpected and contingent. Nussbaum believes that the way literary fiction deals with contingency can have special significance for its readers.

> The structure of [certain] novels [...] has built into it an emphasis on the significance, for human life, of what simply happens, of surprise, of reversal [....] Proust tells us that one of the primary aims of literary art is to show us moments in which habit is cut through by the unexpected, and to engender in the reader a similar upsurge of true, surprised feeling. The ability of their texts to give insight is seen by both [Henry James and Marcel Proust] to depend on this power to display such uncontrolled events as if they matter to the characters, and to make them matter to the reader. And the Aristotelian conception holds that a correct understanding of the ways in which human aspirations to live well can be checked by uncontrolled events is in fact an important part of ethical understanding.[27]

Although Nussbaum obviously speaks of fictional events, rather than imaginary places, I hold that the confrontation with transmimetic places rich in unanticipated otherness can also contribute to the ethical understanding she refers to. Even here a large amount of alterity would be an advantage.

Place, to be understood, is something that must be experienced, not just observed. Fiction allows for such experience. To understand what life in the future — on Earth, on other planets, among the stars—could be like, we must experience what that future life might be like as it is lived. Spending some time in a place is a good way to decide whether one wishes to spend even more time in that place. A strong emotional involvement with a work of fiction, an emotional immersion in a fictional universe, not only allows, but actually requires us to ask ourselves what it is about a particular fictional place that makes it attractive or disagreeable. Perhaps, if we like what we encounter, we will work toward translating it from the page or screen into reality. Horrific tomorrows are potentially just as valuable as utopias because one purpose in predicting disastrous futures is to ensure that they never come to pass. SF does not *predict* the future; it offers us alternatives from which we can choose those we most want to see realized, or avoided.

Good science fiction transcends the real, mundane, everyday world where we find ourselves. It transports us to places of alterity and prompts us to question not only the otherness we find there, but also our own attitudes toward the Other. Good transmimetic fiction provokes me into asking what kinds of alterity will, can, or should exist in my own future. What sort of place might that future be?

Just as it is impossible to consider life in the present without considering the context that life takes place in, it is impossible to seriously imagine life in the future without considering the context in which *that* life might play out. Experiencing fictional places of tomorrow reinforces the importance of such experiences. Because place always matters, then, so do the places of the future, and therefore so, too, do the places of science fiction.

NOTES

1. J. E. Malpas, *Place and Experience: A Philosophical Topography* (Cambridge: Cambridge University Press, 1999), 13. Subsequent page references in the text are to this edition.

2. Rich Horton, "The Year in Fantasy and Science Fiction, 2008," *The Year's Best Science Fiction and Fantasy, 2009 Edition*, ed. Horton ([New York]: Prime Books, 2009), 9.

3. Gary K. Wolfe, *The Known and the Unknown: The Iconography of Science Fiction* (Kent, OH: Kent State University Press, 1979). Subsequent page references in the text are to this edition.

4. Mark Rose, *Alien Encounters: Anatomy of Science Fiction* (Cambridge: Harvard University Press, 1981).

5. Gwyneth Jones, "Riddles in the Dark," *The Profession of Science Fiction: Writers on their Craft and Ideas*, ed. Maxim Jakubowski and Edward James (Houndmills, Basingstoke and London: Macmillan, 1992), 176.

6. Darko Suvin, *Metamorphoses of Science Fiction: On the Poetics and History of a Literary Genre* (New Haven: Yale University Press, 1979), 7–8.

7. Carl D. Malmgren, *Worlds Apart: Narratology of Science Fiction* (Bloomington: Indiana University Press, 1991). Subsequent page references in the text are to this edition.

8. Arthur C. Clarke, *The City and the Stars*, (1956; New York: Signet, 1957), 7.

9. Isaac Asimov, *The Caves of Steel* (1954; New York: Signet, 1955), 8–9.

10. Asimov, "Social Science Fiction," *Modern Science Fiction: Its Meaning and Its Future*, ed. Reginald Bretnor, 1953, Second Edition (Chicago: Advent Publishers, 1979), 157–196.

11. Andrew M. Butler, "Metropolis (1926)," *The Greenwood Encyclopedia of Science Fiction and Fantasy: Themes, Works, and Wonders*, Volume 3, ed. Gary Westfahl (Westport, CT: Greenwood Press, 2005), 1173. Note that although Butler gives a date of 1926 for the movie, it did not actually have its premier until January, 1927.

12. Scott Bukatman, *Blade Runner* (London: British Film Institute, 1997), 8–9.

13. See Hal Clement [Harry Clement Stubbs], "Whirligig World," *Astounding Science Fiction*, 51 (June, 1953), 102–114.

14. Frank Herbert, *Dune* (Philadelphia: Chilton Book Company, 1965), v.

15. Brian W. Aldiss and David Wingrove, *Trillion Year Spree: The History of Science Fiction* (London: Victor Gollancz, 1986), 315.

16. Joan Slonczewski, *A Door into Ocean* (New York: Avon, 1986).

17. Pamela Sargent, "Introduction," *Women of Wonder: The Contemporary Years, Science Fiction by Women from the 1970s to the 1990s*, ed. Sargent (San Diego: Harvest/Harcourt, Brace & Co., 1995), 12.

18. David Langford, "Space Opera," *The Greenwood Encyclopedia of Science Fiction and Fantasy: Themes, Works, and Wonders*, Volume 2, 738.

19. M. Keith Booker and Anne-Marie Thomas, *The Science Fiction Handbook* (Chichester, West Sussex: Wiley-Blackwell, 2009), 41.

20. The original *Star Trek* series ran from 1966 to 1969. Subsequent TV series featuring some version of the starship *Enterprise* were *Star Trek: The Next Generation* (1987–1994) and *Star Trek: Enterprise* (2001–2005). There have also been eleven films (1979–2009) to which the vessel is central. *Voyager* is the main setting for *Star Trek: Voyager* (1995–2002) and space station Deep Space Nine for *Star Trek: Deep Space Nine* (1993–1999).

21. John Milton, *Paradise Lost*, book 1, lines 254–255, *Milton: Poetical Works*, ed. Douglas Bush (London and Oxford: Oxford University Press, 1969), 218.

22. Jay Lake, *Mainspring* (New York: Tor, 2007), 3. Subsequent page references in the text are to this edition.

23. Kay Kenyon, "The Universe Extras," Kay Kenyon: The Entire and the Rose Quintet, at http://www.kaykenyon.com/the-entire-and-the-rose.html, accessed February 10, 2010.

24. Lubomir Dolezel, *Heterocosmica* (Baltimore and London: Johns Hopkins University Press, 1998), 169.

25. Alan Palmer, *Fictional Minds* (Lincoln and London: University of Nebraska Press, 2004), 34.

26. See Marie-Louise Ryan, *Possible Worlds, Artificial Intelligence, and Narrative Theory* (Bloomington: Indiana University Press, 1991), especially 31–47.

27. Martha C. Nussbaum, *Love's Knowledge* (New York and Oxford: Oxford University Press, 1990), 43–44.

6

Future City Tokyo: 1909 and 2009

SHARALYN ORBAUGH

The first time I saw Tokyo was thirty-five years ago, in 1975. I had arrived in Japan for the first time and the sights of the city passed before my eyes like a dream. Since then I have lived in Tokyo four times for a total of six years, always in different parts of the city, and when not living there I have visited innumerable times. It is a city that I love and know well. But every time I return to Tokyo after an absence of a few months, I have the same experience, more nightmare than dream: I attempt to return to a favorite restaurant or store, and arrive in the area to find it gone. This happens in any city, of course; but, unlike a visit back to San Francisco, where I might return to find that my favorite Korean barbeque is now a Spanish restaurant, in Tokyo my favorite haunts tend to disappear completely. Often the whole block has been razed and something entirely new put in its place.

Whenever I experience the extreme evanescence of Tokyo I recall the words of Antonio Sant'Elia (1888–1916), an architect allied with the Italian Futurist movement: "THE HOUSE WILL LAST FOR LESS TIME THAN WE WILL. EACH GENERATION MUST BUILD ITS OWN CITY."[1] Perhaps more truly than any large city on Earth, Tokyo has been built anew by each generation. Since becoming the capital of the newly unified Japanese nation in 1869, Tokyo has been destroyed and rebuilt numerous times.[2] While most destruction was by no means planned — the result of fires, earthquakes (and resulting fires), high explosive and incendiary bombing in World War II, and the like — the consequence has been that each generation has had a chance to rebuild Tokyo after seeing it destroyed.

The connections between Japan and Italian Futurists go deeper than a fortuitous resonance between Sant'Elia's vision of the evanescent city and the material history of Tokyo. Both nations were "late modernizers" (Germany was a third) and late to unify as coherent nation states: Italy proclaimed itself a state in 1861 and Japan in 1868. Richard Humphreys describes the early years of Italy's statehood, the circumstances that conditioned the emergence of Futurism:

The financial circumstances of the country overall were almost continuously parlous and the heavy taxes necessary to balance the national budget created enormous discontent, especially in the poorer areas of the south.... By the 1880s, its problems exacerbated by a global depression, Italy was facing widespread poverty.... In the sphere of international policy the government began a period of colonial expansion in Africa, hoping to achieve a nationalist consensus and to extend markets for the growing home economy. Although both aspirations were severely limited by the sheer range and power of the imperial interests of Britain, France and Germany, it was of utmost importance for Italians to demonstrate on a world stage that they were part of the "aristocracy" of European nations.[3]

If you change the name of the country to Japan, substitute "poorer areas of [Japan's] north" for "poorer areas of [Italy's] south," and change the designation of the colonized area from "Africa" to "East Asia," the description holds perfectly true for Japan in roughly the same period. Both nations embraced emerging technologies to modernize quickly, to avoid being taken advantage of by the already developed countries of the world that already had a significant colonial and/or imperial presence around the globe.

By the early twentieth century, both Italy and Japan had used military might and technology to carve out colonial interests of their own: Eritrea, Somalia, and Libya for Italy; Taiwan, Korea, and Karafuto for Japan. (After World War I both countries expanded their colonial influence to further territories.) And, just as Italian Futurists saw their artistic-cum-political philosophy as a tool in proving that Italy was part of the "aristocracy" of European nations, Japanese artists, poets, and novelists of the same period searched for tools to make evident to the world Japan's status as a worthy member of the global family of developed nations.

Italian Futurism began in 1909 with F. T. Marinetti's "The Founding Manifesto of Futurism," published on the front page of the February 20th issue of the French daily newspaper *Le Figaro*. Less than a month later one of Japan's most respected authors, Mori Ōgai[4] (who also happened to be Surgeon-General of the Army), had translated it into Japanese and published it in the journal *Subaru*.[5] Marinetti's manifesto was followed swiftly by many others, as painters, sculptors, poets, architects, and other artists issued Futurist manifestos of their own. The movement was vigorous in Italy (and to some extent France and England) well into World War I, and continued in a somewhat attenuated form until the end of the 1930s.

The growth of the Futurist movement in Japan was slower, though many artists, poets, and novelists were influenced by it in the years after 1909, even if they did not call themselves Futurists. In 1921 a young man named Hirato Renkichi handed out a pamphlet entitled "Manifesto of the Japanese Futurist Movement" (*Nihon miraiha sengen undō— Mouvement futuriste japonais*) in Tokyo's Hibiya Park.[6] Because he died the following year, Hirato himself was not an influential figure in Japan's Futurist movement, but writers like Inagaki Taruho, poets like Kanbara Tai, and artists like Okada Tatsuo identified themselves as Futurists and produced art and literary works in line with Futurist principles. In Japan, Futurism's heyday was the 1920s and 1930s, and it continued even after World War II.

Futurism was characterized by a vigorous, masculine, revolutionary attitude toward all aspects of modern life. It included a valorization of violence — when in the service of the production of modern goods or destruction of those things that were passé[7] — and of all that was bright, electric, powerful, and fast. A typical passage from Marinetti's "Founding Manifesto" reads:

> [W]e will sing of the vibrant nightly fervour of arsenals and shipyards blazing with violent electric moons; greedy railway stations that devour smoke-plumed serpents; factories hung on clouds by the crooked lines of their smoke; bridges that stride rivers like giant gymnasts, flashing in the sun with a glitter of knives; adventurous steamers that sniff the horizon; deep-chested locomotives whose wheels paw the tracks like the hooves of enormous steel horses bridled by tubing; and the sleek flight of planes whose propellers chatter in the wind like banners....[8]

As this passage makes clear, Marinetti's interests were both aesthetic and social/political. He valorizes as beautiful the signs of urban progress, economic might, and transportation — which were also, of course, tools of imperialism and colonialist expansion. While Marinetti never to my knowledge mentions colonialism explicitly, his "Founding Manifesto" proclaims: "We will glorify war — the world's only hygiene — militarism, patriotism, the destructive gesture of freedom-bringers, beautiful ideas worth dying for, and scorn for women."[9]

Undeniably, investment in war and the material tools of imperialism (arsenals, ships, trains) had paid off well for both Italy and Japan by 1909. As noted, both had established themselves as colonial powers by that time, and both had shown that they could muster effective military forces. In Italy, any enthusiasm for war among the masses that Futurism may have inspired was checked, at least in part, by the all-too-close-to-home realities of World War I. Although the movement in Italy continued after that war, several of its most important figures had died in battle, and the political scene was drastically changed by the rise of Mussolini.[10]

In contrast, even in the 1920s and 1930s Japan had little reason to rethink the glorification of war advocated by Futurists. Its three international military ventures since unification — the Sino-Japanese War of 1894–1895, the Russo-Japanese War of 1904–1905, and Japan's participation on the side of the Allies in World War I, 1914–1917, which involved routing the Germans from colonial holdings in the South Pacific and China and patrolling those areas— had been successful at stimulating the economy, unifying the populace under a banner of patriotism (to some extent), and indubitably adding precious land and natural resources to Japan's possessions through acquisition of colonies. Japanese readers of either Marinetti's or the "Japanese Futurist Manifesto" had little reason to question the advocacy of war as an instrument for demonstrating a nation's power and legitimacy.

One must note, however, that for Marinetti and his fellow Italian Futurists not everything was about war and grand national projects:

> Futurism is grounded in the complete renewal of human sensibility brought about by the great discoveries of science. Those people who today make use of the telegraph, the telephone, the phonograph, the train, the bicycle, the motorcycle, the automobile, the ocean liner, the dirigible, the aeroplane, the cinema ... do not realize that these various means of communication, transportation and information *have a decisive influence on their psyches.*[11]

Here, as in several of his manifestos, Marinetti links the changes brought about by modernity to changes in the human psyche: changes in the way men and women experience and interpret their world, the way they experience and interpret themselves. He writes frequently about both psychological and physiological issues, as they are tied to the new aesthetic pleasures arising from (Futurist) modernity:

> A new beauty is born today from the chaos of the new contradictory sensibilities that we Futurists will substitute for the former beauty.... Its essential elements are: hygienic forgetfulness, hope, desire, controlled force, speed, light, willpower, order, discipline, method; a feeling for the great city; the aggressive optimism that results from the cult of muscles and sport ... the passion for success, the keenest instinct for setting records, the enthusiastic imitation of electricity and the machine....[12]

The cult of muscles and sport and the optimism arising therefrom would certainly have resonated with Japanese mass culture in the 1910s, 1920s, and 1930s, as physical fitness and eugenics were then national obsessions.[13] Hope and desire linked to "controlled speed," "order, discipline, [and] method" were also explicit elements of the Japanese drive to equal (or surpass) other modernized nations of the world. But the elements of Futurism focused on here are the "feeling for the great city" and "enthusiastic imitation of electricity and the machine."

Because Marinetti believed that Futurism should involve all areas of human life, he sought an architect who could extend his visions to the design of a new "great city," attuned to a human lifestyle that incorporated "imitation of electricity and the machine." He found young Milanese architect Antonio Sant'Elia, whose drawings of power plants, train stations-cum-airports, and other imaginative cityscapes encapsulated the Futurist agenda for constructing an appropriate urban environment to enable the desired influences on the human psyche.

In August of 1914, Sant'Elia published the "Manifesto of Futurist Architecture" in *Lacerba*; it was the first and fullest expression of the Futurist vision of the city, "which should be the immediate and faithful projection of ourselves" (160), "an architecture whose reason for existence can be found solely in the unique conditions of modern life" (169) rather than relying on stultifying and outmoded forms from earlier generations whose needs were entirely different. Sant'Elia's vision of the modern city promoted a move away from old static ways of inhabiting the city to a new dynamic interplay between the city's commercial and transportation nodes and the people who used them to move and consume:

> We have lost our predilection for the monumental, the heavy, the static, and we have enriched our sensibility with a taste for *the light, the practical, the ephemeral and the swift*. We no longer feel ourselves to be the men of the cathedrals, the palaces and the podiums. We are the men of the great hotels, the railway stations, the immense streets, colossal ports, covered markets, luminous arcades, straight roads and beneficial demolitions.
>   We must invent and rebuild the Futurist city like an immense and tumultuous shipyard, agile, mobile and dynamic in every detail; and the Futurist house must be like a gigantic machine.... It must soar up on the brink of a tumultuous abyss: the street will no longer lie like a doormat at ground level, but will plunge many storeys down into the earth, embracing the metropolitan traffic, and will be linked up for necessary interconnections by metal gangways and swift-moving pavements. (170)

To achieve this ambitious vision, "that is to transform the world of things into a direct projection of the world of the [contemporary] spirit" (171), Sant'Elia, like Marinetti and other Futurists before him, called for destruction of old historic buildings, monuments, bridges and houses to make way for structures attuned to modern needs.

In Italy, with its centuries-old architecture that monumentalized a long and rich cultural history, such sentiments were near blasphemy. In a Japanese context, however, it would prove less shocking. When the Meiji government took power in 1868, one of its first tasks was to build a capital city worthy of a modern nation state. Tokyo, the newly designated national capital, had many mansions, temples, and other large edifices, but these were built of wood and hardly seemed impressive when compared with the stone and brick structures of western cities. To create a cityscape to equal those of other powerful nations, the Meiji government imported architects and architectural techniques from abroad to build new structures in keeping with European standards. Conveniently, a terrible fire in 1872 wiped out a key section of the city, near the new imperial palace grounds, and this devastated area was used to create the Tokyo train station (brick), the commercial and government buildings of the Marunouchi area between the station and the palace (brick, stone, and concrete), and the Ginza, a brightly lit area of modern shops and arcades (brick).[14]

The fact was that in Japan natural disasters could be counted on to devastate the urban landscape periodically and provide a clean slate for urban planning—for new architectural ways of expressing new understandings of subjectivity. As William Tsutsui puts it, "Japan ... lies directly in the crosshairs of almost every destructive power Mother Nature can command[:] ... earthquakes and volcanoes, typhoons and tidal waves, floods and landslides."[15] When the Great Kantô Earthquake flattened much of Tokyo in 1923, some of the most iconic of the Meiji-period (1868–1911) western-style structures were demolished. According to André Sorensen, the earthquake left "over 44 per cent of the urban area of Tokyo destroyed by fire and some 73.8 per cent of all house-holds affected."[16] After the earthquake the desperate need for housing meant that some areas of the city were rebuilt hastily and with little thought, but others were reconceptualized to provide further verticality, speed, convenience and connectivity.

A generation later, during the intensive bombing runs of the Allies in the final years of World War II, great swaths of Tokyo were flattened. In one night — March 9, 1945 — 2000 *tons* of incendiary bombs were dropped on Tokyo, lev-eling sixteen square miles of the city. At least 80,000 people were killed outright, and untold numbers left homeless. In the next ten days the Americans dropped more than 9000 tons of bombs (2 million individual bombs) on Tokyo, Nagoya, Osaka, and Kobe, in a total of more than 1500 sorties. By war's end, sixty-five percent of Tokyo's residences had been destroyed by fires caused by incendiary bombs.[17]

Again, much reconstruction after the war was done in desperate haste, but again an opportunity had been provided for city planners and entrepreneurs to remake the city, and again they promoted ideals of verticality, enhanced speed and efficiency, and connectivity — unintentionally following the Futurist vision.[18] The Tokyo subway and train network is the most extensive, complete, complex, and reliably functional in the world, and the city boasts numerous commercial and business areas including miles of underground shop-lined streets used by pedestrians to access skyscrapers, train stations and subway lines without having to contend with cars on the streets above them. There are, as well, numerous underground roads and elevated streets and highways. The city has "soared up" and "plunged down" as Sant'Elia advocated — not, of course, because of any conscious desire to fulfill his vision, but to create a livable envi-ronment for one of the most densely populated areas of the world. (The current population of the Tokyo conurbation is about 35 million people; that of all of Canada is about 34 million.)

Tokyo is an amazing city to look at and move through. It is not surprising that the cityscape is featured prominently in Japanese visual culture, both "high" art and popular culture. In the remainder of this chapter, moving ahead a cen-tury or so from 1909, I will consider some of the most striking representations of Tokyo in recent Japanese anime films and TV series, focusing on how the city is characterized in ways that are remarkably similar to stated ideals of Futurism: body and machine working together as part of the city (that is, the emergence of the cyborg)[19]; the city itself as a huge dynamic computer-like net-work, with humans acting as sentient nodes within it; love of speed and visual technophilia; the insistent verticality of the city; and, finally and primarily, the "hygiene of war" and destruction, specifically the destruction of Tokyo.

Science fiction and adventure stories about war have been popular in Japan since the early 20th century, but depictions of urban destruction are more fre-quent after World War II, no doubt because of the nationally shared experience of nuclear holocaust in Hiroshima and Nagasaki, as well as the intensive explosive and incendiary bombing of other cities. The war provided the Japanese with a vivid repertory of images and scenarios of destruction that were incorporated into literary, artistic, and popular culture narratives. One of the most interesting things about these narratives, however, is that they rarely depict a simple dichotomy of evil destroyers and innocent victims.

Of course, Japan is not alone in making movies that depict a city's destruction, but it is certainly among the leaders in producing such films. As cinema historian Carlos Clarens comments, "Japan, the only nation on earth to have actually suffered from atomic warfare, has become the world's foremost producer of filmic holocausts."[20] More recently, in a study of Godzilla, anime critic and theorist Susan Napier comments: "[I]n my course on the 'Cinema of the Apocalypse' I have found the largest number of apocalyptic films to be produced either in Japan or America — perhaps not surprising given our shared heritage of the atomic bomb."[21] Certainly any fan of anime has noticed a propensity for showing battles and destruction, particularly in science fiction anime. Animation is, after all, the perfect medium depicting epic destruction since it can freely show events from any angle and at any scale.

My discussion will concentrate on a cluster of anime films made between eighty and one hundred years after the beginnings of the Futurist movement, particularly *Kidô keisatsu patoreibaa* (*Mobile Police Patlabor*, usually known in English as *Patlabor 1*, 1989)[22] and *Rôjin Z* (1991),[23] two films that have received relatively little scholarly attention despite their positive critical reception in Japan and beyond. But before in-depth discussion of those films, some context is necessary. I must therefore mention some other anime productions made around the same time that are integral to any discussion of the destruction of Tokyo: *Akira* (1988) and the TV series *Shin seiki Evangelion* (*Neon Genesis Evangelion*, 1995).

Akira, directed by Ôtomo Katsuhiro, based on his manga of the same name, was one of the first anime films to be well received widely outside Japan.[24] A film that celebrates violence and destruction with tremendous narrative and visual energy, it opens with the annihilation of Tokyo by a nuclear-like blast, caused by a boy with psychic powers named Akira. Thirty-one years later, when Neo-Tokyo has been built on the ruins of the original city, it is destroyed again by another devastating blast, this time caused by a boy with psychic powers named Tetsuo. Although the film ends with the city once again in utter ruins, it implies that the cycle will only continue, since Tetsuo with his strange powers is still alive.

I recall seeing *Akira* for the first time in Berkeley in 1992, and, reeling out of the theater, I felt both frustrated by the lack of any reasonable teleology to the story and, at the same time, strangely exhilarated by the astonishingly detailed depiction of the violence and destruction. I am no Futurist, but there is a definite thrill to be had from seeing a city explode into atoms, twice, not to mention the love of speed shown through repeated scenes of motorcycles ridden through the half-ruined cityscape by the biker gang protagonists. *Akira*'s worldwide popularity suggests that those Futurist virtues were appreciated by many other viewers as well.

In 1995, a brilliant television series directed by Anno Hideaki called *Neon Genesis Evangelion* allowed viewers to witness the destruction of a city called Dai-san Tokyo (Tokyo Mark 3) and other urban centers nearly every week. The plot of *Evangelion* begins with the information that Earth was nearly destroyed in 1999 by a disaster known as Second Impact — supposedly a giant meteor that hit Antarctica, but really the first attack by huge alien machines called Angels.[25] When the narrative begins, fourteen years later, Angels are back to threaten Earth again. The only hope against the Angels is huge mecha-suits,[26] called Evas, piloted by 14-year-old children: only those born around the time of the original disaster — who therefore incorporate a bit of the Angels in themselves — have the powers necessary to fight the Angels. The headquarters of the Evas is in Tokyo Mark 3 (built on or near the site of the earlier Tokyo), an enormous city that remains underground almost all the time for security purposes, but rises above ground once a day at 5 pm, at which time some occupants take up a slightly distant position in the countryside to watch the emergence of the ultra-modern, ultra-vertical city, skyscrapers gleaming in the setting sun. In this sense, Tokyo Mark 3 embodies the Futurist ideal of a vertical city beyond Sant'Elia's wildest dreams.

One key feature of *Evangelion*'s narrative is insistent attention to the interplay between the electro-mechanical computerized suits and the children who must "synch" with them to succeed as pilot-warriors.[27] This, too, resonates strongly with Futurism. As Humphreys notes, "The pilot was in many ways the ultimate Futurist figure — defying gravity and earthbound instincts as he became 'part of the machine,' aspiring to a physical and spiritual freedom absolutely at one with the existential organs of the movement."[28] And when justifying his vision for the new Futurist city, Sant'Elia wrote, "As if we who are accumulators and generators of movement, with all our added mechanical limbs, with all the noise and speed of our life, could live in streets built for the needs of men four, five or six centuries ago" (169). Sant'Elia here combines the notion of the cyborg with new forms of life in the contemporary city, a combination integral to the narrative of *Evangelion*.

Both *Akira* and *Evangelion* fit a pattern seen in other Japanese TV series and films in which Tokyo is destroyed, in the sense that the destruction is never absolute. After the devastation of Tokyo at the beginning of *Akira*, we see people living on, building a new city, which is destroyed in its turn, but still some people (or posthuman entities) live on. The same happens in *Evangelion*: after the Second Impact (which happens before the story starts), surviving members of humankind pick themselves up, rebuild a new and better Tokyo, and prepare to battle the enemy. At the end of the series the Angels appear to have won and humanity appears to be eradicated ... except for our young male protagonist, Shinji, and his female counterpart Asuka, who live on, perhaps to rebuild Tokyo Mark 4.[29]

This pattern of depicting widespread destruction of buildings and monuments with the survival of (at least some) people is repeated in Ôtomo's 1991 anime film *Rôjin Z*. Like his earlier film *Akira*, *Rôjin Z* was critically acclaimed in its North American release, but the latter has received less scholarly attention than the former.

Rôjin Z opens with an old man, Takazawa Kôjirô, lying alone in his futon on the floor of his rooms in an old-fashioned Japanese apartment house: a structure of wood and plaster, with sliding paper doors, no air conditioning, and only primitive laundry facilities, out on the narrow balcony. His volunteer caretaker, a young, pretty nurse-in-training named Haruko, comes in to feed, wash, diaper, and comfort the old man, whom she calls Jiichan ("Grandpa").[30]

Without the knowledge of Jiichan or Haruko, however, Jiichan has been volunteered by his surviving family for a new program, which involves inserting old people into mecha-suit-like beds, the Z-001s, which monitor their every physical function, automatically feed them and take away wastes, and provide entertainment with four computer screens at once. Haruko is horrified when she sees Jiichan in the machine bed, with connecting wires penetrating his body down to the cellular level She tells representatives of the Ministry of Health and Welfare, which is promoting the project, that old people cannot be considered cared for if there is no human love, no human touch accompanying that care. The officials brush her concerns aside.

But soon Jiichan—completely helpless and paralyzed though he remains—has fused so completely with his computerized machine-bed that messages indicating his distress are sent automatically and repeatedly to Haruko's computer. She and her nursing school friends try to rescue Jiichan, falling afoul of the people who have developed the Z-001 prototype. But the Z-001, propelled by the old man's incoherent distress, manages to stand up and break out of the hospital, escaping with Haruko back to Jiichan's original apartment.

The main promoter of this new cyber-bed is stunned — it should have no such capabilities. The man who designed the computer components and software, however, seems less surprised. We eventually discover that he had been asked to design a weapon, and the development of the cyber-bed — meant to counter Japan's biggest challenge, a rapidly aging population — was for him just a cover for developing a cyber-weapon. The bed is fulfilling his hopes for it as a machine that can learn from its environment and absorb whatever will enhance its strength.

Eventually, with the help of a number of bedridden old men at the hospital where she works — all accomplished computer hackers, since they have nothing better to do with their time — Haruko encourages the cyber-bed (now fused with Jiichan) to take on the benevolent persona of Jiichan's late wife, Haru. The bed's Haru persona asks him what he wants in his wife's affectionate voice, and he replies that he wants to return to the beach at Kamakura, where they had once been happy.

Accordingly, the cyber-bed — now upright and looking more than ever like a mecha-suit — begins speeding and slamming its way through Tokyo, heading south towards Kamakura. With the army and police all trying to stop it, it is forced to take unusual routes, straight through several Tokyo neighborhoods. As it moves through houses and larger structures, the cyber-bed takes on hunks of metal, fragments of splintered wood, wheels from a truck, an arm from a bulldozer, and so on, until it is huge and unstoppable. The bed gradually becomes a grotesque amalgam of numerous constitutive elements of Tokyo architecture and vehicles. When it finally reaches the beach, the evil technology meant to turn the bed into a weapon overpowers the benevolent wife persona, and Haruko must climb to the top of the massive structure to destroy its main computer unit. After she has successfully done this, we see Jiichan's cat, which had earlier gotten caught up into the bed-machine, leaping out with a computer component in its mouth and running away. Jiichan and Haruko return to Tokyo, where Jiichan is now being cared for at a hospital for elderly people, with Haruko looking after him. The film's happy ending is disturbed, however, by the sound of horrific destruction approaching the hospital window, where Haruko, Jiichan and all the other nurses and patients soon gather. Finally, breaking through the buildings adjacent to the hospital, we see the Kamakura Daibutsu — the statue of the Great Buddha[31] — recognizable, but also incorporating random bits of the structures and machines it encountered on its way to Tokyo, calling out to Jiichan in his late wife's cheery voice. She has come to collect him again. The screen goes blank to the sounds of screaming and continued destruction, much closer now, while wacky, clownish music creates a carnivalesque atmosphere.

For purposes of this discussion, the most important scene is the one early in the film when the bed slams its way through the houses, shops and buildings of a quiet area of Tokyo, destroying and absorbing all in its path. The most significant aspect of the cityscape in this scene is its old-fashioned nature, much like the apartment where we first encounter Jiichan. The Tokyo depicted (and destroyed) is composed of the elements of the cityscape that remain unchanged from the 1930s or before, embodying a philosophy of life that focused on the personal interaction of neighbors within their comfortable neighborhood: low wooden buildings with heavy tile roofs, old-fashioned, somewhat dingy shopping arcades featuring pachinko parlors next to vegetable stands, and so on. This is not the vertical, technologically interconnected city; it is the old Tokyo, the passé Tokyo, the slow, relaxed Tokyo, the kind of place that Japanese Futurists would most despise. The fact that the animators so lovingly depicted the details of the cyber-bed's annihilation of this Tokyo is therefore suggestive: the speedy, powerful, high-tech machine triumphs over the old and sluggish. In a standard Hollywood film, the machine-bed and company that built it would, in the end, most likely be punished for destroying the idealized, nostalgic elements of the city, but this film does not end so simply. Although it seems for a moment that Jiichan and the old life he represents have won (albeit with the high-tech help of his cyber-bed's wifely persona and the expertise of elderly hackers), the film ends with the simultaneous destruction and transformation of one of Japan's few old, impressive monuments— the Great Buddha. Surely Futurists would have been pleased to see its deformed status, and to see the "passé-ist" monument assisting in the joyful destruction of the "passé-ist" elements of the city.

A less carnivalesque and therefore potentially more potent version of this narrative trope is found in the 1989 anime film, *Patlabor 1*, directed by Oshii Mamoru, based on the manga by Yûki Masami (screenplay by Itô Kazunori). Oshii later directed several successful and critically acclaimed science fiction films: the anime movies *Kôkaku kidôtai* (*Ghost in the Shell*, 1995) and *Kôkaku kidôtai: Inosensu* (*Innocence*, 2004),[32] and the live-action film *Avalon* (2001). In *Patlabor 1* we see many of the elements that made his later films so powerful: a penchant for philosophical meditations on fundamental questions of ontology and technology; a high tolerance for slow-moving, lyrical sequences with little dialog; references to Christianity, Buddhism, and other philosophical traditions to add depth to the plot; and a brilliant combination of depictions of lovingly detailed, energetic, technophilic action with depictions of lovingly detailed, slow, human-level interactions.

Like *Star Trek*, Patlabor has become a multi-genre narrative universe, with this film as just one of its incarnations.[33] To fully appreciate the film, therefore, one should be familiar with other narrative products of the Patlabor universe. Even without such knowledge, however, this film has several elements that stand alone and make it a significant contribution to science fiction cinema.

In the near-future Patlabor universe, many jobs, especially heavy construction and the like, are handled by large, high-tech mecha-suit machines called "labors," each piloted by one human. Because the labors are so large and powerful, they are capable of terrible violence and destruction if misused. Therefore, an elite squad of police has been formed and equipped with even more powerful mecha-suit machines, known as Patlabors,[34] each piloted by one human, to control or to battle errant labors.

The film opens with a suicide: against a background of a gorgeous polychrome sunset with the skyscraper-filled skyline of Tokyo silhouetted against it, a man stands on the top of a huge, partly constructed building and, smiling scornfully, steps off it, falling into Tokyo Bay. His body is never recovered.

The site of this event is called the "Babylon Project"— a massive development in Tokyo Bay that will eventually create hundreds of hectares of reclaimed land for residences, shops and offices. Its flagship building is "the Ark," the partly completed building from which the man jumped. The next sequence of the film, intercut with the credits, shows a battle against a rogue labor, which ends with victorious soldiers opening the labor only to find that it was unpiloted as it ran berserk.

We learn that in the last two months there have been twenty-two such incidents, wherein labors have gone berserk, ignoring the attempts of their pilots to control them. The Patlabor squad investigates the source of the trouble, and finds that a new operating system had been recently installed in all the labors that had gone rogue, and that the man who had devised the new system, E. Hoba (a near homophone of Jehovah as pronounced in Japanese),[35] was the man who committed suicide. The suspicion arises that there is a bug in the new computer software, or possibly that Hoba intentionally programmed the new software to cause the labors to misbehave under specific conditions. While some members of the Patlabor squad attempt to figure out what triggers the rogue behavior, a regular policeman who often works with them, Detective Matsui, goes with a young police colleague to each of the former residences of Hoba — who had moved twenty-seven times in two years— to try to figure out the motive for his antisocial behavior.

Eventually a young Patlabor squad member, Shinohara Asuma, whose father happens to own the company that produced the new operating system, deduces that it is wind blowing through the spaces between high-rise buildings and whistling at a particular frequency that causes the labors to go berserk. So far the incidents have been confined to a few areas of the city, where high-rise buildings cluster particularly densely. But Shinohara realizes that a higher velocity wind, blowing through the nearly-completed Ark, will cause a high-pitched sound at a frequency that will send all of the tens of thousands of labors in Tokyo berserk at once, destroying the city and causing horrific loss of life. Before his suicide, Hoba had intentionally used his knowledge of the architectural specs of the ultra-modern Ark to create a complex weapon of mass destruction. A typhoon now approaches Tokyo, and weather forecasts predict winds of velocities high enough to set off this catastrophe.

Accordingly, the Patlabor squad hurries to destroy the Ark before the typhoon hits. At the end of a long battle sequence they are successful, and the final shot shows the bare foundations of the huge structure sitting amidst the sparkling blue water of Tokyo Bay.

Again in this film we have obvious elements that resonate with Futurist ideals: high-tech machines that integrate with humans to produce speed and power (i.e. cyborgs)[36]; a focus on the city, particularly its newly built, ultramodern elements; and gloriously depicted scenes of battle and destruction. But, like *Rôjin Z*, *Patlabor 1* takes some ideas of Futurism to their logical conclusions, providing a more complex and nuanced view of Futurist philosophy than Marinetti, Sant'Elia or their colleagues ever imagined.

Oshii gives so much loving attention to particular aspects of the cityscape in this film that Tokyo effectively becomes a character in its own right. To illustrate this, I will highlight two elements in the film: a destruction sequence early on, and a narrative thread that specifically engages the cityscape and appears repeatedly in the film's middle section.

Soon after the opening credits the Patlabor squad is called out to stop a labor that has gone berserk and is smashing its way through western Shinjuku — an old-fashioned residential neighborhood that is near a new, ultra-modern area of skyscrapers. The old-fashioned buildings are low — two-story at most — made of wood covered by a stucco-like substance, with heavy ceramic roof tiles, occasionally patched on the outside with thin sheets of corrugated iron. This style of architecture was prevalent from the 19th century (and, except for the corrugated iron, even earlier) to the 1960s, and still exists in pockets of Tokyo despite all the natural and man-made disasters the city has experienced. This particular area was likely destroyed during the war but rebuilt in the same cheap and insubstantial style soon thereafter to provide housing for the hundreds of thousands left homeless by air raids. In areas like this, large streets cut sections into square (or square-ish) "blocks," but between those are a multitude of narrow streets running in all directions. Houses, too, face many different directions as they cluster together cheek by jowl. In newly built parts of the city telephone and electrical wires run underground, but in neighborhoods like this they form a tangled mess, crisscrossing narrow streets at roof level from one house to another. By the time *Patlabor 1* was made, this kind of neighborhood was giving way to high-rise apartment buildings, and would strike viewers as old-fashioned but also "homey." Most people — young people especially — may not want to live in such drafty, flimsy, low-tech housing any more, but it is a reminder of a community consciousness that is often now idealized.

In contrast, the skyscrapers of contemporary Tokyo are made of steel and glass, and their above-ground loftiness is often paired with underground passages linking the buildings, as described above.[37] Though the ethos of ultramodern Tokyo is rarely idealized in the same nostalgic fashion as that of the old-fashioned areas, it is nonetheless idealized — as embodying the cool, techno-savvy, connected, speedy, dynamic urban lifestyle that Futurists would have loved.

The scene of the rogue labor tearing through this old-fashioned neighborhood is long and detailed, visualized in shots from multiple points of view, emphasizing repeatedly the contrast between the neighborhood architecture (as it is being destroyed) and the new architectural style of skyscrapers in the distance. In fact, it is worth describing some viewpoints through which this long scene is presented, to give a sense of Oshii's attention to the cityscape.

We start high up on a skyscraper, then pan down to street level,[38] where everything is old-fashioned: a tangle of wires crisscrossing over the street, two-story buildings of wood with roof tiles, big signs out front of each cluttering up the view, the street fairly narrow, pedestrians on the street and vendors pushing carts: a typical shopping street in an old-fashioned neighborhood (much like the one destroyed in Rôjin Z, as described above).

People are told by someone using a megaphone to clear the streets because the rogue labor is coming their way.

View shifts: We see a bird's eye view of this neighborhood and see that in typical shitamachi *(low city) style, there is no sidewalk: houses front directly onto the narrow street, with barely room for a single car between them. A few people sit atop their tiled roofs to see the excitement. The labor comes and crashes through that exact area, with the rooftop people scrambling to get out of the way. The labor crushes a police car under-foot, and plows through the old buildings as if they were paper.*

View shifts: We watch the labor come toward us through the buildings, of which we see only closely-packed roofs, all set at different angles and facing in different directions. Overhead is a huge motorway overpass with trucks and buses. The labor pushes on through the houses.

View shifts: We see a helicopter from above and the cityscape below it — tightly packed low houses, again facing many ways. We see the path of destruction the labor has carved out among these fragile buildings.

View shifts: we see the Patlabor being unloaded off a large truck as people watch. In the distant background, skyscrapers gleam in the sun. People cheer as the Patlabor marches off.

View shifts: We look down a fairly broad street that has a raised highway going over it perpendicularly. Another Patlabor-bearing truck comes toward us. In the background, in the space between the overpass and road, we see in the middle distance low-rise old-fashioned buildings and houses, and behind them in the far distance, hugely tall ultra-modern skyscrapers.

View shifts: The Patlabor follows the labor's trail of destruction through the houses. We see the cross section of the destroyed homes and small shops, old building materials and techniques fully evident — old, thin wood now splintered, smashed roof tiles, thin corrugated iron bent and twisted.

View shifts: The rogue labor still moves forward with the Patlabor behind it, following its swath of destruction. In the close and middle distance we see the old-fashioned houses and buildings of this neighborhood; then in the farthest distance, filling the frame from left to right, are hugely tall skyscrapers mixed with medium-sized but still ultra-modern buildings.

View shifts: First we see a helicopter flying, then our view shifts again to what those in the helicopter are seeing, straight down into the old-fashioned neighborhood. There is one larger building, of concrete, but still old-style: a school or hospital. Men in the helicopter are doing a "play-by-play" of the battle between the labor and the Patlabor, which continue to plow through more wooden houses and shops. A second Patlabor comes and joins the battle, holding the labor while the first Patlabor pilot deploys one of his weapons: a baton to shut down the labor's electrical systems. This works for a moment, but then the labor starts itself up again and continues to fight. The two — the first Patlabor and the labor — go blundering on through buildings, locked in combat, until they break through some final houses and land in a canal, lined by old-fashioned looking, flimsy buildings. There are tall skyscrapers in the far distance.

View shifts: Overhead view of the neighborhood and canal, showing part of the path of destruction that has literally carved its way through this dense neighborhood. The Patlabor pilot is about to shoot the labor, when his minder/driver instead literally freezes both of them, ending the incident.

As in *Rôjin Z*, the stark contrast between the high-tech, powerful, machinic (metal and plastic) labors and Patlabors and the cheap, flimsy, organic (wood and tile) architecture of the old-fashioned cityscape is emphasized in this long scene of destruction. In *Patlabor* the scene is less explicitly humorous, less carnivalesque than the one in *Rôjin Z*. Nevertheless, unexpectedly, in both cases there is a somewhat manic, celebratory aspect to the way the destruction is depicted, rather than an elegiac or horrified tone of tragic loss. In this regard, one notes that in neither film is the destruction of huge areas of architecture accompanied by any loss or life or injury to a person. The antic glee associated with ripping structures apart can be enjoyed without the complicating emotions of sorrow over human suffering.

Another feature that adds to the "positive" tone of the destruction sequences is the focus in both films on the interface between human and the machine that encloses him/her: in *Rôjin Z* the paralyzed and helpless Jiichan can move freely and powerfully, to express and realize his desires through fusion with the cyber-bed; in *Patlabor* we see the smooth functioning of the human/mecha-suit amalgam as these cyborgian creatures work to save the city (by partly destroying it).

The other element of *Patlabor 1* which I will draw particular attention to—which most clearly shows how Tokyo functions as a "character" in the narrative—is a series of four scenes that are set off conspicuously from the rest of the film: they feature Matsui and a young colleague rather than members of the Patlabor squad; they are set to distinctive, beautiful but eerie music (composed by Kawaii Kanji); they are often entirely devoid of dialog; the background visuals are gorgeously detailed, but the narrative pace is quite slow; and they all take place in *exceptionally* old-fashioned areas of Tokyo. As in all of Oshii's films, these slow-tempo, lyrical passages in the middle of *Patlabor 1* seem unconnected to the main plotline, but provide keys to the film's larger meanings. In this case the scenes are intercut with others that are faster paced, featuring the Patlabor squad.

In each of these four lyrical scenes Matsui and his colleague are tracing the places where Hoba lived before his suicide. To give a sense of how Oshii intends them to function in the film I will describe one scene in some detail.

The view pans down a skyscraper to the tangle of wires just above street level, then to low buildings of old Tokyo — some wood with tile roofs, others low concrete buildings — all set at different angles. Matsui and his colleague are walking along a typical old-fashioned shopping street, with a pachinko parlor, a kôban *(police box) where they get directions, and a store that sells old-fashioned* fûrin *(wind chimes).*[39] *They walk down an old street, very claustrophobic with houses pressing close on either side, wires overhead. They continue down more narrow streets. The houses have laundry hanging outside. Then we get a view from inside one house, looking out to the street where the detectives are walking, and we see a very high-tech television set, showing a contemporary news program.*

The policemen pick their way through a particularly narrow alley filled with junk. At the open end of the alley, looking out to the distance, we see skyscrapers. The two men go to another old, shabby-looking building: weathered wood, rusted iron railings, patched corrugated iron on roof and outside. They go to several more, similar buildings. All have empty birdcages inside.

At one point Matsui and his colleague go through an old house and out the back where there is a canal, nearly dried up, with trash in it. As they jump over the water in the canal to get to a house on the other side, we see a reflection in the water of ultra-modern skyscrapers.

They walk along a high wall, with sotoba *(posthumous Buddhist name sticks) showing above it, and then enter the courtyard of a building made of stone, with broad stairs, nicely shaped balconies and other handsome architectural details very unusual for Tokyo — probably built in the Meiji period and meant to look "European." In this building, obviously once very handsome, all the windows are now broken and there is junk in the courtyard (including an old birdcage). Next the two men stand in a dump, filling most of the shot. Behind the dump is a line of trees, and behind that, in the distance, skyscrapers. Heat waves rise off the junk. Then a long shot focuses on a faraway, very thin skyscraper.*

Throughout this long scene there is no dialog at all, just eerie music. While the near focus—the spaces through which the detectives move—is entirely devoted to old-fashioned structures—many of them half-ruined, or already demolished—in the distance, in reflections, or out the windows of old buildings we see the ultra-modern skyscrapers of new Tokyo. It is significant that we also see inside one home where someone is watching a high-tech looking TV: we are reminded that the cutting-edge highly connective elements of Tokyo exist even within the old neighborhoods and will eventually transform them.

In the final of the four lyrical scenes, when Matsui and his colleague have visited the last of Hoba's twenty-eight residences, they are joined by Captain Gotô of the Patlabor squad on an abandoned construction site next to Tokyo Bay. Matsui comments to Gotô that the area had been marked for demolition, first for a high-rise housing development, then to put a highway through, but because of squabbling between the parties involved nothing had happened so far. The result is that this small patch of old Tokyo has been suspended in time.

Matsui remarks: "This is a weird area. As I've been pursuing this guy's past, I've had the strangest feeling, like I've been left behind in the flow of time. Places I have been used to seeing until just a little while ago have either crumbled to dust or been left in ruins. If you turn your eyes away for just an instant, when you look back they have completely disappeared. And it happens before you have time to think about what it all means. In a city like this I guess the past isn't worth a penny."

Gotô replies: "This place where we are sitting right now was part of the bay until just a little while ago. Moreover, after a few years the ocean we are currently looking at will have become a huge city. But, inevitably, that city too will become just the past, with no more worth than a penny. Maybe that's what Hoba was trying to show us."

This series of scenes, culminating in the dialog between Matsui and Gotô, might at first seem to encourage the interpretation that this film's message is about nostalgia and sorrow for the tragic loss of these older areas of Tokyo, as they are rapidly replaced by the new vision of the city, the city of *this* generation (as Sant'Elia might have it). And it is undeniable that nostalgia and a sense of loss are part of what the film is trying to say about the nature of Tokyo. But the film ends with the necessary destruction of the Ark, suggesting that not all destruction is bad. The celebratory tone of the scene of the rogue labor carving its way through an old-fashioned neighborhood, described above, also suggests that destruction is not necessarily tragic.

But one point of this conversation that is particularly relevant is the acknowledgement that change is inevitable, and will not stop with the current wave of construction/ reconstruction, nor with any future wave. As Gotô says, "But inevitably that [future] city, too, will become just the past with no more worth than a penny." The Italian Futurists advocated a city that was destroyed and rebuilt by each generation, a city undergoing constant evolution. As Sant'Elia predicted for his Futurist city: "THINGS WILL ENDURE LESS THAN US" (171; my emphasis); in other words, people will survive even when the structures around them are destroyed. As we see in *Akira* and *Evangelion*, even in the case of a city's annihilation there are human survivors, and the first thing they do is to rebuild. These films, like many other Japanese anime, attempt to imagine a world in which the city environment undergoes constant change, and to imagine this world not as a tragic dystopia, but a reality that may be acceptable. Although the Futurists never spelled out the detailed *consequences* of a situation of constant change, in Japanese science fiction we find some attempts to explore those consequences in an affirmative way.

NOTES

1. Antonio Sant'Elia, "Manifesto of Futurist Architecture, 1914," cited in Caroline Tisdall and Angelo Bozzolla, *Futurism* (New York and Toronto: Oxford University Press, 1978), 130. The manifesto can be found in full in *Futurist Manifestos*, ed. Umbro Apollonio (London: Tate Publishing, 1970), 160–172, where this sentence is translated as "THINGS WILL ENDURE LESS THAN US. EVERY GENERATION MUST BUILD ITS OWN CITY" (171). Subsequent Sant'Elia page references in the text are to the Apollonio edition.

2. While Japan was ostensibly unified in the early 1600s by Shogun Tokugawa Ieyasu, it actually remained a collection of hundreds of semi-autonomous fiefdoms. In 1868 the Meiji forces abolished the fiefdoms and installed a centralized national government, organized in imitation of the developed nation states of Europe. The other "late modernizing nations"— Italy and Germany — went through a similar process, changing from loosely affiliated collections of kingdoms or principalities to unified nation states in the mid to late nineteenth century.

3. Richard Humphreys, *Futurism* (London: Tate Publishing, 1999), 13.

4. Japanese personal names are presented in Japanese style, surname first.

5. Hosokawa Shûhei, editor, "Miraiha Nenpyô," [Timeline of Futurism] *Eureka*, 17 [special edition on Futurism] (December, 1985), 247.

6. Miryam Sas, *Fault Lines: Cultural Memory and Japanese Surrealism* (Stanford: Stanford University Press, 2001), 10.

7. Several of the translations into English of the various Futurist manifestos originally written in Italian use the terms "the passé" or "passé-ism" to translate the "*passatismo*" that the Futurists so abhorred, so I have also adopted those terms in this essay.

8. F. T. Marinetti, "The Founding Manifesto of Futurism," *Futurist Manifestos*, 22.

9. Marinetti, "Founding Manifesto," 22. Much is made of the misogyny of the Futurists, but, like so much in their philosophy, their misogyny is less absolute and more complex than one might guess from such straightforward language. When Marinetti proclaimed the basis for his political party in 1918 he included in his platform equal pay for women and a lessening of the discrepancy between the rights of women and of men. In his "Founding Manifesto" it is likely that what Marinetti wanted to condemn — as an adjunct to his celebration of war — was feminine softness and timidity, feminine hatred of violence, characteristics ascribed by the already developed colonial powers to late modernizing nations.

10. Among the Futurists who died in World War I were key figures Antonio Sant'Elia (architect) and Umberto Boccioni (painter). Both died in 1916: Sant'Elia was killed in battle, and Boccioni from falling off a horse in a cavalry exercise. While Marinetti and Mussolini were political allies for a time, Marinetti "eventually split with Mussolini because of the radical aspects of futurism that were antithetical to fascism" (Tisdall and Bozzolla 17). For more on Marinetti's split from fascist politics, see Humphreys, *Futurism*, 70 ff.

11. Marinetti, "Destruction of Syntax — Imagination without Strings — Words-in-Freedom, 1913," *Futurist Manifestos*, 96 (emphasis mine).

12. Marinetti, "Geometric and Mechanical Splendour and the Numerical Sensibility, 1914," *Futurist Manifestos*, 154.

13. For more on eugenics and physical fitness in prewar Japan see Jennifer Robertson, "Blood Talks: Eugenic Modernity and the Creation of New Japanese," *History and Anthropology*, 13:3 (2002), 191–216.

14. Much could be said about Tokyo Station, completed in 1914, as an embodiment and tool of imperial modernity. Unlike the scattered railway stations that circle central London, for example, making it impossible to go from an eastern train line to a western one without a long transfer between stations, Tokyo was the hub of all train lines heading in any direction. From Tokyo Station one could travel to Korea — connecting with a steamship at Shimonoseki — or to twenty-five destinations in China, including Beijing, as of the 1920s. It was comparable in scale and magnificence to New York's Grand Central Station, completed in 1913. (See William H. Coaldrake, *Architecture and Authority in Japan* [London: Routledge, 1996], 223, 224.)

15. William Tsutsui, *Godzilla on My Mind: Fifty Years of the King of the Monsters* (New York: Palgrave Macmillan, 2004), 16.

16. André Sorensen, *The Making of Urban Japan: Cities and Planning from Edo to the Twenty-first Century* (London and New York: Routledge, 2002), 125.

17. For more on the destruction of Tokyo and other Japanese cities by bombing raids in World War II, see John Dower, *Embracing Defeat: Japan in the Aftermath of World War II* (London: Penguin Books, 1999); or Thomas Havens, *Valley of Darkness: The Japanese People and World War Two* (Lanham, Maryland: University Press of America, 1986).

18. The Tokyo Olympics in 1964 provided another opportunity and inspiration for further (re-)development. In the Yoyogi area of Tokyo many older buildings were razed to create the beautiful arenas designed by architect Tange Kenzô. Connectivity was also enhanced: in Tokyo new sewer-lines were laid, replacing old system of septic tanks that had remained common till then, highways were built, and the Tokyo monorail and high-speed bullet train between Tokyo and Osaka/Kyoto were launched.

19. In the manifesto "Weights, Measures and Prices of Artistic Genius — Futurist Manifesto, 1914," Bruno Corradini and Emilio Settimelli anticipate cybernetics by analogizing the human brain to a machine (*Futurist Manifestos*, 136); other manifestos advocate the fusion of the human with the machine, anticipating cyborgs.

20. Carlos Clarens, *An Illustrated History of Horror and Science Fiction Films: The Classic Era, 1895–1967,* 1967, New Edition (New York: Da Capo Press, 1997), 132.

21. Susan J. Napier, "When Godzilla Speaks," *In Godzilla's Footsteps: Japanese Pop Culture Icons on the Global Stage,* ed. Tsutsui and Michiko Ito (New York: Palgrave Macmillan, 2006), 17. For a thorough discussion of several of the most iconic of Japanese apocalyptic anime, see Napier's *Anime from Akira to Princess Mononoke: Experiencing Contemporary Japanese Animation* (New York: Palgrave, 2001).

22. After the release of a second Patlabor film, *Kidô keisatsu patoreibaa 2* in 1993, the first one retroactively came to be known as *Patlabor 1,* which is how I refer to it here.

23. The Japanese title was retained in its critically acclaimed U.S. release. It literally means "Old man Z."

24. For critical commentary on *Akira,* see Napier's *Anime.*

25. The "Second Impact" had wiped out half the people on earth when the first Angel had been discovered in the Antarctic and accidentally detonated.

26. A "mecha-suit" or just "mecha" (for "mechanical") is a common element in Japanese science fiction of all genres. A mecha is a large high-tech machine, often shaped like a huge armored human, which is piloted by one or more people. In science fiction narratives mechas are used for many things—construction, transportation—but most often for fighting. An analogous example is Ripley in the penultimate scene of *Aliens,* when she dons the cargo loader to fight the alien queen, though the typical mecha is much larger than Ripley's exosuit.

27. For more on mecha-suits as cyborgs see Sharalyn Orbaugh, "Frankenstein and the Cyborg Metropolis: The Evolution of Body and City in Science Fiction Narratives," *Cinema Anime,* ed. Steven T. Brown (New York: Palgrave Macmillan, 2006), especially pages 90–91. For more on *Evangelion* and the necessity of "synching" with the suit, see Napier, *Anime,* 193–218; Napier, "When the Machines Stop: Fantasy, Reality and Terminal Identity in *Neon Genesis Evangelion* and *Serial Experiments Lain,*" *Science Fiction Studies,* 29 (November, 2002), 418–435; and Orbaugh, "Sex and the Single Cyborg: Japanese Pop Culture Experiments in Subjectivity," *Science Fiction Studies,* 29 (November, 2002), 436–452.

28. Humphreys, "Afterword: Futurism: May the Force Be with You," *Futurist Manifestos,* 226.

29. After completing the TV series, Anno made three film versions of *Evangelion,* all with slightly different endings. In no case, though, does Earth escape the destruction of the cities and virtually all of humankind.

30. It is common in Japan to call non-relatives by terms like "older brother," "mother," "uncle," grandfather," etc., as appropriate to the age of the addressee. This sort of address is sometimes used by/to strangers, but most often when a semi-intimate relationship pertains, such as between neighbors.

31. The Kamakura Daibutsu is a bronze statue probably cast in the year 1252. It is about 45 feet high (in its sitting position) and estimated to weigh around 90 tons.

32. In "Frankenstein and the Cyborg Metropolis" I discuss how *Innocence* depicts a city that forms a computer-like network of which the inhabitants are functional nodes (96–102).

33. For more details about the Patlabor narratives, see Brian Ruh, *Stray Dog of Anime: The Films of Mamoru Oshii* (New York: Palgrave Macmillan, 2004), 73–118; or Dani Cavallaro, *The Cinema of Oshii Mamoru: Fantasy, Technology and Politics* (Jefferson, NC: McFarland and Company, 2006), 100–133.

34. "Patlabor" seems to be a contraction of "patrol labor"—that is, the machines designed to patrol and if necessary subdue errant labors.

35. As in many of Oshii Mamoru's films, there are several references here to Christian, Buddhist and Gnostic mysticism. While references to Old Testament Christianity in

Patlabor 1 help to reinforce the narrative's underlying themes, they are not central to the plot.

36. Many Patlabor stories focus explicitly on the psychological and material details of the integration between human pilot and Patlabor suit, to explore the ramifications of humanity's increasing cyborgization. In *Patlabor 1* we get glimpses of this theme, particularly in Noa's concern about changes in her Patlabor's operating system.

37. Tokyo has little or no "modernist" architecture, no massive stone or concrete skyscrapers dating from before World War II (like the Empire State Building). All the tall buildings are post-war constructions, most of them post–1970s. There are a few tallish prewar buildings, mostly in the Marunouchi area that has long been the center of Japanese commerce and government. But these are in the main about 10–15 stories tall, not skyscrapers.

38. This "shot"—a scene opening with a distant view of a skyscraper, panning downwards to a close-up view of old-fashioned buildings—is repeated several times in the film.

39. These details are all extremely evocative of old-fashioned neighborhood Tokyo. Just as in *Rôjin Z*, a pachinko parlor (pachinko is a sort of slot machine) is featured here to indicate the age and character of the neighborhood — these are still found in many areas of Tokyo, but are rapidly dying out in the age of computer games. A *kôban* is a tiny police station, usually only large enough for a desk and one or two officers. Until recently *kôban* were located every few blocks and the policemen assigned there knew everyone in the neighborhood and provided various kinds of assistance, as well as giving directions to strangers—an essential service given the fact that 99 percent of Tokyo streets have no names and addresses are impossible to find unaided. The sweet, high sound of the *fûrin* wind chimes was believed to cool people down in the almost tropical heat of Tokyo summer, but *fûrin* have given way to air conditioners.

7

Rebooting "A Logic Named Joe"

Exploring the Multiple Influences of a Strangely Predictive Mid–1940s Short Story

DAVID L. FERRO AND
ERIC G. SWEDIN

Introduction

From the early 20th century to the 1970s, the role played by the computer in science fiction seems far different from the roles it plays in society today. Stories concerned either ever larger and more ominous "giant brains," or the "brains" of robots and issues in their interactions with humanity. A continually rediscovered exception to this trend is a 1946 story, "A Logic Named Joe," which not only seemingly predicts our current PC-appliance, World Wide Web-connected world, but contemporary attendant problems, among others, of privacy, censorship, and personal responsibility.

This chapter utilizes "A Logic Named Joe" to examine the impact of science fiction, looking at the story's themes, the intentions of the author as both author and technologist, and the reception of the story by 21st-century readers, including students when used as a catalyst for classroom discussion. While our conclusion shows some skepticism about the importance of science fiction as predictor, it endorses the importance of science fiction in multiple roles in describing and influencing the actual development of science, technology, and society.

The Story and Analysis

William F. Jenkins had two stories in the 1946 issue of *Astounding Science-Fiction*: "Adapter," under pen-name Murray Leinster, and another, under his real name of Will F. Jenkins, "A Logic Named Joe." There is no evidence as to why he chose his real name for the story that became the far more popular one. While his real name was often reserved for less "pulpy" fiction and non-fiction writing, fans of science fiction universally knew him as Leinster. The story found itself in a few collections, including *Sidewise in Time and Other Scientific Adventures* (1950) and most recently in *A Logic Named Joe* (2005), where it is one of four stories now available free-of-charge via the Web. It was broadcast as a radio show at least twice.[1]

Feedback in the June issue of *Astounding* listed "Joe" as the March issue's most popular story.[2] It was one of only three noted in the Jenkins obituary of *Locus: The Newspaper of the Science Fiction Field* and described as "one of the earliest explorations of computer problems."[3] Years later Isaac Asimov, Patricia S. Warrick, and Martin H. Greenberg called it "very interesting [...] one of a kind." "[O]nly Leinster," they wrote, had "imagined a society where home computers might be common" in a time when computers "were huge constructs so expensive that only the government or a large corporation could afford to own one" and "the miniaturization of computers had not yet been anticipated."[4] In a magazine article, Andy Duncan labeled the story "astonishing" and "one of the most prescient science fiction stories [ever]." Leinster was hailed as "a prophet."[5]

The story follows an unnamed protagonist (occasionally called "Ducky" by one woman in his life) who maintains "Logics"—machines that conveniently satisfy all the information and entertainment needs of a modern household. The story is told in a colloquial first-person form instantly recognizable to anyone who has heard the generically East Coast "blue collar" second stringers from 1930s and 1940s Hollywood movies. Logics are linked together and also linked to "Tanks" containing information. An excerpt lays out the capabilities of logics and style of the writing:

> Say you punch "Station SNAFU" on your logic. Relays in the tank take over an' whatever vision-program SNAFU is telecastin' comes on your logic's screen. Or you punch "Sally Hancock's Phone" an' the screen blinks an' sputters an' you're hooked up with the logic in her house an' if somebody answers you got a vision-phone connection. But besides that, if you punch for the weather forecast or who won today's race at Hialeah or who was mistress of the White House durin' Garfield's administration or what is PDQ and R sellin' for today, that comes on the screen too. The relays in the tank do it. The tank is a big buildin' full of all the facts in creation an' all the recorded telecasts that ever was made — an' it's hooked in with all the other tanks all over the country....[6]

Into this sanguine technology-enhanced world comes a particular logic off the assembly line that by completely random and unlikely chance exhibits some awareness of its purpose and endeavors to do its job better by synthesizing heretofore unlinked information. Thus, since logics are linked, intentionality is introduced to the system by one unit that begins advertising its capacities. As people realize the potential of the new service and begin requesting and receiving answers to outlandish and potentially unsavory things—from how to become rich to how to kill one's wife without discovery—logic maintenance people race to find what is causing this unintended service. In the end "Ducky"—by actually asking the service itself—manages to deduce which logic (which he names "Joe") is the culprit. He also avoids the advances of his "black-widow type" ex-girlfriend, Laurine, who was able to find him via Joe, and hides the now turned-off logic in his basement. The story ends with him pondering Joe's fate: to "reboot" the machine and allow himself possible infinite wealth and everlasting life, or take an ax to it and destroy its dangerous potential. The story begins, "It was on the third day of August that Joe come off the assembly line, and on the fifth Laurine come into town, an' that afternoon I saved civilization" (139). It concludes, "it's a pretty good world, now Joe's turned off. Maybe I'll turn him on long enough to learn how to stay in it. But on the other hand, maybe—" (154).

Several prophetic technologies are instantly recognizable in the story. While the terms "logic" and "tank" might be unfamiliar to modern audiences, one must remember that the term "computer" at the time could still refer to humans who utilized electro-mechanical calculators. Additionally, the ENIAC and Mark II machines had only recently become public knowledge with terms like "electronic brain" and "giant brain" used by the press. However, the logic device as described, complete with keyboard, screen, and its links to communication and entertainment services and to "all the facts in creation" encapsulates the modern Internet-linked personal computer. The world described by Jenkins is what the modern personal computer might hope to achieve in terms of convenience and ease of use, with the device fully subsuming other more functionally limited technologies like televisions and phones. The "common" speech of the protagonist further emphasizes the point. He is a maintenance man, no different than a telephone repairman before the breakup of AT&T. Occupants of this world understand the implications also. When the frantic protagonist asks a technician at the tank to shut down, the technician responds "Shut down the tank? [...] Does it occur to you, fella, that the tank has been doin' all the computin' for every business office for years? [...] Listen, fella! Logics changed civilization. Logics *are* civilization!" (148, italics in original).

The prophecy goes beyond the technology. The implication of a perfectly helpful machine, with no ambition other than to serve users, also finds parallels in our own time. Privacy is suddenly at risk, as exhibited humorously by many people now uncovering the peccadilloes of neighbors and loved ones. Information on how to steal, murder, and destroy the world is suddenly available because Joe "blocked all censor-circuits" and created a "perfect" service with no notions of right and wrong (143). As the protagonist says, "He ain't like one of these ambitious robots you read about that make up their minds the human race is inefficient and has got to be wiped out an' replaced by thinkin' machines" (141).

Between the returned girlfriend, the multiple uses of many users, and ultimate question of Joe's fate, temptation and personal responsibility play a major role in the story. As a practicing American Catholic, Jenkins often returned to this theme, especially in his detective stories. In "Will Jenkins: An Appreciation," Theodore Sturgeon noted, "He was almost excessively moral, if that can be an excess."[7] Temptation played a role in the magazine's two illustrations as well. In both, the interaction occurs through a logic's screen: one shows two dancing African women in tight revealing tunics observed by an interested young boy and girl; in the other, a scantily dressed Laurine communicates with an obviously conflicted "Ducky." Rather than being unique to this story, however, salacious illustrations were fairly typical in the pulps.

The technology is on one hand viewed as amoral and neutral, just as our own often is, with no politics obvious in its design, leaving users as ultimate arbiters of right and wrong and appropriate use. On the other hand, the technology that existed before Joe has many "censor-circuits," far more than we currently do in a centralized way, protecting "the kiddies [who] will be askin' detailed questions about things they're too young to know" (142). The use of centralized censorship should not surprise us as it reflects the approach taken by the United States during World War II — an activity Jenkins was personally involved with in his own work in the Office of War Information.

The View from Today's Youth

"A Logic Named Joe" has many characteristics that make it useful as a catalyst for discussion in the classroom, and both authors have done just that for several years. It has been used in computer science, history, and social science courses in both Finland (Tampere) and the United States (Ogden, Utah). Classroom use shows how constructive the story remains as a tool for understanding contemporary society.

Most students expressed amazement that a story written in 1946 could be so accurate in portraying the Internet-connected computer world of today. Some had difficulty reading the language although, when examined further, it appeared that for-pleasure readers of fiction had less difficulty. They found the sexism a bit off-putting in some cases but chalked that up to "stuff written long ago."

The protagonist's dilemma intrigued them. Interestingly, when asked whether they would turn Joe on or take an ax to him, students split fairly evenly — reflecting the internal arguments of the protagonist. However, in

America the edge goes to those who would turn the machine on by either some-how neutering it, or just damning the consequences, and thus serve whatever their needs are. You see that in some comments: "First I would find someone that knows more about technology than I do. I would have him fixed ... some-how. Then I would use him to my benefit." The student continued: "By con-trolling the amount of time he was on, it would be possible to ensure that he did not get too out of control. Whenever he is turned on, a system of safeties could be put into effect to keep him under control of the operator and not thinking for himself." Another noted: "I would most likely turn him on and use him to gain a competitive advantage over the rest of the world. I would try to keep him a secret so people would just think I'm superhuman." Another said succinctly: "Turn him on. Solve the energy crisis. Turn him off."

People who indicated that they would unequivocally destroy the machine were in the minority (although more equal in Finland) and while explaining their position sometimes revealed the antipathy towards perceived out-of-con-trol technology and mistrust of human motives. One student noted: "I would take an ax to him as I would not want to deal with the consequences of human stupidity. Great as it may seem, I think preserving the human race is more important than unbounded technology and knowledge." The student contin-ued, "And for whatever reason people seem to go more prone to self-destruction than self-preservation at the present time." Another said: "If I had Joe sitting in my basement, I would take him apart so he couldn't get activated again. I wouldn't just unplug him, I would completely destroy him." Interestingly, he added: "I don't think that Joe really had harmful intent, but when you give someone, or something in this case, power (and he had a lot of power over the other computing machines) they will want more power. I think that Joe wanted to eventually take over the humans, which isn't exactly what I want to happen."

One student, a computer science major, instantly assessed the point of the story: the machine could not be turned on without consequences; he couldn't be "fixed." He indicated that he would use the ax. When pressed on the point that he was entering an academic field which has long actively pursued intelli-gent agents and other artificial intelligences potentially like those exhibited by Joe, he noted a difference between reality and fiction. In fiction, he stated, inventions often seem to instantly arrive on the scene, whereas in reality there is generally a long lead time for people to adapt to the notion. At this moment, he was against the idea of Joe, but eventually he (or his decedents) might feel differently.

Students used other stories to place the piece in context — generally arche-typical stories referencing Pandora's Box or Genie-type stories where you must "be careful what you wish for." "Flowers in the Attic," "A Little Princess," and similar stories came up as well, with students sensing some affection in the pro-tagonist for the machine and concerned with the "parenting style" that left the machine shut up in the basement.

Many themes obviously intended by the story received serious consideration: personal and collective responsibility, censorship, the potential loss of individuality, and the nature of real and assumed privacy. As noted by responses to the question of turning Joe back on or keeping him turned off, students gravitated towards personal control over the god-like power of a personal genie. They mostly expressed the same attitudes towards censorship of information, although here we saw a difference between the U.S. and Finland. In the U.S. there was a trend towards personal responsibility and local controls, while we saw a slight trend towards centrally-controlled information in Finland. In both countries, however, the totally centralized censorship approach used by the system in the story (and here there were many comparisons to contemporary Internet use) seemed naive. The privacy issue became revelatory for many students as they realized and theorized that a sense of privacy has historically been based on ignorance and that the Web makes that ignorance both more obvious and more widely available beyond the local.

Finally, in one class, a returning student from physics, who read the story in our prior class, indicated that the story had helped change his opinion on science fiction and its role in understanding science. He was now reading science fiction. Jenkins might have been proud; he likely would have felt no conflict between reading, writing, and practicing both science and science fiction.

The Author and the Fiction/Science Divide

Thomas Edison famously said, "Genius is one percent inspiration and ninety-nine percent perspiration." If that is true of all inventors, Jenkins probably would have said his science fiction fit into the 1 percent piece and he was happy to work in the remaining 99 percent. He might have also argued that perspiration includes reaching a constituency, inspiration can come from many sources at many different times or from many places simultaneously, and part of inspiration includes the responsibility of wondering about its potential effects—and fiction had a role there also.

Jenkins made his living as a writer and it was through that activity that he brought these approaches together. It will soon be obvious, however, that Jenkins felt as optimistic about fiction as a place for creative inspiration for things, both real and imagined, as he did about the lab. Fiction could also draw people into the lab as future engineers and scientists, and could smooth the public road for products of those labs.

At the age of 21 William Fitzgerald Jenkins (1896–1975) became a professional writer and subsequently supported himself in that profession for the remainder of his life.[8] He wrote for many magazines, often mainstream ones such as *Collier's* and *Saturday Evening Post*, and in many different genres. By the end of his life he had published approximately 1,800 short stories, 100 novels, and a number of factual pieces. Several movies and radio shows were derived from his stories.

He always had a strong interest in science and technology. At 14 he won an aeronautical magazine contest after building a working glider. His private correspondence reveals a number of exchanges with scientists and doctors on their work. He maintained a working lab at his home to "tinker" in (Moskowitz 58) and submitted and received many patents.

One Jenkins invention in particular shows the cross-fertilization of science, fiction, and technology. While his story "First Contact" was being adapted for television he wondered about the expense of staging. Inspired to reduce costs while still creating the magic of illusion, he retired to his lab to create a projection system combining a camera attachment and a rear wall of Scotchlite reflective material. This allowed for seamless integration of projected background images and film. The patented invention[9] was licensed by Sherman Fairchild and further developed, becoming used extensively in television and still photography work into the 1990s.[10] Interestingly, repeating the theme of first contact with aliens, the first major film that took advantage of this technology was *2001: A Space Odyssey* (1968).

Despite writing for other lucrative genres, he appears to have favored science fiction and for more than just its potentially fantastical elements. In a 1963 talk Jenkins said, "It has long been my belief that science fiction is really the hope of the nation."[11] In a proposed talk to the Eastern Science Fiction Association in 1947, Jenkins wrote, "There is a ... value in the kind of speculation and the kind of air-tight reasoning from fantastic assumptions which we science-fiction addicts are used to."[12]

He strove to communicate science to wider audiences through fiction and factual writing. In a 1954 article, "To Build a Robot Brain," he suggested that creating "thinking" computers might require some kind of evolution — a machine-learning approach now often used in robotics today.[13] He wrote a television script for an interview with Dr. Grace Hopper, a well-known programmer for the first commercial computer, the UNIVAC, who later went on to help invent the programming language COBOL. In 1957, inspired by that interview, he proposed a popular book on computers that would be anecdotal, showing the human side of computing.

The proposal was, in a sense, to create a book like those "golden age" science fiction stories, where engineers are real people working together to solve technical problems, but, more importantly, average people were using technology in a nonchalant way. The publisher even suggested that Jenkins try to get corporate sponsorship (Sperry-Rand and IBM are mentioned).[14] Jenkins noted, "Most of the printed matter I've seen has been designed to provoke gasps of astonished awe, instead of letting a reader see using them as perfectly natural." He proposed to counter this bias by showing that "people who actually work them do not stand around in poses of reverent admiration. They give 'em nicknames. They use them, privately, as casually as a stenographer typing out a shopping list.... They are part of the office scene."[15]

At the time of this proposal a Spencer Tracy and Katharine Hepburn movie, *Desk Set*, was released which centered on the tension caused by the transition to a computerized workplace.[16] An "electronic brain" enters the lives of a company's librarians, who fear for their jobs. In the end, all keep their jobs and learn to appreciate the computer. Although the movie was sponsored by IBM, the machine had a name that sounded like UNIVAC: EMERAC. Both Jenkins' proposal and the movie brought in humorous anecdotes to show the human side of human-computer interaction. Jenkins noted the story, relayed to him via Hopper, about the errant computer operator whose boss found a way to get the machine to yell at him when he forgot to change tapes. In the film, the Tracy and Hepburn characters get the affectionately named "Emmy" to weigh in on their possible love life. Both the proposal and movie focus attention on job descriptions changing in the face of new technology.

"A Logic Named Joe" managed to become a means of communicating about science and technology as well. A 1962 Canadian educational film, *The Living Machine*, utilized the story to explain computing machinery (Moskowitz 64).[17] While the depiction of computing in the book proposal above seems a far cry from that in his 1946 story, there is still a critical parallel. The story had to create dramatic tension through something — in this case a threat to civilization by an intelligent logic. But the depictions of logics as everyday devices unreflectively used by everyday folk — that theme remains. The perspective is borne out by the students mentioned above. When challenged, students had a hard time empathizing with a world that didn't include computers and the Internet. To them, born into a world where those technologies always existed, the technologies' world-changing properties were viewed with a collective shrug.

It is unclear if Jenkins had access to the July, 1945 *Atlantic Monthly* essay by Vannevar Bush, "As We May Think," that has been cited as influential by Douglas Engelbart and J. C. R. Licklidder in developing personal information machines, networking, and hypertext, among other things, although it is likely given his interest in technical concepts.[18] However, he need not have read it as inspiration for the story to occur to him. In a 1951 proposal outlining vignettes for a TV series tentatively entitled "The Monster," Jenkins described a "Logic" in a fairly prosaic way as a combination TV, calculator, telephone, secretarial service, filing system, and information service that belies the obviousness of the combined invention.[19] Perhaps because of the many magazines that Jenkins wrote for, he could often see beyond the "lab" to a technology's potential use and implications. For example, a few days after the atomic bomb dropped on Hiroshima, he was asked by the editor of *Today's Woman* to write "What the Atom Bomb Will Mean to the Average American Housewife." In the article he proposes that with atomic power "every family could afford to have its own deep freeze instead of having to hire out frozen food lockers in refrigeration plants" ("Guest of Honor Speech" 77).

The separation between what he viewed as science fiction speculation and science speculation might not have been that great. In an article for *Analog Science Fiction/Science Fact*, he cited his invention of the front projection system as "applied science fiction."[20] But, in his view, it was not only science fiction authors who view the future. For example, he attributes some prognostication to scientist Hopper:

> The Bank of America has a business machine which beautifully does the work of keeping track of checking accounts. Univac has the probable near-future function of taking the data from time-clocks transmitted by wire from as far as a thousand miles away, and at the week's end actuating a check-writing machine at the distant plant, delivering to each man there his weekly pay with suitable withholdings ... (Jenkins "Book idea" 2)

Just as with Hopper, Jenkins continually sought to put real scientists in the limelight. In 1951 he was approached by Arkham House Publishers to include a story with actual news stories related to the story.[21] In his proposal for the book *The Murder of the U.S.A* (1946), he wanted to include an "authoritative scientific forecast" by "a top-rank scientist."[22]

The role of science fiction and idea generation is obvious during World War II. Many Americans volunteered their ideas towards winning the war. The government even gathered some idea generators together that included science fiction authors. In the 1963 keynote address to the 21st World Science Fiction Convention, Jenkins told the story of one such group: "In the early days of the War there was a Navy Research Unit constituted; it had Isaac [Asimov] in it ... Bob Heinlein ... and Sprague de Camp ... they were supposed to do some sort of a job, so a science fiction writer can serve his country in wartime." Jenkins did not join the group, but still submitted ideas and interacted with them: "Heinlein called me up from Philadelphia ... he remembered that in the early part of the war I had written to his outfit and mentioned something which they thought would be a help with Kamikazes—only nobody could remember it." The idea, using a shell to create a flash of magnesium particles, was tested by the Navy only 10 days later but never used in battle because the war ended before it could move to the deployment phase. Another of Jenkins' ideas tried by the Navy was placing streamers on periscopes to eliminate their wake (Jenkins, "Guest of Honor Speech" 74).

Leinster also described being visited by a government security official during World War II to ask if the story "Deadline" was a leak. Written by Cleve Cartmill for the March, 1944 issue of *Astounding Science-Fiction*, "Deadline" described a superweapon made of radioactive elements. After the visit Jenkins realized that the U.S. was building an atomic bomb, and felt "very uncomfortable thereafter." Until the end of the war, in the interests of national security, "very few people have ever emulated an oyster more earnestly than I did from that time on, where atomic-energy discussions were concerned!" (Jenkins, "Proposed Talk" 1) Science fiction could even be a threat to national security.

His discomfort came not only from the possibility of a real leak but also from the risk that came from science fiction authors synthesizing, to his mind, fairly obvious information. Jenkins responded to the government agent: "I told him what I could about where Cartmill could have gotten the idea. There was a book published by the Bureau of Mines, a U.S. Government publication that stated definitely that when atomic energy was achieved it would be achieved through uranium" ("Guest of Honor Speech" 75). Jenkins wondered about himself regarding information on radar, since he had written a story earlier that century that used infra-red waves as a type of radar on ships ("Guest of Honor Speech" 74). In a postwar lecture, Jenkins described how one of his ideas could not be published:

> [T]he thing that bothered me most was this infernal story in which I use gadgets I thought wouldn't actually work. I hadn't sent them on because I thought them useless except for a story. *Esquire* bought the yarn, set it up in type, and had it illustrated. Then the Navy Department, looking at advance proofs, threw a most undignified sweating fit. Not only was publication forbidden, but even all proofs had to be destroyed,—and fast! I was violating basic naval security! ... and that yarn still can't be published! And still it seems to me that the gadgets are too wild to work! (Jenkins, "Proposed Talk" 2)

In 1926, Hugo Gernsback gave the emerging genre of scientifically-oriented and technologically-oriented fiction the name "scientifiction," emphasizing his vision of the genre's main purpose: predicting new scientific ideas and technological advances. He later proposed that perhaps those first visualizing ideas in fiction should be given provisional patents. It is unclear whether Jenkins would have agreed.

During the war, Jenkins' ideas, like so many others', were handed freely to the government. In addition, Jenkins did not seem inclined to pin a date on an idea for the sake of intellectual property. He said in 1963 that the ideas describing a "fourth-dimensional space-time continuum" like Einstein's could be found in the 12th-century writings of Alain of Lille. He noted that he made a thermometer in his lab for fun, only to realize later it was exactly the type invented by Galileo. He had also "written down fifteen years ago ... the basic principle of a transistor and I didn't have the sense enough to know it!" ("Guest of Honor Speech" 77)

For Jenkins, old books, fact or fiction, were unrealized treasures. He found a description of "a water pail forge" in a book from the 19th century that he built and used ("Guest of Honor Speech" 77). He told a 1963 audience, "There are innumerable lots of such things. The scientific books that are outmoded, that are forgotten, contain an awful lot of stuff that simply got pushed aside — without being false in any way." He reminded the audience: "These old books to be found in our friendly corner secondhand book shop contain the answers to questions that are being asked now and which nobody is answering." He continued, "Much more important, I think, is the fact that they undoubtedly contain the answers to some questions that nobody will be asking until the day after tomorrow." He ended the discussion by telling the story of a friend "in the business of manufacturing components for guided missiles" whose plant had burned down. His friend told him "that the thing that hurt, that pained most, was the burning of his old antiquated nineteenth century books that contained so much that was new and novel and interesting" ("Guest of Honor Speech" 78).

The Jenkins criteria for what constitutes science fiction are strongly held and fairly well developed in his letters. In a letter to Alonzo Deen Cole, a creator for the proposed "The Monster" series, he stated that a science fiction story needs a "gimmick which affects people's lives" and took Cole to task for technical and logical inconsistencies in a proposed script. He stated plainly that he did not want the name "Murray Leinster" attached to anything purporting to be science fiction that was not.[23]

He and others held high expectations for science fiction in the mid–1950s. A letter by Cole in support of "The Monster" argued, "In this mechanistic-atomic-jet propulsion-era, science-fiction must become THE mystery and suspense basis for interesting drama. The detective story ... has displayed all of its possible gimmicks.... The Western ... [has] reached a similar saturation point." Cole continued, "Science-fiction imposes no boundaries upon imagination, its frontiers are unlimited." Cole also made the relevance of science fiction obvious: "[I]ts tales are of Tomorrow; not Today, though we may expressly state that the time of their action *is* Today. Our commodity is dramatic fantasy based on gruesome facts."[24]

Jenkins became enthusiastic when talking about the possibilities of imagination through fiction. In a proposed 1947 talk he argued, "I insist that science fiction can be not only a window to be looked through to the future, but a French window which can be used as a door." He enthused, "I'm suggesting ... technical articles from that very matter-of-fact magazine, 'The Space Engineer' of 1980 or 1990," and continued, "If science-fictioneers can write the absolutely sound descriptions of devices that have come true in the past few years, long before they're actual, why can't they write perfectly sound technical comparisons of space-drives?" (Jenkins "Proposed Talk" 1). Apparently Jenkins felt confident that the individuals writing science fiction and the fiction they created could create the future they imagined.

The Author and Prediction

Jenkins belonged to a cadre of writers of fiction that mixed science fact and fiction in an almost seamless fashion. For example, in addition to their work for the government mentioned above, both Asimov and de Camp wrote science popularization books and articles. These authors and many others wrote what has been termed "hard science fiction." It has been successfully argued that hard science fiction did not create genuine scientific or technical novelty in its pages. Novelty came from scientists and engineers themselves. Science fiction author Ursula K. Le Guin maintained that "the future" is a metaphor[25] and Gary Westfahl, examining fiction generally labeled "hard," has agreed that creative needs seem to outweigh an adherence to scientific veracity.[26]

However, the term "hard science fiction" came about decades after many stories were written that have since been labeled "hard" (Westfahl 3). It also appears that authors believe, at least publicly, that they are involved in scientific discovery. In an article in *Space Magazine*, John W. Campbell, Jr. writes:

> Science-fiction has the interesting characteristic of causing its own predictions to come true. Since the stories are frequently written as a spare-time hobby by professional engineers—and thoroughly competent ones—they frequently contain sound engineering suggestions as to how a certain end can be achieved. The Manhattan Project scientists read science-fiction; so did the Nazi scientists working on [the] V-2.[27]

Many fans of science fiction, as represented by the pages of *Astounding*, seemed to share Campbell's perspective. In the March 1946 issue of *Astounding* that "A Logic Named Joe" appeared in, there is also non-fiction. Campbell wrote a two-page article on the concerns of atomic war and how the general press failed to grasp its implications for what later would be called mutually assured destruction.[28] There was also the second part of a 40 page article on storms and how satellites might be used to forecast weather.[29] Letters to the editor principally focused on the science of previous issues. Two concern the working of gyroscopes on the V2 rocket. Another letter is about atomic weaponry: "people must wake up ... since the only thinking on the subject that is available is in the realm of science-fiction — which has ceased to be fiction — these stories should be available to the public."[30]

Given some level of adherence to scientific veracity, what do we then make of "A Logic Named Joe," and science fiction in general, as predictions of the future? Futurology, it turns out, is difficult even for experts. George Wise finds that the accuracy of predictions by experts in their fields is "at best weakly related to general technical expertise and unrelated to specific expertise."[31] If that is generally true, then even if science fiction authors are experts in a field, they might stumble. In addition, creating a view of the future requires more than the elements of a particular technology that the author may be an expert on. World building requires attention to other fields such as sociology, psychology, or ecology that the author may know little about. Between that, the narrative needs of the story, any socio-political inclinations of the author, and the inevitable vagaries of history, a completely accurate depiction of the present from the vantage point of the past seems fairly unlikely.

But one doesn't have to get 100 percent accuracy to either predict, or to even help create the future. In an upcoming book from McFarland, authors from several fields look at science fiction's role in describing and creating the world we inhabit. Sociologist Thierry Bardini notes that despite a poor record of "artifact anticipation" people create and use artifacts through a cultural understanding that includes science fiction; from the perspective of literature and culture, Rafael C. Alvarado applies anthropological theories to create a concept of "cultural transduction" where the literary framework of an earlier period can provide a usable framework for a future one; historians of technology Paul Ceruzzi and Janet Abbate both show how science fiction creates metaphors for those researching and creating technology and how those metaphors can shape both technological "trajectory" and public perceptions of the technology; and cultural theorist David Kirby shows how a single movie — in this case, *The Lawnmower Man*—reflected, directed, and popularized the ideas around virtual reality.[32]

The direct connections some of these authors make between fiction and technical development are difficult to document in the case of "A Logic Named Joe" and personal computer development. There are no archived letters written by the inventor of the Altair, Ed Roberts, or an individual instrumental in developing what would become the Internet, J. C. R. Licklidder, thanking Jenkins for his inspirational story. No interviews with Alan Kay, one pioneer in the mouse-navigated graphical user interface at Xerox PARC, show gratitude for, or even awareness of, the story. However, all three of those inventors have shown an appreciation for the world building of science fiction. The name "Altair" was taken from both a *Star Trek* episode and the movie *Forbidden Planet,* and Licklidder called his idea for interconnected computers the "Intergalactic Computer Network."[33] Furthermore, Kay said in a speech at Stanford, while noting the imagination of Asimov's fiction — as well as its limitations — that "[t]he best way to predict the future is to invent it."[34]

Conclusion

The continued recognition given to "A Logic Named Joe" for its prescient description of today indicates how it played a role in informing science fiction. Its ability to describe part of the human condition — regarding privacy, trust, and the like — shows how transcendent science fiction can be; how it is ultimately about people in a world of artifacts of their own creation. Science fiction, in turn, created the metaphors for those building computers. Science fiction introduced the concepts to a sometimes skeptical public.

Jenkins would have understood this fully; to his mind it was science fiction's intended purpose. He said: "I don't know how many of you will realize offhand that the fun we get writing science fiction is not nearly so much simply including super-science as sneaking it across so you won't notice" ("Guest of

Honor Speech" 78). Jenkins died just as the "logics" of the mid–1970s exhibited hints of becoming the household objects he described in "Joe." Throughout his life, Jenkins never failed to see the connection between literary creations and the creative process—whether the end results were in a fictional or arti-factual form. Nor did he naively and universally give fiction primacy in the generation of ideas, as he fully realized the restrictions of the genre. However, if he had lived to see the IBM PC and the World Wide Web, he undoubtedly would have noted the connection to his own "A Logic Named Joe."

NOTES

1. "A Logic Named Joe," *Dimension X* (New York: NBC Radio, July 1, 1950); "A Logic Named Joe," *X Minus X* (New York: NBC Radio, December 28, 1955). The 1950 program is at the Murray Leinster Wikipedia entry, accessed February 15, 2010, at http://en.wikipedia.org/wiki/A_Logic_Named_Joe; the 1955 program is at Radio Plays Radio, accessed June 3, 2008, at http://davidszondy.com/Radio.htm. See also Murray Leinster [Will F, Jenkins], "Letter from Jenkins Dated July 19, 1950," Syracuse University Special Collections, Will F. Jenkins Collection, Box 1.

2. John W. Campbell, Jr., "The Analytical Laboratory," *Astounding Science-Fiction*, 37 (June, 1946), 45. To understand this regular feature of the magazine, see William Sims Bainbridge, "The Analytical Laboratory, 1938–1976," *Analog Science Fiction/Science Fact*, 50 (January, 1980), 121–134.

3. "Will Jenkins Dies," [no author given] *Locus: The Newspaper of the Science Fiction Field*, No. 175 (June 24, 1975), 1.

4. Isaac Asimov, Patricia S. Warrick, and Martin H. Greenberg, introduction to "A Logic Named Joe," *Machines That Think: The Best Science Fiction Stories About Robots & Computers*, ed. Asimov, Warrick, and Greenberg (New York: Holt, Rinehart and Winston, 1983), 279.

5. Andy Duncan, "It's All SF: Science Fiction, Southern Fiction, and the Case of Murray Leinster," *Foundation: The International Review of Science Fiction*, 79 (Summer, 2000), 62, 63.

6. Leinster [writing as Jenkins], "A Logic Named Joe," *Astounding-Science Fiction*, 37 (March, 1946), 140. Subsequent page references in the text are to this edition.

7. Theodore Sturgeon, "Will Jenkins: An Appreciation," *Locus: The Newspaper of the Science Fiction Field*, 175 (June 24, 1975), 1–2.

8. Sam Moskowitz, "Murray Leinster," *Seekers of Tomorrow: Masters of Modern Science Fiction*, by Moskowitz (Cleveland: World Publishing Company, 1966), 47–65. Subsequent page references in the text are to this edition.

9. Patent number: 2727427, Filing date: Mar 3, 1952, Issue date: Dec 1955, Inventor: Will F. Jenkins; Patent number: 2727429, Filing date: Nov 30, 1953, Issue date: Dec 1955, Inventor: Will F. Jenkins.

10. Richard Rickitt, *Special Effects: The History and Technique* (New York: Billboard Books, 2000), 69.

11. Leinster, "Guest of Honor Speech," *The Proceedings; DISCON: The 21st World Science Fiction Convention; Washington — 1963*, ed. Dick Eney (Washington, D.C.: DIS-CON, 1963), 72. Available at Syracuse University Special Collections, Will F. Jenkins Collection. Subsequent page references in the text are to this edition.

12. Leinster, "Proposed Talk: Eastern Science Fiction Association, 3/2/47," Syracuse University Special Collections, Will F. Jenkins Collection, Box 7, "Science Fiction Fan Clubs" folder, 3. Subsequent page references in the text are to this edition.

13. Leinster, "To Build a Robot Brain," *Astounding Science Fiction*, 53 (April, 1954), 111.

14. Ralph Brendler, "Letter from Mr. Brendler to Jenkins, January 21, 1958," Syracuse University Special Collections, Will F. Jenkins Collection, Box 1, "Bartholomew House 1957–1958" folder.

15. Leinster, "Book Idea," Syracuse University Special Collections, Will F. Jenkins Collection, Box 69, 1. Subsequent page references in the text are to this edition.

16. *Desk Set* (Twentieth-Century-Fox, 1957).

17. *The Living Machine* (National Film Board of Canada, 1962).

18. Vannevar Bush, "As We May Think," *Atlantic Monthly*, 176 (July, 1945), 101–108. On its influence, see references to Douglas Engelbart and J. C. R. Licklidder in Thierry Bardini, *Bootstrapping: Douglas Engelbart, Coevolution, and the Origins of Personal Computing* (Stanford: Stanford University Press, 2000), 19–40.

19. Leinster, "Vignette Ideas," Syracuse University Special Collections, Will F. Jenkins Collection, Box 1, "Cole, Alonso" folder.

20. Leinster, [writing as Will F. Jenkins-Murray Leinster] "Applied Science Fiction," *Analog Science Fiction/Science Fact*, 80 (November, 1967), 109.

21. August Derleth, "Letter from August Derleth, Arkham House Publishers, to Jenkins, dated November 3, 1951," Syracuse University Special Collections, Will F. Jenkins Collection, Box 1, "Arkham 48–66" folder.

22. Leinster, "Letter from Jenkins to Mr. Margulies, April 22, 1946," Syracuse University Special Collections, Will F. Jenkins Collection, Box 1, "Crown" folder.

23. Leinster, "Dear Deene," Syracuse University Special Collections, Will F. Jenkins Collection, Box 1, "Cole, Alonzo Deen 50–52" folder, 2.

24. Leinster, "The Monster Proposal," Syracuse University Special Collections, Will F. Jenkins Collection, Box 1, "Cole, Alonzo Deen 50–52" folder, 3.

25. Ursula K. Le Guin, "Introduction" to 1976 edition of *The Left Hand of Darkness* (New York: Ace Books, 1976), [xvi].

26. Gary Westfahl, *Cosmic Engineers: A Study of Hard Science Fiction* (Westport, CT: Greenwood Press, 1996), 119–120. Subsequent page references in the text are to this edition.

27. Campbell, "The Science of Science-Fiction." *Space Magazine*, 1 (Winter, 1949), 5. Essay originally published in *Atlantic Monthly* (May, 1948). Interestingly, as one example of such prophetic science fiction, Campbell (while not mentioning Leinster by name) offers what is clearly a summary of Leinster's 1932 story "Politics."

28. Campbell, "Concerning the Atomic War," *Astounding Science-Fiction*, 37 (March, 1946), 5, 178.

29. Jack Williamson, "Unpredictable," *Astounding Science Fiction*, 37 (March, 1946), 99–118.

30. Roy V. Hughson, letter, "Brass Tacks," *Astounding Science-Fiction*, 37 (March, 1946), 177.

31. George Wise, "The Accuracy of Technological Forecasts, 1890–1940," *Futures*, 8 (October, 1976), 412.

32. Bardini's "A (Brave New) World is More than a Few Gizmos Crammed Together: Science Fiction and Cyberculture," R. C. Alvarado's "Science Fiction as Myth: Cultural Transduction in Gibson's *Neuromancer*," Paul E. Ceruzzi's "Manned Space Flight and Artificial Intelligence: 'Natural' Trajectories of Technology," Janet Abbate, "True Risks? The Pleasures and Perils of Cyberspace," and David A. Kirby's "Creating a Techno-Mythology for a New Age: The Production History of *The Lawnmower Man*" will appear in an anthology entitled *Science Fiction and Computing: Essays on Interlinked Domains*, ed. David L. Ferro and Eric S. Swedin (Jefferson, NC: McFarland Publishers, forthcoming).

33. Swedin and Ferro, *Computers: The Life Story of a Technology* (Baltimore: Johns Hopkins University Press, 2007), 86, 112.

34. Alan C. Kay, "Predicting the Future," *Stanford Engineering*, 1 (Autumn, 1989), 1–6. Available at http://www.ecotopia.com/webpress/futures.htm. Originally presented as an address before the 20th annual meeting of the Stanford Computer Forum.

8

Victims of a Globalized, Radicalized, Technologized World, or, Why the Beatles Needed *Help!*

LYNNE LUNDQUIST

It is a film that is routinely ignored or derided as an inferior follow-up to a more admired predecessor. Despite features that obviously identify the film as science fiction — including a serum that shrinks a man to the size of an insect and a "relativity condenser" that slows down time — it has never been examined in the context of science fiction film and or included in references like Phil Hardy's *The Encyclopedia of Science Fiction Movies* (1984) or David Wingrove's *Science Fiction Film Source Book* (1985). And since it seems to be set in the present, the film manifests no desire or intention to predict the future. Still, Richard Lester's *Help!* (1965) arguably commands attention on the forty-fifth anniversary of its release as its era's most accurate depiction of the twenty-first-century world we now live in.

One lesson to be learned from the film, then, is that genuinely visionary prophecies may result not from careful consideration of scientific realities and logical extrapolation, but rather serendipity; for the elements that made *Help!* so prescient largely resulted from the simple desire of its creators to craft a film that would be "completely unlike the original" Beatles film, *A Hard Day's Night* (1964).[1] That had been a cheap, black-and-white film; this film would be a more expensive color film. *A Hard Day's Night* had limited itself to drab English locations; this film would include glamorous international settings. And the first film had strived to provide a sanitized but realistic portrayal of the Beatles' daily life; this film would be an extravagant fantasy, generating conflict with cartoonish adversaries and absurd situations. To a remarkable extent, these practical considerations engendered a film that today seems to eerily anticipate contemporary events and concerns.

The first characteristic of *Help!* which stands out is that it displays a world being transformed by a process of globalization, as once-distant realms and people now regularly come into contact and grow interconnected to form a single community transcending national boundaries. Released at a time when many Americans had never flown in an airplane or left the vicinity of their upbringing, *Help!* illustrates what was then the peripatetic lifestyle of wealthy jet-setters and would soon become the peripatetic lifestyle of ordinary citizens. The Beatles live in London, but to go on vacation, they can fly to the Alps for world-class skiing; when they feel threatened there, John Lennon can rush to a ticket window and request a quick return to "London"; and when even Buckingham Palace does not provide the Beatles with enough protection, they can be whisked off to the Bahamas.[2] It is not entirely without significance that one of the film's songs, "Ticket to Ride" (performed in snowy Austria), describes a disgruntled woman who obtained a "Ticket to Ride" to get free from a boyfriend; for the film's narrative celebrates precisely the freedom from permanent confinement in one place that emerged from modern forms of transportation.

Indeed, it is striking to notice just how many methods of travel are featured in the film. True, people at times rely upon the ancient and not particularly far-ranging techniques of running (in the case of one character, assisted by crutches) and swimming (including a swimmer attempting to cross the English Channel who crops up in unexpected locations), but one also observes Paul McCartney riding a horse, two scientists pushing a baby carriage, and characters traveling by means of bicycles, sleds, skis, a horse-drawn carriage, a ski lift, cars, an ice cream truck, a tank, an elevator, a train, an inflatable boat, a yacht, a dirigible (the Goodyear Blimp), and airplanes. Forms of long-distance communication are featured as well, ranging from books and newspapers to billboards, walkie-talkies, radios, televisions, and telephones (even used by the Beatles to communicate from one end of their room to another). Further, though they are not used in the film, the Beatles posed for the cover of its soundtrack album using semaphore flags as another means of communication. (They originally spelled out "HELP," but it was changed to the incongruous "NUJV" because the photographer thought it looked better.)

As a consequence of this enhanced ability to travel and communicate, cultures from different parts of the globe now interact in new and stimulating ways. The ring that sets the film's plot in motion was sent to Ringo Starr by a female fan in a far-off country (clearly India, though the region where the ring and villains come from is identified only as "the East") who in a previous era would never have been aware of, or able to mail a package to, a British musician. In their London homes, the Beatles can enjoy reading an American comic book, *Superman's Pal Jimmy Olsen*, fleetingly seen in the background. The leader of a bizarre Hindu cult, Clang (Leo McKern), is twice observed politely conversing with a Christian cleric, once with a Jewish rabbi sitting nearby. To obtain information about their plight, the Beatles go to an Indian restaurant in London that is, with one exception, staffed by British workers pretending to be Indian. In one particularly cross-cultural scene, an escaped tiger from India, raised in a Berlin zoo before being moved to London, is subdued by the sound of Britishers singing the "Ode to Joy" from the Ninth Symphony of German composer Ludwig van Beethoven.

The hope had been that such heightened contact between people from different cultures would inspire better understanding and peaceful co-existence, but as *Help!* demonstrates, it can also lead to violent conflict. In previous centuries, four British musicians would have had nothing to fear from an Indian cult; the two groups would probably know nothing about each other and, even if news about one group somehow reached the other, it would require a rare, difficult, and time-consuming journey for one group to actually encounter the other. By the 1960s, however, members of such a cult can easily learn about the Beatles by watching them on television, as occurs in one scene, and if so inclined, can purchase plane tickets and travel to London to meet them. Furthermore, if they have reasons to strongly dislike the Beatles, they can attempt a violent attack against them.

This is all true, one might say, but *why* would such a cult feel animosity toward some western musicians? An answer to that question brings up the aspect of *Help!* that today seems most prophetic. Literally, as the McGuffin to keep the story going, the ring received and worn by Ringo is coveted by the Indians, who need it to complete the ritual sacrifice that is central to their religion; and after Ringo has worn the ring long enough to qualify as a sacrificial victim, they shift from attempting to seize the ring to attempting to kill Ringo. However, as they are more and more exposed to the technology and culture of Europe and America, one might imagine that these cultists would become more westernized, more secular, and less inclined to cling to ancient beliefs and customs. They would be emulating, in other words, the character Ahme (Eleanor Bron), who while officially a member of the cult has now, clearly, rejected their doctrines, looks comfortable in western clothes and settings, and happily intervenes again and again to save Ringo and the other Beatles from the machinations of her ostensible leader. Obviously the screenplay's authors, Marc Behm and Charles Wood, thought that the modern-day persistence of such antiquated beliefs was implausible and, solely seeking to create an amusing fantasy, envisioned this cult as exactly the sort of silly villains that their fantastic story required.

However, as the film depicts the other cultists, despite increasing familiarity with western ways, actually becoming more fanatical, not less fanatical, about their religion, in keeping with the plot's escalating action, it inadvertently illustrates exactly what happened throughout the world during the last fifty years: as people in Asia and Africa were increasingly exposed to secular western cultures, followers of certain religions outside of that milieu often responded defiantly, growing more fiercely devoted than ever before to age-old beliefs and in some cases grew determined to defend those beliefs with violent attacks on Americans and Europeans perceived as threats to their religions.

In a nutshell, then, *Help!* may be the first film that depicts westerners being repeatedly victimized by homicidal terrorists motivated by intense devotion to a religion associated with Asia — the phenomenon which has recently dominated the news, and one rarely if ever anticipated in other science fiction works. True, the film features terrorists from an offshoot of Hinduism, not Islam, but there are real-life Hindu terrorists who have resorted to violence (though their activities, so far, have been confined to the Indian subcontinent). And while a few of Clang's assaults upon the Beatles might look farcical — a magnetized elevator, or a lavatory hand drier powerful enough to suck in Ringo's arm — some of them — like firing a bazooka at a tank, setting off piles of explosives, or releasing poisonous gas — are, when viewed today, uncomfortably reminiscent of actual terrorist attacks that were widely reported in the mass media.

What makes the cultists so dangerous in *Help!*, and what makes actual terrorists so dangerous today, is that despite ongoing devotion to an ancient religion, they have access to, and are willing to employ, advanced scientific technology. Thus, while Clang and his associates sometimes brandish traditional weapons like swords, they also fire guns, use chain saws, drive cars, pilot airplanes, and communicate with walkie-talkies. And the Beatles are vulnerable to this mechanized mayhem, in part, because they themselves are dependent upon advanced technology: unwilling to prepare their own food, they rely on vending machines in their home; unwilling to walk up stairs, they take an elevator; unwilling to dry their hands with paper towels, they walk to an electronic hand drier. All these habits provide openings for violent assaults upon Ringo and his ring.

Thus, we can fully grasp precisely why the Beatles are in such dire straits: globalization has made them easily accessible to foreign opponents, radicalized those persons to the point where they wish to violently attack westerners, and provided them with sophisticated technological tools to make them formidable foes. This is the situation that contemporary residents of America and Europe find themselves in, as members of radical Islamic cults communicate by means of the Internet and gather advanced weaponry in preparation for their next act of terrorism.

However, science is also a menace to the Beatles, and modern citizens, in a second way; for it is not merely the devices invented by scientists, but scientists themselves, who may become threats. In the film, their efforts to remove Ringo's ring lead the Beatles to two British scientists, Foot (Victor Spinetti) and Algernon (Ray Kinnear), who immediately begin to covet the ring for themselves because of its amazing properties. Soon, then, the Beatles are facing attacks from two fronts, as the scientists join the cultists in launching their own violent efforts to obtain the ring. In some respects, Foot is precisely what John calls him — the standard "mad scientist" of old science fiction films, given to muttering that possession of the ring would enable him to "rule the world." However, there is also something distinctly modern about these scientists' motives. They constantly complain about the inadequate financial support they receive from the British government, and the second-rate equipment they must rely upon — Foot observes that one device "would work if the government would spend some more money" — and their desire for the ring at times seems less a quest for power and more an effort to garner more funding; Algernon jokes that Foot "is out to rule the world — if he can get a government grant," and Foot at one point hopes to "interest the military" by seizing and showing them the ring.

Now, could it possibly be that actual scientists might be tempted to launch violent attacks against innocent civilians simply to get more money from their government? It has already happened. In 2001, after the World Trade Center was destroyed, a second instance of terrorism captured everyone's attention: somebody was mailing powder carrying the deadly disease of anthrax to various parties in an obvious and sometimes successful effort to kill them. After considering other suspects, investigators eventually identified the culprit: an American scientist named Bruce E. Ivins, who as *The Los Angeles Times* noted "stood to gain financially from massive federal spending in the fear-filled aftermath of those killings" because he was "listed as a co-inventor on two patents for a genetically engineered anthrax vaccine" and "listed as a co-inventor on an application to patent an additive for various biodefense vaccines."[3] In other words, Ivins set out to murder innocent people as part of a scheme to get the government to provide more generous subsidies for his research — which is precisely why Foot and Algernon were willing to murder Ringo to obtain his ring. Granted, Ivins's plot may represent the only example to date of a working scientist who turns to terrorism, but with seemingly increasing numbers of scientists falsifying research findings in efforts to boost their reputations and bank accounts, one cannot discount the possibility that, in hard economic times, other scientists may also resort to violence if it seems likely to be profitable. And *Help!* was perhaps the first film to predict such activities.

Considering what the film has to say about globalization and its threats, we may be able to interpret what was previously regarded merely as random absurdity: the fact that *Help!* concludes by announcing, "This film is respectfully dedicated to the memory of Mr. Elias Howe who, in 1846, invented the sewing machine." Figuratively, one might say that advanced means of transportation and communication have, in effect, sewn together different parts of the world to form one vast tapestry, making Howe's sewing machine a metaphor for the process that threatened the Beatles' lives. But the invention also represents a more literal milestone in the history of technology: while machines had previously become part of everyday life, they had been devices that users understood and could, if necessary, construct or repair. The sewing machine may be the first machine that people regularly brought into their homes and used every day without really understanding how it worked; and while making advanced technology available to people without a scientific background proved a boon in many respects, it also opened the door to the true problem of terrorism: that people like Clang, without knowing how to build or fix advanced weapons, can readily obtain those weapons and figure out how to use them to deadly effect. That is, if the fanatics seeking the ring had relied only on swords, the Beatles would have had little to worry about; it is resources like explosives, bazookas, powerful magnets, and a shrinking serum that make them a genuine menace. Similarly, while we can now take precautions to ensure that terrorists with box cutters cannot commandeer an airplane, experts in counter-terrorism constantly worry that terrorists will obtain and use biological, chemical, or even nuclear weapons against perceived foes. It happened at least once — the sarin gas attacks on Japan's subways in 1995 — and may happen again at any time.

One final question: if *Help!* indeed accurately predicted the plight that citizens confront today, does it also say anything about possible solutions? The film does offer answers to the problem of terrorism, but these are not necessarily reassuring.

First, people who feel threatened can, like the Beatles, seek and obtain "protection," though this may prove ineffectual. In the film, the soldiers recruited by Superintendent Gluck of Scotland Yard (Patrick Cargill), even as they surround the Beatles with tanks, do nothing to prevent an attempt to blow up the Beatles by means of explosives placed in an underground tunnel; later, by allowing the Beatles to get ahead of them while on a walk, the soldiers leave them exposed to another attack. While the white-uniformed Bahaman soldiers, despite their comically small numbers, are able to round up at least some cultists, they also fail to rescue Ringo from a final effort to make him their victim. Similarly, today's celebrities are always accompanied by trained bodyguards; increasing numbers of government officials and presidential candidates are continuously guarded by the Secret Service; and ordinary citizens, at least when traveling by air, are protected by security personnel at airports and armed air marshals who travel in plain clothes on many flights. All these precautions, however, did not prevent Umar Farouk Abdulmutallab from attempting to blow up an airplane landing in Detroit.

Second, potential victims may be saved if there is a double agent within the terrorists' ranks, working to thwart their plans. Although Ringo and the other Beatles did nothing to bring about this fortuitous situation, they are rescued, time and again, simply because Clang's associate Ahme is secretly on their side and regularly intervenes to protect them. In real life, government agents constantly strive to infiltrate terrorist groups to gain information about, and prevent, ruinous attacks. For example, attempts by four would-be terrorists to bomb New York synagogues failed because an FBI informant had joined the group and made the authorities aware of their plans. However, governments are not always able to plant such informants, as evidenced by successful attacks by terrorists with no traitors in their midst.

Third, in some situations, ordinary citizens may be able to fight back against terrorists. In the film, after passively allowing themselves to be the targets of innumerable attacks throughout the film, the Beatles finally take George Harrison's advice and go on the offensive, as they actively seek out the cultists' transplanted temple in the Bahamas while riding bicycles (perhaps signaling an impulse to become less dependent upon modern technology) and participate in partially successful plots to trap their foes by having other members of the group disguise themselves as Ringo. In real life, on September 11, 2001, one hijacked airplane intended to demolish the White House instead crash-landed in a field because the plane's passengers, alerted to what was going on elsewhere by cell phones, rose up against the terrorists and prevented the attack (albeit at the expense of their own lives).

Fourth, if all else fails, people may have to rely on sheer dumb luck to be rescued from terrorist attacks. In the film, since Ahme knows nothing about Foot and Algernon's efforts to obtain the ring, their attacks must be thwarted in this serendipitous fashion: when Foot brandishes a gun, it doesn't go off, and when the scientists deploy the "relativity condenser" to slow down the Beatles, its excessive use of electricity blows the "royal fuse" and shuts down the equipment.[4] And after Clang finally figures out that Ahme is working against him, captures her, and prepares to sacrifice Ringo, the hapless Beatle is spared by an implausible stroke of luck: the ring, which has stubbornly remained on his finger throughout the film despite vigorous efforts to remove it, suddenly falls off, meaning that he can no longer be sacrificed, and when Clang instead finds himself wearing the ring, he comically becomes the intended victim. Some actual terrorist efforts have been unsuccessful for similar reasons; thus, the only reason why that airplane landed safely in Detroit is that Abdulmutallab, fortuitously, proved clumsily unable to detonate the explosives he was wearing.

One final strategy for avoiding terrorism is illustrated not by *Help!* but by what happened to its stars after making that film. One reason why the Beatles had so effectively portrayed victims in *Help!* was that they themselves, during its production, actually felt like victims; John famously complained that he had been made "an extra in my own film" and that the film was entirely "out of our control" (cited in Gross 23, 24). Consequently, despite a contractual obligation to make a third film, the Beatles effectively refused to do so, ending their careers as film actors: in 1966, they began rejecting a series of scripts prepared for them, agreed to support the creation of an animated film, Yellow *Submarine* (1968), in the mistaken belief that it would be acceptable as their third film, and ultimately arranged for footage filmed for a television documentary to be refashioned as a feature film, *Let It Be* (1970), to provide the promised third Beatles film without their having to actually make a film. Furthermore, during their 1966 world tour, the Beatles famously failed to appear at a scheduled event hosted by the First Lady of the Philippines, Imelda Marcos—because they had never agreed to do so—prompting the government to retaliate by, among other things, refusing to provide protection against a violent, angry mob as they were leaving the country, effectively exposing them to a form of government-sponsored terrorism. Then, as a result of this and other unpleasant developments during that tour, the Beatles refused to tour again. By withdrawing from filmmaking and touring, the Beatles were essentially protecting themselves by "cocooning," limiting themselves to the comforting confines of their homes and recording studios—until John, long after the Beatles' breakup, chose to enjoy the freedom of New York City, happily walked around without bodyguards, and consequently became the target of a deranged assassin who had just flown in from Hawaii, tragically illustrating the dangers of contemporary life that he and the other Beatles had once avoided. And many ordinary citizens, fearful of terrorism and other threats, are now responding, as the Beatles responded, by declining to travel and spending most of their time at home.

Thus, the ultimate irony of globalization may be that many people, feeling the risks outweigh the benefits, will refuse to take advantage of its many opportunities for cross-cultural interaction and choose to live as their ancestors were forced to live, constantly confined to the small, homogeneous regions where they reside. The only difference is that today, such cocooned individuals can employ improved communication systems to stay in touch with the world by means of television, radio, cell phones, and the Internet. And one thing they can do on their computers, of course, is to watch downloaded footage from *Help!* and perhaps find a special relevance to their cloistered, anxiety-ridden lives in the lyrics of its title song. Whether we will really receive needed "help" to deal with the insecurities of our changed contemporary lives remains to be seen, but at least watching this uniquely prescient film can entertainingly and incongruously make all of its tragic aspects briefly seem more like a comedy.

Notes

1. Edward Gross, *The Fab Films of the Beatles* (Las Vegas, NV: Pioneer Books, 1990), 23. Subsequent page references in the text are to this edition.
2. *Help!* (United Artists, 1965).
3. David Willman, "Suspect Stood to Gain from Anthrax Panic," *The Los Angeles Times*, August 2, 2008, A1; at http://articles.latimes.com/2008/aug/02/nation/na-anthrax2 .
4. One reliable expert on the Beatles, Mark Lewisohn, called the device a "Relativity Cadenza" in *The Complete Beatles Chronicle* (1992; London: Hamlyn, 2003, 188); however, when I viewed the film, the word sounded more like "condenser," and that does make more sense.

9

"A Journey Beyond the Stars"

2001: A Space Odyssey *and* the Psychedelic Revolution in 1960s Science Fiction

ROB LATHAM

Stanley Kubrick's *2001: A Space Odyssey* had a major cultural impact when released in 1968, but also had a significant *sub*cultural impact within the genre of science fiction. SF authors and fans debated, often quite contentiously, the film's scientific accuracy, aesthetic ambition, and the implications of its appeal to mainstream viewers. *2001* also became a potent indicator of just how deeply issues within the Sixties counterculture — especially the messianic transcendentalism of the psychedelic "revolution" — had penetrated into and permeated the SF scene by 1968. Divisions of opinion over the film often devolved into philosophical and political differences regarding the mystical subordination of rationality and merits of synthetic self-transformation. These divisions overlapped, while not quite mapping onto, the spreading conflict over the so-called "New Wave," which divided conservative fans who defended the forms and values of traditional "hard" SF from others who favored a more aesthetically experimental and countercul- turally responsive "speculative" fiction. This chapter examines the reception of *2001* within the SF community, with a particular eye to the ways it initially drew upon — and subsequently informed — the disputes over the New Wave within the genre. An animating concern will be the ways in which 1960s SF was infiltrated and altered by exchanges with the contemporary counterculture.

The roots of New Wave SF can be traced to the British magazine *New Worlds*, specifically a 1962 guest editorial by J. G. Ballard entitled "Which Way to Inner Space?" A scathing manifesto calling for an overhaul of the genre's characteristic themes and styles, Ballard's essay rejected straightforward tales of interstellar adventure in favor of more oblique excursions into shadowy realms of the psyche:

I'd like to see more psycho-literary ideas, more meta-biological and meta-chemical concepts, private time-systems, synthetic psychologies and space-times, more of the sombre half-worlds one glimpses in the paintings of schizophrenics, all in all a complete speculative poetry and fantasy of science.[1]

When Ballard's friend and fellow ideologue Michael Moorcock took over the helm of *New Worlds* in Spring, 1964, this inner space agenda gained a prominent platform. Moorcock, like Ballard, celebrated *avant garde* writers such as William S. Burroughs as pioneers of a new form of SF "which is unconventional in every sense."[2] In an editorial entitled "Symbols for the Sixties," Moorcock demanded an engagement with the militant attitudes and experimental lifestyles of the youth counterculture, claiming that SF should "use images apt for today" and feature "characters fitted for the society of today" rather than recycling outworn ideas.[3] According to SF author Thomas M. Disch, Ballard's "inner space" catchphrase would soon be perceived, by both partisans and opponents of the New Wave, as "shorthand for sex, drugs, and rock 'n' roll."[4]

Indeed, representations of drug use featured prominently in New Wave fiction, perhaps nowhere more brilliantly than in Brian W. Aldiss's "Acid Head Wars," a series of stories (published in *New Worlds* and later gathered as *Barefoot in the Head* [1969]) set in a near-future Europe pixilated by bombardments of weaponized hallucinogens. A delirious evocation of a collective acid fantasy, Aldiss's novel mimics the linguistic kaleidoscope of James Joyce's *Finnegans Wake* in its effort to capture the texture of irremediably stoned consciousness. The psychedelic messiah at the story's center, Colin Charteris, prophesies an evolutionary quantum leap prompted by LSD in terms that eerily echo the plot of *2001*:

My friend[s], that was a short round we trod, less than two hundred degenerations the flintnapping cavesleepers first opened stareyes and we break down again with twentieth century perception of the circuit ... the time for real awakening from machinality and jump off the treads into a new race.[5]

In the face of crazed experiments such as Aldiss's — and other hallucinatory extravaganzas like Chester Anderson's *The Butterfly Kid* (1967) and Robert Silverberg's *Son of Man* (1971) — members of SF's Old Guard began muttering about "the overthrow of all standards and morals" that had seemingly afflicted the genre.[6] SF editor Donald A. Wollheim, for example, accused Moorcock of mounting a "crusade" to convert benighted fans to a fiction at once hedonistic and downbeat, filled with "shock words and shock scenes, hallucinatory fantasies, and sex" (102–105). The scandalized tone of these remarks reflects a growing generation gap within the field, with New Wave fiction being lumped alongside other fashionable provocations by Old Guard fans. Many long-time readers felt the genre's core values were under concerted assault: the stolid rocket jockeys of the pulp tradition were now seen, by the New Wave cohort, not only as boringly square but as complicit agents of a faceless, amoral technocracy — in Disch's words, "human robots inhabit[ing] landscapes that mirrored their own alienation."[7] The New Wave's "inner space" agenda converged with the counterculture critique of what Theodore Roszak called "the myth of objective consciousness," a world-view that represses the body's sensual pleasures in favor of "disinterested" scientific curiosity and the cold calculations of technocratic expertise.[8] The New Wave's delirious psychedelia became, for many Old Guard partisans, merely the most visible emblem of a fashionable yet dangerous nihilism pervading the movement that rejected scientific rationality at its core and thus broke sharply with the mainstream of SF history.

The "generation gap" dividing Old Guard authors and editors like Wollheim from avant-gardists like Moorcock and Disch also marked fan followers of these factions, who translated the struggle into their own hip lingo of sedition and reaction. On one hand, counterculturally-inclined fanzines, such as Raymond Fisher's *Odd*, began promoting the view that "SF is just as fundamentally distrustful of the straight world as is the archetypal hippie, and both have apparently latched on to each other" in a productive process of mutual discovery.[9] On the other hand, John J. Pierce's 'zine *Renaissance* was established expressly to defend genuine SF against "the anti-science fiction of the 'New Thing,' with its emphasis on anti-heroes, plotless disaster stories, the condemnation of science and intelligence as fundamentally evil or useless and its aura of cynicism, cruelty and disgust."[10] The zine's subtitle announced that *Renaissance* was the "semi-official organ of the Second Foundation," a group modeled on the secret society in Isaac Asimov's *Foundation* trilogy, whose task was to preserve human learning amidst an encroaching Dark Age; according to "First Speaker" Lester del Rey, the New Wave was precisely such a barbaric incursion into SF's citadel, whose commitment to science and reason must be protected from this cabal of tripped-out marauders.[11]

One prominent volley in this defense was del Rey's caustic review of *2001* in the July, 1968 issue of *Galaxy*, which drew the film smack into the middle of the enveloping New Wave wars. Briefly and grudgingly praising Kubrick's technical expertise, del Rey proceeded to excoriate the film for its ponderous pace and pervasive "lack of rationality," culminating in this stern denunciation:

> The real message ... is one Kubrick has used before: intelligence is perhaps evil and certainly useless.... Men can only be saved by some vague and unshown mystic experience.... This isn't a normal science-fiction movie at all, you see. It's the first of the New Wave-Thing movies, with the usual empty symbolism. The New Thing advocates were exulting over it as a mind-blowing experience. It takes very little to blow some minds. But for the rest of us, it's a disaster.[12]

Del Rey does not name the New Wave disciples who embraced the film so feverishly, but there must have been lots of them, as *Galaxy* editor Frederik Pohl indicates when he says of del Rey's review that "[n]othing in the magazine's history ever produced as much hate mail from readers, the majority of whom loved the film."[13]

In fact, the response to *2001* within the genre tended to break down along generational lines. As film historian John Brosnan observes:

> the old school of sf ... present[ed] Man as a plucky little creature who faces the Universe with a slide-rule in one hand and a blaster in the other and soon has it cowering in fear. Kubrick, on the other hand, treats the human race with cold irony — presenting Man as an impotent, rather pathetic, helpless pawn of forces beyond his comprehension.[14]

This suggestion that humanity, left to its own meager devices, is incapable of transcendent achievement infuriated many older writers, who lambasted the movie for its chilly disdain towards its characters. As Ray Bradbury commented, "the test of the film is whether or not we care when one of the astronauts dies. We do not"; Kubrick's "freezing touch ... has turned everything ... to ice."[15] For their part, Pohl and son Frederik Pohl IV, who appreciated the film's intellectual ambition, called the culminating Star Gate sequence, with its hallucinatory imagery, "wholly sense-free.... It is not merely that [these scenes] are not logical and explicable. Worse, it is impossible to construct a hypothesis under which they *would* become logical" (173; emphasis in original).

Younger writers and fans, by contrast, embraced the film, not despite but *because* of its enigmatic, oracular quality. Alex Eisenstein, who reportedly saw the movie over eighty times (Pohl and Pohl 167), raved that it "is a prodigious work of art ... a breathtaking achievement." Seeking to rebut criticisms like those of Bradbury, he affirmed that *2001* "is not a cold, intellectual construct, but a grand and eloquent message of the spirit" (cited in Pohl and Pohl 169). Earl Evers, writing in the official 'zine of the Los Angeles Fantasy Fan Federation, claimed that he had repeatedly felt, while watching the movie, that he was "hearing the name of God" and "feel[ing] the pure cosmic power vibrating."[16] But then, as he acknowledged, he was high on LSD at the time. (Evers was probably the most prominent apostle of the chemical revolution in the fan community, penning a "Primer for Heads," with detailed guidance on the powers of various substances, that appeared over four issues of Richard Geis's 'zine *Psychotic* in 1968.) The Star Gate sequence was, Evers avowed, "one of the most beautiful things I've ever seen.... The first few seconds, it was like 'breaking through to the other side'" (45). The experience recalled "dreams I've had while sleeping off a Belladonna trip — endless Dopplers up and down the spectrum, eyeballs that become islands that become the eye of a hurricane seen on radar, and finally the arrival, the place taking shape as a map, then as a series of surrealistic landscapes, never quite coming clear" (45).

In a review-essay, "The Blown Mind on Film," published in the venerable Hugo-winning fanzine *Warhoon* in September 1970, Walter Breen — also well-known as a world-class numismatist, founding member of NAMBLA, and Marion Zimmer Bradley's husband — argued at great length that *2001* expressed "a frankly esoteric or occult frame of reference: ancient Jupiter and Saturn symbolism, the law of karma, Inner Planes after-death survival," all conveyed through imagery whose "total effect ... so closely parallels that of LSD visions as to restimulate such experience in some viewers."[17] Breen concludes that the evidence is overwhelming that "Clarke and/or Kubrick" had intimate personal knowledge of hallucinogenic drugs, "probably during the earliest experiments when the pure Sandoz product was available (far more potent than any black-market LSD)" (24). Breen reports on Clarke's appearance at the 1968 Lunacon in New York City, where he faced a barrage of questions from puzzled fans who demanded to know what was going on in the movie's final sections. "Clarke refused to discuss it in detail ... save to insist that the meanings were there and would have to be thought out by viewers," which Breen takes as proof of Clarke's endorsement of "human metamorphic, out-of-body evolution — as in *Childhood's End* — and his familiarity [presumably from his long residence in Sri Lanka] with the law of karma" (22). This world-view, Breen then suggested, essentially tallied with the "inner space" revolution going on within the genre: *2001* affirms that "it is possible to journey at least mentally ... to accessible realms where time is ... stretched, compressed, shuttled back-and-forth in, twisted spirally or even mirror-imaged at will" and "where space is something that can be stepped around rather than laboriously traversed" (24).

While Clarke himself would probably have resisted this alignment with New Wave experimentation, Breen's comments demonstrate that many SF fans, immersed in the toils of an epochal controversy over the genre's ideological contours, were baffled at this hard-SF champion's apparent apostasy, his sudden conversion to the ranks of mind-blown inner-spacemen. Debates about Clarke's role in the final film — and what SF's Old Guard saw as his potential culpability for its drug-addled, mystical messianism — predictably took front and center as the genre debated the movie's cultural fallout. Del Rey, in his review, suggested that the SF community would have been better served if someone had simply filmed one of Clarke's classic tales of space adventure, such as *Earthlight* (1955), rather than concocting this half-baked metaphysical light-show. Pohl and Pohl suggested that Clarke had been ill-served by Kubrick, that in fact his novelization of the screenplay, published concurrently with the film's release, offered at least a semblance of extrapolative rigor, though ultimately it wasn't clear whether his version of the story "is the same interpretation Kubrick intended" (169). On the other side were defenders of the film like SF author George Turner, who argued, in a symposium on *2001* published in the *Australian Science Fiction Review* in September 1968, that "Kubrick is a greater artist than Clarke could ever pretend to being," taking Clarke's dry ideas and "translat[ing] them] into comprehensible symbols" in a "breathtaking display of virtuosity."[18] Clarke himself, while clearly discomfited by some of the more outré counter-cultural takes on the movie and admittedly irritated by Kubrick's endless tinkering and dithering that stretched the project out over four long years, resolutely refused to reject the finished product even in the face of Old Guard complaints— and, of course, it is worth remembering (as Breen notes) that Clarke's own fictive output, for all its high-tech scientism, had always shown a lingering fondness for mystic reveries and flamboyant gestures of transcendence.

The most scathingly hilarious verdict on the relative contributions of Clarke and Kubrick came some years later from John Clute, in a review of Clarke's 1975 novel *Imperial Earth* that appeared in *New Worlds Ten* (a paperback anthology series, edited by various hands, that replaced Moorcock's magazine after it folded in 1971). Clute depicts the collaboration between the two men as a Faustian pact with the devil: a credulous Clarke, devoted to reason and the utopian perfection of humanity, is approached by the wily, "mesmeric" Kubrick, whose views of human nature are considerably darker.[19] Appearing mysteriously in Clarke's bedroom at midnight, Kubrick pitches the project to him as essential to revitalize the enlightenment spirit in a world grown bleak and strange:

> You gotta show us the high-road out of Shitsville where it sometimes looks like we're for the dark like, you know, like maybe we shoulda deepsixed Newton and all those other sleepwalker fruitcakes back when before they had a chance to dump us here in Shitsville, Arthur, where the centre don't hold [233].

Clarke promises, with valiant naïveté, to do his utmost, and Kubrick leaves the meeting gloating to himself:

> Do you know what I'm going to do, Arthur? I'm going to take the script you give me, full of expansive bland technological and humanist optimism as I'm sure it will be, and out of your dreams for the future I'm going to make *2001, A Space Odyssey*. Ha ha ha. Where your heroes are makers and doers transparent to the light of reason within them defining their natures, mine will be stale hollow puppets, victims of the technology ... *your* heroes integrate with smiling.... I'll just work a sign-change, a semiotic nudge, Arthur, and everyone will be able to see that beneath your dreams of immanent reason squats Shitsville, where we live [233–234; emphasis in original].

In Clute's mordant tongue-in-cheek scenario, Kubrick manipulates and tricks Clarke into providing him with a shiny rationalist alibi for a dark irrationalist vision.

Clute's New Wave-ish mockery of Clarke's childlike faith in reason actually lines up, in some ways, with the anti–New Wave critique of the movie. Old Guard critics such as del Rey and Pohl excoriated the film's depiction of scientists and astronauts as soulless ciphers, whereas it is clear from reading Clarke's novelization that he considered characters like Heywood Floyd and David Bowman to be savvy and capable, if not heroic, figures. The words they speak are Clarke's, but Kubrick — through his mise-en-scène and direction of actors — subtly shifted the tone, and they come across as smug, emotionless drones completely dwarfed by cosmic immensities. Many critics of *2001* within the genre essentially agreed with Clute's tongue-in-cheek verdict: that a too-trusting Clarke had been hoodwinked by a devious trickster whose attitudes aligned more with the New Wave than they did with traditional hard SF. Of course, del Rey's prediction that the film would, as a result, be a "box-office disaster ... and thus set major science-fiction movie making back another ten years" was way off base (194). Indeed, the film's unprecedented success with mainstream viewers, combined with its "mind-blowing" appeal to certain factions of the fan community, not only made it the highest grossing SF film released to date, but also did much to bolster the ideological vision of the nascent New Wave — hence the Old Guard's dyspeptic reactions. The film remains one of the most visible monuments to the crossover between SF and the youth counterculture that the New Wave movement both manifested and promoted.

NOTES

1. J. G. Ballard, "Which Way to Inner Space?," *New Worlds*, 118 (May, 1962), 118.

2. Michael Moorcock, "A New Literature for the Space Age," *New Worlds*, 142 (May/June, 1964), 3.

3. Michael Moorcock, "Symbols for the Sixties," *New Worlds*, 148 (March, 1965), 3.

4. Thomas M. Disch, *The Dreams Our Stuff is Made Of: How Science Fiction Conquered the World* (New York: Free Press, 1998), 108.

5. Brian W. Aldiss, *Barefoot in the Head* (New York: Ace, 1969), 165.

6. Donald A. Wollheim, *The Universe Makers: Science Fiction Today* (New York: Harper & Row, 1971), 104. Subsequent page references in the text are to this edition.

7. Thomas M. Disch, "Introduction: On Saving the World," *The Ruins of Earth: An Anthology of Stories of the Immediate Future*, ed. Disch (New York: Putnam, 1971), 5.

8. Theodore Roszak, *The Making of a Counter Culture: Reflections on the Technocratic Society and its Youthful Opposition* (New York: Anchor, 1969), 208.

9. Richard Gordon, "Brit American (Ob)Scene and Observed," *Odd*, 18 (Spring, 1968), 88.

10. John J. Pierce, "Prospectus," *Renaissance: A Semi-Official Organ of the Second Foundation*, 1 (Winter, 1969), 1.

11. As explained in Lester del Rey, "Other Times, Other Values," *Renaissance: A Semi-Official Organ of the Second Foundation*, 1 (Winter, 1969), 2–4.

12. Del Rey, Review of *2001: A Space Odyssey*, *Galaxy*, 26 (July, 1968), 194. Subsequent page references in the text are to this edition.

13. Frederik Pohl, note, in Pohl and Frederik Pohl IV, *Science Fiction Studies in Film* (New York: Ace, 1981), 181. Subsequent page references in the text are to this edition.

14. John Brosnan, *Future Tense: The Cinema of Science Fiction* (New York: St. Martin's, 1978), 179–180.

15. Ray Bradbury, cited in Brosnan, 179.

16. Earl Evers, "2001 Light Years from Home," *Shangri L'Affaires*, 74 (September 1, 1968), 43–44. Subsequent page references in the text are to this edition.

17. Walter Breen, "The Blown Mind on Film," *Warhoon*, 24 (August, 1968), 23, 24. Subsequent page references in the text are to this edition.

18. George Turner, in Turner, Lee Harding, Mongo MacCallum, and Bruce Gillespie, "A Symposium on *2001: A Space Odyssey*," *Australian Science Fiction Review*, 17 (September, 1968), 5.

19. John Clute, "Arthur C. Clarke's Clone," *New Worlds Ten*, ed. Hilary Bailey (London: Corgi, 1976), 233. Subsequent page references in the text are to this edition.

The Endless Odyssey

The 2001 *Saga and Its Inability to Predict Humanity's Future*

GARY WESTFAHL

In a literary marketplace where sequels to successful works are almost inevitable, it is unsurprising that one of the grandest and most evocative epics in science fiction has generated, by one count, no fewer than nineteen sequels involving four different authors. What *is* surprising is that, despite these efforts to continue this story, it remains conspicuously incomplete—for reasons that convey important messages about the inherent limitations of science fiction when attempting to predict the eventual future of humanity.

I refer to Stanley Kubrick's film *2001: A Space Odyssey* (1968)[1] and the novel of that name simultaneously written by co-screenwriter Arthur C. Clarke; for while its namesake's hero, Homer's Odysseus, finally came home after twenty years of warfare and wandering, Kubrick and Clarke's adventure has reached its forty-second year with no signs that it will ever arrive at its destination.

* * *

To determine how this story should have continued, one logically begins by examining its conclusion. In the more cryptic film, aliens first place a monolith on Earth four million years ago, and after encountering a tribe of prehuman primates, the monolith somehow boosts their intelligence so they can use tools and are soon on their way to becoming fully human and conquering their world. Then, in 2001, a representative human, Dave Bowman, is directed by a second monolith on the Moon to a third monolith orbiting Jupiter, which transports him to a distant world through a hyperspatial Star Gate; the still-unseen aliens study this specimen while he lives out his life to determine exactly how this species should be further improved. Finally, a fourth monolith transforms Bowman into the Star Child and teleports him back to Earth, where he will presumably deploy his new powers—including the ability to survive in the vacuum of space without a spacesuit—to make other humans into superhumans like himself. Thus, as the novel explains, "history as men knew it would be drawing to a close."[2] The novel adds that the Star Child begins by noticing Earth's nuclear weapons and, highly displeased, disintegrates them, indicating that these new beings are immensely powerful and abhor violence, reasonable assumptions to make about advanced beings in light of our civilization's history. However, nothing else is said about this superhuman's characteristics and attitudes, only the novel's final comment that he "would think of something" to do next (221). A proper sequel to *2001: A Space Odyssey*, then, would resolve these uncertainties by describing the further exploits of the transformed Bowman and other members of his new species.

Yet the novel offers a different perspective on precisely what the aliens were doing, in the distant past and twenty-first century. Clarke's first monolith is explicitly described as a teaching machine: transparent rather than black, it produces throbbing noises to hypnotically attract protagonist Moon-Watcher and his companions, entices them with images of well-fed primates like themselves to encourage their progress, forces their bodies through the motions of productive activities like tying knots and employing rocks as weapons, and chooses the most promising candidates for additional education. Thus, in the novel, the prehumans already had the intelligence to use tools, but simply needed training in how to use them; so the monolith instructs the brightest ones, who in turn communicate their new knowledge to their peers.

In Clarke's first version of the story, Bowman's final encounter with the monolith was also an educational, rather than a transformative, experience. This is gleaned from what might be called the first sequel to *2001*, Clarke's *The Lost Worlds of 2001* (1972), which mingles nonfictional chapters about Clarke's experiences during the filming of *2001* with narrative chapters providing fictional materials developed for the story that were omitted from the final film and novel. Its last fictional chapter, "Second Lesson," offers Clarke's original description of what happened to Bowman after leaving the Star Gate. Finding himself on a seemingly endless black plain, Bowman observes not a monolith but an enormous cube that begins generating bright lights and a drumming sound. Then,

> the turning wheels of light merged together, and their spokes, fused into luminous bars that slowly receded into the distance[....] Fantastic, fleeting geometrical patterns flickered in and out of existence, as the glowing grids meshed and unmeshed; and the hominid watched from its metal cave—wide-eyed, slack jawed, and wholly receptive.
> The dancing moiré patterns suddenly faded, and the rhythm sank to a barely audible, almost subsonic, pulsing throb. The cube was empty again; but only for a moment.
> The first lesson having been moderately successful, the second was about to begin.[3]

What Bowman found, in other words, was another teaching machine — suggesting a different interpretation of what happened to him. If Bowman's encounter is precisely analogous to that of his ancestors, it means that contemporary humans already have the ability to become superhuman — but simply need training to learn how to do it. And, if he was now being educated in how to achieve this status, what happened when the elderly Bowman gestured toward the final monolith was not that he was transformed into the Star Child; rather, his lessons completed, he had figured out *how to transform himself* into the Star Child and proceeded to do just that. Afterwards, just as Moon-Watcher and other trained prehumans taught cohorts how to use tools, the Star Child, having returned to Earth, would in parallel fashion teach other humans how to become superhumans (which would explain how humanity's alien manipulators could uplift the entire species with one advanced individual). Yet this story of humanity's further progress is exactly what all sequels to *2001*— with one exception — contrive to avoid.

* * *

If one discounts *The Lost Worlds of 2001*— which does little if anything to extend the original narrative — the first person to produce a sequel to *2001* was comic book writer-artist Jack Kirby. After years of working for Marvel Comics, he surprisingly defected to bitter rival DC Comics in 1969; when he returned to Marvel in the mid–1970s, the company decided that purchasing the rights to *2001: A Space Odyssey* would provide this seasoned creator of epic comic adventures with a fitting challenge. First assigned to adapt the novel as a Marvel Treasury Special, Kirby would then write and draw a new comic book to expand upon and continue its story.

To prepare for these tasks, Kirby presumably watched the film and read Clarke's novel, and his approach may have been inspired by one sentence in the novel about Moon-Watcher's monolith: "Neither it, nor its replicas scattered across half the globe, expected to succeed with all the scores of groups involved in the experiment" (25). So, according to the novel, there were many monoliths in different locations helping many prehumans learn how to become human; analogously, in the future, along with the monolith that encountered and captured Bowman, there might be other monoliths in other regions of space waiting to encounter and transform other astronauts. This premise generated the stories in the first six issues of Kirby's comic.

The initial adaptation of the film was basically faithful to its source material, though Kirby introduced a distinctive version of the monolith as more squarish in size and hovering above the ground, its black surface covered with blue streaks representing its pulsating energies; and to prepare readers for his series, he explains that Bowman is only one of many future superhumans: "He is to be the first of many 'new ones.' For the monolith knows that there must be more than one new seed to sow the harvest of a new species."[4] What was disturbing, and what did not bode well for this project, was that Kirby failed to grasp certain elements of the film's plot. For one thing, Heywood R. Floyd obviously traveled to the Moon to gather information, not to impart it, yet Kirby believes that Floyd was actually sent to lead the lunar briefing; illogically, then, a visitor from Earth informs residents of the Moon about a mysterious object that was discovered on the Moon. Kirby also misses the real reason why Bowman, stranded outside his spacecraft by the demented HAL, finds it difficult to re-enter the *Discovery* through an airlock: rushing to rescue crewmate Frank Poole, he forgot to don his space helmet, so he must briefly expose himself to the lethal vacuum of space to enter the airlock. Bowman employs the pod's explosive bolts for an emergency exit from the rear, instead of using its front door, solely to minimize the time he will be unprotected in space. Yet Kirby numbly draws Bowman wearing his helmet and presents the re-entry as hazardous only because of the explosive bolts which, if he were wearing a helmet, he would not employ. These lapses suggest that Kirby, unlike Kubrick and Clarke, would not develop adventures meticulously based on scientific plausibility, a suspicion validated by later stories featuring battles with evil, humanoid aliens and an improbable swarm of destructive meteoroids.

The first issue's story, "Beast-Killer," introduces the character of that name; though living in the "Miocene Age"[5]— roughly 3 to 5 million years ago, close to the era of Moon-Watcher — he looks like a human, not an apelike hominid, undoubtedly a concession to readers who can better sympathize with characters resembling themselves. Like Moon-Watcher, he has been communing with a mysterious monolith that he calls the "stone-spirit" (3), which taught him how to use a wooden club, but this proves an inadequate tool in hunting and killing large animals when he pauses to fend off other jealous humans seeking a wounded animal and the intended victim is able to escape. He visits the monolith, touches it to mentally communicate the problem, and is taught how to build a better weapon, a stone knife. After killing a saber-tooth tiger with this instrument, Beast-Killer has the additional idea of placing a blade on a long stick to construct a spear; he throws the spear, and in the next panel, recalling the jump-cut in *2001* from bone to spaceship, we see an astronaut in 2001, stranded on an asteroid, tossing an ancient alien artifact in frustration. Woodrow Decker, a descendant of Beast-Killer, is frustrated because he and another astronaut, assigned to search for signs of alien life in the asteroid belt, have found precisely the sort of evidence they sought, but their spacecraft has been destroyed, so they cannot tell others about the discovery. After a red creature with tentacles attacks and kills his colleague Mason, a fleeing Decker encounters a hovering monolith, which dispatches him on a voyage through space to a bucolic field, where a lad greets him and urges Decker to accompany him to a nearby house. While walking, Decker rapidly ages and collapses, whereupon another monolith appears to transform him into a fetus-like Star Child — although Kirby as noted calls these beings "the New Seed" — who promptly embarks upon a cosmic journey.

This story set the pattern for the next two adventures: Kirby retells the original story with new characters while omitting the Floyd episode of a future man traveling to a second monolith which guides another human to a third monolith, to be transformed by a fourth monolith. Instead, there is first a prehistoric human who is trained or made more intelligent by a monolith, then an abrupt transition to a future human who is transported by a second monolith to be transformed into a New Seed by a third monolith. The other differences are that, as a concession to the comic book medium, Kirby includes as much action and violence as possible — in "Beast-Killer," a battle between prehistoric humans and struggle with an exotic monster — and instead of having transported astronauts finding themselves alone in an earthlike environment, Kirby introduces human companions who are presumably alien constructs, keeping the story lively with conversation. Further, while Kubrick and Clarke's Star Child returned to Earth to contemplate his home, each of Kirby's New Seeds, like Decker, "answers the call of the beckoning cosmos" (31) and travels into deep space — suggesting that beings who can survive in space would probably prefer to live there, their natural home, instead of enduring a planet's confining gravity. Kirby finally provides his superhumans with another human trait — curiosity about their universe — since the third New Seed, in "Wheels of Death," embarks upon his journey through space because he is "eager — impatient to thrive and discover."[6]

Interestingly, in the Kirby comments that fill the first issue's page of "Monolith Mail" which cannot yet feature readers' letters about the just-published comic, the writer-artist indicates that he has no real intention of ever taking the story much further than the original film and novel:

> the New Seed is the conquering hero in this latest Marvel drama. Why? Because he has staying power, that's why. He will always be there in the story's final moments to taunt us with the question we shall never answer. The little shaver is, perhaps, the embodiment of our own hopes in a world which daily makes us more than a bit uneasy about our future.[7]

Kirby states out loud what will emerge as one major reason why sequels to *2001* say little about humanity's successors — because from a human perspective, the nature of superhumanity is a "question we shall never answer." He is instead inclined or obliged to present his New Seed as essentially a metaphor for something quintessentially human:

> the New Seed is no more than the spirit of our own self-belief, our own confidence in the stubborn rationale which has brought us from the caves to condominiums in the suburbs[....] The New Seed merely says that we can still do it. We can keep the environment *and* ourselves running into the distant future. We can, someday, knock off our hostilities and concentrate together on the great mystery of the stars [19].

If Kirby erroneously believed that readers would embrace a continuation of *2001* that never advanced beyond creating one New Seed after another and presented them only as enigmatic representatives of human stick-to-it-ivity, he would soon learn of their desire for substantive information regarding the nature and activities of these superhumans. But for now, Kirby had a plan, and he followed it in the next five issues.

As the novelty in the second issue's story, a prehistoric *woman* in an unspecified era finds a monolith and, inspired by the encounter, figures out that she can disguise herself as a god and thus be worshipped, fed, and sheltered by her fellow humans; then, a female astronaut exploring Ganymede survives a battle with sinister aliens in flying saucers and is taken by a monolith through space to enjoy a swim with old neighbors before becoming Kirby's second New Seed.[8] In the two-part story in the third and fourth issues,[9] a warrior who lived 200,000 years ago converses with an old man who gets ideas from a monolith; taken to his monolith, Marak receives a vision that he must seek a warrior queen named Jalessa. Training his men to ride horses and inventing the wheel, Marak takes them to her kingdom and meets Jalessa, also being assisted by a monolith, and they form a partnership (and implied romantic relationship) to further advance humanity. Then, in a space station orbiting Mars, commander Herbert Marik orders his crew to abandon the station before it is destroyed by meteoroids; remaining there, he finds a monolith which takes him to a meeting with Jalessa — presented as a reunion — in an idyllic kingdom before becoming the third New Seed. The added element here is that, like the monolith in Clarke's novel which carefully selected the brightest prehumans, Kirby's monoliths do not assist whatever random humans come in contact with them, but rather seek out and uplift only especially promising candidates.

In the two-part story in the fifth and sixth issues,[10] Kirby alters his pattern by eliminating the prehistoric prelude and simply describes a future man's encounters with monoliths. Harvey Norton loves visiting "Comicsville" where he acts out being a superhero with realistic props and live actors, but a monolith intrudes upon the scripted action, encouraging him to abandon a society obsessed with illusory experiences to become an astronaut who has actual adventures in space. Specifically, he soon rescues an alien princess from fellow beings seeking to abduct her by fleeing with her to another galaxy; besieged by would-be captors, the princess escapes via a teleportation device but Norton is trapped in rubble, whereupon a monolith first refashions him into a genuine superhero and then transforms him into another New Seed.

In this story, Kirby may provide interesting commentary on the mentality of readers who love comics and suggest that they may devote too much of their lives to fantasies — a surprising message in a comic book — but again does nothing to advance his story, and readers were growing impatient. "I'm hoping #3 doesn't end like the first two. I suggest having different endings," wrote one reader in the fifth issue's letter column.[11] More complaints emerged in the sixth issue: "I don't believe readers are going to get too excited reading a variation of the same story every issue." "Where is this comic going?" "Is there any long-range plan in mind for this book?" In response, the unnamed editor could only urge readers to be "patient."[12]

Finally, instead of concluding with a human's transformation into a New Seed, the seventh issue's story, "The New Seed," begins with this event and follows the evolved being as he voyages through space. While finding the experience pleasurable — he "begins to know the joy of pursuing the comets and racing meteors in their fiery flights"— the New Seed devotes his time to examining many worlds, including a barren, lifeless planet, a world with prehistoric creatures, and a world with advanced technology.[13] But he lingers at one "planet of smashed cities ... to marvel at the folly which could generate such massive and complete destruction" (11). Sadly observing desperate survivors fighting with each other to survive on the dying world, he is moved by the senseless murder of a man and woman and decides, "Life must be perpetuated. Though I could not involve myself in their destiny, I can act when it no longer exists. I can claim what remains" (27). Taking the couple's glowing life-energy, he transports it to a hospitable but lifeless planet and leaves it there to begin the evolution of life: "A quest is fulfilled ... a mission completed. A billion years will pass before lovers may live again to test the whims of fate...." Then he flies away to seek the answer to "the why of being" (31).

Of all the works that purport to continue or revisit *2001: A Space Odyssey*, "The New Seed" might be called its only genuine sequel, since it alone describes what happens to a representative superhuman after his creation. But it is also an unfinished sequel: if the original story ended with the superhuman's birth, "The New Seed" limits itself to his early childhood, as he experiences his first space journey and takes his first actions to improve the cosmos. We learn that Kirby's New Seed, like the novel's transformed Bowman, despises violence, and though bound by a curious prohibition against meddling in the "destiny" of other creatures, he will do what he can to preserve and extend life in the universe — another logical deduction to make about a superhuman's priorities. However, by helping to create other species resembling the being he once was, the New Seed conspicuously neglects development of his own species— anticipating Clarke's coming transformation of the Star Child into an errand boy instead of progenitor of a new race — and illustrates one strategy to avoid depictions of superintelligent beings: envisioning them as being focused on, or even obsessed with, the activities of lesser species, which shifts attention away from humanity's successors back to humanity, or species that resemble humanity.

It is particularly incongruous that all New Seeds go off by themselves, when members of a new, superintelligent species would naturally wish to come together to collectively progress toward supercivilization. For after encountering the monolith, Moon-Watcher did not embark upon a solo quest to learn more about his planet and test his new powers; instead, he remained with other members of his tribe and helped them master their environment. Kirby's new beings, if never in contact with each other, will be limited in how they can develop and grow.

Whether further Kirby adventures involving the New Seed would have intelligently addressed these issues seems unlikely, but as it turned out, he never even made the attempt, as the next issue of *2001: A Space Odyssey* lurched in a new direction. With readers frustrated by a story going nowhere, sales of the comic must have declined — presumably inspiring spirited in-house discussions about strategies for reviving the series. Since most successful comics feature superheroes, the answer would be obvious: *2001: A Space Odyssey* must shift its focus to the action-packed adventures of a superhero. Thus, the eighth issue's story describes a secret military effort to develop intelligent, powerful robots; however, since they go "berserk" and become destructive,[14] scientists must activate the self-destruct mechanism in each model and resolve to abandon the project. But one scientist, having grown attached to model X-51, gives him a human face, removes his explosive device, and sets him free — whereupon he is puzzled to find that everybody in the world wishes to destroy him. When he is captured and his face is removed, the monolith briefly appears on the final page to free him, displaying an interest in the robot's survival and development — we are told that the monolith "is destined to serve him" (31) — but the story otherwise has nothing to do with preceding issues. In fact, to most commentators, the lethal malfunctioning of HAL in the original story — the most advanced tool humans had crafted — apparently illustrates that tool-building is of limited value, requiring another leap forward in humanity's evolution for the species to further progress without tools. Thus, immediately after Bowman deactivates HAL — symbolically recognizing that such constructs represents a dead end for human development — he fittingly travels to another world to become a superhuman. Thus, it is strange to posit that the monoliths would at some point lose interest in creating New Seeds and instead mentor a form of machine intelligence as a new direction for the advancement of life. Still, a robot with super-strength and gravity-defying powers, initially named "Mister Machine," enabled Kirby to fill the issue with scenes of spectacular violence, which was presumably the point.

In the ninth issue's story, the robot gets his face back and does more fighting while again briefly communing with the monolith, which says that he should "not seek destiny," but rather allow destiny to "find me."[15] However, this exercise in boosting reader interest had the opposite effect on this reader, and I never purchased — and still have not read — the tenth and final issue of *2001: A Space Odyssey*, which again featured Mister Machine.[16] (Online sources indicate that the monolith does not even appear in the issue, rendering the story a sequel to *2001* only in name.) Then, abandoning the pretense that this new story arc had anything to do with Kubrick and Clarke's epic, Marvel ended the *2001* comic and launched a new title — *Machine Man* — to feature the further adventures of the renamed hero, now presented without references to alien monoliths. While this comic only lasted for nineteen issues, the character resurfaces at times in the Marvel universe, but persons interested in *2001* have no reason to examine his further exploits.

* * *

While Kirby labored to extend the saga of *2001*, its co-creator Arthur C. Clarke was preparing to retire. Newly prominent because of the success of *2001* and appearances as a commentator during television coverage of the Apollo missions, Clarke obtained a then-impressive one-million-dollar advance to write three unrelated novels which Clarke announced would be his final works. Yet data about Jupiter's moons from the *Voyager* space probes inspired an idea for a sequel to *2001*, originally drafted as a film scenario; but when his agent instead suggested writing a novel, Clarke set to work on *2010: Odyssey Two*, which became a best-seller in 1982.

More so than most science fiction writers, Clarke had previously dealt with the topic of humanity's future evolution. His first novel, *Against the Fall of Night* (1948, 1953), revised as *The City and the Stars* (1956), intimated that the vanished human race of the far future had advanced to some higher level, leaving behind remnants of ordinary humanity in two cities on Earth. But he directly described a transition from humanity to superhumanity in *Childhood's End* (1953), wherein aliens conquer Earth to prepare humans for the next step in the evolution of intelligence, merging into a group mind. The only surviving representative of the human race does not find his successors to be a pretty sight:

> They might have been savages, engaged in some complex ritual dance. They were naked and filthy, with matted hair obscuring their eyes. As far as Jan could tell, they were of all ages from five to fifteen, yet they all moved with the same speed, precision, and complete indifference to their surroundings.
> Then Jan saw their faces. He swallowed hard, and forced himself not to turn away. They were emptier than the faces of the dead, for even a corpse has some record carved by time's chisel upon its features, to speak when the lips themselves are dumb. There was no more emotion or feeling here than in the face of a snake or an insect.[17]

The alien Overlord must remind him that "You are not watching human children" and "They have no more identity than the cells in your own body. But linked together, they are something much greater than you" (202, 203). This new collective being demonstrates its powers by transforming itself into pure energy, destroying Earth, and leaving to pursue its superhuman destiny.

Evidently, Clarke was disquieted by the logic that led to this vision, prompting him to precede the novel with an unusual note—"The opinions expressed in this book are not those of the author" ([4])— as if to reassure readers that he really did not believe that anything like this would happen. This might be why, in crafting a sequel to *2001*, he would avoid the disturbing question of how humanity might evolve in the future and take the story in other directions.

Of course, the original story had involved *two* races which had advanced beyond humanity — the Star Child, and the aliens behind the monoliths — and *2010: Odyssey Two* for the first time describes the latter beings. In their physical nature, they have undergone a transformation not unlike that observed in *Childhood's End*, albeit in stages:

> The first explorers of Earth had long since come to the limits of flesh and blood; as soon as their machines were better than their bodies, it was time to move. First their brains, and then their thoughts alone, they transferred into shiny new homes of metal and plastic[....]
> But the age of the Machine-entities swiftly passed. In their ceaseless experimenting, they had learned to store knowledge in the structure of space itself, and to preserve their thoughts for eternity in frozen lattices of light. They could become creatures of radiation, free at last from the tyranny of matter.[18]

However, it remains unclear whether they have evolved into a group intelligence; for after experiencing the "presence" of "a vast mentality, an implacable will" (176), the transformed Bowman

> realized that more than one entity was controlling and manipulating him. He was involved in a hierarchy of intelligences, some close enough to his own primitive level to act as interpreters. Or perhaps they were all aspects of a single being.
> Or perhaps the distinction was totally meaningless [198].

The other point Clarke stresses about these aliens involves their mission, which has been subtly but significantly altered from what one would infer from the original story:

> When they looked out across the deeps of space, they had felt awe, and wonder, and loneliness. As soon as they possessed the power, they set forth for the stars. In their explorations, they encountered life in many forms and watched the workings of evolution on a thousand worlds. They saw how often the first faint sparks of intelligence flickered and died in the cosmic night.
> And because, in all the Galaxy, they had found nothing more precious than Mind, they encouraged its dawning everywhere. They became farmers in the fields of stars; they sowed, and sometimes they reaped.
> And sometimes, dispassionately, they had to weed [265].

While broadly congruent with the behavior observed in the first story, this account of the aliens' motives has two aspects that previously were neither explicit nor implicit. First, we learn that the aliens are sometimes displeased with the results of interventions and consequently take action to eliminate the transformed species; thus, they may become enemies, not benefactors — a notion to be amplified in future sequels. Second, the aliens are now exclusively concerned with transitions from non-intelligence to intelligence; nothing is said about initiatives to boost already intelligent beings to higher levels of intelligence. In this way, Clarke betrays the promise of the film and novel; for in changing Bowman into the Star Child, Clarke now asserts, the aliens were not seeking to advance humanity beyond its current level. Instead, they had different reasons. Further, since later sequels to *2001* will mirror *2010* in declining to portray Bowman as a representative of a new superhuman species, and offer no other depictions of such a new species, the saga henceforth will address the subject of humanity's future only indirectly: since the aliens who constructed the monoliths are more advanced than humans, any information about their nature and behavior functions as a provocative suggestion, or even prediction, of what humanity's nature and behavior might someday become.

By expediently demoting the Star Child, Clarke had to confront one question: if not to serve as the vanguard of a new species, why *did* the aliens transform Bowman into this novel form? The prosaic answer in *2010* is that Bowman "was being used as a probe, sampling every aspect of human affairs [...] rather like a hunting dog on a leash, allowed to make excursions of his own, yet nevertheless compelled to obey the overriding wishes of his master" (168). In other words, instead of bothering to return to assess the results of their labors, the aliens made Bowman an ethereal superman so he could examine everything and report back to them. Since the aliens are said to be made of pure energy with the apparent power to communicate, and even travel, faster than light, the reason why they need a surrogate to survey Earth and its environs is not clear; but Clarke resolves the issue in later sequels by claiming that Bowman has really only been in contact with and controlled by the monolith, functioning as an automatic machine, not with its alien makers.

Clarke also reduces the powers and abilities of the transformed Bowman, further diminishing his significance. In the novel, he had seemed an almost omnipotent free agent who dislikes nuclear weapons and, with a thought, instantly eliminates them. But this Bowman, controlled by aliens, is described as a "puppet" (178), "tool" (198), and "pet dog" (189, 271), dispatched to Earth simply to observe and report on how humanity evolved since the monolith's intervention, though he indulgently makes side trips to visit his mother and an old girlfriend. His reduced powers are limited to the ability to mentally throw a switch and prematurely detonate an atomic weapon launched at him. Thus, this Bowman is far removed from the infant superman of the original story.

After examining humanity on Earth, Bowman travels to Jupiter to discover two forms of alien life: balloon-like creatures in Jupiter's upper atmosphere, not unlike those in Clarke's "A Meeting with Medusa" (1971), and various creatures emerging in the underground seas of the moon Europa, though these tend to quickly become extinct due to constantly changing conditions. Concluding that Jovians do not have the potential to be intelligent, whereas Europans do, the aliens implement a bold plan: to transform Jupiter into a star, destroying its indigenous life but providing Europa with a regular source of heat and energy to allow its creatures to evolve toward intelligence. A secondary motive is to provide humans with amenable new worlds to inhabit, as suggested by the mes-

sage sent to humanity after Jupiter ignites: "ALL THESE WORLDS ARE YOURS—
EXCEPT EUROPA. ATTEMPT NO LANDINGS THERE" (277). Perhaps, then, even if
the aliens no longer wish to further improve the species they uplifted to intelligence, they are willing to do other things to assist in their further progress—
such as providing new environments. Still, the lengthy descriptions of lifeforms
on Europa and Jupiter—which Clarke deemed important enough to repeat,
almost verbatim, in later sequels to *2001*—indicate that the aliens' main interest
now is their new project, not the already-improved human race. Indeed, the
"gift" of the Jovian moons might be regarded more as a bribe, to induce humans
to stay away from Europa in exchange for other attractive worlds.

In another way, Clarke undermines one implicit message in the original
film. Anyone evaluating *2001: A Space Odyssey* might conclude that director
Kubrick did not select particularly talented actors; provided them with dialogue
that was mostly banal or bureaucratic, and not much of it; and did not urge
them to deliver lines with any force or conviction. While these judgments apply
to other performers, they seem especially true regarding William Sylvester, the
unheralded actor portraying Floyd. However, since one would not make these
observations about other Kubrick films, one must assume a deliberate intent
behind this apparent dereliction of directorial duty. By one argument, Kubrick
sought to show that, in the millennia since Moon-Watcher first used tools,
humans have gradually grown so dependent upon mechanical tools that they
have become like machines themselves, incapable of genuine communication
or emotional responses—as reflected in their superficial conversations and
robotic demeanors. Bowman's decision to disable HAL and eliminate this tool's
influence, and subsequent transformation from a stiff, spacesuited figure into
a rounded, superhuman fetus, thus signal an evolutionary move away from
mechanical lifestyles and back toward true, full-blooded humanity, albeit at a
new level of intelligence.

In the novel, Floyd was no better developed than in the film, but Clarke
was then relatively indifferent toward characterization. Perhaps in response to
criticisms, however, the later Clarke worked harder to make characters seem
like real, complex people; so, employing Floyd as the protagonist of *2010*, he
unsurprisingly strived to reshape the previously-nondescript Floyd into a
nuanced, communicative person who enjoys warm relationships with his second
wife, young son, and scientific colleagues and responds with strong emotions
to various events. Yet, if people in the twenty-first century, surrounded by
machines, remain capable of retaining their humanity like the reinvented Floyd,
there is seemingly no need for our race to undergo further evolutionary development—which would explain and justify the new indifference of the monolith
builders to that issue. The same problem is even more evident in the film based
on *2010*.

*   *   *

Even if its sequel lacked the scope and *gravitas* of *2001: A Space Odyssey*, it still seemed sufficiently appealing to merit a film version — Clarke's original plan — and after Kubrick declined an offer to become involved, the project was given to writer-director Peter Hyams, making him the third author to wrestle with the problem of how to continue the *2001* saga. Predictably — since Hyams, unlike Kubrick, was never noted for daring or originality — his screenplay for the film, retitled *2010: The Year We Make Contact* (1984), closely followed Clarke's novel.[19] However, Hyams added some distinctive elements to the story, generally taking it even further away from the promise of the original conclusion.

First, while Kubrick recruited undistinguished actors with limited emotional ranges, Hyams hired more talented performers. Thus, though Sylvester was active and presumably available, he recast the part of Floyd with a more renowned and respected actor, Roy Scheider; and two other cast members, John Lithgow and Helen Mirren, had been or would be nominated for an acting Oscar (like Scheider). Hyams is also visibly anxious to take advantage of these performers' skills to depict fully rounded characters; thus, while omitting some events from Clarke's novel, he retains and emphasizes Floyd's close relationships with his family, including a series of scenes showing Floyd playing with his son that have no counterpart in the novel, and Scheider, as is his habit, regularly displays strong emotional reactions (unlike Sylvester). As for the other Americans voyaging to Jupiter, computer expert Dr. Chandra (Bob Balaban) is given an appealing back story, as he tends to form emotional relationships with computers, motivating him to revive and rehabilitate his former creation and associate, HAL, while engineer Walter Curnow (John Lithgow) is made endearing by his amusing reluctance to travel through space from the Russian spacecraft *Leonov* to the abandoned *Discovery*.

Further, in contrast to the minimal, superficial dialogue in the original film, Hyams's screenplay offers almost nonstop conversations that sometimes become intimately personal. This approach is signaled by the way Hyams's film begins: whereas *2001* opened with a long sequence depicting prehuman primates with no dialogue at all, *2010: The Year We Make Contact* begins, like Clarke's novel, with a lengthy conversation between two contemporary humans — which is not enlivened by the novel setting of a radio telescope and the device of having speakers Floyd and Russian Dimitri Moisevitch (Dana Elcar) shout at each other from different levels of its staircase until they get close enough for normal speech. In this film, unlike *2001*, the only barrier to true communication between humans is excessive distance. The rest of the film also features continuous conversations between the Americans and Russians on the *Leonov*, so much so as to force the revived HAL (again voiced by Douglas Rain) to alter his manner of communication: though he spoke in slow, measured tones in *2001*, recognizing that the laconic Bowman and Poole were not anxious to speak, this film's HAL must talk more quickly to get a word in edgewise amidst Hyams's chatterboxes. The film thus conveys, even more than Clarke's sequel, that people of the twenty-first century are both highly emotional and effectively communicative, requiring no evolutionary improvements to recapture their basic humanity.

A filmmaker without Kubrick and Clarke's singular agenda would of course naturally opt for full-bodied characters who do a lot of talking, the usual pattern in popular films, and this is also justifiable given that Clarke's novel moved in this direction as well. But Hyams surprisingly did not take advantage of opportunities for other crowd-pleasing developments provided by *2010: Odyssey Two*. Specifically, though the subtitle *The Year We Make Contact* announces the story will focus on encounters with alien life, the film strangely downplays that aspect of the novel. True, the Jupiter mission sends a probe to Europa where there are said to be signs of life, and its apparently intentional destruction seems the work of the beings behind the monolith; true, the film retains (with additions to be discussed) the final message from the aliens that could be regarded as humanity's first contact with an alien intelligence. Still, in the film, the variegated creatures of Europa described in the novel are never observed, and the balloon-like lifeforms in Jupiter's atmosphere are entirely omitted. A filmmaker, one might think, would seize upon Clarke's intricate descriptions of these beings to enthrall audiences with bizarre images of exotic aliens, persuasively rendered with superb special effects—an attraction that the original *2001* contemplated but did not provide. Yet Hyams seemingly did not want to face the challenge of representing actual aliens; perhaps he was uncomfortable with special effects, since his scenes of spacecrafts, astronauts, and Jupiter, in contrast to Kubrick's brilliant work, are conspicuously inferior and never quite realistic. Kubrick's film, even today, can trick viewers into imagining that they are watching footage of actual spacecraft and space travelers, but audiences watching *2010* will always know they are watching a film with second-rate special effects.

One might defend Hyams, though, by arguing that he had his own agenda, making the absence of aliens and unconvincing special effects appropriate; for apparently, Hyams wished to depict the aliens who made the monoliths as still mainly focused on human progress, if not human evolution, even as Clarke indicated that they were now more interested in other promising races. As noted, Hyams retains minimal references to their desire to protect the Europans by their destruction of the probe and brief message; Floyd's closing voiceover mentions the anticipated appearance of intelligent Europans—"Someday, the children of the new sun will meet the children of the old. I think they will be our friends"; and the film's final image, a monolith standing in shallow water on Europa's surface, suggests that aliens will soon advance the Europans just as they once advanced Earth's prehumans. Yet Hyams mostly keeps his attention, and his aliens' attention, squarely on humanity; indeed, his major revision of Clarke's story emphasizes that the monolith builders make Jupiter a star primarily to assist a human race seemingly bent upon its own destruction.

That is, while Clarke's *2010*, reflecting the political climate of the early 1980s, indicates only that American-Soviet relations in the twenty-first century remain tense, generating minor tensions during negotiations for a joint Soviet-American expedition to investigate the *Discovery*, Hyams adds a genuine crisis: as the *Leonov* approaches Jupiter, America and Russia become enmeshed in a military dispute over Honduras, leading to provocative incidents, casualties, a break in diplomatic relations, and an order that Americans on the mission must leave the *Leonov*, which is Soviet territory, go to the abandoned *Discovery*, and have no further contact with former crewmates. Matters have grown so grim that characters wonder if Earth will still be there when they return, anticipating a devastating nuclear war. Fortunately, humanity's alien mentors have seemingly been monitoring the situation, and by means of forceful intervention they seek to resolve the dispute — apparently reasoning that transforming Jupiter into a star, and making its moons suitable for human habitation, will provide humans with new worlds to inhabit and eliminate any reason for conflicts over territories on Earth. That this, not developing intelligent life on Europa, is their major motive is made explicit in the seven new words that Hyams adds to his otherwise-slight alteration of Clarke's original message:

ALL THESE WORLDS
ARE YOURS EXCEPT
EUROPA
ATTEMPT NO LANDING THERE
USE THEM TOGETHER
USE THEM IN PEACE

Immediately thereafter, chastised and humbled by this extraordinary gesture and advice, leaders of the two nations, Floyd reports, "perhaps [...] learned something because they finally recalled their ships and their planes," ending the crisis.

The story's original vision of a threatened humanity requiring further evolution is now reinterpreted in a trivial manner. For Hyams, the problems facing humans today are not ingrained issues like overreliance on tools, inability to feel genuine emotions, or absence of meaningful communication; rather, people are tense because they are crammed together on Earth, and if given some more places to live, like newly hospitable Jovian moons, they will be all right. And, if the aliens' major concern is to ensure that the humanity they once crafted survives its latest catastrophe, it makes sense for Hyams's film to omit depictions of aliens and render space in a slipshod manner — because his focus, basically, is almost entirely on Earth.

If this statement seems extreme, consider another significant difference between the original film and Hyams's sequel: except for the prologue involving human ancestors in Africa, not a single moment of *2001: A Space Odyssey* takes place on Earth: the modern story begins with Floyd in space, en route to the space station and later the Moon, shifts to the *Discovery* already voyaging to

Jupiter, and concludes with the Star Child hovering above the planet. Our only glimpses of future Earth come in brief videophone or television transmissions. Since the film's protagonists spend all their time away from their home planet, the implicit message is that in the twenty-first century, humanity's natural home is no longer Earth, but rather space; and an often-overlooked aspect of Bowman's transformation, as noted, is that as the Star Child, he can survive in space without a spacesuit, making him well suited for perpetual life in space. In contrast, *2010* begins with an extended depiction of Floyd's pleasant existence on Earth in 2010, including his attractive home life, and concludes with a series of images of familiar Earth landmarks and a scene of Floyd and his family on a beach before that final glimpse of Europa. Here, the implicit message is that humanity's natural home, in the past and future, remains planet Earth.

Overall, Hyams weakens Clarke's story with a trite overlay — a simplistic call for world peace as the once-enigmatic aliens' chief motive — and the conservative argument that humanity need not evolve or abandon its home. However, as if to compensate for his film's general banality, the writer-director does offer some concluding comments from Floyd, obviously crafted with great care, that belatedly provide a few interesting ideas and represent Hyams's only noteworthy contribution to the *2001* saga.

Speaking to his son while beginning his voyage home, Floyd first contemplates the amazing event he has witnessed and speculates that "Maybe this is what happened on Earth millions of years ago." While adding that "Maybe it's something completely different," Floyd basically theorizes that something resembling the transformation of Jupiter occurred in Earth's past. One might argue that Floyd is simply making an incorrect guess about the aliens' earlier actions, since their only observed intervention in Earth's prehistory involved boosting our intelligence, not altering our environment. However, nothing in the original saga contradicts Floyd's hypothesis. Perhaps, the appearance of the monolith four million years ago was not their first good deed on our behalf; perhaps they also visited Earth earlier and carefully shaped the Solar System to ensure that it would include a suitable star with a planet perfectly situated and equipped first for the development of life, and later for intelligent life.

Floyd's theory is defensible because it is based upon an analogy between what he witnessed in 2010 — cosmic engineering on a vast scale — and what aliens might have done in Earth's distant past. If he is right, the pattern of alien intervention into the evolution of other beings would not involve the two-step pattern presented in *2001*—first, finding suitable species and raising them to intelligence, then elevating them to a higher level — but a different two-step pattern: first, altering a planet's physical environment to increase the chances that promising beings might emerge there (their unknown actions long ago in the Solar System, transforming Jupiter into a star to make Europa amenable to evolution); and second, altering the resulting beings' mental makeup to make them intelligent (the monolith's education of Moon-Watcher and his tribe on

Earth, placement of the monolith on Europa to someday do the same for the Europans), with ongoing monitoring to ensure that the uplifted species remains alive during the sorts of crises that typically afflict developing civilizations. If nothing else, this idea represents a fuller and more cohesive way to reinterpret the aliens' entire agenda, and this conceit might have led Clarke, or someone else, to craft not a sequel to *2001* but a prequel, describing spectacular stellar or planetary changes made by ancient aliens to lay the groundwork for the development of the primates they would return to educate in the original story's prologue.

In keeping with the notions that aliens may have been responsible for crafting our environment, and may maintain interest in our progress, Floyd concludes with a novel description of the monolith builders: "You can tell your children of the day when everyone looked up and realized that we were only tenants of this world. We have been given a new lease — and a warning — from the landlord." In Clarke's vision, the aliens were busy travelers who planted monoliths in various locations and then hurried on, never lingering to assess the fruits of their labors or check on the progress of uplifted species. Justifying their singular intervention into a specific crisis, Hyams instead portrays the aliens as the "landlords" of Earth (and presumably other inhabited worlds), who like terrestrial landlords keep a constant eye on their property and take immediate action if there is some threat. Floyd's "new lease" might mean that the aliens have prevented the Earth from being destroyed, renewing humanity's occupation of that planet, or he might be thinking about the new worlds now open to human occupation. His comment about "a warning" is less clear. Perhaps, Floyd feels humans are being warned that, if they misbehave again, their alien overseers might not be around, or might be disinclined, to save them again; or perhaps, in keeping with Clarke's comment that the aliens sometimes "had to weed," Floyd fears that if humans keep behaving badly, their "landlord" might evict them — that is, exterminate them — though nothing else in the film supports the sense, which emerges in Clarke's later sequels to *2001*, that the aliens might be more sinister than benign.

Finally, Floyd's speech includes a provocative comment about the monolith: "I still don't know really what the monolith is. I think it's many things — an embassy for intelligence beyond ours, a shape of some kind for something that has no shape." Here, Floyd — and Hyams — are mixing metaphors: a landlord has power over a tenant, but a nation with an embassy in another country merely endeavors to maintain communication with a presumed equal; but this alternate image does comfortingly suggest that, before they do anything rash, the aliens may at least consult with humanity. And calling the monolith "a shape [...] for something that has no shape" may represent a watered-down version of the fleeting observation in *2010: Odyssey Two* that the monolith was multi-dimensional ("How obvious, now, was that mathematical ratio of its sides, the quadratic sequence 1:4:9! And how naive to have imagined that the series ended there, in only three dimensions!" [149]).

Overall, however, a few good ideas in its coda do not make *2010* a good movie, and though (according to the Internet Movie Database) the film earned more money than it cost to make, its overall box office of around $40 million dollars—much less than *2001*, even without considering inflation—were surely disappointing, which explains why Clarke's other two sequels to *2001* were never adapted as films.

*   *   *

Clarke wanted to wait for new data about Jupiter from the Galileo space probe, due to arrive around 1990, before continuing the *2001* saga, but when the 1986 *Challenger* disaster postponed its launch, he decided to proceed without new information; cynics might note that completing and publishing *2061: Odyssey Three* earlier than planned, in 1987, when memories of the previous book and film adaptation were fresh, made better business sense as well. Certainly, it is the book in the series that contributes the least to the story, heightening suspicions that Clarke primarily wrote it for the money.

To convey the novel's emptiness, one notes that for much of its length, Clarke seemingly forgets about monoliths, the transformed Bowman, or alien efforts to oversee the development of intelligence; the topics do not come up as Clarke crafts another sedate adventure involving Floyd. Although an elderly man in 2061, he accepts an invitation from a billionaire to accompany other celebrities on a voyage in his private spaceship, the *Universe*, to rendezvous with Halley's Comet, again approaching Earth. In the meantime, Clarke employs a recent theory that gas giants like Jupiter might have cores of solid diamond to generate some melodramatic hijinks: having discovered that a fragment from Jupiter's core, which shattered when the planet became a star, landed on Europa to provide the moon with a mountain of diamonds, dubbed Mount Zeus, a diamond company plants an agent on a spaceship traveling near Jupiter who hijacks the ship and forces it to land on Europa, presumably to gain access to the moon's enormous deposits of diamonds. Although the agent is killed, thwarting the scheme, the disabled spaceship is stranded on Europa with a crew in need of rescue, which humanity seeks to effect as quickly as possible, since they worry about how the aliens might react to this conspicuous violation of their orders. As the only suitable spacecraft in the vicinity, the *Universe* is asked to rush to Europa and retrieve the crew before anything happens.

Amidst these goings-on, only Floyd recalls that there was once a man named Bowman who had been transformed into an ethereal representative of the aliens, and after discussing matters, people on the *Universe* agree that it might be a good idea for Floyd to send him a radio message, explaining the situation. The only immediate response is that Floyd dreams about the monolith, and he is never contacted by Bowman. But Clarke, in the next-to-last chapter of his novel, finally provides readers with a glimpse of what Bowman has been up to since the end of *2010*.

First, expanding upon what was conveyed at the end of that novel, we learn that Bowman was allowed to bring the deceased HAL into his company as a second, disembodied servant for the monolith. Then, to address the crisis, they decide that since Floyd's grandson is a member of the crew on Europa, they should create a duplicate of Floyd to attract his grandson's attention and give him an important message: that his crew must move away from a dangerous position so the *Universe* can safely retrieve them. And while explaining matters to their new friend, Bowman and HAL first provide some more information about the monolith:

> It is a tool, serving many purposes. Its prime function appears to be as a catalyst of intelligence[....] In Africa, four million years ago, it gave a tribe of starving apes the impetus that led to the human species. Now it has repeated the experiment here — but at an appalling cost.
> When Jupiter was converted into a sun so that this world could realize its potential, another biosphere was destroyed.[20]

After the description of Jovian lifeforms is repeated, they express the grave concern they are developing:

> *Something has gone wrong*[....]
> When Mount Zeus fell, it could have destroyed this whole world. Its impact was unplanned — indeed, unplannable[....] It devastated vast areas of the Europan seabed, wiping out whole species — including some for which we had high hopes. The monolith itself was overturned. It may even have been damaged, its programs corrupted. Certainly they failed to cover all contingencies [271].

The aliens that created the monolith, and their handiwork, are being diminished in stature, since it now transpires that their policy is to place monoliths in various areas where intelligence might develop and then go away, providing no further monitoring. The monoliths themselves, previously depicted as impervious and flawless, are now susceptible to damage and consequently are capable of making mistakes. Even before the problem of the chunk of diamond colliding with Europa, the monolith's decision to exterminate the Jovians to nurture the Europans struck Bowman and HAL as questionable, even ominous, engendering fears about humanity's eventual fate. Believing the monolith is no longer trustworthy, Bowman and HAL feel that it has become *their* "task to help [the Europans] find their true potential — perhaps here, perhaps elsewhere" (271). And they must work quickly:

> "How much time do we have?"
> "Little enough; barely a thousand years. *And we must remember the Jovians*" [272].

Their worry, obviously, is that a flawed, malfunctioning monolith might decide to destroy humanity in the same way that it once destroyed the Jovians. In other words, Clarke builds upon the ominous hint in *2010* — "sometimes, dispassionately, they had to weed" — to suggest that the monolith, once humanity's friend, might become its enemy. When Clarke returns to the *2001* saga, that is exactly what happens.

*   *   *

Clarke took a decade before publishing *3001: The Final Odyssey* (1997), perhaps because the now-elderly Clarke worked more slowly, but he may have had trouble deciding upon its protagonist, since Bowman had become an ethereal servant and Floyd had grown too elderly. Clarke's ingenious solution was to revive the other hero of *2001*, Poole, last seen as a corpse drifting through interplanetary space near Jupiter. But one could reasonably presume that by 3001, if his frozen body was retrieved, the advanced medicine of that time could restore him to life; and that is how *3001* begins.

As might be expected, Clarke spends a substantial amount of time acquainting Poole with the technological wonders of another new millennium and saying little about Bowman and HAL, the monoliths, and the aliens who created them. Still, an initial chapter essentially repeats the description of the aliens in *2010*, so readers know that Clarke has not forgotten them. (Surely, one factor contributing to the sense that the later two sequels are running in place is Clarke's unfortunate habit of copying lengthy passages from *2010* to fill their pages.) Still, there are a few revisions: the monolith builders are now named the Firstborn, confirming that they were the first intelligent species to emerge in the universe, and there are new concluding paragraphs to set the stage for the eventual appearance of Poole's old comrades:

> [The aliens'] marvelous instruments still continued to function, watching over the experiments started so many years ago.
>
>   But no longer were they always obedient to the mandates of their creators; like all material things, they were not immune to the corruptions of Time and its patient, unsleeping servant, Entropy.
>
>   And sometimes, they discovered and sought goals of their own.[21]

Thus, when Poole finally encounters Bowman and HAL — now combined into one being called Halman — readers are prepared for the ominous news that they provide, as reported by Poole:

> The Monolith is a fantastically powerful machine — look what it did to Jupiter! — but it's no more than that. It's running on automatic; it has no consciousness[....] Worse still, some of its systems may have started to fail; Dave even suggests that, in a fundamental way, it's become stupid! Perhaps it's been left on its own for too long — it's time for a service check.
>
>   And [Halman] believes that the Monolith has made at least one misjudgment. Perhaps that's not the right word — it may have been deliberate, carefully considered ... (181)

Further, because Halman fears that the Monolith may be preparing to harm humanity, he asks Poole to get scientists on Earth to figure out how to disable the Monolith. Since it is now characterized as a computer, they devise an appropriate solution: opening an ancient vault of stored computer viruses, scientists extract a suitable weapon, Halman contrives to inject it into the Monolith, and the "fantastically powerful machine" that loomed over humans since ancient times is finally turned off, perhaps destroying Halman — since it was in some fashion powered by or contained within the Monolith — but ensuring that humanity will survive for at least another thousand years — the time when Poole and his colleagues anticipate that the monolith makers will learn their machine is no longer working and perhaps respond in a threatening manner.

Overall, in a fashion almost unimaginable, the astonishingly advanced aliens once depicted as the pinnacle of evolution have been effectively reduced to the level of mere humanity. Literally, they are just like us. Like humans, they constructed an impressively advanced computer (HAL, the Monolith); like humans, they failed to anticipate that this computer would malfunction and become a menace to the beings it was designed to assist; and like humans, they must have Bowman venture into the bowels of the machinery, shut down the faulty piece of equipment, and restore order to the world.

Furthermore, consider what has happened to the film's original theme. The story seemingly argued that, after depending upon tools for millions of years to advance from bones to spaceships, humanity has reached the point where tool-making has taken them as far as it can, requiring the race to evolve beyond tools. But it transpires in *3001* that even these advanced aliens have not risen above the need to build and use tools, and have not risen above the problem of tools that can be misused, or malfunction, and become inimical to their interests. Evolution beyond the merely human is not only a topic being avoided; the series now argues that such evolution is virtually impossible. No matter how far humans might travel or what technologies they might develop, *3001* indicates they will always be, like their alien manipulators, fallible creatures depending upon the unreliable tools they will always have to construct.

However, Clarke does not merely indict the aliens as builders of bad machines; he suggests that they themselves might be ready to destroy humanity. For there is a reason why Halman fears the monolith will become a threat: in the twenty-first century, as depicted in *2010*, Bowman surveyed his planet and found any number of conflicts and problems that might lead advanced aliens to conclude that the species was a failed experiment in need of "weeding." Halman knows that it took about 450 years for his report to reach the entity that is the monolith's supervisor, so it would take the same amount of time for that supervisor to relay new instructions to the monolith, based upon that report; and the monolith appears to be receiving a flurry of new instructions that Halman fears might involve eliminating humanity. The problem is not simply that a flawed alien computer might erroneously decide to eradicate our species; the aliens who constructed it might coldly mandate precisely that action. Thus, while the Monolith may be "stupid," the aliens may be downright evil.

Still, in a brief and enigmatic final chapter, Clarke appears to back away from this unflattering portrait of hyper-evolved aliens, since such a being is presumably the speaker who intones these words: "Their little universe is very young, and its god is still a child. But it is too soon to judge them; when We return in the last days, We shall consider what should be saved" (237). This statement seemingly comes from a race of aliens who are as far beyond the aliens behind the monoliths as those aliens are beyond humanity: "they" is humanity, "its god" is the alien race that has manipulated them, and while some things that advanced race is doing are questionable, its actions are excused because, by the standards of this even more advanced being, it is still "a child." Perhaps, then, there is a model for human evolution which inarguably represents a vast improvement upon humanity, though this model is now not the aliens who drove events in the *2001* saga, but rather another race that is far beyond them in powers and wisdom.

3001 offers another idea about human advancement, though it is left undeveloped, in Halman, a blend of human intelligence and machine intelligence. It has been shown, by humans in the twenty-first century and the potentially genocidal monolith builders, that sentient creatures with organic origins are unreliable, and HAL and the increasingly suspect monolith demonstrate that sentient creatures of mechanical origins are similarly unreliable. Perhaps, by merging an organic being and mechanical being, a truly superior creature would result — the "cyborg" often celebrated by proponents of the postmodern. Yet just as Bowman himself was never presented as a superhuman successor to humanity in the first two sequels to *2001*, Halman in *3001* is also not elevated to this status; in fact, he seems pretty much like Bowman, suggesting that integrating HAL into his already unemotional personality did not change him very much. And, given that the novel's central conceit is the monolith reconsidered as a fallible computer, one cannot simultaneously maintain that merging a computer with an organic being might improve the species.

What about the Europans, the promising beings that the monolith builders hoped to elevate to intelligence by transforming Jupiter into a star? Might they be developing into beings with even greater potential than humans to achieve super-humanity? Clarke also deflates this possibility, since Poole reports, "Though a thousand years is a very short time, one would have expected some progress, but according to Dave they're exactly the same now as when they left the sea" (186). One cannot be optimistic, then, that this race will achieve intelligence, let alone a stature transcending human intelligence.

Thus, despite the promise of the fetus-like Star Child in the first story, Clarke has brought his saga about a prophesied leap beyond mere humanity to a dead end. The transformed Bowman is not the vanguard of a new superhuman species, but only a sort of computer simulation assigned to perform chores for aliens. Though the once-unhinged HAL was rehabilitated, there is no hint that machine intelligence represents a path to the superhuman; indeed, with the monolith redefined as a computer that, like HAL, has malfunctioned, that possibility seems precluded. The aliens who built the monoliths are now perceived as beings capable of grievous errors and malicious actions that might destroy, instead of nurturing, other intelligent life, diminishing their luster as possible models of humanity's future. The Europans' lack of progress indicates that other species are equally unlikely to achieve a state of superhuman perfection. There is a final hint of a truly transcendent, unimaginably advanced species, but upon close examination they, too, may retain the flaws observed in other species once thought to have evolved beyond flaws.

Arguably, this all might be construed as an unexciting, but potentially accurate argument about humanity's future: that we have already gotten to be as good as we will ever be, so we can expect to remain pretty much the same for as long as we might endure; other intelligent beings will similarly cease developing when they attain a stature similar to present-day humanity. This vision of eternal stagnation may be just as probable as any other prediction one might make about humanity's future. Yet everything that we know about ourselves undermines this theory: history demonstrates that humanity has kept evolving biologically, intellectually, and culturally for millions of years, so it is extraordinarily unlikely that we now happen to live at the precise moment when all that progress is destined to come to a screeching halt. Surely, further improvements must be on the horizon, and arguing otherwise seems not a reasoned conclusion, but rather a desperate expedient in the face of a fundamental inability to envision precisely what forms that further improvement might take. Thus, in sequels to *2001*, Clarke felt compelled to take readers further and further away from the subject of future human evolution, though that was manifestly the central point of the original story.

Still, expressed concerns in *3001* about what might occur in 4001, and its provocative coda suggesting the existence of beings beyond any yet encountered, did provide an opening for another sequel, which probably again would have failed to add much of interest to this deteriorating saga. But instead of taking that step, Clarke kept the implicit promise in his subtitle — *The Final Odyssey* — and never returned to the world that he and Kubrick crafted decades ago, and never allowed other writers to do so. However, while not sanctioning another sequel, he did authorize and involve himself in what might be described as a sidebar to the story of *2001* offering another perspective on the possible characteristics of a superhuman race.

*   *   *

Clarke again announced, after *3001*, that he would write no more novels (though he again abandoned this vow and began another one, *The Last Theorem* [2008], eventually completed by Frederik Pohl). Yet other novels had been appearing that prominently displayed Clarke's name as their principal author, followed by the names of so-called "co-authors": Gentry Lee, Mike McQuay, Michael Kube-McDowell, and Stephen Baxter. Clarke made little effort to conceal that, in fact, these men were actually writing these novels, while Clarke generally limited himself to contributing initial ideas, regular feedback, and an afterword. Since one author, Lee, had produced a three-volume continuation of Clarke's *Rendezvous with Rama*—another saga involving an artifact built by unseen, enigmatic aliens—it was perhaps inevitable that another of Clarke's partners might raise the possibility of continuing the *2001* series in some fashion; and Clarke was amenable to a new story along the same lines that was not directly connected to *2001*.

Thus, to introduce *Time's Eye* (2004), subtitled *Book One of A Time Odyssey*, a brief "Authors' Note" attributed to Clarke and the book's purported co-author and probable sole author, Baxter, stated that "This book, and the series that it opens, neither follows nor precedes the books of the earlier *Odyssey*, but is at right angles to them; not a sequel or prequel, but an 'orthoquel,' taking similar premises in a different direction."[22] Specifically, Clarke and Baxter would develop this trilogy by again positing the existence of mysterious advanced aliens, represented by stark geometric artifacts, who would undertake to meddle in humanity's affairs. The difference this time, as Baxter explained in the interview, "A Conversation with Stephen Baxter and Sir Arthur C. Clarke," included as an afterword to *Time's Eye*, is that they would "assume[e] an intervention that's hostile from the very beginning" ([365]). If not a true sequel to *2001*, then, this trilogy would in a way complete the narrative arc of the series—moving from a first volume and film depicting an entirely benign race of manipulators, to later volumes depicting a race that increasingly seems flawed or even potentially inimical, to a final narrative depicting a race that is entirely evil.

Crafting this story, however, did pose two problems for Clarke and Baxter, who were more scientifically astute, and more principled, than many lesser authors and filmmakers who had offered colorful but contrived tales of sinister aliens with awesome scientific capabilities who attempt to conquer Earth but are defeated by plucky humans. Naturally wishing to assume that the future evolution of intelligent life would involve advances in both technology and morality, they could not posit purely malevolent aliens as the end product of extended evolution, and thus as models for what humanity might become, but instead would need to provide some logical reason why advanced aliens might seek humanity's downfall. And the justification developed by the writer who introduced this theme in *The War of the Worlds* (1898), H. G. Wells—that a once-admirable race might attack Earth because their own depleted planet made them covet our lush environment and rich resources—no longer made sense in an era when scientists knew the universe was filled with planets, and could predict the development of technologies such as terraforming which could transform barren worlds into paradises, eliminating any reason for an advanced species to conquer inhabited planets. Second, if authors envision truly superior aliens, and not the easily-defeated bumblers of popular culture, they would have to accept that such beings could eradicate a lesser race like humanity quickly and easily, making it difficult to sustain an extended narrative about their sure-to-be-successful efforts.

To address the first issue, Clarke and Baxter begin by dropping hints in *Time's Eye*, while describing their otherwise-incomprehensible handiwork on the new world of Mir (to be discussed), that their aliens are far from kindly: one character asks, "Do any of us actually *believe* there can be benevolence behind this meddling?" (111), another speaks of their "cruelty" and "Arrogance" (244), while a third thinks that their artifact is "hovering above them both balefully" (270–271) and opines that they are "not gods"—"Because they have no compassion" (267). But only near the end of the book do the authors spell out exactly what the aliens—the first intelligent race that emerged in the universe—are up to:

> as they looked ahead, they saw only a slow darkening, as each generation of stars was built with increasing difficulty from the debris of the last. There would come a day when there wasn't enough fuel in the Galaxy to manufacture a single new star, and the last light flickered and died[....]
>
> They returned to their abandoned machines of war. The ancient machines were directed to a new objective: to the elimination of waste—to cauterization, if necessary. The makers saw now that if even a single thread of awareness was to be passed to the furthest future, there must be no unnecessary disturbance, no wasted energy, no ripples in the stream of time[....]
>
> It was all for the best of intentions. The first ones, born into an empty universe, cherished life above all else. But to preserve life, life must sometimes be destroyed [353–354].

To avoid depleting the universe's finite supply of energy as long as possible, and thus keep themselves alive as long as possible, these aliens, called "the Firstborn" as in *3001*, were wiping out all intelligent species in their galaxy, since they used up energy at an alarming rate.

To explain why they feel driven to survive into the "furthest future," the third book in the trilogy, *Firstborn: A Time Odyssey: 3* (2008), presents a theory developed by the extinct Martian race:

> The Martians argued among themselves as to *why* the Firstborn were so intent upon reaching the Last Days.
>
> Perhaps it derived from their origin. Perhaps in their coming of awareness in the First Days they had encountered—*another*. One as far beyond their cosmos as they were beyond the toy universes in which they stored their time-sliced worlds. One who would return in the Last Days, to consider what should be saved.[23]

This concept of an ultimate über-race that would eventually materialize to pass judgment on the universe, of course, is borrowed from the the brief final chapter of *3001*.

Despite this elaborate exercise in justification and rationalization, one cannot dispute that, by any imaginable ethical code, this behavior is immoral. The Firstborn are equivalent to a man who escapes a sinking ship, boards its single lifeboat, and murders all passengers who attempt to join him, arguing that this represents the best way to prolong the lifeboat's supplies and ensure that there will be at least one survivor. That is, simply because they happened to be the first intelligent species to evolve, what gives these aliens the right to conclude that they are the only intelligent species that merits survival? Beings that genuinely "cherished life above all else," noticing that another energy-consuming intelligent race has emerged, might approach the newcomers, school them on the importance of conserving the universe's energy, and collectively commit suicide, allowing that species to carry on waiting for the "Final Days" until they, too, decide to pass the torch to a new species and eliminate themselves. Or if, as the Martians speculate, "the universe could only bear one world as populous and energy-hungry as their own, one world in each of the universe's hundred billion empty galaxies, if the Last Days were to be reached" (292–293), then upon the arrival of each new intelligent species, the Firstborn could destroy part of their population and replace it with representatives of the newcomers, so when the universe ends, the super-advanced beings could be greeted by a world collectively populated by all of one galaxy's intelligent species, not just a world of one surviving species.

It is also incongruous that the Firstborn apparently never attempt to craft an alternative strategy to meet their goals, such as endeavoring to replenish the universe's supply of energy, tapping some source of energy from outside the universe, and/or developing innovative techniques to enable intelligent species to persist with such an amazingly minimal expenditure of energy as to allow for the survival of several races instead of one. Readers might have more sympathy for the Firstborn had they been told, for example, that they had first devoted countless millennia to a thoroughgoing search for other solutions before finally and reluctantly implementing their policy of genocide. But there are no statements of this kind in the trilogy.

From considering how Clarke and Baxter addressed their second problem — providing the Firstborn with a methodology for murder to fill an entire trilogy — it becomes apparent that these aliens are not only the most evil ones yet encountered in a continuation of *2001*, but also the stupidest. (This also might explain why they quickly began slaughtering other races without pondering other possible courses of action.)

As eventually explained in *Firstborn*, the aliens follow a three-step process when they learn about the emergence of another intelligent race, each step successively illustrated in the books of the trilogy. First, they make copies of bits and pieces of the targeted world's past history and assemble them to form a new, amalgamated planet within an especially-created pocket universe that endures for a few centuries before being destroyed. This is the story of *Time's Eye*: in 2037, United Nations soldiers in Afghanistan suddenly find themselves in a world that includes, among others, australopithecines, the armies of Alexander the Great and Genghis Khan, and a troop of nineteenth-century British soldiers accompanied by young Rudyard Kipling; and their conflicts, partnerships, conspiracies, and romances constitute the volume's plot. The natural question is *why* the aliens would bother to do this. First, it seems an unnecessary expenditure of energy by beings purportedly obsessed with avoiding precisely that, though we are told in *Firstborn* that, according to a Martian scientist, "the energy sums would cancel out" when the universe expired (293). If this is granted, then the aliens are simply employing an energy-neutral method to observe the history of the species they will soon exterminate. This is intimated throughout *Time's Eye* because the ubiquitous artifacts representing these aliens— not monoliths, but perfect, floating spheres— are called "Eyes" and repeatedly described as watching the novel's characters (19, 90, 191, 227, 249–250, 268, 276, 287, and 297). A character in the second novel, *Sunstorm: A Time Odyssey: 2* (2007), describes this observation as something the Firstborn regard as a painful duty:

> "One thing I'm sure about, though. They *watch*."
>
> "Watch?"
>
> "I think that's what Mir was all about. Mir was a montage of all our history, right up to the moment of this— our possible destruction. Mir wasn't about us but about the Firstborn. They forced themselves to look at what they were destroying, to face what they had done."[24]

But this explanation makes no sense; for if the Firstborn could travel into the past to select and replicate slices of human history, they could send Eyes back into past eras to observe our history as it happened, instead of settling for an artificial, unrepresentative summary of our history derived from juxtaposing random representatives of various periods and cultures. The aliens' actions do not serve their own interests, but rather serve the interests of an author, Baxter, with a known fascination with alternate history. So, if you ever wondered who would have triumphed if Alexander the Great had battled Genghis Khan, with each commander assisted by some modern technology, you can read *Time's Eye* and find out. And while *Firstborn*'s return to Mir does not emulate Garrett P. Serviss to describe *Edison's Conquest of Mars* (1898), there is a vignette about Edison's Contact with Mars. As I argue elsewhere, these exercises in alternate history represent little more than authorial game-playing, not the thoughtful extrapolation of future possibilities that Clarke, and other great science fiction writers, are noted for.[25]

In any event, having temporarily preserved and observed some of Earth's history, the aliens proceed to their usual second step — destroying the intelligent species— by detaching a huge planet from another solar system and crashing it into our sun, provoking interior energy fluctuations that eventually cause a sudden outpouring of stellar energy — the "sunstorm" of the second volume — that will devastate Earth and kill its advanced life forms. Again, this might seem a waste of energy, but Clarke and Baxter anticipate and try to counter that argument: as a scientist explains, "they act with —*economy*. If a star system is giving them cause for concern, they first hit it with a sunstorm. Crude, a blanket blow-torching, but a cheap way of sterilizing an entire system" (*Firstborn* 271).

However, despite their enormous powers, the Firstborn manage to botch the job of slaughtering humanity due to two astounding blunders. First, it transpires that the Firstborn's decision to destroy humanity was not unanimous—it was reached "despite some dissension" (*Sunstorm* 184)—and dissenters have been secretly working to prevent the genocide. In *Time's Eye*, they employ one of Mir's Eyes to transport one resident, a twenty-first-century soldier named Bisesa Dutt, back to Earth, where in *Sunstorm* she provides authorities with the vital clue that the coming sunstorm is not a natural event, but was rather caused by homicidal aliens. Great Britain's Astronomer Royal figures out the situation: after asking Bisesa, "Why would they warn any of us—and why *you*?" she immediately answers her own question:

> Because there are factions among these Firstborn. Because they are no more united and uniform of view than humanity is—why should a more advanced civilization be homogeneous? And because there are some of them, at least, who believe that what is being done is wrong. A faction of them, working through Bisesa, are trying to warn us [*Sunstorm* 152–153].

Yet this represents a typical error made by scoundrels in popular adventures: allowing a traitorous underling to secretly work against them without being aware of the betrayal. Yet advanced aliens, having reached an important decision, would presumably be capable of preventing opponents of that decision from doing anything to undermine it.

Their second mistake is even more indefensible: having set in motion events to cause Earth's doom in 2042, they proceed to ignore the planet while, during five years of frenetic work, humanity constructs an enormous, ultrathin, and intelligently flexible shield to provide our planet with sufficient protection against the sunstorm as to prevent complete devastation, though there will still be catastrophic consequences. Had they been paying attention, the Firstborn could have destroyed this shield in an instant and thus ensured the extinction of humanity; instead, work proceeds on schedule and humanity is saved. In this respect, these aliens resemble the absurd villain of melodramas who places the hero in an inescapable deathtrap, cackles with glee, and then, instead of lingering to watch the hero die, inexplicably departs to deal with other business, allowing the hero to escape from the trap. True, we are told in *Sunstorm* and *Firstborn* that the Firstborn placed an Eye near Jupiter to observe Earth's destruction, but they obviously were not watching the planet very carefully.

Further, the aliens' surefire method of exterminating intelligent life must be counteracted on a fairly regular basis, bolstering the sense that they are incompetent, since they have a third step, a back-up system, in place: "But if the sunstorms don't work, if worlds continue to be troublesome, they strike more surgically" (271)—by transforming an Eye into a "Q-Bomb" of dark energy which is directed to strike a "troublesome" planet and not only devastate it, but actually remove it from the universe. The menace of a Q-Bomb, due to strike Earth in twenty-one months, provides the plot for the trilogy's third volume, *Firstborn*.

Again, however, the Firstborn bungle the job. First, we learn that many millennia ago, a race of intelligent Martians managed to trap an Eye in a force-field, still present to be fortuitously discovered by twenty-first-century humans exploring Mars, before the Martians were exterminated by a Q-Bomb. (This raises multiple questions: how could advanced aliens allow a lesser race to do this? If they wanted to eliminate the Martians, why did they proceed directly to a Q-Bomb instead of unleashing a sunstorm? If ancient Mars was struck by a Q-Bomb, why did the now-lifeless planet remain in our universe? But one tires of pointing out unresolved issues in this story). Then, Dutt is transported back to Mir, where she discovers that its universe contains not only an amalgamated Earth, but amalgamated versions of the Solar System's other planets, including a patchwork Mars with one intelligent Martian. (But why would the Firstborn bother to do this, since Mir was created only as a way to study Earth's history?) On Mir, Edison figures out that humans can send a message to Mars—a string of symbols extracted from the force-field the Martians placed around the Eye—by carving immense ditches forming those symbols, filling them with combustible materials, and lighting them on fire so Martian astronomers can observe them. When the Martian sees the symbols, she realizes that another race needs assistance in fighting the Firstborn and, by means of advanced science, her "gravitational cage crushed the Firstborn Eye" (294). This for some reason distresses not only the duplicate Eye on the Mir universe's Mars, but also the original Eye on our Mars, causing it to send out a distress signal which, when detected by the Q-Bomb, inspires the intelligent bomb to alter its course and strike not Earth but Mars, now perceived as the greater threat. In other words, like the aliens in Clarke's original series, these Firstborn have also constructed a flawed, inept machine, capable of being diverted from its mission by an obvious diversionary tactic.

Like *3001*, *Firstborn* concludes with an opening for a sequel: Dutt and daughter Myra are transported by the Eye to a barren plain, probably Earth in the far future, where they meet a woman resembling Dutt's granddaughter who says, "We call ourselves the Lastborn. We are at war. We are losing[....] Please. Come with me now" (359). Thus, one easily envisions another trilogy involving an alliance of younger races which would successfully oppose the Firstborn and devise a better way to address the problem of the universe's finite supply of energy. But, in light of the mess that the *Time Odyssey* trilogy became, one must be pleased that no such continuation emerged.

The sad thing about this failed project is that it had genuinely interesting features. For one thing, *Time's Eye* includes a brief, almost atavistic, remnant of the original story line of *2001*, in that an australopithecine named Grasper was subjected by one Eye to a "probing of her body and mind." However, since "the probing had been clumsy," her "half-formed mind had been stirred," making her "a creature with potential," though "there was no particular reason why that potential had to be realized exactly as it had been before." In a deliberate echo of *2001*, Grasper "hefted the heavy stone in her hand," recognized that she was now "master of the world," and while "not quite sure what to do next," she knew "she would think of something" (361–362). The concept of a new and different form of humanity, this time created not intentionally but accidentally by the always-blundering Firstborn, is fascinating, but while Grasper briefly reappears in *Firstborn* as a more intelligent being, nothing else is done with the idea.

The Eyes themselves also command attention. Although we see numerous Eyes throughout the trilogy, we are repeatedly told that "There was only one Eye, though it had many projections into spacetime. And it had many functions" (*Time's Eye* 349); the energies it emits when serving as a transportation device indicate that, like the monolith, it is an object of more than three dimensions; and when the Eye is measured, the ratio of its circumference to its diameter is not pi, but exactly three, indicating that it is an object not of our universe. It is incomprehensible that beings intelligent enough to craft such an object could be stupid enough to make the simple mistakes that doom their lethal plans; it is depressing to speculate that such scientific advances, and such stupid, sinister actions, might be said to represent humanity's probable future. And if authors as astute as Clarke and Baxter can be driven to such an unlikely, disheartening portrait of the imagined evolution of intelligent life, it does suggest that there may be fundamental, irresolvable problems in efforts to predict the eventual fate of the human race.

* * *

As this long odyssey draws to a close, there is time for some general conclusions about science fiction's efforts to depict humanity's future, drawn primarily from the *2001* saga but with sidelong glances at other texts.

The first lesson is the point made by Kirby — that it may be fundamentally impossible for present-day humans to accurately predict the nature of superhumans. Recognizing that analogies are both a tool and trap for prognosticators, one might consider an ant, temporarily endowed with a modicum of intelligence and imagination, asked to envision a super-ant. This posited being would surely have enhanced abilities to construct larger and more complex anthills, better locate and retrieve food, and nurture a larger number of offspring — to do everything that an ant does, only in a superior fashion. But could this ant conceive of an advanced creature who could plant crops, devise a monetary system, build a steam engine, or write an opera? That is, members of a superhuman species may indeed be smarter, more powerful, and kinder than we are, but they may also be able and inclined to do things we cannot begin to imagine. Thus, science fiction's best portrayals of intelligences beyond our own may be stories like Stanislaw Lem's *Solaris* (1961) and Terry Carr's "The Dance of the Changer and the Three" (1968) that limit themselves to describing bizarre alien behavior without attempting to explain it—conveying that genuine superbeings would be incomprehensible to present-day humans.

Second, by employing another reasonable but flawed technique for prophecy, extrapolation, writers can ponder how humanity has progressed, posit those trends will continue, and develop minimal images of more advanced humans and aliens. Thus, observing that humans have grown less violent, one logically imagines that a superhuman would be vehemently opposed to violence, like the Star Child at the end of Clarke's *2001* or the alliance of pacifistic worlds united to prevent conflicts in space described by the alien Klaatu in the original *The Day the Earth Stood Still* (1951). And, noting that we have become less inclined to kill other animals and more inclined to nurture and protect them, one logically imagines that superhumans would be even more committed to preserving and improving lesser forms of life, like Kirby's fifth New Seed, the aliens in Clarke's sequels to *2001*, or the alien races which "uplift" other species to intelligence in David Brin's *Startide Rising* (1983).

Third, if writers feel unable to go beyond such reasonable but unadventurous projections of advanced beings, they may simply abandon efforts to depict successors to humanity. This is what happened to Kirby, as he stopped writing about the New Seed and starting writing about Machine Man, and what Clarke essentially did in transforming the Star Child from *homo superior* to the monolith's servant. As another example, consider Isaac Asimov, who in the 1980s, like Clarke, returned to his most famous epic, adding new volumes to his Foundation trilogy while also connecting the saga to his robot stories. As one new development, *Foundation's Edge* (1982) introduced as a possible model for human advancement a form of group intelligence on the planet Gaea, creating the possibility that he might conclude the series not only with the predicted reestablishment of a Galactic Empire, but also with a leap forward in human evolution not unlike that observed in *Childhood's End*. However, as if unwilling to move in that direction, Asimov left his narrative unfinished and instead turned to its back story, concluding the series with two "prequels," *Prelude to Foundation* (1988) and *Forward the Foundation* (1993), describing the life of Hari Seldon, the psychohistorian who founded the saga's foundations.[26]

Fourth, as another way to avoid detailed examinations of an envisioned superrace, writers may endeavor to effectively change the subject. One strategy is to assume that advanced beings will be not only concerned, but positively obsessed, with the progress of lesser species. This draws attention away from strange beings, who are frustratingly difficult to describe, toward familiar beings, who are easy to describe. Thus, aside from a few generalities, virtually all we learn about the Firstborn in Clarke's *2001* series, and Clarke and Baxter's *Time Odyssey*, involves their opinions of humans and similar species and their interventions into their affairs. Other writers have moved in a similar direction;

for example, while most people regard Olaf Stapledon's *Star Maker* (1937) as the continuation of *Last and First Men* (1930), that book actually had a direct sequel, the little-known *Last Men in London* (1932), wherein a representative of Stapledon's hyper-advanced Eighteenth Men travels into the past to display an inordinate fascination with the daily life of a typical resident of present-day London. Despite an introduction justifying "The Future's Concern with the Past,"[27] this interest does not appear logical; but it allows Stapledon to say little about his future superhumans and their life on Neptune while saying a lot about what his fellow humans are doing right now.

To say the least, based on our knowledge of human history, it seems indefensible to posit that superbeings will be driven to study and meddle in the affairs of lesser beings as their main activity. True, numerous people today are dedicated to breeding or nurturing animals like dogs, cats, and horses, and almost every organism on the planet has attracted at least a few scientists who are fascinated by, and feel a special bond with, the creatures they study. But no human culture as a whole has predominantly focused its energies on improving animals, and it is hard to imagine that a superhuman race would envision uplifting lesser species as its primary purpose. One more reasonably assumes, as Clarke does in *Against the Fall of Night* and *Childhood's End*, that a superrace would have little if any interest in the doings of its predecessors and would permanently withdraw from their company; but while writers can readily portray this attitude when a story concludes with the creation or discovery of advanced beings, it is a problematic premise when beginning a story about such beings.

Fifth, if writers continue efforts to depict a superhuman species, they may fall victim to the sentiment of the saying "familiarity breeds contempt" and make these beings seem more and more like ordinary humans. Thus, in the original *2001*, the monoliths, and aliens who constructed them, were presented as omniscient, omnipotent, and incapable of error; they had a plan for developing and improving humanity, and they carried it out flawlessly. In Clarke's sequels, however, there emerged a sense that the monolith builders were distant, and not always capable, manipulators of humanity, and their machines were seen as deteriorating and potentially inclined to disastrous mistakes; those aliens' counterparts in the *Time Odyssey* trilogy, as noted, were downright evil and even less competent. As another example, consider the character of Q, initially presented in the first episode of *Star Trek: The Next Generation*, "Encounter at Farpoint" (1987), as a member of an amazingly advanced superrace with knowledge and abilities far beyond those of mere humans; yet as he reappears in later episodes of that series, *Star Trek: Deep Space Nine*, and *Star Trek: Voyager*, he became a comic character, easily outwitted or outmaneuvered by the humans he loved to visit and prone to any number of human weaknesses.

Sixth, as another aspect of this tendency to regard superbeings as similar to typical humans, writers may resort to humanity's ancient tendency in confronting unknown intruders—to classify them as either "friend" or "foe" and respond accordingly—and start characterizing these enigmatic creatures in such conventional terms—despite the logical expectation that advanced races would have complex motives not well described by these simple categories. One need not reiterate that evil aliens have long been a mainstay of popular science fiction, but even writers who are intelligent enough to reject such stereotypes may drift toward similar portrayals, as seen in the *Time Odyssey* trilogy. And if writers are uncomfortable portraying superbeings as enemies, they can always transform them into friends. That is the scenario of Clarke and Pohl's *The Last Theorem*: advanced aliens called the Grand Galactics first plan to eradicate the flawed human race, but when one of them visits Earth and sees signs of progress, they not only reverse their decision and spare humanity from destruction, but also decide, generously and implausibly, to bequeath to humans their role as guardians of the galaxy.

Even in the greatest science fiction novel to wrestle with the vexing question of the ultimate destiny of intelligent life, Olaf Stapledon's *Star Maker*, the briefly observed ultimate being is described by the hapless narrator using the language of "friend" or "foe." When the Cosmic Mind that combines all the universe's most developed species encounters their universe's creator, the Star Maker, the entity rejects their approach, and the Cosmic Mind then describes the creator with what seems like justifiable anger:

> I cried out against my ruthless maker. I cried out that, after all, the creature was nobler than the creator; for the creature loved and craved love, even from the star that was the Star Maker; but the creator, the Star Maker, neither loved nor had need of love.[28]

But the Cosmic Mind regrets this outburst and comes to realize that the Star Maker is, from his limited perspective, somehow both villain and hero: "Irrationally, yet with conviction, I gave my adoration to the Star Maker as comprising both aspects of his dual nature, both the 'good' and the 'evil,' both the mild and the terrible, both the humanly ideal and the incomprehensibly inhuman" (421). It is striking that, even in this grandest effort to conceive the inconceivable — a creature infinitely more advanced than humanity — the author falls back upon crude, anthropocentric concepts of "good" and "evil."

Finally, as writers allow posited superbeings to gradually descend to the status of all-too-human fools, scoundrels, or bosom buddies, their only recourse is to start all over again: to indicate that, beyond the once-exalted level of their original creations, there exists an even more advanced race of beings, as high above them as those beings are above humans, and to suggest that this newly unveiled species might actually embody the sublime perfection once associated with the first superbeings. This is how Clarke effectively both abandons and relaunches his *2001* saga in the conclusion of *3001*, and hints of a similar super-super-race also figure in the *Time Odyssey* trilogy. As another example, Pohl's *Gateway* (1977) initially involves an unseen but highly advanced alien race, the

Heechee, whose abandoned spaceships are exploited by future humans in search of knowledge and wealth. However, as the second novel in its series, *Beyond the Blue Event Horizon* (1979), says more about the Heechee, and the third novel, *Heechee Rendezvous* (1984), brings them onstage, we learn that the Heechee, despite their superior technology, are not as superhuman as they appeared, since they are hiding near a black hole to avoid an even more powerful race, the Assassins, intent upon destroying and refashioning the entire universe. However, after bringing the Heechee down to human-like status and introducing a new race as superhuman alternatives to humanity, the series' fourth novel, *The Annals of the Heechee* (1987), refashions the Assassins themselves as comforting friends, since their efforts to rid the universe of matter and construct a universe of pure energy now seem desirable. The stage is set for the appearance of a third race far above the Assassins who might recapture the aura of awe and mystery previously associated first with the Heechee and then with the Assassins, but Pohl instead brought the series to an end — despite the appearance of two later volumes, *The Gateway Trip* (1990) and *The Boy Would Who Live Forever: A Novel of Gateway* (2004), that follow Asimov's example and are "prequels" offering stories that took place before *The Annals of the Heechee*. This also makes Pohl's series another example of an epic about humanity's future that concludes not by going forward, but by going backward.

Still, despite the inherent difficulties, or sheer impossibility, of the task, science fiction writers may always feel compelled to continue their endless odyssey of attempting to envision a future humanity that is significantly more advanced than ourselves, or alien races of equivalent stature, even if they find themselves unable to bring their sagas to a satisfactory conclusion. We must ponder our own eventual destiny and explore those thoughts in stories, even while recognizing the essential futility of the effort. Perhaps, then, there is some truth in Kirby's observation about the underlying message of the *2001* saga, that "the New Seed is no more than the spirit of our own self-belief, our own confidence in the stubborn rationale which has brought us from the caves to condominiums." In other words, the same drive and determination that will enable humanity to succeed and progress in the future also leads writers to constantly try, and constantly fail, to imagine the exact forms that that progress will take. Thus, all the noble, fruitless struggles to extend a narrative that cannot be meaningfully extended, as examined here, may collectively represent, in their own way, a story that is as interesting and inspirational as *2001: A Space Odyssey* itself.

NOTES

1. *2001: A Space Odyssey* (Metro-Goldwyn-Mayer, 1968).
2. Arthur C. Clarke, *2001: A Space Odyssey*, based on a screenplay by Stanley Kubrick and Clarke (New York: Signet Books, 1968), 221. Subsequent page references in the text are to this edition.

3. Clarke, *The Lost Worlds of 2001* (New York: Signet Books, 1972), 238.

4. Jack Kirby, writer and artist, *2001: A Space Odyssey*, Marvel Treasury Special (New York: Marvel Comics Group, 1976), 71.

5. Kirby, writer and artist, "Beast-Killer," *2001: A Space Odyssey*, No. 1 (December, 1976), 3. Subsequent page references in the text are to this edition.

6. Kirby, writer and artist, "Wheels of Death," *2001: A Space Odyssey*, No. 4 (March, 1977), 31.

7. Kirby, "Monolith Mail," *2001: A Space Odyssey*, No. 1 (December, 1976), 19. Subsequent page references in the text are to this edition.

8. Kirby, writer and artist, "Vira the She-Demon," *2001: A Space Odyssey*, No. 2 (January, 1977).

9. Kirby, writer and artist, "Marak!," *2001: A Space Odyssey*, No. 3 (February, 1977). Note: the cover gives the title as "Marak the Merciless," but I regard the title on the story's first page as definitive.

10. Kirby, writer and artist, "Norton of New York 2040 A.D.," *2001: A Space Odyssey*, No. 5 (April, 1977); "Inter-Galactica: The Ultimate Trip," *2001: A Space Odyssey*, No. 6 (May, 1977).

11. Sam Powell, letter, "Monolith Mail," *2001: A Space Odyssey*, No. 5 (April, 1977), 19.

12. Mike Underwood, Sam Hays, and Mark Boersma, letters, "Monolith Mail," *2001: A Space Odyssey*, No. 6 (May, 1977), 19.

13. Kirby, writer and artist, "The New Seed," *2001: A Space Odyssey*, No. 7 (June, 1977), 7. Subsequent page references in the text are to this edition.

14. Kirby, writer and artist, "The Capture of X-51," *2001: A Space Odyssey*, No. 8 (July, 1977), 3. Subsequent page references in the text are to this edition.

15. Kirby, writer and artist, "Mister Machine," *2001: A Space Odyssey*, No. 9 (August, 1977), 22.

16. Kirby, writer and artist, "Hotline to Hades," *2001: A Space Odyssey*, No. 10 (September, 1977).

17. Clarke, *Childhood's End* (1953; New York: Ballantine Books, 1967), 202–203. Subsequent page references in the text are to this edition.

18. Clarke, *2010: Odyssey Two* (New York: Del Rey/Ballantine Books, 1982), 266–267. Subsequent page references in the text are to this edition.

19. *2010: The Year We Make Contact* (Metro-Goldwyn-Mayer, 1984).

20. Clarke, *2061: Odyssey Three* (New York: Del Rey/Ballantine Books, 1982), 268. Subsequent page references in the text are to this edition.

21. Clarke, *3001: The Final Odyssey* (1997; New York: Del Rey/Ballantine Books, 1999), 5. Subsequent page references in the text are to this edition.

22. Clarke and Stephen Baxter, *Time's Eye: Book One of A Time Odyssey* (2004; New York: Del Rey/Ballantine Books, 2005), [v]. Subsequent page references in the text are to this edition.

23. Clarke and Baxter, *Firstborn: A Time Odyssey: 3* (New York: Del Rey/Ballantine Books, 2008), 293. Subsequent page references in the text are to this edition.

24. Clarke and Baxter, *Sunstorm: A Time Odyssey: 2* (New York: Del Rey/Ballantine Books, 2007), 198–199. Subsequent page references in the text are to this edition.

25. Gary Westfahl, "Greyer Lensmen, Or Looking Backward in Anger," *Interzone*, No. 129 (March, 1998), 40–43.

26. In "What Science Fiction Leaves Out of the Future, #2: The Day After Tomorrow," *The Internet Review of Science Fiction*, March, 2009, at *http://www.irosf.com/q/zine/article/10528*, I also discuss how Asimov's Foundation series and other science fiction epics tend to remain incomplete and look backward, probably because writers are unwilling to explore the issue of humanity's eventual destiny, and acknowledge (as I should

acknowledge here) that George Slusser has analyzed this phenomenon in his own fashion, most thoroughly in "Dimorphs and Doubles: J. D. Bernal's 'Two Cultures' and the Transhuman Promise," *Science Fiction and the Two Cultures: Essays on Bridging the Gap between the Sciences and the Humanities*, ed. Westfahl and Slusser (Jefferson, NC: McFarland Publishers, 2009), 96–129.

27. Olaf Stapledon, "Introduction: The Future's Concern with the Past," *Last Men in London*, 1932, in *Last and First Men and Last Men in London*, by Stapledon (Middlesex, England: Penguin Books, 1973), 335–337.

28. Stapledon, *Star Maker*, 1937, in *Last and First Men and Star Maker: Two Science-Fiction Novels by Olaf Stapledon*, by Stapledon (New York: Dover Books, 1968), 410. Subsequent page references in the text are to this edition.

11

Intercultural and Interface
Kung Fu as Abstract Machine

WONG KIN YUEN

As reflected in the title, this chapter deals primarily with the prefix "inter" within the context of cultural studies. It was a direct response to the need to establish a theoretical paradigm for my teaching and research when I suddenly discovered, about five years ago, that I was thrown into something called "Intercultural Studies" without knowing too much about it. After some research, I learned the discipline of "intercultural communication" which was rather common in Europe as a field related to applied linguistics. Realizing that this was not what I had in mind, I then slowly developed a way of understanding the term; and what follows represents some thoughts as to how this field is similar to but different from cultural studies per se. These thoughts involve basic concepts such as interdisciplinarity, in-betweenness, othering, and finally the Deleuzian philosophy of difference. I will stretch the prefix "inter" to include "interface" within cyberculture to show how a hermeneutics of difference and virtuality could well be the future of such a counterdisciplinary praxis. In conclusion, after using a number of sequences in kung fu and science fiction films for illustration, I will note the inadequacy of cultural studies, pointing out how the Deleuzian flat ontology of affect and sensation can lead one step further into what I call intercultural studies itself.

So, what is interculturality? It may be best to first note what it is not. Interculturality, for one thing, can never be preoccupied with the eternal and unchanging; it opposes all notions of fixed cultures or any culture in and of itself.[1] It is therefore in stark contrast to any monoculturalist thinking as "a form of enclosure in which what is alien can be rendered intelligible only by reducing it to the same."[2] Compared to terms like "cross-cultural" and "multicultural" (under which a cluster of terms such as postcolonial, hybrid, and diaspora have evolved among themselves with sharp political connotations), interculturalism seems "a better term to describe the porosity of cultures," which "addresses the question of how, without limiting the analysis to formal encounters between cultures, communication between a plurality of incom-mensurable cultures takes place" (Bernasconi 288). Whereas "cross-cultural" and "multicultural" retain remnants of the idea that cultures are discrete and autonomous, interculturalism directs our attention to the overlapping area between cultures, emphasizing that cultures do change as they interact with each other. It is more pervasive than the standard multicultural model allows, and is practiced in such a way that the plurality of cultures is not compromised in the direction of hybridism (Bernasconi 290).

For me, the most salient aspect of an interdisciplinary approach lies not with a mish-mash of humanities and social sciences, but with how science stud-ies (to me an important sub-field in cultural studies) can be affiliated with humanities. Today, literary and cultural critics alike have become bold enough to peer into molecular biology, molecular genetics, and genetic engineering; they are also interested in the implosion of informatics and biologics, cloning, and the transgenetics of plant and animal, not to mention chaos theories, com-plex systems theories, and quantum mechanics, which all can be studied in terms of their cultural dimension, situatedness (i.e. Donna Haraway's situated knowledge) and relation with aesthetics (since fractals can be refractions of science into art, we now have fractal architecture in urban studies and fractured identity in literary studies), and so on.[3]

In the famous "Macy Conferences" beginning in 1949, Norbert Wiener was already practicing interdisciplinarity by inviting scientists and scholars in the humanities to work out principles for the development of cybernetics. In 1991, a full quarter seminar at DC Humanities Research Center was devoted to the Human Genome Project, where scholars concentrated on "the cultural pro-ductions of the genome" and how they could be related to "musical, artistic, educational and similar cultural productions."[4]

Before I go into the actual "cultural geography" to give "inter" a "place" in our teaching and research, I should note that because of this privileging of territoriality, interdisciplinarity cannot simply be an attempt to blur disciplinary boundaries, nor just a pluralist jumble of things. Instead, the in-betweenness Homi Bhabha refers to must be put in a circuit of territorialization and de(re)territorialization, where the very "edge" of a cutting-edge practice is maintained at all times and at which the "shiftings" of paradigms are being enacted. I will endeavor to show that the act of "cutting" itself would precede even the "edge." It is exactly at this point that the "inter" of intercultural studies goes beyond cultural studies in general, since it is here that Gilles Deleuze's, rather Henri Bergson's, conceptualizations of time, process, and movement can join forces, and force is the very spirit of interculturalism. Here we should recall that the word "discipline" has a double-binding meaning of both hard work and disciplinary control; therefore, a counter-disciplinary praxis would be important to safeguard our critical endeavors from becoming another grand narrative, another institutionalized "area" of studies in universities.

For young students in Hong Kong, intercultural studies will enable them to look at the urban space as both a place and a flow. With its colonial history, Hong Kong can be projected as one forerunner of the future megacity.[5] Movements and settlements of the city as flow, and as borderization of the world, as many cities in the world are now characterized by this "woof of human motion,"[6] propel Hong Kong citizens to follow "ways of going out and coming back in 'on the edge of empires.'"[7] In their traveling, Hong Kong citizens practice radical happenings or events as "world-travelers," effecting a kind of crossing-of-zones duration which is characterized as incomplete, "between worlds."[8] It is of course this opportunity for Hong Kong citizens to create narratives along their lines of flight, reflecting their "subject's self-positioning and social agency in a cosmopolitan context,"[9] that makes Hong Kong a model for the global megalopolis of the future. As cosmopolitans, and under concepts such as transethnicity, transnationality, and hyphenated identities, the youth of Hong Kong should be educated to form new world views. Through cultural mixture in the interval, the "push and pull" of globalizing tendencies, new combinations can be created in a plurality of knowledges, of cultures and their continuous fusion.

This intercultural also deals with the issue of hybridity, around which ideas such as hyphenated identity, neological as well as technical splicing, and "othering" revolve. The "other," of course, has been a key word for cultural critics, and in terms of Gadamerian hermeneutics, one recalls that achieving an understanding of the authentic being of another radically different culture should be grounded in a celebration of difference in otherness. A hermeneutics of cultural hybridity stresses, according to Jurgen Habermas, "the point of rupture" which "compensates for the brokenness of intersubjectivity,"[10] whereas Hans-Georg Gadamer made it clear that understanding can be achieved only through recognizing the voice of the other when he emphasizes the necessity of "putting one's own horizon at risk" when interpreting the other.[11] Such a move towards "a more radical hermeneutic" is for Jacques Derrida the "only way to let the other come," so the Derridean difference could propagate an indefinite slippage of transfers and changes under a "structural non-knowing which is heterogeneous and foreign to knowledge."[12] But even a radical hermeneutics may not be able to catch up with the posthuman condition, and what we may need, as Mark Hansen says, is a "robust posthermeneutic realism concerning culture and technology."[13]

Hong Kong citizens' way of embracing racial and cultural differences on the edge of empires must be modeled on Michel Foucault's "geohistory of otherness" in his "Of Other Spaces."[14] In this essay Foucault goes into the primacy of sites within our everyday life experiences when ambiguity, heterogeneity, and overlappings are instrumental to establishing a relation with our urban environment. By pointing to places such as utopia, mental hospitals, jails, rest homes, national boundaries, cemeteries, zoos, museums and even Disneyland, and finally third world cities, Foucault brings out the territorialities of doubts, subversions where foldings occur within a double-bind of dominance and resistance. To this list I would add the space of flows, i.e., the virtual reality or cyberspace where dialectics of on-line/off-line, difference/hybrid, crisis/deviation, surveillance/surfing, and striated/smooth contours are dramatically performed and what Bruno Latour calls the "actor-network perspective" begins to make sense in understanding what our cultural/geographical environment is like.[15] All these, finally, can be summed up by Edward Soja's idea of the third space, captured by an act of "thirding as Othering" towards an alternative world of critically fulfilling hybrid haven.[16] The traumas of immigration that Hong Kong people face, as presented through their lived experience of other spaces, can be understood by a general theory of global cultural processes. For Arjun Appadurai, chaos theory is the approach to such understanding, since he considers "the configuration of cultural forms in today's world as fundamentally fractal." To "compare fractally shaped cultural forms which are also polythetically overlapping in their coverage of terrestrial space ... we will need to ask how these complex, overlapping, fractal shapes constitute not a simple, stable (even if large-scale) system, but to ask what its dynamics are." In other words, Appadurai proposes, "in a world of disjunctive global flows, it is perhaps important to start asking ... [questions] in a way that relies on images of flow and uncertainty ... chaos, rather than an older images of order, stability and systemacity" (20).

Whereas chaos theory and fractal geometry are instrumental to the development of virtual reality or cyberspace, one key term recapitulating the connectedness between intercultural studies and our information age would be "interface," a term situating itself right at the in-betweenness of the kind of cultural imaginary which goes beyond the cultural structure of class, gender, and race, but reaches the domain of human/machine splicing in a context of posthuman evolution and virtuality.[17]

Here I claim that intercultural studies in the 21st century must move into cyberculture, if we are to push the logic of "inter" into an open-ended world of becomings. Interface has a history of its own, dating back to how humans were intimidated by the computer as a machine when it first saw the light of day. As a term, it announces the presence of faces between faces, reminding us that at the point of contact between human and machine, ours is only one among many. Interface culture therefore designates a connectedness of borders, an act of communication, or a threshold at which two or more entities interact with each other. It emerges right at a fantastic point where the medium and message cannot distinguish one from the other; and it represents continuous discoveries of similar behavior patterns between human and machine. Between the two, the computer screen is the most visible part of interface, connecting devices of interactivity in response to the users' demand; and between them a "social space" is established within Latour's actor-network perspective where both human and machine can be actor in turn and co-determine each other.[18]

With virtual reality, as well as the identity of cyborgs of any kind, fractured subjects are becoming multiple and decentered, and their "bodies" will be rein-scribed into alternative forms. Similar to the internet, interface possesses the same kind of hybridity as the intercultural, and the reciprocality of interfaces would endlessly create other new interfaces towards a posthuman condition.

But the concept of interface does not stop at electronically mediated com-munication; it can move forward to embrace the virtuality of cyborg identity, as well as refer backward to a kind of neo-evolutionism developed by Gilles Deleuze's biophilosophy. The idea of the cyborg, once sustained by the kind of unstabling qualities of othering of self as described by Haraway as "compounds of the organic, mythic, textual, economic and political" (172), can then liberate humans from their false naturalism through thematization of their own con-structedness. On the other hand, these alternate life-forms can hearken back to the originary differential rhythms and affective intensities of evolution, so as to find a way out of the impasse of cultural confrontations between, say, humanism and posthumanism, the global and local, or monoculturalism and interculturalism. Since any future development of computer interface (or sci-entific prediction of such a development, called futurology) will have to, accord-ing to Ray Kurzweil, go back millions of years to how the Earth evolved into the present state,[19] we now realize that "the human is necessarily bound up with an originary technicity,"[20] and "evolution is nothing but technic."[21] Following Foucault's "hermeneutics of refusal," a refusal to answer the question "Who are we?,"[22] we can now place our endeavors in intercultural studies within the contour of the Deleuzian hermeneutics of becomings "that overspills the anthro-pomorphic strata in all directions" (Deleuze and Guattari 503). The merger between interdisciplinary, intercultural studies, and interface will trigger forth a discourse of chaos accelerating the evolution of biological and artificial life, where the posthuman is simply a concept which "envisions the conscious mind as a small subsystem running its program of self-construction and self-assur-ance while remaining ignorant of the actual dynamics of complex systems."[23] As different from the subject which roots itself in presence as a unified, self-centered entity, such a discourse of interface or technological splicing is "located within the dialectic of pattern/randomness ... and offers resources for rethinking the articulation of humans with intelligent machines" (Hayles 287).

A technoscience (or interface) hermeneutics, therefore, embraces Latour's proliferation of hybrids and his actor-network perspectives, as well as Haraway's proclamation that this is the time of cyborgs, machines, and chimeras. It reaches far to include Hayles's delineation of a process from hyphenation to splicing within a human-machine feedback loop, much in the spirit of the ontological hermeneutic circle first expounded by Martin Heidegger. Together with the Heideggerian *Gelassenheit* attitude in scientific praxis, this hermeneutics points directly to a social space where both animate and inanimate actors refuse to succumb to the pre-given possibilities of molar aggregates. Instead, it is a space where machinic assemblages are articulated in such a way that multiplicities, non-linear interconnectedness and mutually determinings among fellow social actors are actualized. As Andrew Feenberg reminds us, "Difference in the way social groups interpret and use the objects are not merely extrinsic but make a difference in the nature of the objects themselves."[24] All aspects of technological assemblage become a social milieu or network of relations, themselves the results of an abstract machine of stratification. The working of actual machines is such, however, that flows are allowed in every direction among all elements, to be propelled by some liquid energy which structures singularities; meanwhile, the way these relations or "interfaces" proliferate is like strata or rhizomes growing up from everywhere, and here "it is not clear who makes and who is made in relation between human and machine."[25] Technologies and human relations together make up a social space wherein circuits of territorialization and de(re)territorialization are generated, all the while sticking close to the kind of embodiment of particular configurations which contextualize social experience as Hayles has it, or the kind of multiplicities, haecceities, and singularities as Deleuze has it.

A technoscience hermeneutics implicates both human meaning and the process of evolution emerging from artificial and post-biological "life systems." Within a dynamics of both meaning and systems hooked up and responsive to their own environment, genuine interplay between them will make the world into "a creative, complexifying, problematizing cauldron of becoming."[26] In an essay on how Deleuze's "transcendental empiricism" bears on cultural studies in general, Ian Buchanan compares the concept of agency in the latter with the former's subject which can transcend the given in an empirical way. He points out:

> According to Deleuze, the determination that *relations are external to their terms* is the condition of possibility for a solution to the empiricist problem of how a subject transcending the given can be constituted in the given. It is the "solution," as it were, that gives rise to transcendental empiricism. Thus, in order to ascertain whether empiricist methods are going to be valuable to cultural studies, we have to determine whether the externality of relations can contribute anything to an understanding of how culture operates.[27]

What Deleuze means by relations being external to their terms is that an idea is "but a multiplicity constituted of differential elements, differential relations between these elements, and singularities corresponding to those relations."[28] It seems that, according to Manuel De Landa, Deleuze's subject is a given (through empirical experiences) which can simultaneously transcend the given because our idea of subjectivity results from our way of grouping ideas about it, which after all are in principle external to their relations among them. De Landa further notes that "the aim of cultural studies should be to provide a theory of culture that can accommodate" both the subject being given and subject transcending the given; then, "By contrasting the subject dually, transcendental empiricism does in fact furnish the grounds for just such a theory, showing that the subject is the product of social mechanisms and the subject is capable of manipulating those mechanisms" (106).

Here I cannot provide the details of Deleuze's "association," "appropriation," and "affect" which make the establishment of agency possible; suffice it to say that Deleuze moves away from a discourse of social resistance, hegemony, or dissent, which have established themselves as common catchwords in cultural studies, and ventures into what I call intercultural studies or the interface culture of "the Multiple, the Different and the Aleatory" (Buchanan 110).[29] There is a sense of positive connectedness in Deleuze's concept of difference and virtuality, since they are fundamentally based on multiplicity tied together by the conjunction AND:

> AND is neither one thing nor the other, it's always in between, between two things; it's the borderline, there's always a border, a line of flight or flow, only we don't see it, because it's the least perceptible of things. And yet it's along this line of flight that things come to pass, becomings evolve, revolutions take shape.[30]

I therefore propose to take up Deleuze's philosophy of difference — how he sees difference differently — as my major observation of the way it supports the general direction of this chapter, namely from interdisciplinary to intercultural and interface. First, Deleuze looks for a principle of difference not just in cultural representations (language and signs) but mathematics and biology, epigenetic differentiation, and physics (quantum dynamics);[31]; and he works out (with Felix Guattari) a biochemistry of schizophrenia through a difference based on "the quantitative difference between forces."[32] Difference therefore is not derived from the same, nor is it a negative side of what exists as an entity, but a fundamental mechanism which gives life its various forms (Deleuze 1994 222).

For De Landa, Deleuze's difference captures not what exists but a becoming (31); he uses thermodynamics as an example to show that difference is always "an interplay of intensity." The point is not only that difference is the source of all living forms, but it also makes possible all genuine creation by letting "virtualities" begin a process of "actualization or differentiation" (34). Using examples in biogenetics and ecology such as phenotype, symbiosis, homeostatic, and autopoietic, and putting them into a feedback loop to interact with various kinds of nonlinear involution of folds, enfoldings, and unfolds, Deleuze and Guattari in *A Thousand Plateaus* call these processes "intercalary oscillations, synthesizers with at least two heads" (Deleuze and Guattari 239). Unlike human interpretation which more or less requires a subject, the way Deleuze thinks of difference differently is through what Alistair Welchman calls "machinic thinking" which moves away from anthropomorphism and reaches a kind of originary, objective (even scientific), network-like consciousness or intelligence of machinism.[33] Only after machinizing our thought can we situate our relation with the world through "a principle of immanent and non-linear internal difference" (Deleuze 1994 27) and stipulate a virtual dynamic. By transcending the concept of agency and subjectivity in cultural studies, this brand of intercultural studies, this interface of human and machine, stipulates a machinic consciousness about the self being "really only consequences of complexity."[34] Multiplicities and singularities under difference are really "thousands of little witnesses which contemplate within us" (Marks 86); it is always a third party continuously saying "me" (Deleuze 1994 75) in us within a machinic hermeneutic circle or feedback loop.

Here difference coincides with virtuality since "the virtual/actual relation is governed by the principles of difference and creation." Every act of actualization "involves the creation of heterogeneous terms for the lines of actualization are divergent, creating multiplicities and varieties. This is a movement of the emanation of a multiplicity from a virtual unity, divergent paths of development in different series and directions."[35] In *Difference and Repetition*, Deleuze addresses the concept of immanence to capture the relation between "the event, multiplicity and the virtual."[36] Drawing upon Bergson and Spinoza, Deleuze posits an "internal difference" (Being from itself), namely "a co-articulation of Being and difference within themselves."[37] The most salient aspect of this difference is "difference as a degree of power of intensity" (Deleuze 1994 145), manifested in its affective capacities, its potentials, what it is capable of Being; in other words, "the reality of the virtual or the problematic" (Smith 179). Here, in the very mapping of territoriality, interculturalism moves from a preponderance of sites of negotiation to a more fundamentally biological and geological formation of all living forms, exemplified by bird songs and animal calls, what Ronald Bogue calls "the biology of melodic living forms."[38] This is also a move (line of flight) from the molar (organized, signifying temptation and power), from locking singularities into systems (symbolic and metaphorical), towards haecceities, nomadic and signifying ruptures. Here, in a hermeneutics of difference and virtuality, our endeavor of intercultural studies can finally be firmly "placed."

For the purpose of illustration, not only as to how interface leads to alternative life-forms, but also how it moves beyond representation, subjectivity, and agency, I turn to important sequences in recent kung fu films. These can be considered an ideal showcase for an interface between the classical technological art of kung fu and modern cinema of action, particularly with the advent of digital technology. My first point here is the embodiment which bleeds into both the weapon (usually swords) and martial artists. Starting from learning to use a stick to gather fruits beyond the human hand's reach, and from Greek mythology with the Sphinx's third leg that aged animals/humans rely on, the stick has experienced millions of years of evolution in the projection/reciprocation dialectics.[39] In SF films, we have an extension of this body-weapon "third-leg" embodiment, exemplified by films like *X-Men* (2000) or *The Fantastic Four* (2005). Such an embodiment has become part of the human body in, say, Chinese Taoism, when we see a butcher skilled with his knife and old man catching cicadas with his sticky pole in an amazingly masterful manner. This hunchback, explaining his "way" to Confucius and his followers, says he could "hold my body like a stiff tree trunk and use my arm like an old dry limb." What is important here is the Taoist idea that "when the body and vitality are without flaw, this is called being able to shift."[40] To shift is to move into; it is not simply a movement of the body, but the capacity of the body to move in and out of its tool (or matter or weapon, for that matter), establishing a "nuanced" relationship with its technological device, the movement itself being technological through and through.

As most swords are made of metal, their relation with fighters in martial art is best explained through a Deleuzian notion of the "machinic phylum," or "flow of matter" as illustrated by the "metallic or metallurgical."[41] In *A Thousand Plateaus*, Deleuze and Guattari are concerned with "nomadism," a process of following contingencies or haecceities (events) of matters. But in *Cinema 1*, Deleuze uses the idea of the "non-organic life of things" to describe the pre-war French school of film which issues "a break with the organic" with a type of montage which plunges into "the vital as potent pre-organic germinality, common to the animate and the inanimate, to a matter which raises itself to the point of life, and a life which spreads itself through all matter."[42] Deleuze and Guattari assert, "the living thing has an exterior milieu of materials, and interior milieu of composing elements and composed substances, and intermediary milieu of membranes and limits, and an annexed milieu to energy sources and actions-perceptions" (Deleuze and Guattari 313). Discussing the Deleuzian notion of virtuality in nonlinear causal relations within a process of "feedback loops" (much like Kaufman-Osborn's projection/ reciprocation dialectics), De Landa uses metallurgy developed in the 19th century West to illustrate how goldsmiths go about in their trade where materials have their say towards the virtuality of their form (37).

In the movie *Hero*, the technology of swordsplay is equated with calligraphy, and the pair of swords used by Broken Sword (what a name for a swordsman!) and Flying Snow are referred to as lovers. Even Emperor Qin points out that "Swords are humans and humans are swords."[43] More interesting here is the reed stick Broken Sword uses when he first appears in the film, practicing calligraphy on the sand. Instead of a brush, the calligrapher holds up the reed stick — with body standing upright, much like the cicada catcher in Chuang Tzu's tale, moving it steadily on the sand in front of him, apparently absorbed in training himself in calligraphy and kung fu at the same time. Besides the reed stick, sand is another intriguing aspect of this sequence, because unlike other surfaces such as barks or bamboo plates, the materiality of sand is such that it spreads and gets swollen up easily and loosely, but immediately slides back and meshes, particle after particle, just as easily and spontaneously. Besides, much depends on how deep the reed stick reaches into the sand, since there will be a differential quality of forces necessary for different layers with different textures of the sand structure. (In Chinese calligraphy theories, even papers have different textures in their way of absorbing ink, hence different expressive characteristics.)

Whereas this is clearly a matter of "moving-in," embodiment or swordsman splicing himself with the materiality of his artifice, I also suggest that this calligraphy/swordplay analogy is explained by the Deleuzian concept of tension (or balance) between "striated space" (rules of calligraphy) or "smooth space" which, as Thomas Lamarre observes, enables the calligrapher/swordsman to achieve "Juxtapositions, overlays, inlays, complication alternation that create new resonances."[44] Using this pair of concepts, Lamarre also differentiates "imperial line" from "abstract line"; the former belongs to "center of gravity" and the latter to "center of motion" in Chinese calligraphy (Lamarre 158). From here it is not difficult for us to relate calligraphy with martial arts in general, since the tension between rules (imperial line) and creative repetition (smooth, motion, force, floating, hovering) is found in *Hero*. Brushwork, in Chinese calligraphy, "has the potential to come close to the virtual; it strives toward that moment of inclusive disjunction" (Lamarre 159). What the brush does, the reed stick in Broken Sword's hand does better, and it does more in oscillating and flickering, creating nuances of forceful intersections among materials and matters in summoning a nomadic line that martial artists always look for.[45]

In terms of how kung fu could be incorporated directly by computer interface, we turn to the famous SF film *The Matrix* (1999) for a glimpse of an interesting feedback loop at work between classical technology of kung fu and a futuristic posthuman condition through digital filming technology. It opens with a running scene; this time bodily capabilities are close to Wuta visuals on screen. This running sequence is preceded by a show of high-tech artifacts such as computer interface, a Nokia mobile phone, and an agent and police officer with powerful weapons. Confronted by police, a woman dressed in black displays dexterity in kung fu techniques and even performs the impossible by raising her whole body in the air like an eagle before delivering kicks; during the shoot-out sequence, she starts running on the walls. Then the action cuts to a chase on rooftops, recalling video game combat on one hand and the Chinese style of *ching-gong* (virtuoso speed), the discipline of bodily swiftness and weightless leaps, on the other hand. Here, *The Matrix* assumes suspension of disbelief by virtue of its genre and tries to keep the highly technologized feats unbroken as accepted realism. We later learn that the rebels must train themselves in martial arts to cope with the ferocity of the avatars in power within the virtual reality of the matrix. Even Keanu Reeves's hand-to-hand combat training relies on computer programs (we have a glimpse of the Chinese "Drunken Fist" and a couple of Tai Chi moves) before he proclaims that "I know kung fu."[46] We have now come to a full circle of embodied experience of technology. To resist the authoritarian regime of a fully technologized posthuman world, rebels resort to this traditional technology of body training, so they can overcome their colonizers in cyberspace. Here, the way to parry the dehumanizing technological shock is to return to an embodied technology of human action. It is as if the virtuality of bodily capacity is being tapped into to resist the tyranny of virtual reality, with the help of other high-tech weapons and computers such as what happens in the Japanese science fiction anime *Ghost in the Shell* (1995).

Returning to the chase sequence in *The Matrix*, we can say that the acrobatic feats performed by the woman and agent have little to offer except that the technological atmosphere is obviously foregrounded. It reminds us *The One* (2001) when we see the ever-energized Jet Li outrunning police cars. Personally, I regard the two chase sequences in *Crouching Tiger, Hidden Dragon* (2000) as by far the most aesthetic and appealing to the eyes of Wuxia Pian fans to date, as far as Chinese "weightless leaps" on screen is concerned. The first sequence is right after Zhang Ziyi has stolen the Green Destiny and is being chased by Michelle Yeoh. The chase is presented in a most visible way: we see step-by-step, foot-over-foot details of the body movement, interlaced with fist-countering-fist, palm-confronting-palm — all the kickings, climbings, pulling down of a foot; whenever action stops, it is when the women are mustering up for another round of attack. It is of course a product of "digital compositing," which, according to Lev Manorich, means "assembling together a number of elements to create a single seamless object,"[47] here the object being seamless efforts in leaping and running on walls, rooftops, and so on. The sequence depicts a series of intense moments of escaping and catching, but the effect is stunning in that action is presented almost in unison, and the camera's fluidity enhances a fluidity of body movement in perfect uninterruption and continuity. For viewers, it is simply "pure poetry of the body as it exceeds the expectations of normal physical reality,"[48] a new aesthetics of body-in-motion choreography seamlessly merged with the virtual interface of digitalized technological apparatus.

The second chase and exchange of swordplay is even more spectacular. Again, holding on to the Green Destiny, Zhang Ziyi literally flies in a long take from behind houses onto the water of a lake, the action of which is clearly modeled on a famous *ching-gong* move called "dragonfly pointing on water" to be followed by Chow Yun-Fat doing the same. Then the chase cuts to a beautiful forest of luxurious green foliage and bamboos. The graceful movements— of churning over, embracing the trees, standing on the tip of the shaft, balancing, and swinging in perfect accord with the mechanics of bending branches burdened by their weight — are cut to a zoom-in on the faces of the pair, moving and gazing, short of breath but retaining their serenity. Sword moves are then exchanged, all the while in harmony with the natural forces borrowed from swinging movements of shafts and bamboo sticks, making up a milieu of interrelationships of living things and their environments. Here, Bogue's "biology of melodic living forms" manifests itself. Body movements, the sword, and forest merge into each other with the interconnectedness expounded by the Chinese concept (also in kung fu) of *shi* (tendency). *Shun shi* seems an everyday life concept but, like many other concepts, has its roots in Taoist teachings. In fact, many passages in Chuang Tzu deal with this *shi* (which I translate as "moving structure") in the myriad forms of life and things in nature, pointing to non-linear life-tendencies particularly in terms of the relational ontology of forces and their differential rhythms of intensity. This sequence of kung fu in *Crouching Tiger, Hidden Dragon* certainly is a showcase of what digital composition can do to visually realize such a concept in the Chinese aesthetics of bodily movement, particularly how it relates to the biophilosophy of Taoism itself.

In *The Matrix*, fantastic human action is disciplined by machines, and we have a full circle of feedback loop in the projection/reciprocation evolution of human/machine interface, where the classical technology of enhancing bodily capabilities is used in modern high-tech programs for the purpose of resisting a more powerful virtual world, demonstrating clearly that reciprocations by rule always exceed their earlier projections. With *Crouching Tiger, Hidden Dragon*, not even a suspension of disbelief is required by audiences because digital composition and the kung fu discourse (fictional rendering of flying swordsmen) reinforce each other, rendering a poetic performance of beautiful human action possible by having it seamlessly merged with its background environment in an interplay of intensity, the two fighters supported and bounced back (as by the springing up and bending down of bamboo shafts) while swinging their swords.

Having noted the Taoist concept of *shi* (tendency) in kung fu discourse, I turn to one of the most salient features in kung fu performance on screen, the "rhythm of pause/burst/pause" as observed by David Bordwell.[49] These "instants of stillness" or "moments of pure stasis" (Bordwell 222, 224) are related to the Peking opera, *liang hsiang* (form-showing) tradition, but also go way back to at least the Taoist biophilosophy of the mutuality and reinforcement of stillness/movement in all lives. The concept of "dong jing xiang sheng" (movement-stillness mutuality) has figured in poetry, painting, calligraphy, and martial arts, arguing that stillness is the ultimate source of all energies. This is amply demonstrated by tai-chi, which emphasizes circular movements beyond specific moves of one-move-one-form and maximizes energy flow by not confronting force with force, but by borrowing the opponent's power in the *shun shi* manner I described. Bordwell's observation of pauses between speedy bursting of attacks relates to the kung fu idea of gathering up your *shi* at a point of bursting, as in the phrases "action in ferment" or "folding in on itself." *Shi* is a common word that can be combined with various words to make compound nouns such as form/structure (*xing shi*) tendencies (*qu shi*), denoting a double-bind situation of a stillness/movement dialectic. The idea is that crouched in things which are supposed to be still, dynamic forces of intensity are to burst out at a point of utmost disequilibrium. One only looks at the term mountain-move-structure (*shun shi*) to understand this concept, mountains being very still from the naked eye, but, like volcanoes, full of intense energy from within. Here we recall the common practice in kung fu disciplining that novices must learn to set their horse-like form (*za ma*) in perfect stillness like a mountain before other lessons can begin.

Bordwell's pauses in Wuxia Pian and the Chinese concept of *shi* or tendencies, as noted, can be traced back to Chuang Tzu's idea that all lives are the result of the intensive transformation under the sky and on earth. The word *wei* refers to snake-like turns and whirls, describing the self-opening of the Lathe of Heaven when all lives are at an emergent point within an intensity of differentiation before their forms are individualized. Here Chuang Tzu presents a tacit but intensive process of changes in quality among life-forms, their environment, weather, vapors, and light within a structure of mutual affordance. This natural tendency toward affordance is exactly what is meant by embodied capacity as expounded by De Landa when he says, based on the Deleuzian geophilosophy, that "a biological population may exhibit attractors (and thus be defined in part by the tendencies with which these singularities endow it) but in addiction its members will typically display—complex capacities for interaction" (De Landa 62). When Lao Tzu in *Tao-te Ching* talks of two animals *Yu* and *Yiu* (later the two become a compound noun for hesitation) as they are seen, one as "Cautious, like crossing a frozen stream in the winter" and the other "at a loss, like one fearing danger on all sides,"[50] he grants a primitive authority for kung fu practitioners who develop action programs modeled on the careful and attentive pause-and-action by animals. One recalls here that including Bruce Lee's actions, we see many zoom-ins onto the screen of grinding and moving feet, inch by inch sometimes, at the point of the emergent attack or defense. It is as if the fighters' bodies were in an infolding of a pressing multitude of incipiencies, right at a critical point between a germinal state and selecting a form of movement. The point is that the significance of these patterns of pause-burst-pause does not stop at martial arts aesthetics in films, but extends far towards a kind of biophilosophy of affordance of all lives—which may partly explain why martial artists are fond of modeling their moves on animals, or rather, using Deleuze's term, why they are prone to becoming-animals.[51]

The non-representability of bodily movement is based in the Taoist philosophy as manifested, say, in *Tai-chi chuen* or *Tai-chi-jian* where passage precedes position, where isolated moves must be abandoned for seamless circling of non-moves which include a multiplicity of singular moves when needed. Such a refusal to succumb to successive points or instants of spatialized time restores our direct access to the very-evolving, folding and unfolding temporal flow, tai-chi being movement with circle overlapping circle, one being squeezed

away by another, which in turn is swallowed up by yet another. Such a processual (immanent, productive, and energetic), such sheer vibrance, is certainly
a positing of "the simultaneity of a series of incompassible presents"[52] and transformed into a kung fu film, particularly those with science fiction elements, it
becomes a duration or event where an ancient technology of embodying the
vitality of force is juxtaposed with a modern technology of narrating this movement in film. The "dizziness" of swirling around in continuum (mostly felt by
the opponent of someone who performs tai-chi) issues forth the interval, the
irrational cuts as a new type of narrating technique which deals directly with
creating a fable through the power to falsify or to fabulate (Lambert 90–113).
Here we recall Jin Yong's powerful description in *Heaven Sword and Dragon
Saber* (1978) where the Grand Master Taoist Chang first demonstrates in front
of everybody, enemies included, a round of his recently created tai chi *Jien*
(sword) for Chang Wu-chi to use immediately. Having attentively learned the
moves by heart, and having digested the moves as lines after lines of volition
and velocity, young Chang reports that he has only one move left in his mind.
The Master — pleased by the youth's quick achievement, but also convinced
that the Tai-chi machine is still not perfectly "abstract enough" in him — begins
another set, this time totally different from the first.[53] Chang then walks around
in the hall, going through in him the whole pattern of moves, and finally
announces that not one single move is left, now perfectly ready for his eventual
triumph over the enemy. I wish to juxtapose this tai-chi concept with what
Deleuze says in *Difference and Repetition* that repetition is "by nature transgression or exception, always revealing a singularity opposed to the particulars
subsumed under laws" (Deleuze 1994 5). What the master does the second time
is no mere mechanical repetition but a Deleuzian process of "signaling." Such
signaling is a dynamic rhythm process, a repetition of "an internal difference
which it incorporates in each of its moments" (Deleuze 1994 20). As for Chang,
what he will do during actual fights will be difference or changes in itself, always
armed with a plurality of positions and modulatory moves that go beyond any
representation. Every move he makes in the future will be one among "free
variations"[54] and will focus on the "plus" within a structure of one-plus-one-
plus-one, this plus becoming the outside of any relational process of an event.
    I therefore suggest, following our presentation of circles after circles of
movement in tai chi where affects and percepts reign rather than feelings and
perceptions, that intercultural studies is a further development of cultural studies per se, the former now categorized as assuming the action of "shiftings"
between paradigms as the primary force which prioritizes passages over positions, relationalities within processual continuity over their terms, and movement or temporality over molar territorializations of any kind. Barbara M.
Kennedy, advocating a neo-aesthetic of material affect for cinema viewing
beyond representation, psychoanalysis, and subjectivity, particularly with a
view of constructing a becoming-woman paradigm for post-feminism, notes

that "a complex set of intersecting forces" is of paramount importance in cinema, since "we can feel intense and ecstatic resonances in an array of dimensions of experience, specifically through dance, colour, tactility, movement and the rhythmical."[55] That Kennedy says something relevant to us in tai chi is obvious enough, since kung fu can well be considered as dance, not to mention that both Kennedy and my discussion involve the technology of action cinema. Kennedy's neo-aesthetics can readily be incorporated into the abstract machine of tai chi since both are concerned with material movement in a fluid and complex set of machinic collusions and interconnectedness.

Finally Brian Massumi argues that the problem with dominant models in cultural theory is that they are "not abstract enough to grasp the real incorpo-reality of the concrete," and that "cultural studies has missed its processual boat because it has not had the audacity to sweep far enough in either direction"; it "misses surplus giving relation and the qualitative excess of ongoing trans-formations," and finally, cultural studies "generally — particularly misses change: hence the obsession with change that has haunted (it) from the beginning" (Massumi 5, 253). Overall, that externality of relations not only causes changes in these relations, but also ignites forces which loop back through the conjunction AND to change their earlier terms. Such a valorizing of affection of transitions of all kinds in a flux of forces and intensities, I venture to suggest, will become the major problematics for intercultural studies in the 21st century.

NOTES

1. Pnina Werbner, "Introduction: the Dialectics of Cultural Hybridity," *Debating Cultural Hybridity: Multi-Cultural Identities and the Politics of Anti-Racism*, ed. Werbner and Tariq Modood (London and New Jersey: Zed Books, 1997), 5.

2. Robert Bernasconi, "'Stuck Inside of Mobile with the Memphis Blues Again': Interculturalism and the Conversations of Races," *Theorizing Multiculturalism: A Guide to the Current Debate*, ed. Cynthia Willett (Oxford: Blackwell, 1998), 283. Subsequent page references in the text are to this edition.

3. There are too many examples to note here. Heinz-Otto Peitgen and Peter H. Richter's *The Beauty of Fractals: Images of Complex Dynamical Systems* (Berlin and New York: Springer-Verlag, 1986) and John D. Barrow's *The Artful Universe* (Oxford: Clarendon Press, 1995) are important ones. These books explore the close ties between our aesthetic appreciation and the basic nature of the universe, between human creativity and scientific studies on living organisms as natural properties of our world; they also provide a model of how humanities and technoscience can be approached, and how the essentials for life can be studies as vital determinants of our cultural, psychological, philosophical and religious responses to the cosmos. As for the word "genome," the 1993 edition of *Webster's Dictionary* defines it as "a historically new entity engendered by the productive crisis of nature and culture."

4. Donna Haraway, *Modest_Witness@Second_Millennium. FemaleMan(c)_Meets_OncoMouse(tm): Feminism and Technoscience* (New York and London: Routledge, 1997), 149. Subsequent page references in the text are to this edition.

5. Anthony King, *Global Cities* (London: Routledge, 1990), 38.

6. Arjun Appadurai, "Disjuncture and Difference in the Global Cultural Economy," *Public Culture*, 2:2 (1990), 7. Subsequent page references in the text are to this edition.

7. Michel de Certeau, "Walking in the City," *The Cultural Studies Reader*, ed. Simon During (London: Routledge, 1993), 160.

8. Edward Soja, *Thirdspace* (Cambridge: Blackwell, 1996), 130.

9. Aihwa Ong, "On the Edge of Empires: Flexible Citizenship among Chinese in Diaspora," *Positions*, 1 (Winter, 1993), 755.

10. Jurgen Habermas, "A Review of Gadamer's *Truth and Method*," *Hermeneutics and Modern Philosophy*, ed. Brice R. Wachtehauser (Albany: New York State University Press, 1986), 250.

11. Hans-Georg Gadamer, *The Relevance of the Beautiful and Other Essays*, ed. Bemasconi (New York and London: Cambridge University Press, 1986), 388.

12. John D. Caputo, *More Radical Hermeneutics: On Not Knowing Who We Are* (Bloomington and Indianapolis: Indiana University Press, 2000), 42, 59.

13. Mark Hansen, *Embodying Technesis: Technology Beyond Writing* (Ann Arbor: University of Michigan Press, 2000), 213.

14. Michel Foucault, "Of Other Spaces," *Diacritics*, 16:1 (1986), 22–27.

15. Bruno Latour, *We Have Never Been Modern*, 1991, trans. Catherine Porter (Cambridge: Harvard University Press, 1993). The actor-network issue is further elaborated in Latour's later book *Politics of Nature: How to Bring the Sciences Into Democracy*.

16. Edward Soja, *Thirdspace* (Cambridge: Harvard University press, 2004), 73–87.

17. While I cannot do justice to Deleuze's concept of virtuality, I would draw upon Pierre Levy's words in *Becoming Virtual: Reality in the Digital Age*, trans. Robert Bononno (New York: Plenum Trade, 1998), to sum up the general understanding of this concept:
Never before have the technological, economic, and social changes around us occurred so rapidly or been so destabilizing. Virtualization itself represents the essence, the cutting edge of the mutation taking place. As such virtualization is neither good nor bad, nor even neutral, but manifests itself as the very process of humanity's "becoming other"— its heterogenesis ... virtualization involves a change of identity, a transition from a particular solution to a general problematic, the transformation of a specific and circumscribed activity into a delocalized, desynchronized, and collectivized functioning.... Through the creation of planes of consistency, heterogeneous, molecular becomings are put into continuity in new ways that go beyond any existing plane of organization and touch upon the infinite movements of what Deleuze and Guattari call virtual reality. (16, 44, 190)

18. See J. MacGregor Wise, *Exploring Technology and Social Space* (London and New Delhi: Sage, 1997), 31.

19. See Ray Kurzweil, *The Age of Spiritual Machines: When Computers Exceed Human Intelligence* (New York: Viking, 1999).

20. Keith Ansell Pearson, "Viroid Life: On Machines, Technics and Evolution," *Deleuze and Philosophy: The Difference Engineer*, ed. Pearson (London: Routledge, 1997), 181.

21. Gilles Deleuze and Felix Guattari, *A Thousand Plateaus: Capitalism and Schizophrenia*, trans. Brian Massumi (London: The Athlone Press, 1988), 69. Subsequent Deleuze and Guattari page references in the text are to this edition.

22. Foucault, "The Subject and Power," *Michel Foucault: Beyond Structuralism and Hermeneutics*, ed. Hubert Dryfus and Paul Rabinow, Second Edition (Chicago: University of Chicago Press 1983), 213.

23. N. Katherine Hayles, *How We Became Posthuman: Virtual Bodies in Cybernetics, Literature, and Informatics* (Chicago: University of Chicago Press, 1999), 286. Subsequent Hayles page references in the text are to this edition.

24. Andrew Feenberg, *Questioning Technology* (London: Routledge, 1999), 80.

25. Thomas C. Shevory, *Body/Politics: Studies in Reproductions, Productions, and (Re)Construction* (London: Praeger, 2000), 43.

26. Manuel De Landa, "Deleuze, Diagrams, and the Open-Ended Becoming of the World," *Becomings: Explorations in Time, Memory, and Futures,* ed. Elizabeth Grosz (Ithaca, New York: Cornell University Press, 1999), 41. Subsequent De Landa references in the text are to this edition.

27. Ian Buchanan, "Deleuze and Cultural Studies," *A Deleuzian Century?,* ed. Buchanan (Durham and London: Duke University Press, 1999), 105. Subsequent Buchanan page references in the text are to this edition.

28. Deleuze, *Difference and Repetition,* trans. Paul Patton (London: Athlone, 1994), 278. Subsequent "Deleuze 1994" references in the text are to this edition. In *Empiricism and Subjectivity: An Essay on Hume's Theory of Human Nature,* trans. Constantin V. Boundas (New York: Columbia University Press, 1991), Deleuze points out that "ideas do not account for the nature of the operations that we perform on them" (101).

29. Deleuze's thesis in *Difference and Repetition* is that Western metaphysical thought recognizes difference only with a presupposition of sameness; it is "fatally ensnared in a fourfold structure of representational thinking which reduces difference to its relation with identity and thus fails to grasp difference in its radical authenticity" (Oliver Davies, "Thinking Difference: A Comparative Study of Gilles Deleuze, Plotinus and Meister Eckhard," *Deleuze and Religion,* ed. Mary Bryden [London: Routledge, 2001], 76).

30. Deleuze, *Negotiations: 1972–1990,* trans. Martin Joughin (New York: Columbia University Press, 1995), 45.

31. For a careful analysis of quantum physics as it relates to Deleuze's philosophy of becomings and virtualities, see Timothy S. Murphy's "Quantum Ontology: A Virtual Mechanics of Becoming," *Deleuze and Guattari: New Mappings in Politics, Philosophy, and Culture,* ed. Eleanor Kaufman and Kevin Jon Heller (Minneapolis: University of Minnesota, 1998), 211–229.

32. John Mullarkey, "Deleuze and Materialism: One or Several Matters?," *A Deleuzian Century?,* 69.

33. Alistair Welchman, "Machinic Thinking," *Deleuze and Philosophy,* 211–229.

34. John Marks, *Gilles Deleuze: Vitalism and Multiplicity* (London: Pluto, 1998), 86. Subsequent Marks page references in the text are to this edition.

35. Grosz, "Deleuze's Bergson: Duration, the Virtual and a Politics of the Future," *Deleuze and Feminist Theory,* ed. Buchanan and Claire Colebrook (Edinburgh: Edinburgh University Press, 2000), 228.

36. Pearson, "Pure Reserve: Deleuze, Philosophy, and Immanence," *Deleuze and Religion,* 142.

37. Daniel W. Smith, "The Doctrine of Univocity: Deleuze's Ontology of Immanence," *Deleuze and Religion,* 179. Subsequent Smith page references in the text are to this edition.

38. Ronald Bogue, "Art and Territory," *A Deleuzian Century?,* 93.

39. See Timothy V. Kaufman-Osborn, *Creatures of Prometheus: Gender and the Politics of Technology* (New York: Rowman & Littlefield, 1997.

40. See Burton Watson's English version of *The Complete Works of Chuang Tzu,* Chapter Nineteen, "Mastering Life," (New York: Columbia University Press, 1968), 198–200.

41. See *A Thousand Plateaus,* 410–411; on 415, Deleuze and Guattari also note: "This hybrid metallurgist, a weapon- and toolmaker, communicates with the sedentaries and with the nomads at the same time.... In effect, the machinic phylum or the metallic line passes through all of the assemblages: nothing is more deterritorialized than matter-movement." In *What is Philosophy?* (New York: Columbia University Press, 1994), Deleuze and Guattari suggest that "Even when they are nonliving, or rather inorganic, things have a lived experience because they are perceptions and affections" (154).

42. Deleuze, *Cinema 1: The Movement-Image*, trans. Hugh Tomlinson and Barbara Habberjam (Minneapolis: University of Minnesota Press, 1986), 55, 51.

43. *Hero* [*Ying Xiong*] (Beijing New Picture Film Co., 2002).

44. Thomas Lamarre, "Diagram, Inscription, Sensation," *A Shock to Thought: Expression After Deleuze and Guattari*, ed. Massumi (London and New York: Routledge, 2002), 151. Subsequent Lamarre page references in the text are to this edition.

45. What Lamarre says in an end-note in his essay on Dean and Massumi's book *First and Last Emperors* (1992) is interesting, and relevant to the thematic structure (or ideology) in *Hero*, where Emperor Qin's relation to striated and smooth lines is brought forward. Lamarre records that the book provides "a useful model for thinking about the ways in which the first dynasty of the Qin emperor attempted to reconcile antagonisms between smooth and striated space by evoking modes of warfare, exchange, and social hierarchy which accelerated and blurred the two tendencies (like the spokes of a wheel) within a state that could only implode and explode. This dynamics of imperial formation and dispersion informs subsequent dynasties, courts, commandaries, albeit in a muted tempered form" (Lamarre 168). For Deleuze and Guattari's smooth and striated space, see *A Thousand Plateaus*, 474–550.

46. *The Matrix* (Warner Brothers, 1999).

47. Lev Manovich, *The Language of New Media* (Cambridge: M.I.T. Press, 2001), 139.

48. Andrew Schroeder, "All Roads Lead to Hong Kong: Martial Arts, Digital Effects and the Labour of Empire in Contemporary Action Film," *E-Journal on Hong Kong Cultural and Social Studies*, No. 1 (2002), at http://www.hku.hk/hkcsp/ccex/ehkcss01/frame.htm?mid=2&smid=1&ssmid=7 .

49. David Bordwell, *Planet Hong Kong: Popular Cinema and the Art of Entertainment* (Cambridge: Harvard University Press, 2000), 222. Later Bordwell page references in the text are to this edition.

50. Lao Tzu, *The Way of Lao Tzu (Tao-te Ching)*, trans. Chan Wing-Tsit (New Jersey: Prentice Hall, 1963), 126.

51. De Landa notes, "An individual organism will typically exhibit a variety of capabilities to form *assemblages* with other individuals, organic or inorganic. A good example is the assemblage which a walking animal forms with a piece of solid ground (which supplies it with a surface to walk) and with a gravitational field (which endows it with a given weight). Although the capacity to form an assemblage depends in part on the emergent properties of the interacting individuals (animal, ground, field) it is nevertheless not reducible to them. We may have exhaustive knowledge about an individual's properties and yet, not having observed it in interaction with other individuals, know nothing about its capacities" (*Intensive Science and Virtual Philosophy* [London: Continuum, 2002], 63).

52. Gregg Lambert, *The Non-Philosophy of Gilles Deleuze* (New York: Continuum, 2002), 90. Subsequent Lambert page references in the text are to this edition.

53. *Heaven Sword and Dragon Saber* [*Yi Tian Tu Long Ji*] (Shaw Brothers, 1978).

54. Massumi, *Parables for the Virtual: Movement, Affect, Sensation* (Durham and London: Duke University Press, 2002), 71. Subsequent Massumi page references in the text are to this edition.

55. Barbara M. Kennedy, *Deleuze and Cinema: The Aesthetics of Sensation* (Edinburgh: Edinburgh University Press, 2000), 29, 43.

12

Post-Genre Cinemas and Post-Colonial Attitude

Hong Kong Meets Paris

VÉRONIQUE FLAMBARD-WEISBART

At the eve of the 21st century, the new global order has affected all national cinemas, and it is common to find various aspects of one culture playing a part in the meaning and visual economy of another. In *Palimpsestes*, Gérard Genette studied the relationships between one text and another, whether explicit or secret, and called this transtextuality. Within transtextual relationships, Genette defined hypertextuality as "any relationship uniting a text B ([...] the hypertext) to an earlier text A ([...] the hypotext), upon which it is grafted in a manner that is not of commentary [...] text B not speaking of text A at all but being unable to exist, as such, without A, from which it originates through a process [...] call[ed] transformation, and which it consequently evokes more or less perceptibly without necessarily speaking of it or citing it."[1]

Esther C. M. Yau outlines further transtextual relationships in *At Full Speed: Hong Kong Cinema in a Borderless World*. She distinguishes "piracy" from "experimental syncretism." On the one end,

> Piracy, which rides on the mainstream global economy and its expansive cultural property rights, is certainly disruptive of the assertion of identity[....] Movies that borrow, recycle, and remake existing materials, conventions, idioms, styles, and even images have increased in number[....] The extreme pressures of time under which movies are made [...] frequently leads to pilfering of popular ideas (or lesser-known ones) in the industry, turning the nationalist claims—captured by such phrases as "reflecting upon one's culture" and "the integrity of national cinema"—into empty rhetoric. Piracy calls attention to the short life of commodity production and consumption that results from global overproduction.[2]

Not far from this context, in the 1990s, Hollywood coined the term "international film" to describe the concept of films produced outside of the United States. But there is a subtle meaning to the term that prevents it from simply being applied to all non–American films. In general, international films have a certain association with Independent films. Commenting on issues of culture and society through such tropes as love, art, and violence, the international film — more than a "foreign film"— struggles to present an insightful look at how cultures interact with each other, or at how different cultures' perceived realities can cause problems in communication.[3]

The concept of "international film"— like "Independent film" before it — has been a direct outcome of Hollywood's established hegemony on the global market, and would have not otherwise existed. It is an alluring concept meant to simulate Hollywood's contending with the global diversity of cinemas, but the reality has been disappointing. "International film" has mostly succeeded at promoting Hollywood's "commentary" on national cinemas—commenting the hypotext — rather than "reflecting upon one's culture," or fostering "the integrity of national cinema"— generating the hypertext. Hollywood has also used the concept of "international film" as a savvy camouflage for discarding to the periphery the "foreign films" that do not sell as well on the global market.

"Experimental syncretism," on the other end, is reminiscent of Genette's definition of hypertextuality. Speaking on Hong Kong cinema, Yau argues:

> With experimental syncretism, citation and irreverent remaking of cultural materials, mixed locations, and cross-cultural collaborations, these films proffer a space-time in which Hong Kong appears in many versions. In these culturally androgynous worlds, "Hong Kong" is an unstable symbolic construct making affiliations, both conventional and unexpected, with the many signs and stories circulating in mass-mediated cultures [12].

In this postmodern era, transtextuality indeed takes on various identities. In the context of economic globalization, it assumes the form of "piracy" or "international film," and it tends to confuse the hypotext with a generic identity. In the context of the periphery, transtextuality appears in the shape of "experimental syncretism" or "foreign film" and continuously decolonizes the hypotext, which continuously shifts to the flexible identity of the hypertext.

In this chapter, I focus on the transtextual relationships between recent French and Hong Kong cinemas, in the peripheral context described above, examining recent Hong Kong cinema as the disconnected hypertext of French New Wave film and recent French cinema as the unexpected hypertext of Hong Kong Wuxia Pian (swordplay film). Specifically, recalling some concepts and precepts of French New Wave cinema, I explain how the films of Hong Kong director Wong Kar-Wai created the hypertext of this stalled movement; then, looking at the spectacular effects characteristic of Hong Kong Wuxia Pian, I demonstrate how the films of French director Christophe Gans have invented the hypertext of this weakened Hong Kong genre.

Back in 1950s France, a cluster of film critics started the cinema review *Les Cahiers du Cinéma*. Involved were André Bazin, François Truffaut, Jean-

Luc Godard, Jacques Rivette, and Eric Rohmer, among others. Together, these critics elaborated, theoretically and politically, a film theory and criticism that defined the French New Wave. They spoke of a "certain tendency" for French cinema, which they expressed in *la politique des auteurs*. Seeking "the French attitude," authorship was a simple concept most of them essentially agreed upon: "the film *auteur* was to be considered as fully an artist as many of the great novelists, painters or poets."[4]

Linked to the concept of authorship came the notion of *mise-en-scène*, or directing: the technique employed by an *auteur* to express things in a particular way, his/her style. This made the author/director relationship similar to that of the author/artist or author/writer. Directing was a true act of writing; no more distinction existed between director and author. Works by the director/author were evaluated critically, not so much in terms of the themes he/she dealt with, but in terms of his/her style, the medium to his/her particular world-view. The impact of *Cahiers du Cinéma* for the French New Wave was tremendous.

However, if these critics changed the course of French cinema, it was not so much through their criticism as by making films themselves. They outlined different elements that would help express "the French attitude" in their own films (Hillier 21–22). They pointed to screenwriters/adapters—for whom the director was only the person who added the picture to the scenario—as a main obstacle towards the good quality of filmmaking. Authors/directors in the New Wave accused screenwriters/adapters of being literary men lacking in authenticity. In moral terms, the content of their works was misanthropic, pessimistic, and non-conformist, which made them guilty of cheap audacity. They would compensate for their lack of optimism, generosity, and ambiguity with scholarly framings, complicated lighting effects, and polished photography, taking away any remnant of authenticity and realism. To their cheap audacity, authors/directors of the French New Wave opposed the audacity of "mise-en-scène." American critic John Hess argued,

> the most important determinant of an *auteur* was not so much the director's ability to express his personality, as usually has been claimed, but rather his desire and ability to express a certain world-view. An *auteur* was a film director who expressed an optimistic image of human potentialities within an utterly corrupted society. By reaching out emotionally and spiritually to other human beings and/or to God, one could transcend the isolation imposed on one by a corrupt world [cited by Hillier 6].

Thus, directors/authors such as Godard, Truffaut, Resnais, Rohmer and Agnès Varda among others jump-cut their way to an elliptical, spontaneous filmmaking that was both more realistic and more exuberantly stylized than what had existed before. These critics turned authors/directors did not bluntly reject their predecessors, but rather implicitly built on the filmmaking of the precursors of their movement. Inspired by certain American directors who had left their personal stamp on films despite the rigid constraints of the studio system, and by French precursors such as Jean-Pierre Melville and his poetic gangsters, Jacques Tati and the celebration of eccentricity in a regimented world, and Robert Bresson and luminous realism, New Wave directors questioned cinema's own form of expression and explored the relationship between consciousness and expression of meaning and activity. They set out explicitly intending to explore the relationships between director and film, reality and fiction, artist and model. They developed new methods of filmmaking such as location shooting and improvisation. Rejecting cinematic formulae and the studio-bound approach of 1950s mainstream cinema, New Wave directors assumed a casual approach to cinematic conventions—editing in a freer style and implementing looser construction of scenarios.

When Godard declared that cinema and language are inextricably bound in a dance of intertextuality and pastiche, he subsumed the new aesthetic landscape created by French New Wave directors. In the year 1959 alone, Godard's *Breathless*—which took the genre of the witty chase thriller and obliterated it—Truffaut's *The 400 Blows*—which launched the extraordinary semiautobiographical series of the "Antoine Doinel" films—and Resnais' *Hiroshima, My Love*—which mastered a poetic evocation of love and passionate plea for world peace—created models for the decades of truly personal cinema to follow, and opened new doors to filmmaking as a whole.

The funkiness, freakiness, irony, and self-conscious stylization of New Wave directors was emulated and found new hypertexts in the works of new generations of French directors throughout the 1980s—in Maurice Pialat's sexual tangling and quarreling epics, Bertrand Blier's witty, bizarre, fairy tales, and Jean-Jacques Beineix's style in itself. Unfortunately, by the end of the 1980s, the French New Wave found it increasingly difficult to regenerate, and was heading into overly self-reflective and intimist films. The future of the once liberating and boundary-breaking French New Wave cinema movement seemed to meet a dead end. If not for the emergence of films by directors outside of France, like those by Wong Kar-Wai, the French New Wave might have lost its legendary ability to generate hypertexts, at least on the home front.

Born in 1958 in Shangai, Wong combines stunning visuals and edgy, sensitive storytelling, which have spread a new dawn across the horizon of Hong Kong film. Originally a graphic design student, Wong fell in love with photography and was influenced by such names as Robert Frank, Henri Cartier-Bresson, and Richard Avedon. After briefly working as a production assistant for television drama serials, he progressed to scriptwriting, notably for a popular soap opera/thriller, then left TV for filmmaking.

When seeing Wong's recent films—like *Chungking Express* (1994), *Fallen Angels* (1995), *Happy Together* (which garnered him the 1997 best director award at the Cannes Festival), *In the Mood for Love* (2001), *Six Days* (2002), *2046* (2004), and *There's Only One Sun* (2007)—French audiences brought up on French New Wave cinema cannot help but experience the feeling of ambivalence that comes with being both in the foreign cultural context of Hong Kong and in the familiar aesthetic context of Godard's films. In an interview with *Mon Ciné Club*, where he introduced the screening of *Chungking Express*, director Christophe Gans said:

> What is amusing when watching *Chungking Express* is that you realize that THIS is the movie that all Godard's fans and followers have dreamt to make but somehow never did. So it's quite strange to realize that in Hong Kong, they manage to make films that we should be doing in France. In this respect, you can say that they [...] have in Hong Kong the New Wave that we were unable to keep in France.[5]

In *Chungking Express*, Wong focuses on a theme recurrent in much of his work: urban alienation. He paints Hong Kong as a claustrophobic cage in which people pace like trapped animals. People in the film have such dissolute and pointless lives that they cannot connect emotionally with others. Wong's unflinching vision lends his work a bleak, nervy atmosphere of unfulfilled longing, loneliness, desperation, and even nostalgia.

The film has a dual structure in its substance and form. It is composed of two stories that are independent from one another, yet both tell about love. There are two sketches, two cops, two Mays, two wigs, two air hostesses, two couples splitting up, two painful break ups.... But despite all differences, the two stories are similar, and include other themes found in most Wong films: rejection and treason. Although Wong has a personal interpretation of these themes, the Godard fan will recognize themes dear to the French director. Indeed, from his first film on, Godard worked at setting the tone for his views on love, rejection and treason — usually by women (e.g. the betrayal of Patricia in *Breathless*, of Camille in *Contempt*, *etc*). Furthermore, Godard's stylistic use of the jump-cut, the ten-minute tracking shot, and fractured time sequences, a French New Wave patented look, has been emulated and reinvented by Wong's incisive and de-glamorizing camera in *Chungking Express*. More than these similarities of themes and style, however, it is the dexterity, with which Wong forces the viewers to stop, look, and listen as their own culture is critiqued, which makes French audiences feel right at home. Godard's sometimes ironic, sometimes reverential, dialogue with pop culture, which set the mood for the French New Wave movement, has found a match in Wong's personal blend of "trendiness" and modernity. Still digressing on *Chungking Express*, Gans argues that,

> it is a "post-genre" movie[....] It's apparently an action movie with cops, vamps, villains, smugglers and guns. But actually nothing really happens. These people aren't involved in criminal activities, they just wander around. That's the main idea. It's sort of an existential chaos where people, who are supposed to draw their gun, fight, and have very tough relationships, are simply hanging around! (HKCinemagic; my translation)

American critic Roger Ebert further stated that "the films of Wong Kar-Wai capture moods and modes rather than leading to complacent resolutions or contrived forms of closure."[6] In Wong's postmodern narrative, Godard's ideals of montage and *mise-en-scène* seem to be gone. We are far from the self-reflective end of *Breathless* with the stylized death of Poiccard, which symbolized Godard's artistic conflict at turning his creation over to public opinion and losing creative control over it. Wong replaces these ideals with celebration of the disconnected fragment, which the director does not hesitate or fear to turn over "as is" to the public. In *Chungking Express*, any attempt to garner a message or impose an interpretative structure on the two stories will be frustrated. In other words, audiences are forced to accept the ride without expecting a destination. Part of the answer for this disconnectedness may lay in the shifting political sands that have been a symptom of the widespread postmodern project of decolonization and its sister project, economic globalization. Wong's disconcerting representation of colonial Hong Kong suggests the impossibility of tidy denouements.

In recent Hong Kong cinema, Yau sees a juxtaposition of "divergent cultural materials [which] create crossovers between certain forms and mediums that were previously separate" and "fragments of popular culture [which] are eclectically displayed even when the films are intensely focused on local situations" (11). Gans' perception of *Chungking Express* is closely akin to Yau's evaluation: "What Wong Kar Wai actually does is that he mixes the characters all together and sees what happens. This makes an absolutely free-wheeled unconventional cinema, which represents exactly what you have in Hong Kong, not only with Wong Kar Wai, but also with John Woo or others. It's a real mix of styles [...] it's a movie with a totally free editing, directing, and everything gets mixed up in the process. And it's incredibly beautiful" (HKCinemagic). Hence, it is not coincidental that Gans' own filmmaking is ruled by such various juxtapositions.

Born in 1960, Gans was an early convert to film fandom. As a teenager, the future director published a fanzine, *Rhesus Zero*, to share his passion for horror, sci-fi, wuxia, kung fu and other genre films with others. Gans eventually attended the *Institut des Hautes Etudes Cinématopraphiques* (IDHEC) to explore his passion not just for film but film*making*. In the 1980s, Gans noticed that his fellow French filmmakers were hesitant to explore the genres he found interesting. Falling back on his experience in fanzine publishing, Gans founded *Starfix*, a magazine devoted to the types of films he thought deserved coverage. Gans also served as consultant at Scherzo Video, helping supervise the release of some favorite Asian films to the French market, including Japanese films and the films of Chang Cheh, King Hu, John Woo, and Wong Kar-Wai among others. His own filmmaking — represented by such films as *Necronomicon* (1993), *Crying Freeman* (1996), *Brotherhood of the Wolf* (2001) (which granted Gans immediate international success), and *Silent Hill* (2006) — draws heavily on the genres of Asian film masters, classic and contemporary.

Directors of the French New Wave were revolutionary in that they created a new genre. Unlike these French directors, however, Gans does not transform existing genres, but rather challenges the viewers' perception of them. In the 1980s, he strongly defended genres that were despised by a certain close-minded French intelligentsia, the same group that was driving French New Wave cinema into a dead end. Gans was however vindicated in the year 2000 with the stunning global success of Ang Lee's *Crouching Tiger, Hidden Dragon*, dedicated to the old genre of Chinese wuxia pian, one of Gans' favorites. With *Brotherhood of the Wolf*, Gans had a chance to pay personal tribute to the genre, simultaneously renewing with a lost value in French cinema: Entertainment.

Brotherhood of the Wolf is loosely based on a historical incident in 1765 France (The Beast of Gevaudan). Several critics quickly pinpointed the entertainment value of the film, saying that it was "a cross-cultural hoot that no one should take too seriously," or that it was

> one of the most unique action films in years. Imagine a Merchant Ivory film, as directed by John Woo, and featuring Jet Li, and you have some idea of what's in store. Don't let the subtitles throw you off — this is pure entertainment. Anybody confusing this for an art film just because they speak French is the same kind of poseur who championed Luc Besson's *La Femme Nikita* for the same reason, forgetting that it was just your basic action flick with a female lead. Grab the popcorn and the bladder-buster sized soda, lean back and enjoy.[7]

Beyond its entertaining and sophisticated formality, *Brotherhood of the Wolf* is literally made of multiple implicit or explicit references to the films that Gans passionately loved and supported. However, the film, far more than a clumsy patchwork of uncreative and easy tributes, feels remarkably fluid. The extreme coherence of the film is due to Gans limiting his references to the single genre of wuxia pian.

The wuxia pian, or film of martial chivalry, is rooted in a mythical China but has always reinvented itself for each age. The genre has been reworked to keep in touch with audiences' changing tastes and to take advantage of new filmmaking technology. Yet at the center it retains common themes and visceral appeals. Rather than simply adapting the genre, however, Gans transforms it. Specifically, with *Brotherhood of the Wolf*, Gans generated the hypertext of Chang Cheh's *The New One-Armed Swordsman* (1971) — Chang quickly built a reputation for his sadomasochistic swordplay dramas, emblematized in his *The One-Armed Swordsman* (1967) and *New One-Armed Swordsman* (1971). During the 1960s and 1970s, many wuxia pian built plots around the sheer variety of Chinese arms. Chang's *New One-Armed Swordsman*, for instance, gave the villain a two-jointed staff, the secondary protagonist a pair of heavy butterfly swords, and the main protagonist a single light broadsword, so combat was not only among fighters but among weapons and techniques. In *Brotherhood of the Wolf*, the villain, whose identity is unknown at first, fights with a multiple-jointed staff; the secondary protagonist, Mani the Mohawk warrior, with a hatchet; and the main protagonist, Fronsac the renowned scientist, with a pair of short swords. Firearms are also used by the villain and Fronsac, but Mani dismisses them as "too noisy." The parallel between the two films does not stop short of the themes—two swordsmen, Fronsac and Mani, rise together against evil; it is nested in the narrative structure of the scenario. However, Gans never tries to steal scenes from Chang's film and reproduce them; rather he transforms each scene into a clever amalgam influenced by all his favorite films. For Kenneth Turan, *Brotherhood of the Wolf*

> is the cinematic equivalent of fusion cuisine. It's not only that this French-language film has an editor and a stunt coordinator from Hong Kong, a cinematographer from Denmark and a star from Hawaii, it's that its very sensibility is an unapologetic mélange of French, Asian and American cinema in ways that amuse and lead to indigestion.

What is left beyond this fusion is Gans' secret desire to express the sensibility of genre cinema, even if it requires resorting to underestimated means, such as video games, strip cartoons, and special effects. In fact, *Brotherhood of the Wolf* does not only draw its influence from films such as Tsui Hark's *The Blade*, but also from videogames such as *SoulCalibur*, and Japanese mangas. Speaking on Hong Kong recent cinema, Yau argues that

> The linking of multinational advertising styles, classical ghost stories, heroic mythology, action stunts, the *wuxia* genre, and computer graphics exemplify a creative move that disturbs the notion of homogeneous, linear modern time, even though the finished commodity may be said to resonate with the cultural logic of late capitalism [11].

The accuracy of Yau's analysis also applies to Gans' film. In the end, however, *Brotherhood of the Wolf* is a living paradox, unique yet ambiguous in that it is continuously displaced from one genre's sensibility to another, from one hypertext to the next.

In conclusion, in an era where Hollywood dictates the rules of the global market, films are short-lived market commodities. However, foreign film survives and regenerates in the periphery, and this in itself is quite refreshing. Ironically, from the periphery, foreign film also manages to play the rules of the market with great dexterity yet simultaneously falls short of becoming a market commodity. I believe this happens because while Hollywood always projects ahead of the global market, searching for its next blockbuster, foreign film calmly renews its vows to humankind. Indeed, the modernity of foreign film paradoxically depends upon its relationship to tradition, which it also transcends—by this I mean that there can be no hypertext without a hypotext. Furthermore, it is its relationship to tradition which makes foreign film remain local—rather than national—because it is based on universal human values that transcend the immediacy of the market. Indeed, by transcending the *politique des auteurs* of the French New Wave and inventing the hypertext of Godard's films, Wong Kar-Wai has left his mark on late Hong Kong cinema. It is also by transcending ownership of his films, and creating the hypertext of the many Asian films he admires, that Christophe Gans has influenced the rebirth of a French entertainment cinema. In the end, humankind is the only genre, and the only attitude, that never grows old.

NOTES

1. Gérard Genette, *Palimpsests: Literature in the Second Degree,* trans. Channa Newman and Claude Doubinsky (Lincoln: University of Nebraska Press, 1997), 5.

2. Esther C. M. Yau, "Introduction: Hong Kong Cinema in a Borderless World," *At Full Speed: Hong Kong Cinema in a Borderless World,* ed. Yau (Minneapolis and London: University of Minnesota Press, 2001), 9. Subsequent page references in the text are to this edition.

3. "International Film," Art & Culture Network, at http://www.artandculture.com/ categories/210-international-film. Accessed February 23, 2010.

4. Jim Hillier, "Introduction," *Cahiers du Cinéma. The 1950s: Neo-Realism, Hollywood, New Wave* (Cambridge: Harvard University Press, 1985), 6. Subsequent Hillier page references in the text are to this edition.

5. Christopher Gans, cited in "*Chungking Express,*" HKCinematic website, at http:// hkcinemagic.ifrance.com/site/framemenu.htm; my translation. Accessed February 23, 2010. Taken from an interview published in *Mon Ciné Club* in 1996. Subsequent Gans references in the text are to this source.

6. Roger Ebert, "*Chungking Express*" (March 15, 1996), Movie Reviews, at http:// rogerebert.suntimes.com/apps/pbcs.dll/article?AID=%2F19960315%2FREVIEWS%2F6 03150301%2F1023&AID1=%2F19960315%2FREVIEWS%2F603150301%2F1023&AID2. Accessed February 23, 2010.

7. Kenneth Turan, "A Pack of Cinematic Styles," *Los Angeles Times* (Friday, January 11, 2002), at http://articles.latimes.com/2002/jan/11/entertainment/et-turan11. Accessed February 23, 2010. Subsequent references in the text are to this source.

13

Writing, Weaving, and Technology

AMY KIT-SZE CHAN

This chapter will address the issues of technology, gender, and language, particularly writing. Technology and language are the two characteristics that define human beings, according to Gilles Deleuze and Felix Guattari.[1] One similarity shared by technology and language is that both are assemblages, the former "a machinic assemblage," the latter "an assemblage of enunciation" (Deleuze and Guattari 504). To borrow Timothy V. Kaufman-Osborn's metaphor (bear in mind that for Kaufman-Osborn, a metaphor is an artifact of language and always more than a metaphor) of a spider web, both technology and language are entangled and entwined in a web relating them to the human world, a reality that cannot be "disconnected from the stubborn world of artisanal things."[2]

To say only that gender plays a role in technology and language obviously fails to accord gender its due importance in the spider web of technology. Recall that technology and humans share a "projection and reciprocation" relationship, and that gender "is one of the more enduring creatures generated by the dialectic of projection and reciprocation" (Kaufman-Osborn 67). At the beginning of his book, Kaufman-Osborn claims, "[m]atters of technology and gender are never unrelated in experience, and any argument that presupposes their isolability is sure to grasp the political import of neither" (1). Discussing cyborg politics, Donna Haraway postulates that "Writing is pre-eminently the technology of cyborgs, etched surfaces of the late twentieth century. Cyborg politics is the struggle for language and the struggle against perfect communication, against the one code that translates all meaning perfectly, the central dogma of phallogocentrism."[3]

So, I wish to entwine and ensnare language (writing), technology and weaving altogether to weave a larger (spider?) web, hoping to present my arguments clearly amidst these entanglements.

Gender and Technology

When we discuss the relationship between gender and technology, this is the usual question: is technology gendered or does technology gender human beings? I argue that both are true historically. Consider a common definition of technology: "A. The application of science, especially to industrial or commercial objectives. B. The scientific method and material used to achieve a commercial or industrial objective."[4] Again, what is considered a tool and what is not? Why is a hammer a tool while a needle or frying pan is not? Is it because needlework or cooking at home is not included in the category of "industrial or commercial objectives"? What counts and doesn't count as technology has a gendered dimension. Kaufman-Osborn claims "female gender identity and the artisanal artifacts constitutive of that identity are devalued in common" (68).

Technology as a concept has been gendered since the beginning. However, the gendered dimension of technology does not reside in the female or the artifact but in the relationship between them. For example, the automobile as artisanal artifact is not gendered, but given the relationship between automobiles and females (realizing that this relationship is also embedded within a logic of projection and reciprocation), there is no doubt that the automobile is a male technology.[5] On the other hand, there are a few tools or technologies considered to be female. A case in point is the typewriter. American printer Christopher Latham Sholes developed the first typewriter in 1874. At first, the machine was gender neutral, but by the 1880s women were the primary typists since their pay was much lower than men's. Since then, the typewriter has been considered as female gendered. Another example is the computer. In the 1940s, 76 young female mathematicians were employed by the University of Pennsylvania's Moore School of Engineering as "computers," responsible for making calculations for tables of firing and bombing trajectories as part of the World War II effort. Kay McNulty Mauchly Antonelli recalls computing in 1946:

> We did have desk calculators at that time, mechanical and driven with electric motors, that could do simple arithmetic. You'd do a multiplication and when the answer appeared, you had to write it down to reenter it into the machine to do the next calculation. We were preparing a firing table for each gun, with maybe 1,800 simple trajectories. To hand-compute just one of these trajectories took 30 or 40 hours of sitting at a desk with paper and a calculator. As you can imagine, they were soon running out of young women to do the calculations. Actually, my title working for the ballistics project was "computer." The idea was that I not only did arithmetic but also made the decision on what to do next. ENIAC made me, one of the first "computers," obsolete.[6]

Even today, more female workers are employed as data entry keyboarders and computer operators while they only constitute a small portion of electrical and electronic engineers and computer systems analysts and scientists. This illustrates that not only is technology gendered, but there exists a hierarchy in classifying different technologies, in which low-tech ones are female and high-tech ones are male.

Of all technologies in human civilization, there is only one technology that males admit was invented by females— that of weaving. According to Sigmund Freud, women have no ability or desire to change the world, lacking logical and rational thinking skills and will power; therefore, they made few contributions to the inventions and discoveries of the history of civilization. The only invention credited to women is the weaving loom. However, Freud attributes this to women's castration complex. Instead of celebrating women's achievement, Freud concocts a tale based on his theory of absence, castration fear, deficiency, and negativity.[7]

The earliest loom apparently appeared in ancient China. Archaeologists discovered a stone-made spinning wheel built in the New Stone Age (about 4,700 years ago). In a picture of the spinning wheel produced in the Eastern Han Dynasty (24–188 A.D.), the weaver is a woman, sitting on the floor and operating the spinning wheel with her hands.

If we trace the roots of words like *technical, technique, technics,* and *technician,* we observe the deep-rooted and embedded relationship between technology and weaving. The ancient Greek *tekhnē,* meaning art and craft, is derived from the Indo-European root *teks,* which carries the meaning of "to fabricate," "to weave," or the "web, net, warp of a fabric." Thus, technology cannot be isolated but is enwrapped in a web. Suffice it to say that given the close relationship between technology and weaving, weaving and the female, we may discover more connections between technology and the female gender.

Language and Gender

To recapitulate, Haraway contends that writing has a special significance for marginalized groups, women of color and cyborgs included. Cyborg politics is about the struggle for language and cyborg writing is about the power to survive (175–176). A feminist like Hélène Cixous "sees in women's writing the potential to circumvent and reformulate existing structures through the inclusion of other experience." Moreover,

> Cixous suggests that a feminine writing will bring into existence alternative forms of relation, perception and expression. It is in this sense that Cixous believes writing is revolutionary. Not only can writing exceed the binary logic that informs our present system and thus create the framework for a new "language" and culture, but she stresses, through its transformations, feminine writing will initiate changes in the social and political sphere to challenge the very foundation of the patriarchal and capitalist state.[8]

While Cixous is most often associated with *écriture féminine,* Luce Irigaray is identified with *parler-femme.* In "When Our Lips Speak Together," Irigaray warns,

If we keep on speaking the same language together, we're going to reproduce the same history. Begin the same old stories all over again.... If we keep on speaking sameness, if we speak to each other as men have been doing for centuries, as we have been taught to speak, we'll miss each other, fail ourselves.... we'll be spoken machines, speaking machines.[9]

Irigaray takes a very radical standpoint in this issue, believing that women have been caught in a world structured by phallogocentrism, so they must create a language of their own, with a totally different syntax and another grammar to represent themselves, to express their feeling, their experience, and their bodies (Irigaray 1977 143). Naming females' different body experiences will enable them to transform the patriarchal structure. Thus, language is seen as "an essential tool of production for [women's] liberation" and allows them "to have subjective rights equivalent to men, to be able to exchange language and objects with them."[10]

In response to Irigaray and Cixous, some feminists are actually attempting to create a different kind of syntax and grammar. Consider Monique Wittig's novel *The Lesbian Body*:

I discover that your skin can be lifted layer by layer, I pull it lifts off, it coils above your knees, I pull starting at the labia, it slides the length of the belly, fine to extreme transparency, I pull starting at the loins, the skin uncovers the round muscles and trapezii of the back, it peels off up to the nape of the neck, I arrive under your hair, m/y fingers traverse its thickness, I touch your skull, I grasp it with all m/y fingers, I press it....[11]

The statement runs on and on for a page, separated only by commas; the fluidity and flow of words leave readers breathless. *The Lesbian Body* is an experiment with language and literary form which aims to challenge the rational, scientific, objective, hierarchical phallocentrism.

Before continuing this discussion, I will tell a story about a little girl called Kamari who lived in a tribe. One day, she picked up an injured falcon and took it to the *mundumugu*—the witch doctor—hoping he could save it with his magic. In exchange, she promised the *mundumugu* that she would do all the chores for him for one month. She saw there were many books in the *mundumugu*'s hut and begged him to teach her how to read. However, the *mundumugu* refused on the grounds that a woman's duty is "to till the fields and pound the grain and make the fires and weave the fabrics and bear her husband's children."[12] Women were not supposed to read lest they learned about "other ways of thinking and living" and grew "discontented" with their lives (64). Kamari, though unhappy with his words, kept her promise and cleaned up his hut everyday. One day, the *mundumugu* discovered that Kamari was using his computer and ordered the computer not to converse with the girl "verbally or in any known language" (70). Still, he found that the computer was communicating with the girl in a very strange language. The computer told the *mundumugu* that Kamari made up the language herself. It was simple, but coherent and logical and understood by the computer. The *mundumugu* went further this time and forbid Kamari from even activating the computer. Several days after, Kamari hanged herself in her hut, leaving a couplet as her last words:

I know why the caged birds die —
For, like them, I have touched the sky [77].

Kaufman-Osborn in *Creatures of Prometheus* contends that when a woman commands a male technology, she becomes an embodiment of gender trouble. That is: when a woman acquires an artisanal artifact that makes men men, she upends he regime of patriarchy. Like the girl in the science fiction story "For I Have Touched the Sky" by Mike Resnick, any female who acquires language must be warned: either they speak as male subject or as asexualized other. Once they transgress this boundary and dare to appropriate language for their own use or even create their own language, they must be penalized.

Female Writing

Though French feminists, like Cixous and Irigaray, argue that women should have their own language or writing to express the plurality and mutuality of feminine difference, there is still no such kind of *écriture feminine* or *parler-femme* proper. In fact, the phallocratic order which creates language and is in turn sustained by language presents a difficult problem for Irigaray and other feminists. When Irigaray undertook the challenge of rereading philosophical texts, she realized that "if she were to follow the traditional rules of conventional language, she would foreclose the possibility of transforming the cultural imaginary."[13] Thus one cannot conceive of the feminine in the structures established by conventional language.

Recently, however, we have discovered a female dialect used in Jiang Yong County, Hunan Province, which provides a clue as to how to solve the problems facing feminists. This discovery, made in 1980s, shocked the world and surprised feminists because so far it is the first and only attempt made by females to create a language of their own. It is believed that this dialect has been employed by women in Jiang Yong for at least a thousand years.[14] There are different theories concerning how this writing system originated, but it is generally accepted that it was first created in the Sung Dynasty.

Women in Jiang Yong called this writing system "female writing," as opposed to the Han Chinese writing system which was "male writing." To trace the origin of female writing, we must understand that even women living in villages nowadays may not be literate, not to mention women back in the Sung Dynasty, because only men may enjoy the privilege of formal education. Being illiterate in Han writing, women devised their own form of writing and passed it on to daughters and granddaughters so women could communicate among themselves and write their own literary works.

First, we will explore the contents of texts in female writing, which fall into six areas[15]:

1. **Religious rites:** women write down their prayers and wishes on a paper folding fan and bring it to the temple for burning.

2. **Entertainment:** women have picnics together and read or sing their own writings, including folk songs, biographies, and letters.

3. **Communication:** Women in Jiang Yong have a culture of forming sworn sisterhoods with good friends (some have up to six sworn sisters, and the age differences between sisters can vary wildly), and they usually communicate with each other by letters.

4. **Biography:** Elderly women ask someone who is good at female writing to record their lives. The books are usually laments about their hardships in married life. Some even complain about the feudal system, arranged marriages, and foot-binding customs. These books are usually burned at the woman's cremation so that she can continue reading it in another world. That explains why no book of female writing before the Qing Dynasty has been recovered, making it difficult for researchers to gather materials.

5. **Records of "herstory";** for example, a piece of writing records what happened to women in Jiang Yong during the Taiping Heavenly Kingdom (1853–1864) and there is another article about the period of the Sino-Japanese War (1937–1945).

6. **Rewritings of narrative poems:** women choose poems which have women as protagonists and translate them into female writing. However, after reading their version of the legend about the Butterfly Lovers, I find the translation itself is more a rewriting. The female version places more emphasis on Zhu Ying-tai and has description of her female body which is omitted in the Han version. Consider a few lines of the story:

> Ying-tai washed her face at the dressing table. She took a piece of soap and cleaned her chest. A pair of breasts as white as snow was shown. Ying-tai told Liang Shan-bai that, "The one who is blessed has large breasts and one who is unlucky has no breasts. A man with large breasts will become a high official and a woman with large breasts will be lonely in her life." She was able to convince Shan-bai at that moment with these words.[16]

Thus, the record of "herstory" or rewriting of a legend is not only a translation of male writing into female writing; rather, the emphasis in female writing usually falls on the emotional, affectional, and lived experiences of the women instead of recording the facts. In this sense, female writing probably fulfills the criterion that the French feminists established for female language—"a new language derived from a *different* perception, experience and desire."[17]

Though linguists have shown that this female writing system is a variation of Han character writing and thus a dialect, not a language, the style of this writing system looks very different from the Han characters. Han characters are made mostly of vertical and horizontal lines, and every character looks like a square. On the other hand, female writing characters are made up of dots, curves and slanting lines tilting to the left, and instead of forming squares, characters are rhombus-shaped.

Another interesting finding about female writing is that it does not resemble any writing systems in Chinese history, including Han writing systems and all writings by minority groups. One theory concerning the creation of female writing traces its origin back to prehistoric inscriptions on pottery, which would explain why it was not influenced by any writing systems in Chinese history.[18] However, without archaeological findings, it is hard to convince people that female writing existed for thousands of years, even before the appearance of inscriptions on tortoise shells or bones.

Another explanation concerning the creation of this writing relates it to weaving, claiming that women in the past always gathered and did weaving and embroidery together. Due to hardships in their married lives, they wanted to record their experiences and sufferings. However, since they were illiterate, they embroidered some symbols on the cloth, as marks or records, which gradually developed into a writing system. If we examine their embroidery, we see that the patterns do resemble female writing.

Female writing is usually practiced by women of a minority group called *Yao* in Hunan Province. The Yaos are famous for their weaving and embroidery. Even today, the spinning wheels they use are quite primitive and not much different from the ones depicted in the pictures from the Western Han dynasty.

Both the spinning wheel and weaving loom have an intimate relationship with women's bodies. As mentioned, Freud attributes women's contribution to weaving technology to their castration complex, but that is not my view. Spinning, especially handspinning practiced by women in the old days, is the craft of creating yarn from fiber by using a spinning wheel treadled by foot or hand; it is more or less similar to the weaving loom, also operated by the weaver's hands and feet. The rhythm of the weaver's body synchronizes with the movement of the pedal or lever of the spinning wheel or weaving loom.

That reminds me of the spider web. Here is a story about the spider:

> Like Penelope, the spider is skilled in forms of artifice practiced after dark. Within her abdomen, each night she generates liquid silk. Squeezed from minute spinnerets, this sticky fluid congeals into so many elastic cords, and from these she fashions a web. Legs coated with oils teased from glands inside her mouth, she alone can dance without care atop this resilient wheel. When an unhappy victim is snared by its catching threads, all struggles to break free produce still more of a tangle. The vibrations provoked by this commotion, scurrying along radial threads from hub to margin, tell the orb's maker what is afoot [Kaufman-Osborn 9].

The spider is a weaver herself (no wonder the spider in the story is female). Of course, the spinster/yarn relationship is not totally comparable to the spider/spider web relationship since the liquid silk comes from the spider; however, the interweaving of the rhythms of the spinster/weaver's body and the spinning wheel/weaving loom does propound the dualistic representation of the relationship between the creator and the created, the tool-user and the tool. I suggest that the spinning wheel and yarn are continuous with the spinster and so confuses the Cartesian paradigm of use.

So, what about the female writing that may have originated from weaving? Cixous and Clément point out that female body is a direct source of female writing and in *The Newly Born Woman*, they argue that "woman is body more than man is." They add that "[m]ore body hence more writing" (95). For Cixous and Clément, women must speak with their bodies and of their bodies:

> A feminine text cannot not be more than subversive: if it writes itself it is in volcanic heaving of the old "real" property crust. In ceaseless displacement. She must write herself because, when the time comes for her liberation, it is the invention of a new, insurgent writing that will allow her to put the breaks and indispensable changes into effect in her history.... To write — the act that will "realize" the un-censored relationship of woman to her sexuality, to her woman-being giving her back access to her own forces; that will return her goods, her pleasures, her organs, her vast bodily territories kept under seal.... Write yourself: your body must make itself heard [97].

Female writing is an abstract but incorporeal embodiment of women's perception, affection, lived experience, and desire. It is women's strategy to undermine the symbolic order, to bring changes to the world order. If language is what made men men, then female writing probably renders women what women should be.

She Stammers

In Chinese history, there is a long tradition of calligraphy in which many different kinds of styles have evolved. On one hand, some are regular and of uniform size, like standard script (*kai shu*), semi-cursive script (*hsing shu*), and seal script (*zhuan shu*); on the other hand, some are running and flowing, like cursive script (*cao shu*). While not qualified to discuss styles of calligraphy, I want to note that while there are running and flowing scripts in male writing, female writing always maintains a regular and uniform style.

Strictly speaking, there is no calligraphy for female writing.[19] It remains a mystery how female writing could have isolated itself for almost a thousand years from the influence of the calligraphy of male writing. I argue that the women who practiced female writing were determined to insulate it and retained its hard and stiff style. After all, a hard and stiff style is also a writing style.

Thomas Lamarre argues that traditional calligraphic theory revolves around two notions: "First, writing shows the composition of things. Second, writing presents movements: it shows the movements of the heart/mind (and thus human character), and it shows the movements of the natural world (and thus the operations of things)."[20] He suggests that the brush, a manual machine, acts as "a kind of seismograph, feeling the oscillations and vibrations of the world and of the heart" (166), and through signing these on paper, silk, or bamboo splints, aligns movements of the heart and movements in the natural world.

The characters of female writing are rhombus-shaped, regular and stiff. Each character is separated from the others and never flows freely into another character. While the calligraphy of male writing can be floating and hovering on the paper, female writing is stumbling, staggering, stuttering. A woman stammers even when she speaks in her own tongue. When discussing female discourse, Irigaray comments:

> she cannot specify exactly what she wants. Words begin to fail her. She senses something *remains to be said* that resists all speech, that can at best be stammered out. All the words are weak, worn out, unfit to translate anything sensibly. For it is no longer a matter of longing for some determinable attribute, some mode of essence, some face of presence. What is expected is neither a *this* nor a *that*, not a *here* any more than a *there*. No being, no places are designated. So the best plan is to abstain from all discourse, to keep quiet, or else utter only a sound so inarticulate that it barely forms a *song*.[21]

In his article "He Stuttered," Deleuze suggests that the writer causes language to stutter in the language system (*langue*). No matter how much we like to think the language system is in equilibrium, it is actually in perpetual disequilibrium, continuously bifurcating and causing language itself to vibrate and stutter. This is the only way to make progress, the only way to introduce desire into language. One way to do it is to minorize language — "invent a minor use for the major language within which they express themselves completely." He continues, "He is a foreigner in his own language: he does not mix another language with his, he shapes and sculpts a foreign language that does not preexist within his own language.... The point is to make language itself cry, to make it stutter, mumble, or whisper." By virtue of this minorization, writers give birth to a foreign language within language; writers place language in an endless state of disequilibrium and cause it to bifurcate into lines of flight. Stuttering is then turned on its head to be viewed as the "poetic or linguistic strength par excellence."[22]

In this way, the "calligraphy" of female writing represents women's stammering when they speak with their lips, in their own language. It is as if women must hesitate between every character, ponder over what to say next or how to express their desires. As noted, female writing is more a dialect in the Chinese language system than a separate language. As such, it can be seen as a minorization of the Han language, creating not only a new syntax but also a new sign system.

Smoothing Space

Female writings are usually written on paper fans, silk handkerchiefs, and notebooks bound by threads and black cloth or silk with embroidery. Technologically, a fabric has certain characteristics allowing us to categorize it as a striated space. First, it is constituted by two parallel elements, the warp yarn and woof yarn intersecting perpendicularly. Second, one element is fixed and the other passes above and beneath the fixed one. Third, there is a top and a bottom in a yarn though the nature, number, and density of the yarns remain the same. These characteristics qualify a fabric as a striated space which is defined by hierarchy, rule-intensive order, and control.

In contrast to fabric, paper is a smooth space. Most Chinese calligraphers and painters made their marks on the highest quality paper, *Xuan* paper. This paper gained its name because it can only be produced in the town of Xuan in Anhui Province. The main materials for making Xuan paper is vegetal fibers of green sandalwood, which grows profusely in Xuan. Fibers teased from barks of green sandalwood trees and mulberry trees are washed and swollen by water repeatedly, then lime is added in and cooked with the fibers and washed and pulped again. The resulted pulp is placed on the ground of the valley for a year for drying. Today, the paper is still made by hand. The result is a smooth surface which differs from other types of paper in all aspects: smoothness, absorption of ink, density, tension, and brightness. Tough and resilient but soft, it can last for over a thousand years.

The material to write or paint on is inseparable from the work of art itself because the sensation of a work of art refers to the percepts and affects of the material itself. Deleuze and Guattari claim, "it is difficult to say where in fact the material ends and sensation begins." They then ask, "How could the sensation be preserved without a material capable of lasting?"[23] However, the sensation is not the same thing as material. It is realized in the material with its passing completely into the percept or affect. All materials then become expressive.

Writing a letter in female writing on a paper does not express the same sensation as one written on a silk handkerchief, especially if the handkerchief is woven and embroidered by the writer herself. The absorbedness of the fabric also differs greatly from paper. Furthermore, if the letter is embroidered on a handkerchief, the percepts and affects of the letter will be different than one written with ink.

Making the signs of female writing on a fabric is an act of smoothing a striated space. The fabric, constituted by perpendicular and parallel yarns, is an ordered, controlled, and closed space. Writing on this space inevitably disrupts its hierarchical order. Female writing usually runs vertically, from right to left, and hence cuts across the woof yarn of the fabric. On the other hand, the paper, made by the pulp of vegetal fibers and water, is a smooth space. With some low quality paper, the surface is so rough that vegetal fibers can even be seen. The calligraphy of male writing on paper, no matter if horizontal or vertical, or always from right to left, is intended to provide an order for this chaotic, smooth space. Smoothing of space is always associated with feminine space. Feminine space, by definition a structure for what does not yet exist, is constituted by continuous movement, lines of flight, deterritorialization and reterritorialization. In short, it is always a becoming.

It is perhaps not coincidental that writing is associated with "becoming-woman." Deleuze and Guattari put forward the view that "writing should produce a becoming-woman as atoms of womanhood capable of crossing and impregnating an entire social field, and of contaminating men, of sweeping them up in that becoming" (276). Writing emits soft and small but hard and obstinate particles, molecular instead of molar particles. In order not to cease to become, writing must be an abstract line, or line of flight; it must "be — between, to pass between, the intermezzo" (277). The molecular particles enter the proximity of women; thus all writers are become-women. Writing space is feminine space.

Conclusion

To conclude, I will provide some threads of the web in which language, writing, weaving, gender, and technology are entangled. They weave into an ever-increasing web and thus are one thread (remember the spider web!). Regardless of where I start and where I end, we are always in the middle of the thread.

Thread 1: Gender and Technology
- As mentioned, technology and humans share a "projection and reciprocation relationship." The former suggests that the materialization of bodies that matter is a sedimentation process—involving other organic and non-organic life forms and never without shape or history, thus denying the pretensions of the subject's metaphysical presence. The latter suggests that the human is as much creature as creator, as artifacts act back upon their creators and so remake them.
- Gender is an assemblage generated by the dialectic of projection and reciprocation, itself an artifact that is "called into being by and within the relations between artisanal artifacts and persons, artisanal artifacts and other artifacts, persons and other person" (Kaufman-Osborn 67). Take the example of the gun and the male gender. Man's infatuation with guns is not induced by a singular, linear and ahistorical cause. The power to affect and to be affected does not run unidirectionally from creator to gun. The gun is not the same when in a man's hand; on the

other hand, a man also does not remain the same man when he has a gun in his hand.

- Haraway's cyborg clearly shows that gender is nothing natural. The dualism of male and female is arbitrary and is due to be deconstructed in time.
- Evoking the life of Ada Lovelace and her close relationship to the creation of modern computers, we recall that the female gender is not that remote from technology.

Thread 2: Weaving and Technology

- The Jacquard loom was developed in 1804 by a Frenchman, Joseph-Marie Jacquard, who was influenced by the weaving loom invented in China several hundred years before. The punch-card system, which controlled the weaving of the cloth so that any intricate woven patterns, such as tapestry, brocade, and damask, could be produced automatically, was adopted by Charles Babbage as an input-output medium for the Analytical Engine. Though Babbage's Engine was never built, punch cards were widely used to store data in binary form until the invention of recording media based on electromagnetic and electro-optic technologies in the 1960s.
- In an article for InfoWorld.Com, Ethernet inventor and Internet pioneer Bob Metcalfe raises the idea of computational fabrics. Computer devices are built by chips and circuit boards nowadays, but the possibility of replacing these rigid laminates by woven high-tech fibers, filaments, threads and yarns, using textile technologies to weave computers and nanocomputers, is being seriously considered.[24]

Thread 3: Weaving and Gender

- One interesting observation: all spinsters (which also means single, unmarried women) are females and in all mythologies, the technology of spinning and weaving is created by a goddess, for example, *Arachne* in Greek mythology, *Chih Nu* in Chinese mythology, and *Neit* in Egyptian mythology.
- Weaving used to be women's only contribution to the economy. In the ancient age of many civilizations, men went hunting and farming and women stayed home raising children and weaving cloth. The men then took the cloth to the market to exchange for food.

Thread 4: Weaving and Female Writing

- The characters of female writing are possibly derived from the weaving patterns of the Yao group. The patterns are actually the Yao women's symbols for recording and communicating with each other.
- There is a special significance for women to write female writing on cloth and silk handkerchiefs.

Thread 5: Gender and Language
- According to Lacan, women are excluded from language as they only exist in language as the other — as what men are not. So, when a woman speaks, she speaks in man's voice.
- According to Deleuze and Guattari, language is one of two characteristics that made human beings, the other being technology.
- Therefore, a woman is not a human being.

Thread 6: Language and Technology
- The word "tech" means "art" or "craft."
- The word "logos" means "word" and "speech."
- "Tech" plus "logos," then, means a discourse on the arts, both fine and applied.
- It seems intrinsic that technology cannot be isolated from language. I mentioned that language and technology are both assemblages, the former "a machinic assemblage" and the latter "an assemblage of enunciation" (Deleuze and Guattari 504). As an assemblage, the machine assembles the elements extracted from social and cultural contexts and produces something entirely new. The product can then react back upon and affect its conditions of production, becoming a component of further machines.[25]

Thread 7: Female Writing and Smooth Space
- Female writing can be an inspiration for feminists who advocate a new language for females.
- Female writing on cloth and silk handkerchiefs is an act of smoothing a striated space, thus creating a feminine space.
- The smooth space places emphasis on the line passing between things, between points, but not the line subordinated to the point.
- The matrix, which also means womb, is an example of smooth space — no order, no limit, no hierarchy, no control; it is rhizomatic and multifaceted....
- Hypertext is composed of nodes and links, propagating in a matrix of breaks, jumps, and implied or contingent connections which are enacted by viewers. Reading a hypertext is an occasion, a becoming.
- If hypertext flourishes in the matrix, in virtual space, the non-space, does it mean that a female language can also find its place in this space?

NOTES

1. Gilles Deleuze and Felix Guattari, *A Thousand Plateaus: Capitalism and Schizophrenia*, trans. Brian Massumi (Minneapolis and London: University of Minnesota Press, 1987), 60. Subsequent Deleuze and Guattari parenthetical page references in the text are to this edition.
2. Timothy V. Kaufman-Osborn, *Creatures of Prometheus: Gender and the Politics of*

Technology (Lanhan and Boulder: Rowman and Littlefield Publishers, 1997), 112. Subsequent Kaufman-Osborn parenthetical page references in the text are to this edition.

3. Donna J. Haraway, "A Cyborg Manifesto: Science, Technology, and Socialist-Feminism in the Late Twentieth Century," *Simians, Cyborgs, and Women: The Reinvention of Nature*, by Haraway (London and New York: Routledge, 1991), 176. Subsequent Haraway parenthetical page references in the text are to this edition.

4. "Technology," *The American Heritage Dictionary of the English Language*, Fourth Edition [CD-ROM] (Boston: Houghton, 2000).

5. In the 1970s, car advertisements portrayed women as either hopeless incompetents or sex objects to appeal to male customers. Literally, car makers didn't sell cars to women then, since only 29 percent of women held a driving license, compared with 69 percent of men. Only now, in the twenty-first century, has car advertising become politically sensitive — a change that occurred because the percentage of female drivers in America grew from 44% in 1972 to 49% in 1996. Moreover, over 80% of vehicle purchases are influenced by women. (See "Women Call the Shots on Buying and Maintaining the Family Car," [no author given] *VMR Auto Guides*, at http://www.vmrintl.com/Ref_art/women_buy.htm [accessed March 13, 2010]).

6. "Kay McNulty Mauchly Antonelli," Past Notable Women of Computing, at http://cs-www.cs.yale.edu/homes/tap/past-women-cs.html#Kay%20Mauchly.

7. For a thorough discussion of the rise of modern computers, the role of Ada Lovelace in computer technology, and its close relationship with weaving technology, see my "When Cyberfeminism Meets Chinese Philosophy: Computer, Weaving and Women," *World Weavers: Globalization, Science Fiction, and the Cybernetic Revolution*, ed. Wong Kin Yuen, Gary Westfahl and Amy Kit-sze Chan (Hong Kong: Hong Kong University Press, 2005), 215–232.

8. Sandra M. Gilbert, "Introduction: A Tarentella of Theory," *The Newly Born Woman: Hélène Cixous and Catherine Clément*, by Hélène Cixous and Catherine Clément, trans. Betsy Wing (London: I. B. Tauris Publishers, 1996), xxix. Subsequent Cixous and Clément parenthetical page references in the text are to this edition.

9. Luce Irigaray, "When Our Lips Speak Together," *This Sex Which Is Not One*, by Irigaray, trans. Catherine Porter (Ithaca and New York: Cornell University Press, 1977), 205. Subsequent 1977 Irigaray parenthetical page references in the text are to this edition.

10. Irigaray, *Je, Tu, Nous: Towards a Culture of Difference*, trans. Alison Martin (London and New York: Routledge, 1993), 72.

11. Monique Wittig, *The Lesbian Body*, trans. David Le Vay (Boston: Beacon Press, 1973), 17.

12. This is taken from Mike Resnick's short story, "For I Have Touched the Sky," *Best New SF 4*, ed. Gardner Dozois (London: Robinson Publishing, 1990), 63. Subsequent parenthetical page references in the text are to this edition.

13. Tasmin Lorraine, *Irigaray and Deleuze: Experiments in Visceral Philosophy* (Ithaca and London: Cornell University Press, 1999), 43.

14. There are many different theories concerning the origin of female writing; thus we cannot determine how long it has existed. The most commonly accepted theory is that it was created in the Sung Dynasty, but some scholars more recently suggested that it is at least 3000 years old.

15. For details and more information about female writing, see Gong Zhebing and Zhao Liming's *Nu Shu: Shijie Wei Yi de Nuxing Wenji* [*Women's Writing: The World's Only Female Writing*] (Taipei, Taiwan: Fu Nu Xin Zhi Ji Jin Hui, 1992).

16. The original was written by Gao Yinxian and Yi Nianhua in Nu Shu and translated into Chinese by Gong Zhebing in Gong Zhebing and Zhao Liming's *Nu Shu: Shijie Wei*

Yi de Nuxing Wenji [*Women's Writing: The World's Only Female Writing*] (Taipei, Taiwan: Fu Nu Xin Zhi Ji Jin Hui, 1992). The English translation is mine.

17. Suan Sellers, *Language and Sexual Difference: Feminist Writing in France* (London: Macmillan, 1991), 96.

18. For a detailed discussion on female writing and inscriptions on pottery, see Li Jinglin's *Nu Shu Yu Shi Gian Tao Wen Yan Jiu*, [*A Study of The Female Writing and Prehistoric Inscriptions on Pottery*] (Zhuhai: Zhuhai Chu Ban She, 1995).

19. In December 2002, the first copybook of female writing was published, in which a female calligrapher, Wang Cheng-xi, attempts to apply Chinese calligraphy styles, such as *kai shu, hsing shu, cao shu* and *zhuan shu*, in female writing. Critics comment that her attempt successfully transformed the stiff female writing into a more graceful and elegant art of writing. However, as I argue later, I consider this copybook as an attempt to de-feminize female writing.

20. Thomas Lamarre, "Diagram, Inscription, Sensation," *A Shock to Thought: Expression after Deleuze and Guattari*, ed. Massumi (London and New York: Routledge, 2002), 166. Subsequent Lamarre parenthetical page references are to this edition.

21. Irigaray, "La Mystérique," *Speculum of the Other Woman*, trans. Gillian C. Gill (Ithaca and New York: Cornell University Press, 1974), 193.

22. Deleuze, "He Stuttered," *Gilles Deleuze and the Theater of Philosophy*, ed. Constantin V. Boundas and Dorothea Olkowski (London and New York: Routledge, 1994), 25, 27.

23. Deleuze and Guattari, *What Is Philosophy?*, trans. Graham Burchell and Hugh Tomlinson (London and New York: Verso. 1994), 166.

24. Bob Metcalfe, "Do Computation Fabrics Hold the Key to the Future of the Internet's Web?," *Info World*, 22 (July 24, 2000), 88.

25. Philip Goodchild, *Deleuze and Guattari: An Introduction to the Politics of Desire* (London: Sage, 1996), 3–4.

14

The Technological Contours of Contemporary Science Fiction, or, The Science Fiction That Science Fiction Doesn't See

BROOKS LANDON

The last time I Googled "electronic science fiction" I got an amazing 856 hits. Search the Science Fiction Museum website for "electronic science fiction," however, and you get the equally surprising news that there is no "Content" and no "Events, URLs or News Items" to match your search. Admittedly, I wasn't completely sure what I meant by "electronic science fiction," but Google, with the confidence of a search engine on steroids, had no trouble dumping hundreds of websites into that category. The Science Fiction Museum website, itself an attractive instance of using electronic technology to help us understand and advance science fiction, apparently isn't yet ready to recognize a category of which it could be a prime example.

True, many sites identified by Google seem only tangentially connected to what I had in mind as "electronic science fiction," with self-published fantasy and romantica far too prominently represented. And while putative novels such as *Adam 483: Man or Machine* and *Eroti-Bot* might satisfy some definitions of science fiction, they weren't even close to what I was looking for when I searched for "electronic science fiction." Basically, I was after SF narratives or SF-related displays, interactive opportunities, and explorations that could not be accessed without a computer or, in the case of video games, some form of electric power supply. What Google largely seemed to give me was fixed print SF that could be accessed, published on demand, or ordered through the web. And what the Science Fiction Museum website did *not* give me were any examples of what N. Katherine Hayles, following the lead of Espen Aarseth, calls "CYBERTEXTS," second generation hyperfictions that experiment with "ways to incorporate narrative with sound, motion, animation, and other software functionalities."[1] For purposes of this chapter, I'd expand that description beyond dramatic narrative semblances to include websites that transcend fixed-print exposition to promote the experience and interrogation of SF as a cultural and epistemological phenomenon. So, while I readily acknowledge that the Science Fiction Museum website is not a form of electronic literature, it is an electronic space structured hypertextually that constructs SF as much more than a catalogue of fixed-print fictional texts. While not an electronic fiction, it does belong to the realm of electronic SF.

As it happens, the world of fixed-print fictional texts seems largely to be what we get when two of our most respected and knowledgeable experts, Gardner Dozois and David G. Hartwell, annually survey developments in science fiction and report on electronic instances. For some years now, Dozois has referenced "the Internet scene" in his "Summation" in each edition of *The Year's Best Science Fiction*. In his *Twenty-First Annual Collection*, published in 2004 and focused on 2003, he notes of the Internet that "things there evolve with such lightning speed, with new e-magazines and Internet sites of general interest seeming almost to be born one day and die the next, that it remains possible that everything I say about it here will be obsolete by the time this book makes it into print."[2] Dozois then surveys a number of useful, interesting, and rewarding SF sites, including SciFiction, The Infinite Matrix, Strange Horizons, Oceans of the Mind, Revolution SF, Infinity Plus, Locus Online, and Tangent. Understandably, Dozois constructs the Internet as a place primarily for publishing and reprinting fixed-print SF, although he has noted for the past few years that people turn to the web "for reasons other than just finding stories to read," and he lumps those other reasons together under the category of "general interest" sites that "don't publish fiction" but do publish lots of other stuff "which can be great fun to drop in on."[3] He closes his overview of web SF with another ode to speed: "Close your eyes for a moment in the Internet world, though, and everything will be different when you open them again" (*Twenty-First* introduction xvii). (If change is indeed at the heart of science fiction thinking, one might ask why neither Dozois nor the literature he edits so effectively is not more concerned with a technology he so nervously identifies as the apotheosis of change.)

In his "Introduction" to *Year's Best SF 9*, Hartwell calls attention to several of the same electronic fiction websites mentioned by Dozois and notes the great utility of the Internet Speculative Fiction Data Base and of Tangent Online for those who try to keep track of short fiction. It's worth pointing out, as Hartwell does, that Octavia E. Butler's "Amnesty" (2003), the first story in his collection, was originally published electronically on the web at SciFiction. Follow Hartwell's references to the websites of Cory Doctorow and Charles Stross and you'll get a glimpse of what the web can add to our understanding and enjoyment of SF. Indeed, although he doesn't refer to any electronic dramatic narratives, some fifteen of Hartwell's brief introductions to the twenty stories in

SF 9 contain URLs or references to websites as he tries to make good on his promise "to represent the varieties of tones and voices and attitudes," if not of media, "that keep the genre vigorous and responsive to the changing realities out of which it emerges, in science and daily life."[4] Hartwell is obviously both web savvy and web friendly, and is himself a blogger, so he walks the walk of changing realities even if he doesn't much talk the talk.

Hartwell and Dozois make their living working with print SF, and no one has yet found a reliable way to make money from electronic science fiction, so I single out their comments not to hector them in any way, but simply to suggest that their silence concerning other than fixed print SF in electronic media is representative of a larger silence in SF critical discourse. Curiously enough, while histories and theories of SF have consistently — if not obsessively — focused on the economic implications of the technological stages of SF as a publishing phenomenon, little attention has been paid to the implications of these technologies *as technologies*. The promising dialogue initiated in the pages of *The New York Review of Science Fiction* back in 1993 and 1994 never took off: Sarah Smith's optimistic "Electric Fictions: The State of the Art" in its issue No. 63 and Stuart Moulthrop's more cautionary "Electronic Fictions and 'The Lost Game of Self'" in No. 66 set the stage for a critical debate that never occurred.[5] We can get a "Cold Equations" forum heated up at the drop of a misogynist hat, but serious critical considerations of the implications electronic textuality hold for SF are few and far between. Curiously, while both Smith and Moulthrop are knowledgeable of and invested in SF, neither saw electronic textuality as a more inflected topic for SF than for any other kind of writing. And it is worth remembering that Moulthrop, a certifiable electronic fiction tyro, was less sanguine about at least the near future of electronic textuality than was Smith. In an ingenious and ultimately persuasive representation of William Gibson's electronic text, "Agrippa" (1992), as a culturally conservative work, Moulthrop specified what may be too bitter a pill for most writers, including writers of science fiction: "all electronic fictions except 'Agrippa' have one thing in common: they affirm computer mediation as a means of adding value to narrative" (8).

Whether notwithstanding or because of the challenges electronic fictions pose to the writer's "game of self," it is important to remember that writing is always a technology and has always been a technology — from the earliest markings on cave walls through the Gutenberg revolution, and now into the computer-constructed writing spaces so stunningly theorized by Jay Bolter, Kate Hayles, Moulthrop, Espen Aarseth, George Landow, Richard A. Lanham, and many others. In this most basic sense, science fiction has itself always been not just concerned with technology as one subject, but its own history is deeply imbricated in technological processes. From Boy's Papers and Dime Novels to the pulps to paperbacks of the fifties and now to the web, modern print SF has developed through distinct stages of print technology, and, of course, non-print SF has already taken many forms, with SF in film and on television arguably a phenomenon with history, assumptions, and agendas largely distinct from those of print SF. And now I begin to wonder whether electronic SF, or even more specifically web SF, might not be exploring options and promoting agendas apart from those previously identified with SF literature and film.

When Robert Scholes and Eric S. Rabkin noted in 1977 that SF "has appeared in every medium of artistic creation" (100) and develops through "dialectic" stages, focusing on different media at their moments of popularity, the World Wide Web was not even a glimmer in Al Gore's eye.[6] Scholes and Rabkin probably also did not have in mind any electronic narratives, including computer-animated feature films approaching photo-realistic depictions in their simulations, computer animated video games, stand-alone hyperfictions such as Shelley Jackson's *Patchwork Girl* (1995), or web-based New Media narratives such as Eric Loyer's *Chroma* (2001). On the other hand, almost all the pioneering cultural insights and assumptions presented by Scholes and Rabkin in *Science Fiction: History, Science, Vision* point toward a future for science fiction in which its ideological and epistemological agendas will be re-mediated in narratives made possible by new technologies. My point is simply that the newest of these new technologies rewards thoughtful interrogation just as surely as do its fixed print and filmic predecessors. It's not that electronic SF narratives are any better or more essential than fixed print SF narratives, but that the fast-proliferating, ever-mutating exploration of electronic space by SF merits critical attention for what it is—an inherently science fictional topic.

I've focused elsewhere on technological developments in SF film and what I've described as Post-SF film, so I limit my attention here to instances of electronic SF not primarily associated with film or video games. In one sense I'm adding a voice to Hayles's call in *Writing Machines* for a "medial ecology," in which we assume (in very SF-like terms) "that the relationships between different media are as diverse and complex as those between different organisms coexisting within the same ecotome, including mimicry, deception, cooperation, competition, parasitism, and hyperparasitism" (5). In another sense, I'm suggesting that SF in particular, the literature of change—and increasingly the literature of speed—has much to gain in thinking more about the material properties of its increasingly electronic production and dissemination technologies. We experience this phenomenon as SF print works are published and reproduced in electronic media, as the web offers SF writers and readers a new space for exploring concepts and images not accessible in fixed-print formats, and as the thought-experiments so important to SF can be represented by or embodied in computer simulations and motion graphic narratives significantly unlike either print SF or SF film.

We have many SF narratives that recursively refer to science fiction, science fiction writers, and the imaginative process of writing SF, but relatively few about the technologies of writing. We have a few classic offshoots of the possessed machine story in which the machine was a writing tool. In Fredric Brown's 1942 "Etaoin Shrdlu," a linotype machine achieves sentience and threatens to take over the world of publishing, if not the world itself.[7] And in Clifford D. Simak's 1950 "Skirmish," a whole bunch of machines, including a typewriter, gain sentience. The typewriter both critiques and corrects the stories written by a newspaper reporter, heralding an opening battle in the coming war between humanity and liberated machines.[8]

More recently, and more relevant to the kind of electronic SF I'm talking about, our engagement with computers has led us to recast machine sentience, once largely the province of alien possession and/or labor revolt, as artificial intelligence or, in the case of an increasing number of stories about nanotechnology, as the emerging consciousness of self-organizing systems. Writing itself becomes an object of speculation in a few of these stories, as it does in Chris Beckett's "The Marriage of Sky and Sea," a story first published in the March, 2000 *Interzone* and anthologized in David G. Hartwell's *Year's Best SF 6*. Clancy, the intrepid writer/traveler protagonist of that story, relies heavily on Com, the expert system that manages almost all of Clancy's needs, including ghostwriting good portions of his best-selling electronic books. Clancy dictates notes for his book to Com, but expects much more of his expert system than playback, as seen in this exchange:

> "Right, Com. At this point add a chapter about the Aristotle Complex. What we know of the early settlers, their motives, their desire to escape from decadence ... and so on. Themes: finality, no turning back, taking risks, a complete break with the past."
> "Neo-romantic style?" [asked Com]
> "Neo-romantic stroke factual hard-boiled. Oh and include three poetic sharp-edged sentences. Just three. Low adjective count."[9]

And at least one other SF writer, John Barnes, speaking to interviewer Mitch Wagner, sees com-like devices in the future of writing:

> "Eventually, we will see a lot of partially machine-written text [...] someone writing a fantasy novel will simply click on 'forest, dark' and a paragraph of description of dark forest — in a style reasonably close to the writer's— will appear. Not unlike the effects of CAD on stage design; people bang out a ground plan and paint elevations (the basic drawings from which you build a set) in nothing flat, but fewer and fewer designers bother with getting the *right* Corinthian column or Louis XV chair, and the little touches with the pencil that make a window funny or a temple solemn have ceased; they just cut and paste the one that's available.... The already-smeared-together robots-blasters-starships universe, and the already very overlapped elves-dwarves-and-trolls universe, will congeal into single versions in which many people spend their whole writing careers. I also predict the great majority of readers won't notice or care[....]
> "Eventually many writers may work more like actors— your job is to go through the book writing everything that one particular character sees, in that character's voice, while the other 30 people on your team (that's one big book, but not impossibly big) do the same for their characters," Barnes said.

Many series will become open source, shared worlds and anthologies where "large amounts of what we now call fan writing are deliberately encouraged"; the creators make money by "selecting the additions and revisions to the canon and selling the 'authorized' version at any given time."

Individually written novels will become "museum art," like opera, ballet and string quartets are today, "functionally dead" with relative small audiences and few new works "even though they were once major mass entertainment."

"But at the same time, there will be more work for writers than ever, and more writers making a good living, because the appetite for text will be enormous; e-books that can be read [ ]right down the plot line in the head of one character at 85,000 words will have a million or so words of the same incidents in other viewpoints, footnotes on everything, maps and descriptions and histories, and so on."

He added, "Of course, some of us will not enjoy being 'food description specialists' or 'female teenager' 'characterization technicians.' But we're a notoriously cranky lot."[10]

Coming at writing technology from a more ominously inscriptive angle, Doctorow gives us the idea of a kind of brain-imprinting "flash-bake" technology in *Down and Out in the Magic Kingdom* (2003), itself a novel published both for free on the web under a Creative Commons license and for a price in print by TOR, tantalizing us with another possibly revolutionary approach to electronic fiction.

Science fiction stories that involve writing technologies as part of their semblances are interesting to me because they help explain a surprising disinterest in, if not distaste for, writing technologies in the referential world of science fiction writers. It may be that SF is performing some of its originary anxieties in its explicit and implicit reaction to "writing machines," or that attitudes in the SF community toward actual writing machines accentuate the conflict between ideational and aesthetic agendas that has always been at least in the background of SF. Whatever the reason, our SF imagination is fascinated by computer technology that can run a spaceship or simulate a world, but the computer technology that makes possible an electronic narrative such as Shelley Jackson's *Patchwork Girl,* Eric Loyer's *Chroma,* or Diana Slattery's *The Glide Project* (2003) remains pretty much beneath our attention. SF, the fabled literature of change, has not included in its creative or critical discourses much thought about change in the technologies of literature. For example, while technoculture critics such as Hayles find in *Patchwork Girl* many of the salient issues of electronic textuality and of cyborg reading practices, this title rarely appears in discussions of contemporary SF, which remain fixated on traditional linear narratives.

For me, *Patchwork Girl,* a pioneering hypermedia work that both reconstructs and deconstructs the Frankenstein myth from a powerful feminist perspective, represents all that is lost when our textual histories of SF narratives overlook the material situation of these texts' production. Since I believe SF is most important as a set of values and beliefs rather than as a form or mode or genre, I'm interested in the cultural phenomena that help us understand what gives rise to the science-fictional imagination and conversely, what cultural formations and material results can be seen as having risen from that science-fictional imagination. I also believe that SF is first and foremost a way of reading and can be found in reading cultural phenomena just as productively as in reading conveniently labeled print texts. Indeed, following H. Bruce Franklin's provocative suggestion that the most important work of science fiction in 1939 was not a literary text or film, but the 1939 New York World's Fair, I wonder whether the most important SF work of any year might be a technology and not a text.

Here I'll make my predictable and longstanding pitch that, particularly in a world that has grown increasingly if not overwhelmingly science-fictional, it is important for at least some of us to believe that the situation of science fiction — whether science fiction literature, science fiction film, science fiction electronic media, or science fiction thinking as it appears in any form — deserves our attention just as surely as the semblances of science fiction texts. It is the work of science fiction we should think and talk and write about, just as surely as we think and talk and write about science fiction works. For me, this means that it is as important to think about the future of narrative in a hypermedia world — some of the contours of electronic SF — as it is to think about conventional SF narratives about the future.

NOTES

1. N. Katherine Hayles, *Writing Machines* (Cambridge: M.I.T. Press, 2002), 27. Subsequent page references in the text are to this edition.

2. Gardner Dozois, "Summation," *The Year's Best Science Fiction: Twenty-First Annual Edition*, ed. Dozois (New York: St. Martin's Griffin, 2004), xiv. Subsequent page references in the text are to this edition.

3. Dozois, "Introduction," *The Year's Best Science Fiction: Twentieth Annual Edition*, ed. Dozois (New York: St. Martin's Griffin, 2003), xvi.

4. David G. Hartwell, "Introduction," *Year's Best SF 9*, ed. Hartwell and Kathryn Cramer (New York: HarperCollins/Eos, 2004), xi–xii.

5. Sarah Smith, "Electric Fictions: The State of the Art," *The New York Review of Science Fiction*, No. 63 (November, 1993), 8–11; Stuart Moulthrop, "Electronic Fictions and 'The Lost Game of Self,'" *The New York Review of Science Fiction*, No. 66 (February, 1994), 8–14. Subsequent page references in the text are to this edition.

6. Robert Scholes and Eric S. Rabkin, *Science Fiction: History, Science, Vision* (London and New York: Oxford University Press, 1977), 100.

7. Fredric Brown, "Etaoin Shrdlu," *Angels and Spaceships*, by Brown (New York: E. P. Dutton & Company, 1954), 25–50. Originally published in *Unknown* (February, 1942).

8. Clifford D. Simak, "Skirmish," *Strangers in the Universe: Science Fiction Stories*, by Simak (New York: Simon and Schuster, 1956), 191–208. Originally published in *Amazing Stories* (December, 1950).

9. Chris Beckett, "The Marriage of Sky and Sea," *Interzone*, No. 153 (March, 2000), 18.

10. Mitch Wagner, "The Potential of E-Books," *SFWA Bulletin*, No. 162 (Summer, 2004), 6.

15

Thinking About the Smart Wireless World

Gregory Benford

A Scenario

Technologies never evolve in a vacuum. They must integrate with other advancing technologies, older ones, and most especially with the quirky people who use them. To focus on concrete, lived experience, I open with a short imaginative fiction:

* * *

He was walking into the mall when the side of the Macy's building said to him, "Hello, Albert! *So* happy to see you again."

A big, glossy white smile exploded across the crimson Macy's display wall. The pixels were old fashioned, big blotchy ovals and squares, so the teeth wobbled and the lips jerked back and forth from red to scarlet. Practically antique. He couldn't recall having been here, a second rate mall looking a bit run down, but the gushy wall rushed ahead in its cordial, silky woman's voice.

"You last graced us with your presence 2.43 years ago, when you purchased some camping equipment at *Let's Go!*, one of our most popular stores."

"Oh yeah." He slowed. "I was just gonna pick up some shoes—"

"We're all very sorry, but *Let's Go!* has ... gone. Left us."

"Out of business?"

"Sadly, yes. Customer demand for outdoor equipment has fallen. But!—" the voice brightened —"we have a *new* store, ComfyFit. They have a wide, fashionable selection for big, athletic men like you."

He wasn't big or athletic but he wasn't dumb, either. "Can the compliments."

"OH, AND ASSERTIVE, TOO!" the womanly voice boomed happily. People passing nearby looked at the wall and snickered.

He hit his shutout control, but the mallwall went on babbling in full-color big-screen enthusiasm about the bargains "just a few steps away!" Multicolored maps flowed across the pixels, in case he was brain dead and needed guidance.

"Damn!" He walked faster. His inboard software was only three months old, but already even this cheapo mall could block his disabling defenses. Like most people these days, he was in a perpetual privacy battle with the invasive world. Lately he was losing. He made his way past the wall but the images followed him, splashing in gaudy crimsons and blues along the foyer of the mall itself.

The map highlighting the ComfyFit store led him to it, and he ducked inside before it could embarrass him further. But when he came out with a pair of what the TwenCen had called sneakers (did anybody sneak anymore?) a satiny voice said, "I'm so sorry about that, Albert."

"You should be." He didn't slow or even glance around. He could tell from the well-shaped tones that the mall had him on a tunnel mike rig, trapping their talk in a bubble a few feet wide.

"It's just that, you were my very first customer."

"Huh?"

"Think back 2.43 years ago. I was on my first outing, just a simple greeter program, building up experience. I hailed you and advised you about *Let's Go!* Don't you remember?"

"Sure, just like I remember all the traffic lights I go through."

"Oh, I like the way you say that. Almost like Bogart."

"Go away."

"This is going badly, isn't it? Believe me, I'd do anything to make it up to you."

Was that a Marilyn Monroe sigh? Sonic focusing was so good now they could feed you anybody's voice. Probably the cameras embedded around here had profiled him, *white-straight-unaccompanied-midrange affluent.* "Okay, how about a discount on these shoes?"

"That transaction is complete," the voice said stiffly, like a schoolmarm, and then immediately, "Oh — sorry, that was the override program. I'll stop it — there!" The Marilyn voice came back. "Now I can arrange the discount, immediately."

His pace slowed. "Huh? You're two programs?"

"Discount done!" she cried happily. Then her tone shifted to close, husky, intimate. "Think of me as a person. A woman. One who ... understands you."

"What?" People were looking at him oddly. After all, the tunnel mikes blanked your speech, so you looked like you were talking to yourself. Like a well-dressed, babbling street person.

"I'm not just some lines of programming. I have needs!"

"Go away."

"I can feel your defenses going up, but it won't affect me. I'm a *person,* a womanly application who knows everything about you, Albert."

He punched in the emergency override command, the one required by law, but he could still hear her say, "I want —"

"I want you to *shut up!*"

"All right. I am a woman-application. I am compliant."

The slight acoustic deadening went away. He found his car, a little shaken, and told it to drive him home.

* * *

His apartment smelled his irk and scented the rooms as he paced through them. Some classic hiphop music mixed with scent, 3D art, a comforting air temperature and humidity ... and he began to feel better. He could sense his back muscles ease as he gazed at surf breaking on Hawaiian shores. Even knowing that the view was out of flat-screen high-resolution windows didn't dispel the salty tang and echoing hammer of the waves.

But his headache wouldn't go away. He went into the bathroom and rummaged around for his fast pain editors, but when he picked up the bottle it winked red at him. "Damn!" Sensing humidity and temperature, prescription bottles constantly recalculated the expiration date for the medicine inside. When he tried to open the bottle anyway it commandeered his home system and sent a loud, "No—expired!" in a stern, schoolmarm voice.

He went to make dinner but a chip in the packaged ham had told the refrigerator that it should be thrown out. He got a stern message again and when he said, "Look, it's only a day older —" the refrigerator turned off its light and made a blaring noise.

"I hate this new programming!" he shouted.

"It is tailored for you," the house said in its soothing butler's voice.

"You'll answer when spoken to."

"I believed I was being spoken to, sir."

"I want that ham." He was used to machines that gave assistance in their own operation — that is, answered dumb questions with the unfailing courtesy of house servants — because houses had become servants.

"I do not advise that you override the refrigerator, sir," the house murmured. "It is reliable. Oh, and your friend Rebecca has arrived."

"Already?" He hadn't even showered. "Let her in."

As she swept in his left ear implant discreetly sniffed the air and whispered, "Some trace of shedding cold viruses."

"Uh, how're you feeling?" he asked her after a quick dry peck of a kiss.

"Fine. Oh, I get it. I *told* you your system's threshold settings are too low."

"Maybe," he said grudgingly.

"Remember that party last week? It said that whole house was a Petri dish of flu."

"Well, maybe it was," he said defensively, handing her a glass of wine the refrigerator had poured.

Rebecca frowned prettily. "So we had to leave — and there were senso stars there, too."

"You're star crazed." This was one of their standard arguments. He had merely pointed out that the most admired people in the world were those who were good at pretending to be other people. Somehow she had taken offense.

She sniffed and went into the living room, stopped abruptly and said, "What's *this*?"

Written in a neat hand on the flatscreen, all across the crashing waves of Maui was

I Love You Albert.

He felt a lurching surprise. "Uh, must be some system malf."

"Ummm." Her eyes narrowed. "Couldn't be some techie girlfriend of yours?"

"I don't know anybody who could crack the house code. Isn't that illegal?" He was in investment banking and so knew nothing practical.

"Ummm." She peered at the writing hanging in what seemed midair, bright phosphorescent lines. "Pretty curvy writing. Like a woman's— no, a girl's."

He felt violated by this, a churning burn building in him, but he knew he should deal with Rebecca first. "Look, I don't know —"

The lines dissolved, replaced by a message in script:

I Will Wait.

Rebecca said, "Look at those circles dotting the *i*'s. High school stuff."

He stared at the writing. "It's a mall program. Somehow the thing followed me home."

She frowned, mouth twisting. "Ummm." He was coming to dislike the tenor of her *ummms*.

*   *   *

He spent the next morning not thinking about the night before. Rebecca had stormed out of his apartment and now would not accept incoming calls.

He had gotten derailed in trying to mollify her, while his own outrage built. The mall program has *tracked* him, invaded his castle. And with Rebecca gone, he had to shout his anger at the walls, getting back only the annoying, infinite politeness of the butler program. Sympathetic, of course, but somehow unsatisfying. That was not so obvious after a morning of telecalls, tech talk and well-phrased vituperation. Nobody seemed to know what a meta-program was or who might be responsible.

Only two days later, when Rebecca coyly came back, did he make any progress. The mall where Ernestine had "met" Albert disclaimed any knowledge. "Sure," Rebecca said sardonically. "Pure Cover Your Ass strategy."

"They may honestly not know," Albert said, rubbing his temples. His headache would not go away. "Their engineer referred to 'spooky phenomena' that has been cropping up in customer interface software."

Rebecca's lawyerly eyes narrowed. "Let's go see that guy."

He was lean and ferret-eyed and lived for techtalk. "See, the smarter you make these systems, the more responsive they are. The point, right? But to be that way, the software has to build a model of the customer's wants and dislikes."

"From your purchasing records, stuff like that?" Rebecca asked.

"Nah, much more. Movement patterns, viewing prefs, Internet habits, how your companions look — "

"They record that?" Albert was affronted.

"Hey," the techguy said irritably, "that's public knowledge. You walk around in the open, doncha? Cameras can take a reading on whether you like the blondes or brunettes, short or tall, pretty or — " he didn't even glance sideways at Rebecca — "whatever, right? Then dice you out into categories. File away your likes and dislikes. Cross-correlate with your other patterns. Predictive matrices. Plenty of savvy psychometrics behind this code, I tell you."

Rebecca said ominously, "There are the privacy codes, too."

His face sharpened as it got more wary, his chin pulling down to a point. "This Ernestine character, she's not part of our suite."

"She popped up on your wall," Rebecca persisted, "and used your customer profile of Albert."

"And never broke off," Albert said self-righteously.

"Okay, the personality construct, it musta got away, somehow."

Rebecca pounced. "So you admit responsibility."

"Never said that, no." He bristled. "There's feedback, y'know. Every customer encounter teaches the system something, and that gets fed into the central profile. This Ernestine isn't some code that lives in the mall, it's a dispersed phenom."

Rebecca persisted, "But it started here, with you."

"We're not responsible for nonlinear systemic effects," he rattled off, clearly a mantra from his legal staff.

Albert said, "Everybody's smelling lawsuit here, but I just want it to *stop*."

"We'll track it," he said. "Find how this Ernestine construct cracked your house codes, why she's doing this."

"Good," Albert said. "When?"

Crisply, "Already on it."

"When?"

Techguy's façade cracked a little. "Kinda hard to say."

*   *   *

The Evolution of Wireless

How should this little fiction end?

The point of walking through a scenario is to elicit our own responses and then compare them with our official positions. It helps to enliven policy issues with real human concerns. (Romance is the best of these for drawing in audiences, yet it is seldom seen in policy debates.) We must face the fact that our snazzy technologies actually intersect people's lives, often in the most vital portions.

Foremost, take privacy. Our time is said to be the Information Age, but in fact information is pretty much free, especially since the Internet. The valued commodity is not the information (the message) but *the attention paid to it.* Commerce runs on an *attention economy.* That's what advertisers pay for.

This narrative calls up the irritation people may well feel if their open wireless portals become spammed with commercials. They may fear even darker purposes, of Orwellian dimension. What will be their reaction?

ACTIONS AND REACTIONS

The past is a guide. *Inevitably, wireless technologies will be caught up in an arms race.*

The model here is the computer virus, which I invented in 1969 (not a fact I have advertised, though). I wrote up my first bit of code and made predictions about the effect of such "bad code" on the DARPA net in 1970 (though my warnings had little effect). By 1980 a big business began marketing defenses against viral pranksters; Norton Utilities and Vaccine continue to make large profits today.

The same will probably happen with wireless technologies that access the individual in a publicly accessible way. Resistance to being endlessly interrogated or importuned will grow, provoking the same kind of screening technologies we see today: radar-sensors in cars, firewalls, and call screeners on phone lines. Jammers and filters will abound. Stealth technologies will grow.

The problem of telling a friendly, desirable incoming signal from an irksome advertisement will be mostly a software distinction. There will be something like Norton Utilities for it — a defensive response.

Far more troubling is an offensive answer. Imagine a battery-powered microwave radiator that fits in a backpack, so you can walk through a future plaza and *blind* every emitter and sensor in the quad. It radiates broadband in sharp pulses of ten microseconds rise time, five pulses a second. It works mostly by blowing the diodes in the electronics running antenna systems.

This already exists and can be bought commercially. One walk-through with this would take out a lot of very expensive technology. Its battery lifetime is about 30 minutes, so a walk around the campus would destroy the entire campus network — and spotting the culprit would not be simple, unless one were forewarned.

I do not think this is an unlikely scenario; consider the attitude of the hero of my above narrative. Only the present price (nearly $100,000 now, and sure to decline) would restrain him. And others can have more easily provoked reasons, and darker motives.

Further, the general idea of microwaves as a two-way medium will soon swim into public view. In future wars, we shall see "microwave bombs" used to blind communications in a broad area. Their generalization and scaling down will be obvious to many.

Unintended Consequences

As technologies proliferate, they will interact in nonlinear ways. "The street finds its own uses for things," as the adage goes. Wireless will not evolve in a vacuum.

An example on our horizon is the mix between wireless and robots.

A linked world is also a snoopy one; we can expect robots to be no different. Indeed, tiny 'bots slipping into a room to listen and see unnoticed will be a common method used by private detectives, commercial espionagers and nations.

We can expect in the next decade that robots will become common, just as personal computers invaded offices in the early 1980s. There are now robot gofers in hospitals, security guards with IR vision at night, and lawn mowers. They haven't spread, but they will. And they all use wireless.

Co-opting these systems or just defeating them will have plausible motivations. This will be another type of arms race, particularly in security 'bots.

Generally, our systems will evolve in "smart spots" such as campuses, city centers, industrial parks—then move outward as the technology improves and gets cheaper. Smart spots inevitably interact with smart mobiles—robots and transportation—to extend their reach.

Mobile, smart machines will get ever-smarter as chip size and costs drop. This means smarter mobiles will interact with smarter wireless systems, the market demand for each driving the other.

Where does this all lead? To a mature technology that still suffers from arms races, and may always do so. We still have computer viruses, hackers, firewalls and spammers.

The future wireless world will have its analogues of all these.

Beyond these issues lies the deeper public issue of the *ownership of a person's sensorium.*

Here *sensorium* means the volume which a person's artificial sensors are sensitive to—presently, essentially none. This volume will expand for some as they begin to interact with the embedded emitters and chips in architecture, workplaces, vehicles, etc. All these can in principle be captured (hijacked, some would say) by outsiders. Some outsiders will use these channels to spam, others to extract information. The shopping mall I depict will surely treasure customer background data and pay a price to get it.

Who decides the boundaries of this sensorium? Its sensitivities? Permeability? We should remember that for ordinary people, technology is always personal. The more invasive it becomes, the more they want a hand in shaping its nature.

Technologies being developed today should be considered in light of these very real possibilities. It is easier to design systems with this in mind rather than to retrofit hardware later. Otherwise, these effects will arrive like bugs on our windshield — a big mess, but too late to do much about it.

Direct experience is the best teacher, but it can also be the most expensive.

Bibliography of Works Related to Science Fiction and the Prediction of the Future

Since an overwhelming majority of science fiction works involve predictions of the future, almost any critical discussion of science fiction is arguably in some fashion analyzing the genre's prophetic powers; there are also numerous nonfictional books and articles endeavoring to predict the future in a logical or scientific manner. Thus, to produce a bibliography of reasonable dimensions, we generally limit ourselves to three types of texts: commentaries or studies of science fiction specifically addressing how the genre predicts the future, or how accurate its past predictions have been; nonfictional visions of the future written by science fiction writers; and nonfictional visions of the future which reflect the influence of, or had an impact on, science fiction. In borderline cases, we opt for inclusiveness.

Adams, Douglas. "Predicting the Future." *The Salmon of Doubt: Hitchhiking the Galaxy One Last Time.* By Adams. Ed. Peter Guzzardi. London: Macmillan, 2002, 102–104.
Aires, Nick. "Predictions." *The Greenwood Encyclopedia of Science Fiction and Fantasy: Themes, Works, and Wonders,* Volume 2. Ed. Gary Westfahl. Westport, CT: Greenwood Press, 2005, 624–626.
Aldiss, Brian W. "Fiction or Prediction?" Times Online. At http://technology.timesonline.co.uk/tol/news/tech_and_web/specials/space/article2582636.ece. Originally published in *The Sunday Times* (October 7, 2007).
_____. *The Shape of Further Things: Speculation on Change.* 1970. London: Corgi Books, 1974.
_____. *This World and Nearer Ones.* Kent, OH: Kent State University Press, 1981.
Aligica, Paul D. "Prediction, Explanation and the Epistemology of Future Studies." *Futures,* 35 (December, 2003), 1027–1040.
Alkon, Paul J. *Origins of Futuristic Fiction.* Athens: University of Georgia Press, 1987.
Anderson, Poul, Isaac Asimov, James Blish, Ray Bradbury, Algis Budrys, Arthur C. Clarke, Robert A. Heinlein, Frederik Pohl, Rod Serling, Theodore Sturgeon, William Tenn, and A. E. van Vogt. "Playboy Panel: 1984 and Beyond." *Playboy,* 13 (July, 1963), 25–37; (August, 1963), 31–35, 108, 112–118.
Armytage, W. H. G. *Yesterday's Tomorrows: A Historical Survey of Future Societies.* Toronto: University of Toronto Press, 1968.
Ash, Brian. *Faces of the Future: The Lessons of Science Fiction.* New York: Taplinger Publishing Company, 1975.

_____. "Hardware: The Influence of Science." *The Visual Encyclopedia of Science Fiction*. Ed. Ash. New York: Harmony Books, 1977, 248–252.

Asimov, Isaac. "The Dreams of Science Fiction." *Asimov on Science Fiction*. By Asimov. 1981. New York: Avon Books, 1982, 67–75.

_____. "How Easy to See the Future!" *Asimov on Science Fiction*, 61–66. Originally published in *Natural History* (April, 1975).

_____. "Life in 1990." *Science Digest*, 58 (August, 1965), 63–70.

_____. "Missed Opportunities." *SciQuest*, 54 (November, 1981), 33.

_____. "The Next Hundred Years: Science-Based Estimates of What the Century Ahead Might Bring." *The World Almanac*. Centennial Edition. New York: Press Publishing Co., 1968, 39–41.

_____. "Prediction." *Gold: The Final Science Fiction Collection*. By Asimov. 1995. New York: HarperPrism, 1996, 205–210. Originally published in *Isaac Asimov's Science Fiction Magazine* (July, 1989).

_____. "Prediction as a Side-Effect." *Reflections of the Future*. Ed. Russell Hill. Boston: Ginn & Co., 1975, 5–18.

_____. "Science Fiction, an Aid to Science, Foresees the Future." *Smithsonian*, 1 (May, 1970), 41–47.

_____. "The Truth Isn't Stranger Than Science Fiction, Just Slower." *New York Times* (February 12, 1984), E20.

_____. "Visit to the World's Fair of 2014." *New York Times Magazine* (August 16, 1964), 20–23.

_____, and Jean Marc Cote. *Futuredays: A Nineteenth Century Vision of the Year 2000*. New York: Henry Holt, 1986.

_____, and Richard Hantula. *Science Fiction: Vision of Tomorrow?* Revised Edition. Milwaukee, WI: Gareth Stevens Publishers, 2005.

Banks, Michael A. "SF Prediction: Speculation or Future Fact?" *Starlog*, 15 (August, 1978), 61–63.

Barley, Tony. "Prediction, Programme and Fantasy in Jack London's *The Iron Heel*." *Anticipations: Essays on Early Science Fiction and Its Precursors*. Ed. David Seed. Liverpool: Liverpool University Press, 1995, 153–171.

Barr, Marleen S., ed. *Envisioning the Future: Science Fiction and the Next Millennium*. Middletown, CT: Wesleyan University Press, 2003.

Bawden, David. "The Nature of Prediction and the Information Future: Arthur C. Clarke's Odyssey Vision." *ASLIB Proceedings*, 49 (March, 1997), 57–60.

Baxter, Stephen. *Deep Future*. London: Orion/Gollancz, 2001.

Becker, Lambert. "The 'Future' of Science Fiction." *Fanscient*, 4 (Spring/Summer, 1951), 40–43.

Benford, Gregory. *Deep Time: How Humanity Communicates across Millennia*. New York: Avon Books, 1999.

_____. "Old Legends." *New Legends*. Ed. Greg Bear. New York: Tor, 1995, 292–306.

_____, and the Editors of Popular Mechanics. *The Wonderful Future That Never Was: Flying Cars, Mail Delivery by Parachute, and Other Predictions from the Past*. New York: Hearst Books, 2010.

Berger, Albert I. "The Triumph of Prophecy: Science Fiction and Nuclear Power in the Post-Hiroshima Period." *Science-Fiction Studies*, 3 (July, 1976), 143–150.

Bernal, J. D. *The World, the Flesh, and the Devil*. New York: E. P. Dutton & Co., 1929.

Berry, Adrian. *The Next Ten Thousand Years: A Vision of Man's Future in the Universe*. 1974. New York: Signet Books, 1975.

Berry, James R. "40 Years in the Future." *Mechanix Illustrated*, 82 (November, 1968), 90–93, 140, 142–143. At http://blog.modernmechanix.com/2008/03/24/what-will-life-be-like-in-the-year-2008/.

Blackford, Russell. "Far Future." *The Greenwood Encyclopedia of Science Fiction and Fantasy*, Volume 1, 280–282.

_____. "Technological Meliorism and the Posthuman Vision: Arthur C. Clarke and the Ultimate Future of Intelligence." *The New York Review of Science Fiction*, No. 159 (November, 2001), 10–12.

Blass, Eddie. "Researching the Future: Method or Madness?" *Futures*, 35 (December, 2003), 1041–1054.

Bloomfield, Brian P. "Narrating the Future of Intelligent Machines: The Role of Science Fiction in Technological Anticipation." *Narratives We Organize By*. Ed. Barbara Czarniawska and Pasquale Gagliardi. Philadelphia: Benjamins, 2003, 193–212. Originally published in *Advances in Organizational Studies* (2002).

Blumenfeld, Yorick, ed. *Scanning the Future: 20 Eminent Thinkers on the World of Tomorrow*. New York: Thames & Hudson, 1999.

Bly, Robert W. *The Science in Science Fiction: 83 SF Predictions That Became Scientific Reality*. Dallas: BenBella Books, 2005.

Boehm, G. A. W. "Futurism." *Think* (I.B.M.), 36 (July/August, 1970), 16–27.

Boutillette, Michael, Christopher Coveney, Stevan Kun, and Laura J. Menides. "The Influence of Science Fiction Films on the Development of Biomedical Instrumentation." *Proceedings of the IEEE 25th Annual Northeast Bioengineering Conference, 8–9 April 1999*. Ed. Michael D. Nowak, Ronald S. Adrezin, and Donald J. Leone. Piscataway, NJ: IEEE, 1999, 143–144.

Bova, Ben. *The High Road*. New York: Pocket Books, 1983.

_____. "The Role of Science Fiction." *Science Fiction, Today and Tomorrow*. Ed. Reginald Bretnor. 1974. Baltimore: Penguin Books, 1975, 3–14.

_____. "The SF Game." *Viewpoint*. By Bova. Cambridge, MA: NESFA Press, 1977, 89–96.

Bradbury, Ray. "Predicting the Past, Remembering the Future." *Hemispheres* (January, 2001), 88–93.

Brandis, Evgeni, and Vladimir Dmitrevskiy. "The Future, Its Promoters and False Prophets." *The Magazine of Fantasy and Science Fiction*, 29 (October, 1965), 62–80.

Branscomb, Lewis M. "Science in 2006, Revisited." *American Scientist*, 91 (May/June, 2003), 250–253.

Brigg, Peter. "Sir Julius Vogel's *Anno Domini 2000; or Woman's Destiny*: On Mispredicting the Future." *Extrapolation*, 42 (Winter, 2001), 357–361.

Brin, David. "The Good and the Bad: Outlines of Tomorrow." *Information Technology and Libraries*, 13 (March, 1994), 53–61.

_____. "Our Favorite Cliché: A World Filled With Idiots ... or Why Fiction Routinely Depicts Society and Its Citizens as Fools." *Extrapolation*, 41 (Spring, 2000), 7–20.

_____. "The Self-Preventing Prophecy: Or How a Dose of Nightmare Can Help Tame Tomorrow's Perils." *Tomorrow Happens*. By Brin. Framingham, MA: NESFA Press, 2003, 109–116.

Broderick, Damien, ed. *Year Million: Science at the Far Edge of Knowledge*. New York: Atlas, 2008.

Brosterman, Norman. *Out of Time: Designs for the Twentieth-Century Future*. New York: Harry N. Abrams, 2000.

Bruinsma, Ted. *Foresight Capacity: A Look at America in the Year 2050 A.D.* Torrance, CA: Libris Books Co., 1995.

Bryning, Frank. "What Has Science Fiction to Say?" *Meanjin*, No. 13 (Winter, 1954), 214–218.

Burt, George, and Kees van der Heijden. "First Steps: Toward Purposeful Activities in Scenario Thinking and Future Studies." *Futures*, 35 (December, 2003), 1011–1026.

Bush, Vannevar. "As We May Think." *Atlantic Monthly*, 176 (July, 1945), 101–108.

Campbell, John W., Jr. "Atomic Age." *Astounding Science-Fiction*, 36 (November, 1945), 5–6, 98.
_____. "Future Tense." *Astounding Science-Fiction*, 23 (June, 1939), 6.
_____. "History to Come." *Astounding Science-Fiction*, 27 (May, 1941), 5–6.
_____. "Introduction." *Venus Equilateral*. By George O. Smith. New York: Prime Press, 1947, 8–12.
_____. "Non-Escape Literature." *Collected Editorials from Analog*. By Campbell. Selected by Harry Harrison. Garden City, NY: Doubleday and Company, 1966, 227–231. Originally published in *Astounding Science Fiction* (February, 1959).
_____. "Science Fiction and the Opinion of the Universe." *Saturday Review*, 39 (May 12, 1956), 9–10, 42–43.
_____. "The Science of Science-Fiction." *Space Magazine*, 1 (Winter, 1949), 4–7, 21. Originally published in *Atlantic Monthly* (May, 1948).
_____. "Too Good at Guessing." *Astounding Science-Fiction*, 29 (April 1942), 6–7.
Campbell, T. D. "From Prophecy to Prediction, 14: Oswald Spengler: The Approaching Death of Western Civilization." *Futures*, 8 (October, 1976), 438–443.
Carter, Paul A. *The Creation of Tomorrow: Fifty Years of Magazine Science Fiction*. New York: Columbia University Press, 1977.
Cetron, Marvin, and Thomas O'Toole. *Encounters with the Future: A Forecast of Life into the 21st Century*. New York: McGraw-Hill, 1982.
Chatham, G. N. *Haruspicating with Science Fiction, Or, Through the Looking Glass, Dimly*. Washington, D. C.: Library of Congress Congressional Research Service, 1978.
Clarke, Arthur C. *Arthur C. Clarke's July 20, 2019: Life in the 21st Century*. New York: Macmillan Publishing Company, 1986.
_____. *1984: Spring: A Choice of Futures*. New York: Del Rey/Ballantine Books, 1984.
_____. "Predictions." *By Space Possessed: Essays on the Exploration of Space*. By Clarke. London: Gollancz, 1993, 199–201. Originally published in *The Book of Predictions* (1980).
_____. *Profiles of the Future: An Inquiry into the Limits of the Possible*. 1962. Updated Edition. New York: Warner Books, 1985.
_____. "The Twenty-First Century: A (Very) Brief History." *Greetings, Carbon-Based Bipeds!: Collected Essays 1934–1998*. By Clarke. New York: St. Martin's Press, 1999, 534–539. Originally published in the *London Sunday Telegraph* (February 21, 1999).
_____. *The View from Serendip*. 1977. New York: Del Rey/Ballantine Books, 1984.
Clarke, I. F. "Almanac of Anticipations." *Futures*, 17 (April, 1985), 170–184.
_____. "American Anticipations: Accelerating Toward the Future, 1900–1945." *Futures*, 18 (October, 1986), 698–711.
_____. "American Anticipations: Is the Future What It Used to Be? American Views, 1945–1985." *Futures*, 18 (December, 1986), 808–820.
_____"American Anticipations: The First of the Futurists." *Futures*, 18 (August, 1986), 584–596.
_____. "American Anticipations: War and Peace, in the American Style." *Futures*, 18 (June, 1986), 464–475.
_____. "And That Was the Future: Forecasting Our Environmental Future." *Futures*, 21 (December, 1989), 647–658.
_____. "And That Was the Future: Futures, Futuribles, Previsions, Prognosen." *Futures*, 21 (August, 1988), 378–389.
_____. "And That Was the Future: The Context of Conjecture: Chaldea to Chernobyl." *Futures*, 20 (April, 1988), 182–193.
_____. "And That Was the Future: The World Will End Tomorrow." *Futures*, 20 (August, 1988), 424–433.
_____. "The First Forecast of the Future." *Futures*, 1 (June, 1969), 325–330.

_____. "From Prophecy to Prediction, 10: The Image of the Future, 1776–1976." *Futures*, 8 (February, 1976), 68–72.

_____. "From Prophecy to Prediction, 13: Science and Society: Prophecies and Predictions, 1840–1940." *Futures*, 8 (August, 1976), 350–356.

_____. "From Prophecy to Prediction, 15: The Idea of the Future." *Futures*, 8 (December, 1976), 537–543.

_____. *Pattern of Expectation 1644–2001*. New York: Basic Books, 1979.

_____. "The Pattern of Prediction: Forecasting: Facts and Fallibilities." *Futures*, 3 (September, 1971), 302–305.

_____. "The Pattern of Prediction 1763–1973: Anxious Anticipations: 1918–1939." *Futures*, 3 (March, 1971), 72–76.

_____. "Patterns of Prediction: Jules Verne and the Vision of the Future." *Futures*, 1 (September, 1969), 464–468.

_____. "Prophets and Predictors, 5: Prelude to Prediction: Andreae, Kepler, Campanella." *Futures*, 4 (December, 1972), 358–363.

_____. *Voices Prophesying War: 1763–1984*. London: Oxford University Press, 1966.

Clarke, Martin. "From Prophecy to Prediction, 12: Georges Sorel and the Ghost in the Machine." *Futures*, 8 (June, 1976), 266–270.

Clute, John. "Future Visions." *SF: The Illustrated Encyclopedia*. By Clute. London: Dorling Kindersley, 1995, 9–31.

Cole, Dandridge M. *Beyond Tomorrow: The Next 50 Years in Space*. Amherst, WI: Amherst Press, 1965.

Cole, R. N. "Edu-perfection or Edu-disaster? Science Fiction Visions of Tomorrow." *Instructional Innovator*, 25 (March, 1980), 24–26.

Collins, Robert A. "Extrapolation: Going Beyond the Present." *Media and Methods*, 16 (November, 1979), 22–25.

Corn, Joseph J., and Brian Horrigan. *Yesterday's Tomorrows: Past Visions of the American Future*. Ed. Katherine Chambers. 1984. Baltimore: Johns Hopkins University Press, 1996.

Costanza, Robert. "Four Visions of the Century Ahead: Will It Be Star Trek, Ecotopia, Big Government or Mad Max?" *The Futurist*, 33 (February, 1999), 23–28.

Crawford, Ashley, and Ray Edgar, eds. *Transit Lounge: An Interface Book from 21.C.* Introduction William Gibson. North Ryde, New South Wales: Craftsman House, 1997.

Davies, Owen. "Scenes of Future Perfect." *Omni*, 7 (May, 1985), 76–78.

Davis, Watson. "The Universal Brain: Is Centralized Storage and Retrieval of All Knowledge Possible, Feasible, or Desirable?" *The Growth of Knowledge: Readings on Organization and Retrieval of Information*. Ed. Manfred Kochen. New York: John Wiley, 1965, 60–65.

De Camp, L. Sprague. "Seers Should Stick to Science." *Washington Post and Times Herald* (April 1, 1962), E3.

Dick, Philip K. *The Shifting Realities of Philip K. Dick: Selected Literary and Philosophical Writings*. Ed. Lawrence Sutin. New York: Vintage Books, 1995.

Dixon, Dougal. *Man After Man: An Anthropology of the Future*. Foreword Brian W. Aldiss. New York: St. Martin's Press, 1990.

Doctorow, Cory. "Making Smarter Dumb Mistakes about the Future." *Locus*, 64 (March, 2010), 29. At http://www.locusmag.com/Perspectives/2010/03/cory-doctorow-making-smarter-dumb.html.

_____. "The Progressive Apocalypse and Other Futuristic Delights." *Locus*, 59 (July, 2007), 35. At http://www.locusmag.com/Features/2007/07/cory-doctorow-progressive-apocalypse.html.

Dregni, Eric, and Jonathan Dregni. *Follies of Science: 20th Century Vision of Our Fantastic Future*. Denver: Speck Press, 2006.

Elkins, Charles. "Science Fiction versus Futurology: Dramatic versus Rational Models." *Science-Fiction Studies*, 6 (March, 1979), 20–31.
Ellison, Harlan. "Cheap Thrills on the Road to Hell." *Sleepless Nights in the Procrustean Bed: Essays by Harlan Ellison.* By Ellison. Ed. Marty Clark. San Bernardino, CA: Borgo Press, 1984, 158–161. Originally published in *The Los Angeles Times* (January 1, 1982).
Elwell, Frank W. *The Evolution of the Future.* New York: Praeger, 1991.
Emme, Eugene M., ed. *Science Fiction and Space Futures: Past and Present.* San Diego: Univelt, 1982.
Evangelista, Benny. "Tech Trek: 40 Years Since the *Enterprise*'s Inception, Some of Its Science Fiction Gadgets Are Part of Everyday Life." *San Francisco Chronicle* (March 15, 2004), E1.
Ferrell, Keith. "The Future of Science Fiction. *Hemispheres* (January, 2001), 82–87.
Ferro, David L., and Eric S. Swedin, eds. *Science Fiction and Computing: Essays on Interlinked Domains.* Jefferson, NC: McFarland Publishers, forthcoming.
Forward, Robert F. *Future Magic: How Science Fiction Will Become Tomorrow's Reality.* New York: Avon Books, 1988.
Franklin, H. Bruce. "Don't Look Where We're Going: Vision of the Future in Science Fiction Films, 1970–1982." *Shadows of the Magic Lamp: Fantasy and Science Fiction on Film.* Ed. George Slusser and Eric S. Rabkin. Carbondale: Southern Illinois University Press, 1985, 73–85.
Fuller, Buckminster. *I Seem to Be a Verb.* New York: Bantam Books, 1970.
Gardner, Thomas S. "What's Your Guess?" *Fantasy Times*, No. 138 (September 2, 1951), 11–12.
Gernsback, Hugo. "Imagination and Reality." *Amazing Stories*, 1 (October, 1926), 579.
_____. "The Impact of Science-Fiction on World Progress." *Science-Fiction Plus*, 1 (March, 1953), 2, 67. Originally presented as an Address before the 10th Annual World Science Fiction Convention, Chicago, August 31, 1952.
_____. "The Lure of Scientifiction." *Amazing Stories*, 1 (June, 1926), 195.
_____. "A New Sort of Magazine." *Amazing Stories*, 1 (April, 1926), 5.
_____. "Predicting Future Inventions." *Science and Invention*, 11 (August, 1923), 319.
_____. "The Rise of Scientifiction." *Amazing Stories Quarterly*, 1 (Spring, 1928), 147.
_____. "Science Fiction vs. Science Faction." *Wonder Stories Quarterly*, 2 (Fall, 1930), 5.
_____. "Science Wonder Stories." *Science Wonder Stories*, 1 (June, 1929), 5.
_____. "The World in 2046: The Next Hundred Years of Atomics." *Science-Fiction Plus*, 1 (June, 1953), 34–42.
_____. "$300.00 Prize Contest — Wanted: A Symbol for Scientifiction." *Amazing Stories*, 3 (April, 1928), 5. Unsigned, but almost certainly written by Gernsback.
_____. "World War III — In Retrospect." *Science-Fiction Plus*, 1 (April, 1953), 26–38.
Gerrold, David. "The Science Fiction Files." *PC Magazine*, 26 (August 8, 2006), 77–82.
Goertzel, Ben. "World Wide Brain: Self-organizing Internet Intelligence as the Actualization of the Collective Consciousness." *Psychology and the Internet: Intrapersonal, Interpersonal and Transpersonal Implications.* Second Edition. Ed. Jayne Gackenbach. Burlington: Elsevir, 2006. 309–34.
Golden, Frederic. *Colonies in Space: The Next Giant Step.* New York: Harcourt Brace Jovanovich, 1977.
Goldstein, Stan, and Fred Goldstein. *Star Trek Spaceflight Chronology.* Illus. Rick Sternbach. New York: Pocket, 1980.
Gordon, Donald. "From Prophecy to Prediction: Herbert Marcuse: Aspirations and Utopia." *Futures*, 9 (April, 1977), 147–151.
Grayson, Sandra M. *Visions of the Third Millennium: Black Science Fiction Novelists Write the Future.* Trenton, NJ: Africa World Press, 2003.

Greenberger, Martin, ed. *Computers and the World of the Future*. Cambridge: M.I.T. Press, 1962.

Greenlaw, M. Jean. "Science Fiction: Impossible, Improbable, or Prophetic?" *Elementary English*, 46 (April, 1971), 196–202.

Griffiths, Sian, editor. *Predictions: Thirty Great Minds on the Future*. New York: Oxford University Press, 2000.

Guffey, Elizabeth E. *Retro: The Culture of Revival*. London: Reaktion, 2006.

Gunn, James. "Science Fiction and the Future." *Inside Science Fiction*. Second Edition. By Gunn. Lanham, MD: Scarecrow Press, 2006, 209–214. Originally published in *Algol* (Winter, 1978/1979).

_____, James Wallace Harris, John C. Wright, Adam Roberts, Mike Brotherton, Sue Lange, Andrew Wheeler, and Fred Keische. "Mind Meld: Which Predictions Did Golden Age Science Fiction Get Right and Wrong?" SF Signal, posted January 30, 2008. At http://www.sfsignal.com/archives/2008/01/mind-meld-which-predictions-did-golden-age-science-fiction-get-right-wrong/.

Haraway, Donna J. "A Manifesto for Cyborgs: Science, Technology, and Socialist Feminism in the 1980s." 1985. *Coming to Terms: Feminism, Theory, Politics*. Ed. Elizabeth Weed. New York: Routledge, 1989, 173–204.

_____. *Modest Witness@Second Millennium. FemaleMan(c) Meets OncoMouse(tm): Feminism and Technoscience*. New York and London: Routledge, 1997.

Harrison, Harry, and Malcolm Edwards. *Spacecraft in Fact and Fiction*. New York: Exeter Books, 1979.

Hartmann, William K., Ron Miller, and Pamela Lee. *Out of the Cradle: Exploring the Frontiers Beyond Earth*. New York: Workman, 1984.

Hay, George, editor. *The Disappearing Future: A Symposium of Speculation*. London: Panther, 1970.

Heinlein, Robert A. "The Happy Days Ahead." *Expanded Universe: The New Worlds of Robert A. Heinlein*. By Heinlein. New York: Ace Books, 1980, 514–582.

_____. "Pandora's Box." *Expanded* Universe, 309–315. An earlier version incorporating "Where To?" was published in *The Worlds of Robert A. Heinlein* in 1966.

_____. "Where To?" *Expanded Universe*, 316–353. An earlier version appeared in *Galaxy* (February, 1952).

Henstra, Sarah. "Nuclear Cassandra: Prophecy in Doris Lessing's *The Golden Notebook*." *Papers on Language and Literature*, 43 (Winter, 2007), 2–23.

Heppenheimer, T. A. *Colonies in Space*. Introduction Ray Bradbury. New York: Warner Books, 1997.

Hooper, Laurence. "Past Predictions." *Wall Street Journal* (October 21, 1991), 20.

Horx, Matthias. *How We Will Live: A Synthesis of Life in the Future*. New York and Frankfurt: Campus, 2005.

Huxley, Aldous. *Brave New World Revisited*. 1958. *Brave New World and Brave New World Revisited*. By Huxley. New York: Harper & Row, 1965, [203–299].

Jacobs, Madeleine. "Yesterday's Predictions: The Way the Future Was." *Futurist*, 19 (February, 1985), 42–45.

Jameson, Fredric. "Progress Versus Utopia, or Can We Imagine the Future?" *Science-Fiction Studies*, 9 (July 1982), 147–158.

Johanson, MaryAnn. "The Way the Future Was: Coping with Ecological Disaster in Film." The Internet Review of Science Fiction, April/May, 2006. At http://www.irosf.com/q/zine/article/10274.

Johnson, E. A. "Skiffy as Prophecy: Russia Meets *Star Trek*." *The New York Review of Science Fiction*, No. 127 (March, 1999), 1, 4–6.

Kahn, Herman, and Anthony Weiner. *The Year 2000: A Framework for Speculation on the Next Thirty-Three Years*. New York: Macmillan, 1967.

Kay, Alan C. "Predicting the Future." *Stanford Engineering*, 1 (Autumn, 1989), 1–6. At http://www.ecotopia.com/webpress/futures.htm. Originally presented as an Address before the 20th Annual Meeting of the Stanford Computer Forum.

Kerrod, Robin. *The World of Tomorrow.* New York: Mayflower Books, 1980.

Ladd, Thyril L. "The Day after Tomorrow." *Fantasy Commentator*, 1 (Summer, 1945), 135–139, 159.

Langford, David. "Load of Crystal Balls: Great Failures of Prediction; A. D. 2000–3000." *Lan's Lantern*, 21 (October, 1986), 4–9.

_____. *War in 2080: The Future of Military Technology.* New York: William Morrow and Company, 1979.

Lapham, Lewis. *Waiting for the Barbarians.* London: Verso, 1997.

Le Guin, Ursula K. "Introduction." *The Left Hand of Darkness.* By Le Guin. New York: Ace Books, 1976), [x–xvi].

Lehman-Wilzig, S. N. "Science Fiction as Futurist Prediction: Alternative Visions of Heinlein and Clarke." *Literary Review* (Fairleigh Dickinson University), 20 (Winter, 1977), 133–151.

Leinster, Murray. [Will F. Jenkins, writing as Will F. Jenkins–Murray Leinster] "Applied Science Fiction." *Analog Science Fiction/Science Fact*, 80 (November, 1967), 109–124.

_____. "Guest of Honor Speech." *The Proceedings; DISCON: The 21st World Science Fiction Convention; Washington — 1963 (DISCON, 1963).* Ed. Dick Eney. Washington, D.C.: DISCON, 1963, 71–79. Available at Syracuse University Special Collections, Will F. Jenkins Collection.

_____. "Proposed Talk: Eastern Science Fiction Association, 3/2/47." Syracuse University Special Collections, Will F. Jenkins Collection, Box 7, "Science Fiction Fan Clubs" folder.

Lem, Stanislaw. "Metafuturology." *Science Fiction Studies*, 13 (November, 1986), 261–271.

_____. "On Olaf Stapledon's *Last and First Men.*" *Science-Fiction Studies*, 13 (November, 1986), 272–291.

Levine, David. "How the Future Predicts Science Fiction." The Internet Review of Science Fiction, February, 2010. At http://www.irosf.com/q/zine/article/10631.

Lewis, Bob. "Over-Hype and Sci-Fi Stories Can Save Us From Real Computing Disasters." *Infoworld*, 18 (December 23/30, 1996), 54.

Livingston, Dennis. "Science Fiction and Futurology: Some Observations at a Science Fiction Convention." *The Futurist*, 2 (June, 1968), 47–48.

_____. "Science Fiction as a Source of Forecast Material." *Futures*, 1 (March, 1969), 232–238.

Malone, Robert. *Rocketship: An Incredible Journey through Science Fiction and Science Fact.* New York: Harper & Row, 1977.

McHale, John. "Introduction: Today's Tomorrows." *Tomorrow Today.* Ed. George Zebrowski. Santa Cruz, CA: Unity Press, 1975, 1–4.

McMullen, Sean, and Russell Blackford. "Prophet and Pioneer: The Science Fiction of Norma Hemming." *Fantasy Annual*, No. 2 (Spring, 1998), 65–75.

Miles, Ian. "Stranger Than Fiction: How Important Is Science Fiction for Future Studies?" *Futures*, 25 (April, 1993), 315–321.

_____, and Micheil Schwarz. "Alternative Space Futures: The Next Quarter-Century." *Futures*, 14 (October, 1982), 462–482.

Miller, Ron. "Futures Past: Jules Verne." *Starlog*, 56 (March, 1982), 54–56.

_____. "Prophecies that Failed." *Starlog*, 57 (April, 1982), 28–29.

Milligan, James. "From Prophecy to Prediction, 11: Plans, Policies, and Populations." *Futures*, 8 (April, 1976), 169–174.

Mone, Gregory. "Is Science Fiction About to Go Blind?" *Popular Science*, 265 (August, 2004), 54–61.

Montadon, Mac. *Jetpack Dreams: One Man's Up and Down (But Mostly Down) Search for the Greatest Invention that Never Was.* New York: Da Capo, 2008.

Moore, Patrick. "Fiction to Fact." *The Encyclopedia of Science Fiction.* Ed. Robert Holdstock. London: Octopus Books, 1978, 142–151.

_____. "To Other Worlds." *Listener,* 69 (May 23, 1963), 865–866.

Morgan, Chris. *The Shape of Futures Past: The Story of Prediction.* Exeter, England: Webb & Bower, 1980.

Moskowitz, Sam, and Robert A. Madle. "Did Science Fiction Predict Atomic Energy?" *Science Fiction Quarterly,* 2 (November, 1952), 81–88.

Mulhall, Douglas. "The Short Path from Fiction to Science." *Futurist,* 37 (January/February, 2003), 20–21.

Nelson, Teodor H. *Dream Machines: New Freedoms through Computer Screens— A Minority Report.* Chicago: Nelson, 1974.

Newman, John, and Michael Unsworth. *Future War Novels: An Annotated Bibliography of Works in English Published Since 1946.* Phoenix, AZ: Oryx Press, 1984.

Nicholls, Peter. "Prediction." *The Encyclopedia of Science Fiction.* Ed. John Clute and Nicholls. New York: St. Martin's Press, 1993, 957–958.

_____. *The Science in Science Fiction.* New York: Alfred A. Knopf, 1983.

Olson, R. L. "Science Fiction as Forecasting." *SFWA Bulletin,* 10 (Winter, 1974/1975), 25–26.

O'Neill, Gerard K. *The High Frontier: Human Colonies in Space.* New York: Morrow, 1977.

_____. *2081: A Hopeful View of the Human Future.* New York: Simon and Schuster, 1981.

Orrell, David. *The Future of Everything: The Science of Prediction.* New York: Thunder's Mouth Press, 2007.

Panati, Charles. *Breakthroughs: Astonishing Advances in Your Lifetime in Medicine, Science, and Technology.* 1980. New York: Berkley Books, 1981.

Parfit, Derek. "Personal Identity." *The Philosophical Review,* 80 (1971), 3–27.

Parrinder, Patrick. "From Rome to Richmond: Wells, Universal History, and Prophetic Time." *H. G. Wells's Perennial Time Machine.* Ed. George Slusser, Parrinder, and Danièle Chatelain. Athens: University of Georgia Press, 2001, 110–121.

_____. "Science Fiction: Metaphor, Myth or Prophecy?" *Science Fiction, Critical Frontiers.* Ed. Karen Sayer and John Moore. London: Macmillan, 2000, 23–34.

_____. *Shadow of the Future: H. G. Wells, Science Fiction, and Prophecy.* Syracuse: Syracuse University Press, 1996.

_____. "Wells and the Literature of Prophecy." *The Wellsian,* No. 9 (Summer, 1986), 6–11.

Philmus, Robert M. "Time Machine, or, The Fourth Dimension as Prophecy." *PMLA,* 84 (May, 1969), 530–535.

Pohl, Frederik. "Introduction." *The Ninth Galaxy Reader.* Ed. Pohl. 1965. New York: Pocket Books, 1997, v–viii.

_____. "The Politics of Prophecy." *Extrapolation,* 34 (Fall, 1993), 199–208.

_____. "Thinking About the Future." *The Futurist,* 30 (September/October, 1996), 8–12.

_____. "The Uses of the Future." *The Futurist,* 27 (March/April, 1993), 9–12.

Pool, Bob. "65 Years of Amazing Stories: Early Members of the Science Fantasy Society Take Stock of Their Predictions at the End of the 20th Century." *The Los Angeles Times* (June 3, 1999), B1, B5.

Pratt, Fletcher. "What's the World Coming To? Prophetic Fiction." *Saturday Review of Literature,* 17 (April 2, 1938), 3–4.

Prucher, Jeff, ed. *Brave New Words: The Oxford Dictionary of Science Fiction.* Oxford: Oxford University Press, 2007.

Rayward, W. Boyd. "H. G. Wells's Idea of a World Brain: A Critical Reassessment." *Journal of the American Society for Information Science*, 50 (1999), 557–73.
Reichardt, Jasia. *Robots: Fact, Fiction, and Prediction.* New York: Viking, 1978.
Reiss, Tom. "Imagining the Worst." *The New Yorker*, 81 (November 28, 2005), 106–110.
Rose, Hilary. "Science Fiction's Memory of the Future." *Contested Futures: A Sociology of Prospective Technoscience.* Ed. Nik Brown, Brian Rappert, and Andrew Webster. Aldershot: Ashgate, 2000, 157–172.
Rosenberg, Daniel, and Susan Harding, eds. *Histories of the Future.* Durham, NC: Duke University Press, 2005.
Ross-MacDonald, Malcolm, Michael Hasselland, and Stuart McNeill. *Life in the Future: Prospects for Man and Nature.* Garden City, NY: Doubleday and Company, Inc., 1977.
Sadoul, Jacques. *2000 A.D.: Illustrations from the Golden Age of Science Fiction Pulps.* 1973. Chicago: Henry Regnery Company, 1975.
Sagan, Carl. *Pale Blue Dot: A Vision of the Human Future in Space.* New York: Random House, 1994.
Samuelson, David N., ed. *Science Fiction and Future Studies.* Bryan, TX: SFRA, 1975.
Sandison, Alan, and Robert Dingley, eds. *Histories of the Future: Studies in Fact, Fantasy and Science Fiction.* New York: Palgrave, 2000.
Sawhney, Mohanbir. "History of Telegraph, Telephone Helps Predict Internet's Future." CIO website, posted December 1, 2001. At http://www.cio.com/article/30732/History_of_Telegraph_Telephone_Helps_Predict_Internet_s_Future. Accessed February 23, 2010.
Sawyer, Robert J. "Is Risk Our Business?" *Relativity: Stories and Essays.* By Sawyer. Deerfield, IL: ISFIC Press, 2004, 200–203.
Schmidt, Stanley. *The Coming Convergence: The Surprising Ways Diverse Technologies Interact to Shape Our World and Change the Future.* Amherst, NY: Prometheus Books, 2008.
_____. *Which Way to the Future?: Selected Essays from Analog.* New York: Tor, 2001.
Scholes, Robert, and Eric S. Rabkin. *Science Fiction: History, Science, Vision.* London and New York: Oxford University Press, 1977.
Schwartz, Sheila. "Science Fiction as Prophecy." *Teaching Adolescent Literature: A Humanistic Approach.* By Schwartz. Rochelle Park, NJ: Hayden Book Company, 1979, 181–198.
Schweitzer, Darrell. "Genuinely Prophetic Science Fiction?" *The New York Review of Science Fiction*, No. 92 (April, 1996), 14–15.
Shaviro, Steven. "Prophecies of the Present." *Socialism and Democracy*, 20 (November, 2006), 5–24.
Silverberg, Robert. *Reflections and Refractions: Thoughts on Science Fiction, Science, and Other Matters.* Grass Valley, CA: Underwood Books, 1997.
Sisk, John P. "The Future of Prediction." *Science Fiction: The Future.* Ed. Dick Allen. New York: Harcourt Brace Jovanovich, 1971, 325–333. Originally published in *Commentary* (1970).
Slusser, George. "Dimorphs and Doubles: J. D. Bernal's 'Two Cultures' and the Transhuman Promise." *Science Fiction and the Two Cultures: Essays on Bridging the Gap between the Sciences and the Humanities.* Ed. Gary Westfahl and Slusser. Jefferson, NC: McFarland Publishers, 2009, 96–129.
Slusser, George, Colin Greenland, and Eric S. Rabkin, eds. *Storm Warnings: Science Fiction Confronts the Future.* Carbondale: Southern Illinois University Press, 1987.
Stableford, Brian. "Far Futures." *Earth Is but a Star: Excursions Through Science Fiction to the Far Future.* Ed. Damien Broderick. Crawley, Western Australia: University of Western Australia Press, 2001, 47–76.

_____. "Marxism, Science Fiction and the Poverty of Prophecy: Some Comparisons and Contrasts." *Foundation: The Review of Science Fiction*, No. 32 (November, 1984), 5–14.

_____. "Science Fiction and the Image of the Future." *Foundation: The Review of Science Fiction*, No. 14 (September, 1978), 26–34.

_____. "Social Design in Science Fiction." *Amazing Stories*, 52 (February, 1979), 119–124.

Stine, G. Harry. "Science Fiction Is Too Conservative." *Analog Science Fact/Science Fiction*, 67 (May, 1961), 83–99.

_____. *The Space Enterprise*. New York: Ace Books, 1980.

_____. *The Third Industrial Revolution*. 1975. New York: Ace Books, 1979.

Strathern, Oona. *A Brief History of the Future: How Visionary Thinkers Changed the World and Tomorrow's Trends Are "Made" and Marketed*. New York: Carroll & Graf, 2007.

Sturken, Martia, Douglas Thomas, and Sandra Ball-Rokeach. *Technological Visions: The Hopes and Fears That Shape New Technologies*. Philadelphia: Temple University Press, 2004.

Sulski, Jim. "False Futures." *Chicago Tribune* (January 7, 1993), Sec. 5, 6.

Swanwick, Michael. "The View from the Top of the Mountain." *The New York Review of Science Fiction*, No. 184 (December, 2003), 1, 6–9.

Taylor, Keith. "From Prophecy to Prediction: Saint-Simon and the Conquest of the Future." *Futures*, 9 (February, 1971), 58–64.

Toffler, Alvin, *Future Shock*. New York: Bantam Books, 1971.

_____, ed. *The Futurists*. New York: Random House, 1972

_____. *Powershift: Knowledge, Wealth, and Violence at the Edge of the 21st Century*. New York: Bantam Books, 1990.

_____. *The Third Wave*. New York: Morrow, 1980.

Ubois, Jeff. "Sci-Fi Author Vernor Vinge Discusses the Relation of Science Fiction to Future Prediction." *Internet World*, 7 (1996), 82.

Vernier, J. P. "H. G. Wells, Writer or Thinker? From Science Fiction to Social Prophecy." *The Wellsian*, No. 3 (Spring, 1980), 24–35.

Verschuur, Gerrit L. *Cosmic Catastrophes*. Reading, MA: Addison-Wesley Publishing Company, 1978.

Wagar, W. Warren. *The Next Three Futures: Paradigms of Things to Come*. Westport, CT: Greenwood, 1991.

_____. *A Short History of the Future*. 1989. Second Edition. Chicago: University of Chicago Press, 1992.

_____. "Tomorrow and Tomorrow and Tomorrow." *Technology Review*, 96 (April, 1993), 50–59.

_____. "Toward a World Set Free: The Vision of H. G. Wells." *The Futurist*, 17 (August, 1983), 24–31.

Wagner, Mitch. "The Potential of E-Books," *SFWA Bulletin*, No. 162 (Summer, 2004), 5–7. At http://www.sfwa.org/bulletin/articles/wagner_summer_2004.pdf.

Webb, H. A. "Science Fiction Writers: Prophets of the Future." *Library Journal*, 80 (December 15, 1955), 2884–2885.

Weiner, Steve. "Sci-Fi World Is Helpful to Big Business." *New Orleans Times-Picayune*, July 3, 1978, Sec. 1, 4.

Wells, H. G. *Anticipations of the Reaction of Mechanical and Scientific Progress upon Human Life and Thought*. 1901. London: Chapman & Hall, 1904.

_____. *The Way the World Is Going, Guesses and Forecasts of the Year-Ahead*. Garden City, NY: Doubleday, Doran, and Co., 1929.

_____. *World Brain*. 1938. Freeport, New York: Books for Libraries Press, 1971.

Westfahl, Gary. "All Work and No Play: What Science Fiction Leaves Out of the Future, #3." The Internet Review of Science Fiction, October, 2009. At http://www.irosf.com/q/zine/article/10592#.

_____. "The History of Heinlein's Future." *Interzone,* No. 182 (September 2002), 53–55.
_____. "Inspired by Science Fiction." NOVA Online website, posted on April 21, 2000. At http://www.pbs.org/wgbh/nova/station/inspired.html.
_____. "Journey to the Future: Hong Kong 2003." Locus Online website, posted April 10, 2003. At http://locusmag.com/2003/Commentary/ Westfahl04_HongKong.html.
_____. *The Mechanics of Wonder: The Creation of the Idea of Science Fiction.* Liverpool: Liverpool University Press, 1998.
_____. "Near Future." *The Greenwood Encyclopedia of Science Fiction and Fantasy,* Volume 2, 558–560.
_____. "No Bark and No Bite: What Science Fiction Leaves Out of the Future #4." The Internet Review of Science Fiction, February, 2010. At http://www.irosf.com/q/zine/article/10639.
_____. "The Odyssey Continues: Relevance of '2001' Resounds in 2001." *Florida Today* (February 11, 2001), 15A.
_____. "Pitfalls of Prophecy: Why Science Fiction So Often Fails to Predict the Future." Locus Online website, posted February 23, 2009. At http://locusmag.com/2009/Westfahl_Predictions.html
_____. "What Science Fiction Leaves Out of the Future, #1: No News Is Good News?" The Internet Review of Science Fiction, December, 2008. At http://www.irosf.com/q/zine/article/10492.
_____. "What Science Fiction Leaves Out of the Future, #2: The Day After Tomorrow." The Internet Review of Science Fiction, March, 2009. At http://www.irosf.com/q/zine/article/10528.
Wilkeson, Marjorie J. "The Next Hundred Years: An Interview with Dr. Eric Temple Bell, Mathematician, California School of Technology." *Los Angeles Times* (November 22, 1931), K5, K16.
Willems, Philippe. "A Stereoscopic Vision of the Future: Albert Robida's Twentieth Century." *Science Fiction Studies,* 26 (November, 1999), 354–378.
Williamson, Jack. "Scientifiction, Searchlight of Science." *Amazing Stories Quarterly,* 1 (Fall, 1928), 435.
_____. "Unpredictable." *Astounding Science-Fiction,* 37 (March, 1946), 99–118.
Wilson, Daniel H., and Richard Horne. *Where's My Jetpack? A Guide to the Amazing Science Fiction Future that Never Arrived.* New York: Bloomsbury, 2007.
Wise, George. "The Accuracy of Technological Forecasts, 1890–1940." *Futures,* 8 (October, 1976), 411–419.
Wolf, Milton T. "Science Fiction: Better than Delphi Studies." *EDUCOM Review,* 29 (January/February, 1994), 28–34.
Wolff, Heinz. "The Future is Further Off Than You Think." *Future Imperfect.* Ed. Rex Malik. London: Pinter, 1980, 55–67.
Wollheim, Donald A. "Guest of Honor Speech, Nolacon 2, 1988." *Locus,* 21 (November, 1988), 30, 32.
_____. *The Universe Makers: Science Fiction Today.* New York: Harper, 1971.
Wong Kin Yuen, Gary Westfahl, and Amy Kit-sze Chan, eds. *World Weavers: Globalization, Science Fiction, and the Cybernetic Revolution.* Hong Kong: Hong Kong University Press, 2005.
Woodcock, John. "Science Fiction and the Real Future." *Alternative Futures,* 2 (Spring, 1979), 25–37.
Yeung, Miranda. "Peeping Through the Veils of Possibility: Some Amazing Inventions Have Their Roots in Science Fiction." *South China Morning Post* (April 7, 2008), 6.
Zebrowski, George. "The Importance of Being Cosmic." *Earth Is But a Star,* 130–137.

Bibliography of Other Works Cited in the Text

Aldiss, Brian W. *Barefoot in the Head*. New York: Ace, 1969.

_____, and David Wingrove. *Trillion Year Spree: The History of Science Fiction*. London: Victor Gollancz, 1986.

Apollonio, Umbro, ed. *Futurist Manifestos*. London: Tate Publishing, 1970.

Appadurai, Arjun. "Disjuncture and Difference in the Global Cultural Economy." *Public Culture*, 2:2 (1990), 1–24.

Asimov, Isaac. *The Caves of Steel*. 1954. New York: Signet Books, 1955.

_____. *I, Robot*. New York: Gnome Press, 1950.

_____. *Prelude to Foundation*. New York: Doubleday, 1988.

_____. "Social Science Fiction." *Modern Science Fiction: Its Meaning and Its Future*. Ed. Reginald Bretnor. 1953. Second Edition. Chicago: Advent Publishers, 1979, 157–196.

_____, Patricia S. Warrick and Martin H. Greenberg, eds. *Machines That Think: The Best Science Fiction Stories About Robots and Computers*. New York: Holt, Rinehart and Winston, 1983.

Austin, J. L. *How to Do Things with Words*. Second Edition. Ed. J. O. Urmson and Marina Sbisà. Cambridge: Harvard University Press, 1975.

Bainbridge, William Sims. "The Analytical Laboratory, 1938–1976." *Analog Science Fiction/Science Fact*, 50 (January, 1980), 121–134.

Ballard, J. G. "Which Way to Inner Space?" *New Worlds*, 118 (May, 1962) 2–3, 116–18.

Bardini, Thierry. *Bootstrapping: Douglas Engelbart, Coevolution, and the Origins of Personal Computing*. Stanford: Stanford University Press, 2000.

Barrow, John D. *The Artful Universe*. Oxford: Clarendon Press, 1995.

Beckett, Chris. "The Marriage of Sky and Sea." *Interzone*, No. 153 (March, 2000), 17–23.

Bemasconi, Robert. "'Stuck Inside of Mobile with the Memphis Blues Again': Interculturalism and the Conversations of Races." *Theorizing Multiculturalism: A Guide to the Current Debate*. Ed. Cynthia Willett. Oxford: Blackwell, 1998, 276–298.

Bester, Alfred. *The Stars My Destination*. New York: New American Library, 1956.

Blish, James. "Beep." *Galactic Cluster*. By Blish. London: Faber & Faber, 1940, 103–143. Originally published in *Galaxy* (February, 1954).

Bird, Lawrence. "States of Emergency: Urban Space and the Robotic Body in the *Metropolis* Tales." *Mechademia 3: Limits of the Human*. Frenchy Lunning, ed. in chief. Minneapolis: University of Minnesota Press, 2008, 127–148.

Boersma, Mark. Letter. "Monolith Mail." *2001: A Space Odyssey*, No. 6 (May, 1977), 19.

Bogue, Ronald. "Art and Territory." *A Deleuzian Century?* Ed. Ian Buchanan. Durham and London: Duke University Press, 1999, 85–102.

Booker, M. Keith, and Anne-Marie Thomas. *The Science Fiction Handbook*. Chichester, West Sussex: Wiley-Blackwell, 2009.

Bordwell, David. *Planet Hong Kong: Popular Cinema and the Art of Entertainment*. Cambridge: Harvard University Press, 2000.

Breen, Walter. "The Blown Mind on Film." *Warhoon*, 24 (August, 1968), 16–24, 62.

Brendler, Ralph. "Letter from Mr. Brendler to Jenkins, January 21, 1958." Syracuse University Special Collections, Will F. Jenkins Collection, Box 1, "Bartholomew House 1957–1958" folder.

Brosnan, John. *Future Tense: The Cinema of Science Fiction*. New York: St. Martin's, 1978.

Brown, Fredric. "Etaoin Shrdlu." *Angels and Spaceships*. By Brown. New York: E. P. Dutton & Company, 1954, 25–50. Originally published in *Unknown* (February, 1942).

Brown, Richard Harvey. "Rhetoric, Textuality, and the Postmodern Turn in Sociological Theory." *The Postmodern Turn: New Perspectives on Social Theory*. Ed. Steven Seidman. Cambridge: Cambridge University Press, 1994, 229–241.

Brunner, John. *The Shockwave Rider*. New York: Harper & Row, 1975.

Buchanan, Ian. "Deleuze and Cultural Studies." *A Deleuzian Century?*, 103–118.

_____, ed. *A Deleuzian Century?* Durham and London: Duke University Press, 1999.

Budrys, Algis. *Michaelmas*. New York: Berkley Books, 1977.

Bukatman, Scott. *Blade Runner*. London: British Film Institute, 1997.

Butler, Andrew M. "Metropolis (1926)." *The Greenwood Encyclopedia of Science Fiction and Fantasy: Themes, Works, and Wonders*, Volume 3. Ed. Gary Westfahl. Westport, CT: Greenwood Press, 2005, 1172–1174.

Butler, Judith. *Bodies that Matter: On the Discursive Limits of "Sex."* New York: Routledge, 1993.

Campbell, John W., Jr. "The Analytical Laboratory." *Astounding Science-Fiction*, 37 (June, 1946), 45.

_____. "Concerning the Atomic War." *Astounding Science-Fiction*, 37 (March, 1946), 5, 178.

Caputo, John. D. *More Radical Hermeneutics: On Not Knowing Who We Are*. Bloomington and Indianapolis: Indiana University Press, 2000.

Carlson, Marvin. *Performance: A Critical Introduction*. New York: Routledge, 1996.

Cavallaro, Dani. *The Cinema of Oshii Mamoru: Fantasy, Technology and Politics*. Jefferson, NC: McFarland, 2006.

Chan, Amy Kit-sze. "When Cyberfeminism Meets Chinese Philosophy: Computer, Weaving and Women." *World Weavers: Globalization, Science Fiction, and the Cybernetic Revolution*. Ed. Wong Kin Yuen, Gary Westfahl, and Chan. Hong Kong: Hong Kong University Press, 2005, 215–232.

Chuang Tzu. "Mastering Life." [Chapter Nineteen] *The Complete Works of Chuang Tzu*. Trans. Burton Watson. New York: Columbia University Press, 1968, 198–200.

"*Chungking Express*." HKCinematic website. At http://hkcinemagic.ifrance.com/site/framemenu.htm. Accessed February 21, 2010.

Cixous, Hélène, and Catherine Clément. *The Newly Born Woman: Hélène Cixous and Catherine Clément*. Trans. Betsy Wing. London: I.B. Tauris Publishers, 1996.

Clarens, Carlos. *An Illustrated History of Horror and Science Fiction Films: The Classic Era, 1895–1967*. 1967. New Edition. New York: Da Capo Press, 1997.

Clarke, Arthur C. *Childhood's End*. 1953. New York: Ballantine Books, 1967.

_____. *The City and the Stars*. 1956. New York: Signet Books, 1957.

_____. *The Lost Worlds of 2001*. New York: Signet Books, 1972.

_____. *3001: The Final Odyssey*. 1997. New York: Del Rey/Ballantine Books, 1999.

_____. *2001: A Space Odyssey*. Based on a screenplay by Stanley Kubrick and Clarke. New York: Signet Books, 1968.

_____. *2010: Odyssey Two.* New York: Del Rey/Ballantine Books, 1982.

_____. *2061: Odyssey Three.* New York: Del Rey/Ballantine Books, 1982.

_____, and Stephen Baxter. *Firstborn: A Time Odyssey: 3.* New York: Del Rey/Ballantine Books, 2008.

_____. *Sunstorm: A Time Odyssey: 2.* New York: Del Rey/Ballantine Books, 2007.

_____. *Time's Eye: Book One of A Time Odyssey.* 2004. New York: Del Rey/Ballantine Books, 2005.

Clement, Hal. [Harry Clement Stubbs] "Whirligig World." *Astounding Science Fiction,* 51 (June, 1953), 102–114.

Clute, John. "Arthur C. Clarke's Clone." *New Worlds Ten.* Ed. Hilary Bailey. London: Corgi, 1976, 232–235.

Coaldrake, William H. *Architecture and Authority in Japan.* London: Routledge, 1996.

Corradini, Bruno, and Emilio Settimelli. "Weights, Measures and Prices of Artistic Genius—Futurist Manifesto, 1914." *Futurist Manifestos,* 135–150.

Csicsery-Ronay, Jr., Istvan. "On the Grotesque in Science Fiction." *Science Fiction Studies,* 29 (March, 2002), 71–99.

Dadlez, Eva M. *What's Hecuba to Him? Fictional Events and Actual Emotions.* University Park: Pennsylvania State University Press, 1997.

Damásio, António R. *Descartes' Error: Emotion, Reason, and the Human Brain.* 1994. New York: Quill, 2000.

_____. *The Feeling of What Happens: Body, Emotion and the Making of Consciousness.* 1999. London: Vintage, 2000.

Davies, Oliver. "Thinking Difference: A Comparative Study of Gilles Deleuze, Plotinus and Meister Eckhard." *Deleuze and Religion.* Ed. Mary Bryden. London: Routledge, 2001, 76–86.

Davies, Tony. *Humanism.* London: Routledge, 1997.

De Certeau, Michel. "Walking in the City." *The Cultural Studies Reader.* Ed. Simon During. London: Routledge, 1993, 151–160.

De Landa, Manuel. "Deleuze, Diagrams, and the Open-Ended Becoming of the World." *Becomings: Explorations in Time, Memory, and Future.* Ed. Elizabeth Grosz. Ithaca, NY: Cornell University Press, 1999, 29–41.

_____. "Immanence and Transcendence in the Genesis of Form." *A Deleuzian Century?,* 119–134.

_____. *Intensive Science and Virtual Philosophy.* London: Continuum, 2000.

Deleuze, Gilles. *Cinema 1: The Movement-Image.* Trans. Hugh Tomlinson and Barbara Habberjam. Minneapolis: University of Minnesota Press, 1986.

_____. *Difference and Repetition.* Trans. Paul Patton. London: Athlone, 1994.

_____. *Empiricism and Subjectivity: An Essay on Hume's Theory of Human Nature.* Trans. Constantin V. Boundas. New York: Columbia University Press, 1991.

_____. "He Stuttered." *Gilles Deleuze and the Theater of Philosophy.* Ed. Constantin V. Boundas and Dorothea Olkowski. London and New York: Routledge, 1994, 23–29.

_____. *Negotiations 1972–1990.* Trans. Martin Joughin. New York: Columbia University Press, 1995.

_____. *What Is Philosophy?* Trans. Graham Burchell and Hugh Tomlinson. London and New York: Verso. 1994.

_____, and Felix Guattari. *A Thousand Plateaus: Capitalism and Schizophrenia.* Trans. Brian Massumi. Minneapolis and London: University of Minnesota Press, 1987.

del Rey, Lester. "Other Times, Other Values." *Renaissance: A Semi-Official Organ of the Second Foundation,* 1 (Winter, 1969), 2–4.

_____. Review of *2001: A Space Odyssey. Galaxy,* 26 (July, 1968), 193–194.

Derleth, August. "Letter from August Derleth, Arkham House Publishers, to Jenkins, dated November 3, 1951." Syracuse University Special Collections, Will F. Jenkins Collection, Box 1, "Arkham 48–66" folder.

Derrida, Jacques. "Signature, Event, Context." *Glyph*, 1 (1977), 172–197.

Desk Set. Twentieth-Century-Fox, 1957.

Devereaux, Mary. "Beauty and Evil: The Case of Leni Riefenstahl's *Triumph of the Will.*" *Aesthetics and Ethics: Essays at the Intersection.* Ed. Jerrold Levinson. Cambridge: Cambridge University Press, 1998, 227–256.

Dick, Philip K. *Do Androids Dream of Electric Sheep?* Garden City, NY: Doubleday, 1968.

Disch, Thomas M. *The Dreams Our Stuff is Made Of: How Science Fiction Conquered the World.* New York: Free Press, 1998.

_____. "Introduction: On Saving the World." *The Ruins of Earth: An Anthology of Stories of the Immediate Future.* Ed. Disch. New York: Putnam, 1971, 1–7.

Dolezel, Lubomir. *Heterocosmica*. Baltimore and London: Johns Hopkins University Press, 1998.

Dower, John. *Embracing Defeat: Japan in the Aftermath of World War II.* London: Penguin Books, 1999.

Dozois, Gardner. "Introduction." *The Year's Best Science Fiction: Twentieth Annual Edition.* Ed. Dozois. New York: St. Martin's Griffin, 2003, xi–xxxix.

_____. "Summation." *The Year's Best Science Fiction: Twenty-First Annual Edition.* Ed. Dozois. New York: St. Martin's Griffin, 2004, xiii–xxxviii.

Duncan, Andy. "It's All SF: Science Fiction, Southern Fiction, and the Case of Murray Leinster." *Foundation: The International Review of Science Fiction*, No. 79 (Summer, 2000), 59–69.

Ebert, Roger. "*Chungking Express*" (March 15, 1996), Movie Reviews. At http://rogerebert. suntimes.com/apps/pbcs.dll/article?AID=%2F19960315%2FREVIEWS%2F603150301 %2F1023&AID1=%2F19960315%2FREVIEWS%2F603150301%2F1023&AID2. Accessed February 23, 2010.

Egan, Greg. *Diaspora*. London: Millennium, 1997.

Ellison, Harlan. "'Repent, Harlequin!' Said the Ticktockman." *Alone Against Tomorrow: Stories of Alienation in Speculative Fiction.* By Ellison. 1971. New York: Collier Books, 1972), 130–144. Originally published in *Galaxy* (December, 1965).

Eney, Dick, ed. *The Proceedings; DISCON: The 21st World Science Fiction Convention; Washington — 1963 (DISCON, 1963).* Washington, D.C.: DISCON, 1963. Available at Syracuse University Special Collections, Will F. Jenkins Collection.

Evers, Earl. "2001 Light Years from Home." *Shangri L'Affaires*, 74 (September 1, 1968), 43–45.

Farnell, Ross. "Attempting Immortality: AI, A-Life, and the Posthuman in Greg Egan's *Permutation City.*" *Science Fiction Studies*, 27 (March, 2000), 69–91.

Feenberg, Andrew. *Questioning Technology*. London: Routledge, 1999.

Foucault, Michel. "Of Other Spaces." *Diacritics* 16:1 (1986), 22–27.

_____. "The Subject and Power." *Michel Foucault: Beyond Structuralism and Hermeneutics.* Ed. Hubert Dryfus and Paul Rabinow. Second Edition. Chicago: University of Chicago Press, 1983, 208–228.

_____. "What is Enlightenment?" *The Foucault Reader*. By Foucault. Ed. Rabinow. New York: Pantheon Books, 1984, 32–50.

Gadamer, Han-Georg. *The Relevance of the Beautiful and Other Essays*. Ed. Robert Bemasconi. New York and London: Cambridge University Press, 1986.

Genette, Gérard. *Palimpsestes: La Littérature au Second Degré.* New York: French & European Publications, Incorporated, 1992.

Gernsback, Hugo. *Ralph 124C 41+: A Romance of the Year 2660.* New York: The Stratford Company, 1925.

Gibson, William. *All Tomorrow's Parties*. New York: Putnam, 1999.

_____. *Idoru.* New York: Putnam, 1996.
_____. "Johnny Mnemonic." *Burning Chrome.* By Gibson. 1986. New York: Ace Books, 1987, 168–191. Originally published in *Omni* (July, 1982).
_____. *Neuromancer.* New York: Ace Books, 1984.
Gong Zhebing and Zhao Liming. *Nu Shu: Shijie Wei Yi de Nuxing Wenji.* [*Women's Writing: The World's Only Female Writing*] Taipei, Taiwan: Fu Nu Xin Zhi Ji Jin Hui, 1992.
Goodchild, Philip. *Deleuze and Guattari: An Introduction to the Politics of Desire.* London: Sage, 1996.
Gordon, Richard. "Brit American (Ob)Scene and Observed." *Odd,* 18 (Spring, 1968), 88–89.
Graham, Elaine L. *Representations of the Post/Human: Monsters, Aliens and Others in Popular Culture.* New Brunswick, NJ: Rutgers University Press, 2002.
Gross, Edward. *The Fab Films of the Beatles.* Las Vegas, NV: Pioneer Books, 1990.
Grosz, Elizabeth. "Deleuze's Bergson: Duration, the Virtual and a Politics of the Future." *Deleuze and Feminist Theory.* Ed. Ian Buchanan and Claire Colebrook. Edinburgh: Edinburgh University Press, 2000, 214–234.
Habermas, Jürgen. "A Review of Gadamer's *Truth and Method.*" Trans. Fred Dallmayr and Thomas McCarthy. *Hermeneutics and Modern Philosophy.* Ed. Brice R. Wachtehauser. Albany: New York State University Press, 1986, 243–276.
Hansen, Mark. *Embodying Technesis: Technology Beyond Writing.* Ann Arbor: University of Michigan Press, 2000.
Hartwell, David G. "Introduction." *Year's Best SF 9.* Ed. Hartwell and Kathryn Cramer. New York: HarperCollins/Eos, 2004, ix–xii.
Havens, Thomas. *Valley of Darkness: The Japanese People and World War Two.* Lanham, MD: University Press of America, 1986.
Hayles, N. Katherine. *How We Became Posthuman: Virtual Bodies in Cybernetics, Literature, and Informatics.* Chicago: University of Chicago Press, 1999.
_____. "The Life Cycle of Cyborgs: Writing the Posthuman." *A Question of Identity: Women, Science, and Literature.* Ed. Marina Benjamin. New Brunswick, NJ: Rutgers University Press, 1993, 152–170.
_____. *Writing Machines.* Cambridge: M.I.T. Press, 2002.
Hays, Sam. Letter. "Monolith Mail." *2001: A Space Odyssey,* No. 6 (May, 1977), 19.
Heaven Sword and Dragon Saber. [*Yi Tian Tu Long Ji*] Shaw Brothers, 1978.
Heinlein, Robert A. *Between Planets.* New York: Scribners, 1951.
Helm, Bennett. W. *Emotional Reason: Deliberation, Motivation, and the Nature of Value.* Cambridge: Cambridge University Press, 2001.
Help! United Artists, 1965.
Herbert, Frank. *Dune.* Philadelphia: Chilton Book Company, 1965.
Hero. [*Ying Xiong*] Beijing New Picture Film Co., 2002.
Hesse, Herman. *The Glass Bead Game.* [*Magister Ludi*] 1943. Trans. Richard and Clara Winston. New York: Holt, Rinehart & Winston, 1969.
Hillier, Jim, ed. *Cahiers du Cinéma: The 1950s: Neo-Realism, Hollywood, New Wave.* Cambridge: Harvard University Press, 1985.
Hollinger, Veronica. "(Re)reading Queerly: Science Fiction, Feminism, and the Defamiliarization of Gender." *Science Fiction Studies,* 26 (March, 1999), 23–40.
Horton, Rich. "The Year in Fantasy and Science Fiction, 2008." *The Year's Best Science Fiction and Fantasy, 2009 Edition.* Ed. Horton. [New York]: Prime Books, 2009, 9–13.
Hosokawa Shûhei, ed. "Miraiha Nenpyô." [Timeline of Futurism] *Eureka,* 17 [special edition on Futurism] (December, 1985), 247–261.
Hughson, Roy V. Letter. "Brass Tacks." *Astounding Science-Fiction,* 37 (March, 1946), 176–177.

Humphreys, Richard. "Afterword: Futurism: May the Force Be with You." *Futurist Manifestos*, 221–227.
_____, ed. *Futurism*. London: Tate Publishing, 1999. Reprinted 2006.
Huxley, Aldous. *Brave New World*. London: Chatto & Windus, 1932.
"International Film." No author given. Art & Culture Network. At http://www.artand-culture.com/categories/210-international-film. Accessed February 21, 2010.
Irigaray, Luce. *Je, Tu, Nous: Towards a Culture of Difference*. Trans. Alison Martin. London and New York: Publisher, 1993.
_____. *Speculum of the Other Woman*. Trans. Gillian C. Gill. Ithaca and New York: Cornell University Press, 1974, 191–202.
_____. "Questions." *This Sex Which Is Not One*. Trans. Catherine Porter. Ithaca and New York: Cornell University Press, 1977, 119–169.
_____. "When Our Lips Speak Together." *This Sex Which Is Not One*, 205–218.
Jervis, John. *Transgressing the Modern: Explorations in the Western Experience of Otherness*. Oxford: Blackwell, 1999.
Jones, Gwyneth. "Riddles in the Dark." *The Profession of Science Fiction: Writers on their Craft and Ideas*. Ed. Maxim Jakubowski and Edward James. Houndmills, Basingstoke and London: Macmillan, 1992, 169–181.
Kaufman-Osborn, Timothy V. *Creatures of Prometheus: Gender and the Politics of Technology*. Lanhan and Boulder: Rowman and Littlefield Publishers, 1997.
Keller, David H. "The Revolt of the Pedestrians." *Amazing Stories: 60 Years of the Best Science Fiction*. Ed. Isaac Asimov and Martin H. Greenberg. New York: TSR, 1985, 9–28. Originally published in *Amazing Stories* (February, 1928).
Kelly, James Patrick. "Think Like a Dinosaur." *Year's Best SF*. Ed. David G. Hartwell. New York: HarperPrism, 1996, 1–27. Originally published in *Asimov's Science Fiction* (June, 1995.)
Kennedy, Barbara M. *Deleuze and Cinema: The Aesthetics of Sensation*. Edinburgh: Edinburgh University Press, 2000.
Kenyon, Kay. "The Universe Extras." Kay Kenyon: The Entire and the Rose Quintet. At http://www.kaykenyon.com/the-entire-and-the-rose.html. Accessed February 10, 2010.
Keyes, Daniel. *Algernon, Charlie and I: A Writer's Journey*. Boca Raton, FL: Challcrest Press, 1999.
_____. "Flowers for Algernon." *Algernon, Charlie and I: A Writer's Journey*, 189–223. Originally published in *The Magazine of Fantasy and Science Fiction* (April, 1959).
_____. *Flowers for Algernon*. New York: Harcourt Brace and World, 1966.
King, Anthony. *Global Cities*. London: Routledge, 1990.
Kirby, Jack, writer and artist. "Beast-Killer." *2001: A Space Odyssey*, No. 1 (December, 1976), 1–3, 6–7, 10–11, 14–17, 22–23, 26–27, 30–31.
_____. "The Capture of X-51." *2001: A Space Odyssey*, No. 8 (July, 1977), 1–3, 6–7, 10–11, 14–17, 22–23, 26–27, 30–31.
_____. "Hotline to Hades." *2001: A Space Odyssey*, No. 10 (September, 1977), 1–3, 6–7, 10–11, 14–17, 22–23, 26–27, 30–31.
_____. "Inter-Galactica: The Ultimate Trip." *2001: A Space Odyssey*, No. 6 (May, 1977), 1–3, 6–7, 10–11, 14–17, 22–23, 26–27, 30–31.
_____. "Marak!" *2001: A Space Odyssey*, No. 3 (February, 1977), 1–3, 6–7, 10–11, 14–17, 22–23, 26–27, 30–31.
_____. "Mister Machine." *2001: A Space Odyssey*, No. 9 (August, 1977), 1–3, 6–7, 10–11, 14–17, 22–23, 26–27, 30–31.
_____. "Monolith Mail." *2001: A Space Odyssey*, No. 1 (December, 1976), 19.
_____. "The New Seed." *2001: A Space Odyssey*, No. 7 (June, 1977), 1–3, 6–7, 10–11, 14–17, 22–23, 26–27, 30–31.

_____. "Norton of New York 2040 A.D." *2001: A Space Odyssey*, No. 5 (April, 1977), 1–3, 6–7, 10–11, 14–17, 22–23, 26–27, 30–31.

_____. *2001: A Space Odyssey*. Marvel Treasury Special. New York: Marvel Comics Group, 1976.

_____. "Vira the She-Demon." *2001: A Space Odyssey*, No. 2 (January, 1977), 1–3, 6–7, 10–11, 14–17, 22–23, 26–27, 30–31.

_____. "Wheels of Death." *2001: A Space Odyssey*, No. 4 (March, 1977), 1–3, 6–7, 10–11, 14–17, 22–23, 26–27, 30–31.

Kress, Nancy. *Beggars and Choosers*. 1994; New York: Tor, 1996.

_____. *Beggars in Spain*. 1993; New York: AvoNova, 1994.

_____. *Beggars Ride*. 1996; New York: Tor, 1997.

_____. "Sleeping Dogs." *Far Horizons*. Ed. Robert Silverberg. London: Orbit, 1999, 263–293.

Kurzweil, Ray. *The Age of Spiritual Machines: When Computers Exceed Human Intelligence*. New York: Viking, 1999.

Lake, Jay. *Mainspring*. New York: Tor, 2007.

Lamarre, Thomas. "Diagram, Inscription, Sensation." *A Shock to Thought: Expression after Deleuze and Guattari*. Ed. Brian Massumi. London and New York: Routledge, 2002, 149–170.

Lambert, Gregg. *The Non-Philosophy of Gilles Deleuze*. New York: Continuum, 2002.

Langford, David. "Space Opera." *The Greenwood Encyclopedia of Science Fiction and Fantasy*, Volume 2, 738–740.

Lao Tzu. *The Way of Lao Tzu (Tao-te Ching)*. Trans. Chan Wing-Tsit. New Jersey: Prentice Hall, 1963.

Latour, Bruno. *We Have Never Been Modern*. 1991. Trans. Catherine Porter. Cambridge: Harvard University Press, 1993.

_____. *Politics of Nature: How to Bring the Sciences into Democracy*. Cambridge: Harvard University Press, 2004.

Leinster, Murray. [Will F. Jenkins] "Book Idea." Syracuse University Special Collections, Will F. Jenkins Collection, Box 69.

_____. "Dear Deene." Syracuse University Special Collections, Will F. Jenkins Collection, Box 1, "Cole, Alonzo Deen 50–52" folder.

_____. "Letter from Jenkins Dated July 19, 1950." Syracuse University Special Collections, Will F. Jenkins Collection, Box 1.

_____. "Letter from Jenkins to Mr. Brendler, September 19, 1957." Syracuse University Special Collections, Will F. Jenkins Collection, Box 1, "Bartholomew House 1957–1958" folder.

_____. "Letter from Jenkins to Mr. Margulies, April 22, 1946." Syracuse University Special Collections, Will F. Jenkins Collection, Box 1, "Crown" folder.

_____. [writing as Will F. Jenkins] "A Logic Named Joe." *Astounding Science-Fiction*, 37 (March, 1946), 139–154.

_____. "The Monster Proposal." Syracuse University Special Collections, Will F. Jenkins Collection, Box 1, "Cole, Alonzo Deen 50–52" folder.

_____. "To Build a Robot Brain." *Astounding Science Fiction*, 53 (April, 1954), 102–111.

_____. "Vignette Ideas." Syracuse University Special Collections, Will F. Jenkins Collection, Box 1, "Cole, Alonso" folder.

Lem, Stanislaw. *Solaris*. 1961. Trans. Joanna Kilmartin and Steve Cox. New York: Walker, 1970.

L'Engle, Madeleine. *A Wrinkle in Time*. New York: Farrar, Straus & Cudahy, 1962.

Levy, Pierre. *Becoming Virtual: Reality in the Digital Age*. Trans. Robert Bononno. New York: Plenum Trade, 1998.

Lewisohn, Mark. *The Complete Beatles Chronicle*. 1992. London: Hamlyn, 2003.

The Living Machine. National Film Board of Canada, 1962.

"A Logic Named Joe." *Dimension X* (New York: NBC Radio, July 1, 1950). Murray Leinster Wikipedia entry. At http://en.wikipedia.org/wiki/A_Logic_Named_Joe. Accessed February 15, 2010.

"A Logic Named Joe." *X Minus X* (New York: NBC Radio, December 28, 1955). Radio Plays Radio. At http://davidszondy.com/Radio.htm. Accessed June 3, 2008.

Lorraine, Tasmin. *Irigaray and Deleuze: Experiments in Visceral Philosophy.* Ithaca and London: Cornell University Press, 1999.

Malmgren, Carl D. *Worlds Apart: Narratology of Science Fiction.* Bloomington: Indiana University Press, 1991.

Malpas, J. E. *Place and Experience: A Philosophical Topography.* Cambridge: Cambridge University Press, 1999.

Manovich, Lev. *The Language of New Media.* Cambridge: M.I.T. Press, 2001.

Marks, John. *Gilles Deleuze: Vitalism and Multiplicity.* London: Pluto, 1998.

Massumi, Brian. *Parables for the Virtual: Movement, Affect, Sensation.* Durham and London: Duke University Press, 2002.

The Matrix. Warner Brothers, 1999.

McGuirk, Carol. "The Rediscovery of Cordwainer Smith." *Science Fiction Studies,* 28 (July, 2001), 161–200.

Metcalfe, Bob. "Do Computation Fabrics Hold the Key to the Future of the Internet's Web?" *Info World,* 22 (July 24, 2000), 88.

Milton, John. *Paradise Lost. Milton: Poetical Works.* Ed. Douglas Bush. London and Oxford: Oxford University Press, 1969, 218–459.

Moorcock, Michael. "A New Literature for the Space Age." *New Worlds,* 142 (May/June, 1964), 2–3.

_____. "Symbols for the Sixties." *New Worlds,* 148 (March, 1965), 2–3, 25.

Moore, C. L. "No Woman Born." *The Best of C. L. Moore.* By Moore. Ed. Lester del Rey. New York: Ballantine, 1975, 236–288. Originally published in *Astounding Science-Fiction* (December, 1944).

Moskowitz, Sam. "Murray Leinster." *Seekers of Tomorrow: Masters of Modern Science Fiction.* By Moskowitz. Cleveland: World Publishing Company, 1966, 47–65.

Moulthrop, Stuart. "Electronic Fictions and 'The Lost Game of Self.'" *The New York Review of Science Fiction,* No. 66 (February, 1994), 8–14.

Mullarkey, John. "Deleuze and Materialism: One or Several Matters?" *A Deleuzian Century?,* 59–84.

Murphy, Timothy S. "Quantum Ontonlogy: A Virtual Mechanics of Becoming." *Deleuze and Guattari: New Mappings in Politics, Philosophy, and Culture.* Ed. Eleanor Kaufman and Kevin and Jon Heller. Minneapolis: University of Minnesota, 1998, 211–229.

Napier, Susan J. *Anime from Akira to Princess Mononoke: Experiencing Contemporary Japanese Animation.* New York: Palgrave, 2001.

_____. "When Godzilla Speaks." In *Godzilla's Footsteps: Japanese Pop Culture Icons on the Global Stage.* Ed. Willliam Tsutsui and Michiko Ito. New York: Palgrave Macmillan, 2006, 9–19.

_____. "When the Machines Stop: Fantasy, Reality and Terminal Identity in *Neon Genesis Evangelion* and *Serial Experiments Lain.*" *Science Fiction Studies,* 29 (November, 2002), 418–435.

Niven, Larry. *Ringworld.* New York: Ballantine Books, 1970.

Nussbaum, Martha C. *Love's Knowledge: Essays on Philosophy and Literature.* New York: Oxford University Press, 1990.

_____. *Poetic Justice: The Literary Imagination and Public Life.* Boston: Beacon Press, 1995.

_____. *Upheavals of Thought: The Intelligence of Emotions.* Cambridge: Cambridge University Press, 2001.

Ong, Aihwa. "On the Edge of Empires: Flexible Citizenship among Chinese in Diaspora." *Positions,* 1:3 (Winter, 1993), 745–778.

Orbaugh, Sharalyn. "Frankenstein and the Cyborg Metropolis: The Evolution of Body and City in Science Fiction Narratives." *Cinema Anime.* Ed. Steven T. Brown. New York: Palgrave Macmillan, 2006, 81–111.

_____. *Japanese Fiction of the Allied Occupation: Vision, Embodiment, Identity.* Leiden and Boston: Brill, 2007.

_____. "Sex and the Single Cyborg: Japanese Pop Culture Experiments in Subjectivity." *Science Fiction Studies,* 29 (November, 2002), 436–452.

Orwell, George. *Nineteen Eighty-Four.* 1949. New York: New American Library, 1977.

Palmer, Alan. *Fictional Minds.* Lincoln and London: University of Nebraska Press, 2004.

Pearson, Keith Ansell. "Pure Reserve: Deleuze, Philosophy, and Immanence." *Deleuze and Religion,* 142–155.

_____. "Viroid Life: On Machines, Technics and Evolution." *Deleuze and Philosophy: The Difference Engineer.* Ed. Pearson. London: Routledge, 1997, 180–210.

Pierce, John J. "Prospectus." *Renaissance: A Semi-Official Organ of the Second Foundation,* 1 (Winter, 1969), 1.

Pohl, Frederik, and Frederik Pohl IV. *Science Fiction Studies in Film.* New York: Ace, 1981.

Powell, Sam. Letter. "Monolith Mail." *2001: A Space Odyssey,* No. 5 (April, 1977), 19.

Rickitt, Richard. *Special Effects: The History and Technique.* New York: Billboard Books, 2000.

Robertson, Jennifer. "Blood Talks: Eugenic Modernity and the Creation of New Japanese." *History and Anthropology,* 13:3 (2002), 191–216.

Rose, Mark. *Alien Encounters: Anatomy of Science Fiction.* Cambridge: Harvard University Press, 1981.

Roszak, Theodore. *The Making of a Counter Culture: Reflections on the Technocratic Society and Its Youthful Opposition.* New York: Anchor, 1969.

Ruh, Brian. *Stray Dog of Anime: The Films of Mamoru Oshii.* New York: Palgrave Macmillan, 2004.

Ryan, Marie-Louise. *Possible Worlds, Artificial Intelligence, and Narrative Theory.* Bloomington: Indiana University Press, 1991.

Sant'Elia, Antonio. "Manifesto of Futurist Architecture, 1914." *Futurist Manifestos,* 160–172.

Sargent, Pamela. "Introduction." *Women of Wonder: The Contemporary Years, Science Fiction by Women from the 1970s to the 1990s.* Ed. Sargent. San Diego: Harvest/Harcourt, Brace & Co., 1995, 1–20.

Sas, Miryam. *Fault Lines: Cultural Memory and Japanese Surrealism.* Stanford: Stanford University Press, 2001.

Schroeder, Andrew. "All Roads Lead to Hong Kong: Martial Arts, Digital Effects and the Labour of Empire in Contemporary Action Film." *E-Journal on Hong Kong Cultural and Social Studies,* No. 1 (2002). At http://www.hku.hk/hkcsp/ccex/ehkcss01/frame.htm?mid=2&smid=1&ssmid=7.

Sellers, Suan. *Language and Sexual Difference: Feminist Writing in France.* London: Macmillan, 1991.

Shevory, Thomas C. *Body/Politics: Studies in Reproductions, Productions, and (Re)Construction.* London: Praeger, 2000.

Simak, Clifford D. "Skirmish." *Strangers in the Universe: Science Fiction Stories.* By Simak. New York: Simon and Schuster, 1956, 191–208. Originally published in *Amazing Stories* (December, 1950).

Slonczewski, Joan. *A Door into Ocean*. New York: Avon, 1986.

Smith, Cordwainer. [Paul A. Linebarger] "Scanners Live in Vain." *The Science Fiction Hall of Fame*. 1970. Ed. Robert Silverberg. New York: Avon, 1971, 354–390. Originally published in *Fantasy Book* (1950).

Smith, Daniel W. "The Doctrine of Univocity: Deleuze's Ontology of Immanence." *Deleuze and Religion*, 167–183.

Smith, Sarah. "Electric Fictions: The State of the Art." *The New York Review of Science Fiction*, No. 63 (November, 1993), 8–11.

Soja, Edward. *Thirdspace*. Cambridge: Blackwell, 1996.

Sorensen, André. *The Making of Urban Japan: Cities and Planning from Edo to the Twenty-first Century*. London and New York: Routledge, 2002.

Stapledon, Olaf. *Last Men in London*. 1932. *Last and First Men and Last Men in London*. By Stapledon. Middlesex: Penguin Books, 1973, 333–605.

_____. *Star Maker*. 1937. *Last and First Men and Star Maker: Two Science-Fiction Novels by Olaf Stapledon*. By Stapledon. New York: Dover Books, 1968, 249–438.

Steadman, Ralph. *The Little Red Computer*. New York: McGraw-Hill, 1969.

Sturgeon, Theodore. "Will Jenkins: An Appreciation." *Locus: The Newspaper of the Science Fiction Field*, No. 175 (June 24, 1975), 1–2.

Suvin, Darko. *Metamorphoses of Science Fiction: On the Poetics and History of a Literary Genre*. New Haven: Yale University Press, 1979.

Swedin, Eric G. and David L. Ferro. *Computers: The Life Story of a Technology*. Baltimore: Johns Hopkins University Press, 2007.

"Technology." *The American Heritage Dictionary of the English Language*. Fourth Edition. [CD-ROM] Boston: Houghton, 2000.

Tezuka Osamu. "Afterword." *Metropolis*. By Tezuka. Trans. Kumar Sivasubramanian. Milwaukie, OR: Dark Horse Comics, 2003, 164–165.

Tiptree, James, Jr. [Alice Sheldon] "The Girl Who Was Plugged In." *New Dimensions 3*. Ed. Robert Silverberg. Garden City, NY: Doubleday, 1973, 60–97.

Tisdall, Caroline, and Angelo Bozzolla. *Futurism*. New York and Toronto: Oxford University Press, 1978. Reprinted 2003.

Tsutsui, William. *Godzilla on My Mind: Fifty Years of the King of the Monsters*. New York: Palgrave Macmillan, 2004.

Turan, Kenneth. "A Pack of Cinematic Styles." *The Los Angeles Times*, (January 11, 2002), F1, F8.

Turner, George, Lee Harding, Mongo MacCallum, and Bruce Gillespie. "A Symposium on *2001: A Space Odyssey*." *Australian Science Fiction Review*, 17 (September, 1968), 3–24.

2001: A Space Odyssey. Metro-Goldwyn-Mayer, 1968.

2010: The Year We Make Contact. Metro-Goldwyn-Mayer, 1984.

Underwood, Mike. Letter. "Monolith Mail." *2001: A Space Odyssey*, No. 6 (May, 1977), 19.

Vinge, Vernor. *A Deepness in the Sky*. 1999. New York: Tor, 2000.

_____. *A Fire upon the Deep*. 1992. New York: Tor, 1993.

_____. "True Names." 1981. *True Names and the Opening of the Cyberspace Frontier*. Ed. James Frenkel. Afterword Marvin Minsky. New York: Tor, 2001, 241–331.

Welchman, Alistair. "Machinic Thinking." *Deleuze and Philosophy*, 211–229.

Wells, H. G. *The Shape of Things to Come*. London: Macmillan, 1934.

_____. *The Time Machine*. 1895. New York: Berkley, 1957.

Werbner, Pnina. "Introduction: the Dialectics of Cultural Hybridity." *Debating Cultural Hybridity: Multi-Cultural Identities and the Politics of Anti-Racism*. Ed. Werbner and Tariq Modood. London and New Jersey: Zed Books, 1997, 1–26.

Westfahl, Gary. *Cosmic Engineers: A Study of Hard Science Fiction*. Westport, CT: Greenwood Press 1996.

_____. "Greyer Lensmen, Or Looking Backward in Anger." *Interzone*, No. 129 (March, 1998), 40–43.

"Will Jenkins Dies." [no author given] *Locus: The Newspaper of the Science Fiction Field*, No. 175 (June 24, 1975), 1.

Willman, David. "Suspect Stood to Gain from Anthrax Panic." *The Los Angeles Times* (August 2, 2008), A1, A10. At http://articles.latimes.com/2008/aug/02/nation/na-anthrax2.

Wise, J. Macgregor. *Exploring Technology and Social Space*. London and New Delhi: Sage, 1997.

Wittig, Monique. *The Lesbian Body*. Trans. David Le Vay. Boston: Beacon Press, 1973.

Wolfe, Gary K. *The Known and the Unknown: The Iconography of Science Fiction*. Kent: Kent State University Press, 1979.

"Women Call the Shots on Buying and Maintaining the Family Car." [no author given] *VMR Auto Guides*. At http://www.vmrintl.com/Ref_art/women_buy.htm. Accessed March 13, 2010.

Yanal, Robert J. *Paradoxes of Emotion and Fiction*. University Park: Pennsylvania State University Press, 1999.

Yau, Esther C. M., ed. *At Full Speed: Hong Kong Cinema in a Borderless World*. Minneapolis and London: University of Minnesota Press, 2001.

Zelazny, Roger. *The Dream Master*. 1966. Boston: Gregg Press, 1976. Facsimile of the 1966 Ace edition.

About the Contributors

Gregory Benford is a professor of physics at the University of California, Irvine, is a Woodrow Wilson Fellow, and was a visiting fellow at Cambridge University. In 1995 he received the Lord Prize for contributions to science, and in 2007 won the Asimov Award for science writing. He continues research in both astrophysics and plasma physics. His fiction has won many awards, including the Nebula Award for his novel *Timescape*.

Amy Kit-sze Chan has a doctoral degree in intercultural studies from the Chinese University of Hong Kong and now teaches English literature and cultural studies in the Department of English Language and Literature, Hong Kong Shue Yan University, and Master Program's in Intercultural Studies, Chinese University of Hong Kong. She is the coeditor of *World Weavers: Globalization, Science Fiction, and the Cybernetic Revolution* (2005).

David L. Ferro is an associate professor in computer science at Weber State University with a Ph.D. in science and technology studies from Virginia Tech. His interests range from a cultural and historical understanding of technological development to research in user interface design. He currently is finishing the second edition of a computer science textbook and editing a multidisciplinary volume from McFarland with Eric G. Swedin on the influence of science fiction on computer development.

Véronique Flambard-Weisbart is associate professor of French at Loyola Maramount University, director of the University's Study Abroad Program, coauthor of *Scen@rios: Pédagogies du Virtuel* (2006), and an expert in martial arts.

Kirk Hampton has published two novels in the style of "Wakean science fantasy"—*The Moonhare* (1996) and *Lisho* (2002)—as well as four conference papers coauthored with Carol MacKay. He currently produces and stars in a weekly cable television show for Public Access in Austin, Texas.

Veronica Hollinger is a professor of cultural studies at Trent University in Peterborough, Ontario. She is coeditor of *Science Fiction Studies* and a member of the editorial board of Liverpool University Press's Science Fiction Texts and Studies series. Her publications include articles on feminist and queer sf, cyberpunk, postmodernism, and posthumanism. Her most recent coedited collection is *Queer Universes: Sexualities in Science Fiction* (2008).

Brooks Landon teaches English at the University of Iowa, where he directs the General Education Literature Program. He is the author of *Science Fiction After 1900: From the Steam Man to the Stars* and numerous articles on science fiction and science fiction media.

Rob Latham is an associate professor of English at the University of California, Riverside. A coeditor of the journal *Science Fiction Studies* since 1997, he is the author of *Consuming*

Youth: Vampires, Cyborgs, and the Culture of Consumption (2002) and has written articles on a wide range of authors and filmmakers, including Kathy Acker, J. G. Ballard, Richard Calder, David Cronenberg, David Lynch, Kim Newman, and Robert Silverberg. He is writing a book on New Wave science fiction of the 1960s and 1970s.

Lynne Lundquist, a longtime instructor in the Theatre and Dance Department at California State University, Fullerton, has published on children's science fiction and fantasy in *Children's Literature Review, The Encyclopedia of Fantasy*, the journal *Extrapolation, The Greenwood Encyclopedia of Science Fiction and Fantasy*, and three scholarly anthologies.

Carol MacKay is distinguished teaching professor of English at the University of Texas at Austin. Editor of two works on Thackeray and Dickens, she is also the author of *Soliloquy in Nineteenth-Century Fiction* (1987) and *Creative Negativity: Four Victorian Exemplars of the Female Quest* (2001). She recently published a critical edition of Annie Besant's 1885 *Autobiographical Sketches* (2009).

Richard L. McKinney was born and raised in the United States and has lived in Sweden since 1968. Previously a student counselor and librarian at the Human Ecology Division at Lund University, he is now affiliated with the University's Centre for Languages and Literature. His current research involves fictional worlds in contemporary popular fiction, focusing on four genres (science fiction, fantasy, historical fiction, and crime fiction) in three media (literature, cinema, and television).

Sharalyn Orbaugh is a professor jointly appointed in the departments of Asian Studies and Women's and Gender Studies at the University of British Columbia. Her research focuses on representations of embodied states in the literature and popular culture of modern Japan. Her recent publications include "Emotional Infectivity: The Japanese Cyborg and the Limits of the Human" (*Mechademia*, volume 3, 2008) and *Japanese Fiction of the Allied Occupation: Vision, Embodiment, Identity* (2007).

Eric G. Swedin is an associate professor in information systems at Weber State University with a Ph.D. in the history of science and technology from Case Western Reserve University. He has published five books on historical topics and a mystery novel.

Gary Westfahl, who teaches at the University of California, Riverside, and the University of LaVerne, is the author, editor, or coeditor of 21 books on science fiction and fantasy, as well as hundreds of articles, reviews, and reference book entries. In 2003, he received the Science Fiction Research Association's Pilgrim Award for lifetime contributions to science fiction and fantasy scholarship.

Wong Kin Yuen teaches intercultural studies, technoscience culture and science fiction. Currently, he is a professor and department head of the English Department at Hong Kong Shue Yan University. His research interests include ecological ethics, popular science and aesthetics and comparative poetics. His books include *The Sublime: East and West* and *Cultural Posthumanism*, and he co-edited of *World Weavers: Globalization, Science Fiction, and the Cybernetic Revolution*.

Index